CHRISTIAN WORDS, UN-CHRISTIAN ACTIONS

JOHN STODDARD KLAR

CHRISTIAN WORDS, UN-CHRISTIAN ACTIONS

GEORGE W. BUSH AND THE DESECRATION OF CHRISTIANITY IN MODERN AMERICA

Pleasant Word
A Division of WINEPRESS PUBLISHING

© 2006 by John Stoddard Klar. All rights reserved.

Pleasant Word (a division of WinePress Publishing, PO Box 428, Enumclaw, WA 98022) functions only as book publisher. As such, the ultimate design, content, editorial accuracy, and views expressed or implied in this work are those of the author.

No part of this publication may be reproduced, stored in a retrieval system or transmitted in any way by any means—electronic, mechanical, photocopy, recording or otherwise—without the prior permission of the copyright holder, except as provided by USA copyright law.

Unless otherwise noted, all Scriptures are taken from the Holy Bible, New International Version, Copyright © 1973, 1978, 1984 by the International Bible Society. Used by permission of Zondervan Publishing House. The "NIV" and "New International Version" trademarks are registered in the United States Patent and Trademark Office by International Bible Society.

Scripture references marked KJV are taken from the King James Version of the Bible.

Scripture references marked NASB are taken from the New American Standard Bible, © 1960, 1963, 1968, 1971, 1972, 1973, 1975, 1977 by The Lockman Foundation. Used by permission.

ISBN 1-4141-0699-8
Library of Congress Catalog Card Number: 2006901031

Dedication

This book is dedicated to
Jesus Christ, our almighty Savior and Lord.
May His Truth soon reign.

Questions, comments, criticisms
or other correspondence may be directed to:
RevElation Press, LLC
P.O. Box 106
Irasburg, Vermont 05845

TABLE OF CONTENTS

Acknowledgements ix
Introduction xiii

1. The Christian Duty to Stand for Christ 23
2. Accountability and Tort Reform 69
3. Politics and Christianity: Darkness and Light 101
4. Compassionate Conservatism,
   the "Underclass," and the Privileged 139
5. No Child Left Better Off 197
6. Compassion for God's Creation 221
7. The Rich, the Deficit,
   and What Trickles Down 243
8. "Christian" Leadership into the
   Horrors of War: Iraq and the
   Doctrine of Preemptive War 301
9. Abu Ghraib,
   the Modern Symbol of America 399

10. Bonesman or Christian?	523
11. Do the End Times Justify the Means?	585
Bibliography	599

ACKNOWLEDGEMENTS

Grateful acknowledgment is made to the following for permission to reprint previously published material:

Strang Communications: Excerpts from The Faith of George W. Bush, by Stephen Mansfield, Charisma House, 2003. Used with Permission.

Friends Committee on National Legislation: Excerpts reprinted from the *Washington Newsletter*, as noted in footnotes.

The Prince, by Niccolo Machiavelli, translated by Leo Paul S. de Alvarez, reprinted by permission of *Waveland Press, Inc.*, Long Grove, IL; Waveland Press, Inc., 1980 [reissued 1989]. All rights reserved.

Excerpt from The Creature from Jekyll Island: A Second Look at the Federal Reserve, reprinted by permission of G. Edward Griffin, American Media, Westlake Village, CA, Copyright 1994, 1995, 1998.

Dark Majesty: The Secret Brotherhood and the Magic of a Thousand Points of Light: excerpts reprinted by permission of Texe Marrs, Power of Prophecy, Austin, TX Copyright 1992, Texe Marrs.

Beyond Good Intentions: A Biblical View of Politics, by Doug Bandow, copyright 1988, pp. XII, XIII, 15, 16, 17, 23, 183, 199, 202, 205, 206, 207, 227, 229, 230, 231. Used by permission of *Crossway Books*, a ministry of *Good News Publishers*, Wheaton, Illinois 60187, www.crossway.com.

The Pursuit of God: The Human Thirst for the Divine Excerpts reprinted from *The Pursuit of God* by A.W. Tozer, copyright © 1982, 1993 by *Zur, Ltd*. Used by permission of *WingSpread Publishers*, a division of *Zur, Ltd.*, 800-233-4443.

Today's Isms: Communism Fascism Capitalism Socialism, by William Ebenstein: Excerpts reprinted by permission of Prentice-Hall Inc., Englewood Cliffs, NJ, © 1970.

The Westminster Dictionary of Christian Ethics, James F. Childress and John Macquarrie, eds. Excerpts reprinted by permission of Westminster John Knox Press © 1986.

Reagan and the World: Imperial Policy in the New Cold War, by Jeff McMahon: excerpts reprinted by permission of Monthly Review Press, © 1985.

With the Contras: A Reporter in the Wilds of Nicaragua, by Christopher Dickey: excerpts (pp. 17, 18, 45, 69-70) reprinted by permission of Simon & Schuster, © 1985.

The World Affairs Companion: The Essential One-Volume Guide to Global Issues, by Gerald Segal: excerpts (pp. 44, 55, 56, 87, 122, 194-196, 254) reprinted in U.S.

and Canada by permission of Simon & Schuster Adult Publishing Group, © 1987, 1988, 1991, 1993.

Are We Living in the End Times?, by Tim Lahaye and Jerry B. Jenkins, excerpts used by permission of Tyndale House Publishers, Inc., Wheaton, IL, 1999.

The Perils of Prosperity, 1914-32, by William E. Leuchtenburg, pp.245, 246, 259, used by permission of The University of Chicago Press, © 1958 by The University of Chicago. Published 1958 Eleventh Impression 1966. Printed in the United States of America.

Secrets of the Tomb, by Alexandra Robbins. Copyright © 2002 by Alexandra Robbins. Excerpts pp. 3, 7, 132, 134, 149, 180, used by permission of Little, Brown and Co., Inc.

Arrogant Capital, by Kevin Phillips. Copyright © 1994, 1995 by Kevin Phillips. Excerpts pp. xiii, xiv, xv, xviii, 60, 61, 62, 63, 64, 65, 66, 198 used by permission of Little, Brown and Co., Inc.

1984, by George Orwell. Excerpts used by permission of Harcourt, Inc.

Excerpts from The Culture of Contentment, by John Kenneth Galbraith. Copyright © 1992 by John Kenneth Galbraith. Reprinted by permission by Houghton Mifflin Company. All rights reserved.

Shrub: The Short But Happy Political Life of George W. Bush by Molly Ivins and Lou Dubose, copyright © by Molly Ivins and Lou Dubose. Used by permission of Random House, Inc.

America's Prisoner by Manuel Noriega and Peter Eisner, copyright © 1997 by Manuel Noriega and Peter Eiener. Used by permission of Random House, Inc.

Excerpts from <u>Hitler's Scientists</u>, by John Cornwell, copyright © 2003 by John Cornwell. Used by permission of Viking Penguin, a division of Penguin Group (USA) Inc.

<u>Bread in the Wilderness</u>, by Thomas Merton, copyright © 1953 Our Lady of Gethsemane Archives: excerpts used by permission of The Liturgical Press.

Excerpts from <u>My Utmost for His Highest</u> by Oswald Chambers, © 1935 by Dodd Mead & Co., renewed © 1963 by the Oswald Chambers Publications Assn., Ltd. Used by permission of Discovery House Publishers, Grand Rapids, MI 49501. All rights reserved.

Excerpts from <u>Why America Slept</u> by Gerald Posner, copyright © 2003 by Gerald Posner. Used by permission of Random House, Inc.

Excerpts from <u>Reflections on the Psalms</u>, Copyright © 1958 by C.S. Lewis, renewed by Arthur Owen Barfield 1986, reprinted by permission of Harcourt, Inc.

Excerpts from "When tests' cheaters are the teachers," "Soft vs. hard energy path: the political lines harden," "US already moving toward a flat tax," and "US stand against torture: firm enough?" reprinted by permission of *The Christian Science Monitor.*

INTRODUCTION

The particular challenge of this book has been to address two entirely disparate audiences–the non-Christian liberals who might be drawn to the subject of Mr. Bush's hypocrisy, who have no interest in learning about Scripture; and the conservative Christians who put him in power, for whom Christian Scripture is perhaps the only tool which may pierce the falsehood which has replaced the promise of a Christian influence in a morally-decaying nation. To non-Christian readers, I invite you to two options–learn enough Christian theology in this book to understand more fully the issues shaping this Christian conflict, or skip Chapter One and indulge me my Christian faith where it crops up elsewhere, for there is a great deal of detailed, "secular" proof offered in these pages which proves the case of the utter failure of the worst president in our nation's history.

And here I risk alienating Christian readers before they've read the Scriptural foundation which animates this book. To these readers, I submit that I have written these pages with guidance from the words of Jesus Christ. I beseech Christians to read Chapter One with charity and Christian prayer, to absorb the concept that not only must George W. Bush not be allowed a free ride based solely on Romans 13, but that to do so is sinful and contrary to Scripture. Also of particular significance to Christian readers is Chapter 10, which scratches the surface of the very disturbing yet very real Bush W. flirtation with Satan worship while at Yale. This association is uncontroverted by Bush biographers and defenders, and is documented by numerous credible sources. The unfortunate thing about the nation's largest and most powerful and influential Satanic Cult is that it's not very forthcoming with details of its operations or worship schedule. Yet the evidence is ample of the spiritual reality and terrifying influence of this organization. And if it is, in fact, innocuous, why does George W. Bush so ardently cling to the benefits of membership, and of secrecy, and refuse to denounce his known relationship with such dark worship?

There is material in this book for every reader—America's dearth of intelligent moral discourse must end, and the questions raised herein must be considered. If George W. Bush is a fraud, then what is the nation's moral compass? Does it have one any longer? Can it regain moral consensus in the face of moral relativism and an alienation of much of the public from the way of Christ?

Who I am does not matter. What matters is Jesus Christ–even to non-Christians, for Christianity is a clear code by which George W. says he lives. The acceptance of the deity of Jesus Christ is not necessary to hold this president to the standards he says he holds and which (solely) got him into the White House. Further, Jesus Christ and His teachings must not be judged by the actions of George W. Bush, or by those of any other human.

As I researched this book, I was increasingly alarmed and astonished by what I learned–this information must be shared. If we choose to inquire, the evidence of the truths asserted in this book is overwhelming, and only willful ignorance (or false hope) keeps Christians enthralled by this man who talks a good talk while he leads a nation and the world to destruction and chaos. In the course of my research, I encountered a startling (secular) book by political commentator and erstwhile Republican, Kevin Phillips. I cannot over-emphasize how useful Mr. Phillip's book is in uncovering much of the history of our current president and his family–it is well-researched and impressive. Mr. Phillips encountered the same journey as I, though from a secular perspective:

> Unfortunately,…[through my research] I found a greater basis for dismay and disillusionment than I had imagined. The result is an unusual and unflattering portrait of a great family (great in power, not morality) that has built a base over the course of the twentieth century in the back corridors of the new military-industrial complex and in close association

with the growing intelligence and national security establishments....I am not talking about ordinary lack of business ethics or financial corruption.... Four generations of building toward dynasty...have infused the Bush family's hunger for power and practices of crony capitalism with a moral arrogance and backstage disregard of the democratic and republican traditions of the U.S. government. As we will see, four generations of involvement with clandestine arms deals and European and Middle Eastern rogue banks will do that....deceit and disinformation have become Bush political hallmarks.[1]

It was as if Mr. Phillips found in his secular research the counterpart to my Christian inquiry: the roots indeed go deep and far, and many are hidden from view. Phillips includes an entire Appendix devoted to the subject of Bush family "Deception, Dissimulation, and Disinformation," and three chapters of his book echo moral topics covered herein: Chapter 5, "The Enron-Halliburton Administration," Chapter 4, "Texanomics and Compassionate Conservatism," and Chapter 7, "The American Presidency and the Rise of the Religious Right."

But there is another tendril that ties in with Mr. Phillips' work. Throughout the creation of this book, I was drawn to the teachings of Niccolo Machiavelli because they seemed to jibe so tightly with the moral behaviors of this administration, and with Skull and Bones, the Yale secret society linked to the Illuminati

---

[1] Kevin Phillips, <u>American Dynasty: Aristocracy, Fortune, and the Politics of Deceit in the House of Bush</u>, pp. ix, xi.

which Bush proudly joined (like his father and both his grandfathers). The further I dug (see bibliography), the more this connection seemed unavoidable. Kevin Phillips brought it together by reporting that Lee Atwater, Bush W.'s political mentor and perhaps political idol, reread Machiavelli yearly, and that "Karl Rove, the even more influential advisor to [George W. Bush], is widely known as a Machiavelli aficionado."[2] The implications of this "revelation" are much greater than might at first appear. Why would a supposedly Christian leader employ as his chief political advisors proponents of a frighteningly immoral creed? Machiavelli's teachings were much more than non-Christian–they were blatantly immoral. The picture which continues to emerge of America's president is of a man perfectly trained and conditioned to lead the nation on its current disastrous and irreversible course. But then, God said it would be so, that before Christ again came to earth there would be a mass turning away from Christianity, led by a false leader who would lead Christians astray and non-Christians to revile the faithful. George W. Bush is fulfilling Biblical prophecy, but in the worst way. This book thus compares Mr. Bush's actions to the moral code of Christianity, but also to that of Machiavelli and Skull and Bones. Actions speak louder than words, and in this case those actions show a clear pattern of conduct linked irrefutably to one of these two latter standards, but not linked to Jesus Christ.

    I am not politically motivated, having long ago lost faith in either American political party. Americans

---

[2] Ibid., p. 345.

continue to vote for one of the two entrenched, corrupt political Parties. But third parties have entered American politics before, and such a party is the only hope for the future (if there is any such hope, for only Jesus Christ will bring honest government to man). But to expect George W. Bush to climb through the corruption of worldly politics and retain Christian integrity is absurd, and were he to do so would be to institute a dangerous theocracy. Jesus Christ advocated a separation of Church and state, for Christians cannot walk in both light and darkness. This is why Christians are told to "give Caesar his due," not to try to become Caesars. The world corrupts, and nowhere more powerfully than in politics. This is established in this book–by Christian writers more qualified than I, and by Scripture. It is thus inherently suspect that George W. Bush believes that God chose him to become president: a comparable position would be to proclaim that God chose someone to be a Christian prostitute. Both are absurd notions, and America's Christians should have known better. Of course, God's purpose is served in all things, even in George W's influence: but this does not mean that the actions of this administration should be emulated or supported by those who wish to serve Jesus.

I suffer from the perhaps naïve assumption that if Christian Americans have been completely misled by George W. Bush, they would like to know about it. Alas, for many people, truth cannot dent their loyalty to George W. Bush, perhaps because to do so would be to admit their own failing in not being more vigilant, or the greater sin that they have wedded themselves to a false political ideology in place of their professed Lord, Jesus Christ. And this is the true purpose of this book–to hold Christian Americans to account for their gross error in vaulting this man into power without researching his resume, allowing him to simply hide behind Jesus, and then once in power to hide Jesus behind himself. Two thousand years ago, Paul cried tears day and night for the deception now unfolding in America (See Acts 20: 27-31), and warned over and over in the New Testament of this deception, knowing still that it was unavoidable because it was part of God's plan. I now cry those tears, as thousands of children are killed abroad in His name, and thousands of "enemy combatants" are tortured with impunity.

But God is real, and the stench of America's sin is reaching to heaven. He will withdraw his protection from a nation that, like America, calls itself Christian in willful denial that it is the world's, and history's, capital of pornography, homosexuality, materialism, capitalism, corporate influence, pedophilia, family decay, alcoholism, gluttony, and hypocrisy. I will be attacked personally rather than my charges of immorality and hypocrisy directly addressed, for these charges are not answerable in moral truth, and because that's how Rove, Bush W., and other Machiavellians operate. Yes, it's sinister, but it's today's American reality, as reflected in a deeply disturbed nation. And now, Americans must choose between the two images they have heretically wedded together–their flag and its destructive nationalism, or the visage of Jesus Christ–for they no longer go together, if they ever did. Jesus belongs to no party, and he belongs to no nation.[3] In America, worldly laws protect the flag from desecration, but not the image of Jesus. If a Christian must choose between loyalty to a flag in conflict with the teachings of Christianity, or loyalty to Jesus Christ at risk of conflict with a flag or a nation, which shall he or she choose? It is time for all to choose between faith in Christ and faith in worldly illusions—this is the choice God gives us.

I am God's imperfect vessel, as are we all. My intellect is a gift from my God, and I use it in the following pages to be as true to Jesus Christ as I am in my flawed capacity able. This book aims at truth, and if it fails it is my failing. But all Christians are called most powerfully to join this fray, for "…this is your hour to act, when the power of darkness rules" (Luke 21:53, KJV). Act, Christians, and choose, for time is short and Jesus comes quickly. As to non-Christians, perhaps as the bird flu, America's debt load and approaching Armageddon in the Middle East demonstrate worldly proof of the reliability of God's Word (and reveal as utter illusion the arrogant misperception that man can control his world), they will search their hearts and realize that this world, and its obvious battle between good and evil, did not arise from a random collision of molecules in a mud puddle. My brain is not so great as to understand the universe, nor is any other human brain—mankind

---

[3] "Behold, the nations are as a drop of a bucket, and are counted as the small dust of the balance….All nations before him are as nothing; and they are counted to him less than nothing, and vanity." Isaiah 40:15, 17 KJV. Nations, like corporations, do not possess souls: God blesses individuals. Neither does God have a relationship with nations, but directly with every human soul who seeks Him.

grows so confident in its expanding knowledge, ignoring that each new discovery raises more proofs that there is infinitely more that we don't know, than that which we do. Here again we see the difficulty in addressing two audiences at once who hold diametrically opposed belief systems. To both audiences, I humbly beg indulgence–suspend disbelief long enough to openly consider my moral, logical proofs. May God bless you in your individual spiritual journey. Amen.

Chapter 1

THE CHRISTIAN DUTY TO STAND FOR CHRIST

"Let every soul be subject unto the higher powers. For there is no power but of God: the powers that be are ordained of God. Whosoever therefore resisteth the power, resisteth the ordinance of God: and they that resist shall receive to themselves damnation. For rulers are not a terror to good works, but to the evil. Wilt thou then not be afraid of the power? Do that which is good, and thou shalt have praise of the same."[4]

Romans 13:1-3 is often cited as Christian doctrine requiring that Christians resist questioning government. And yet, Americans emphasize the divine nature of freedom, particularly as embodied in the American political system. Surely when Paul tells us in Romans not to "resist" worldly powers he does not mean that we lay down our "rights" to peaceful, Christian free speech

---

[4] <u>Holy Bible</u>, King James Version. (KJV)

in a democratic form of government. On the contrary, Christians are compelled to hold Christian governments to Christian standards, especially in modern America, when the world looks to the United States as not just economic and technological innovator or military-industrial behemoth, but as the moral champions we and our leaders trumpet ourselves to be. Paul also tells us in Romans 13:11 that "...knowing the time, that now it is high time to awake out of sleep: for now is our salvation nearer than when we believed."[5] American Christians can no more afford to rely upon their government blindly than could Iraqis have ignored the moral failings of Saddam Hussein, whom few would argue was allowed by God to rule to do good, though he was permitted by God to do much evil: Saddam ruled with God's omniscient permission, but Christians would be poorly counseled to support such a leader unquestioningly, in reliance solely upon a misinterpretation of Romans 13.

Clearly Paul's concern in Romans 13 was the appearance of Christ's worldly church to worldly government powers: that is, how Christians should conduct themselves toward Caesar so that Christians would not be persecuted in their worship, and so that worldly leaders would have little complaint against Christian worship. But this standard is quite different from the standard Paul would have Christians apply to the leaders of Christ's church, a high standard about which Paul

---

[5] Ibid.

was quite vocal.[6] Thus, to excuse George W. Bush from Christian accountability based on Romans 13 is to apply a standard or code of conduct, intended to be directed toward worldly leaders, to a supposed Christian leader, and to simultaneously excuse that Christian leader (also a political, worldly leader) from the loving scrutiny mandated for all Christians.

Indeed, no governments escape the imperfection of humanity, and their integrity can only be maintained via the vigilance of individuals and their moral codes. In America, we have historically been assisted in our morality by the gospels of Jesus Christ, and we have tried to navigate our nation through its glory but also through its moral failings (slavery, imperialism, inequality of wealth, the mistreatment of native populations and of women). Currently we are living in, or very close to, End Times, so it has not ever been more vital that we get it right. And we are told by the Word of God (who keeps His promises) that in these times, most Christians will be deceived, following false teachers into sin, and leading nonbelievers to reject Christ.

Americans, then, have long been suspicious of government, and this formed the foundation for the political freedom and integrity that led the world in innovation in technology and various government and free-market institutions. The colonial designers of our republican system were vigilant indeed. Thomas Paine wrote in <u>Rights</u>

---

[6] Twice in Acts, (Acts 15:2, "fierce argument"; Acts 15:39, "sharp argument," Today's English Version (TEV)), Paul engages in sharp if not bitter dispute with other Christians–something he did not do with the worldly, unchristian leaders whom he instead impacted by his passive though impassioned preaching.

of Man that "When I contemplate the natural dignity of man,...I become irritated at the attempt to govern mankind by force and fraud, as if they were all knaves and fools, and can scarcely avoid disgust at those who are thus imposed upon....Lay then the axe to the root, and teach Governments humanity. It is their sanguinary punishments which corrupt mankind."[7]

Though lacking souls, governments all manage to take on an existence of their own, bureaucracies which only grow larger in size and influence, always increasing their reach. Inevitably the interests of the "state," (corrupted by commercial, aristocratic or other influences) and those of the individual (particularly religious and other freedoms) conflict, for "What are incompatible–not always, but surely in the long run–are the sovereignty of the state and the sovereignty of the people...."[8] America has become just such a bureaucracy, especially since the military-industrial build-up occasioned by America's response to the challenges of World War II:

> Over the last half century, a Washington swollen by expansions in peace and war has become what ordinary citizens of the 1780s and even some architects of the US Constitution feared–a capital city so enlarged, so incestuous in its dealings, so caught up in its own privilege that it no longer seems controllable or even swayable by the general public....Yet despite Republican control of the presidency for twenty out of twenty-four years between 1968 and 1992, the

---

[7] Thomas Paine, Rights of Man, pp. 35, 24.
[8] John Lukacs, The End of the Twentieth Century and the End of the Modern Age, p. 261.

occupancy of the White House was not, as events turned out, matched by an ability to take control of Congress or to create a new establishment, as GOP strategists originally hoped. Washington's influential classes had been sinking their roots too broadly and deeply–history's familiar danger signal–to be displaced as before.[9]

The study of political history teaches us that "…a political structure which embodies obsolete or displaced private relationships may resist new necessities. In such cases the political structure loses its claim to legitimacy; it is at odds with society itself. The consequence is decline, instability or even revolution."[10]

The United States government has incurred debt in its citizens' names beyond any accumulated in the history of mankind, even while presiding over an economic system which decries, and whose markets regularly and historically punish, such a lack of frugality. The current administration has overseen a war in Iraq, runaway budget deficits, Abu Ghraib, broad liberation of corporate restraints, No Child Left Behind, and the repudiation of a number of the foreign policy initiatives of previous administrations, Democratic and Republican. And this administration represents itself to be acting with Christian precepts for guidance, in a country whose image of itself is in decay because its economic future is uncertain and its moral condition is dubious at best, a country where "…we worry about our national soul."[11]

---

[9] Kevin Phillips, <u>Arrogant Capital: Washington, Wall Street, and the Frustration of American Politics</u>, pp. xiii, xiv.
[10] Richard N. Goodwin, <u>The American Condition</u>, p. 338.
[11] George W. Bush, <u>A Charge To Keep</u>, p.228.

It's fair to hold this federal government of ours accountable, and to hold the current administration accountable to Jesus Christ whom George W. Bush says he serves. In the absence of moral accountability in government in a world of liberalism carried to its (ill)logical conclusion, moral relativism, we will be left with a society without moral compass other than, perhaps, majoritarianism, itself patently corrupt. Do Americans yield their moral yoke to government process, to the soulless determination of future by a State that pretends to be democratic while it is utterly manipulated by special interest groups and gargantuan financial, industrial and political interests? Meanwhile, our attention is held by the much-esteemed two-party system, which permits the illusions both of political freedom and of competing moral platforms. Yet, both parties are financially supported in large part by corporate and other influences who have therefore bought both horses in every race: ultimately, our moral compass is thus strongly influenced by these interests. We are living Orwell's fiction, allowing government to shape our morality by default; for economic and other functions all have moral consequences, and so the more government control and influence is expanded, the more we surrender our present and future welfare to the morality of the free market, and the more we encounter the moral counterpart to the economic concept of "economies of scale." The government becomes our trusted protector and benefactor, commanding our loyalty as representative of our national interest, and we hear the cry "America right or wrong" in the name of patriotism.

Yet, what faith is to be placed in the moral reliability, or accountability, of government action without testing it against the greater moral standards we say our society lives by? Otherwise, have we not abdicated our moral obligation as a free democratic society, as Christians, as Americans? Are we simply obedient to the "Party" like Winston Smith in George Orwell's 1984?: "Besides, the Party was in the right. It must be so: how could the immortal, collective brain be mistaken? By what external standard could you check its judgments? Sanity was statistical. It was merely a question of learning to think as they thought."[12]

Never has America's role in the world been so vitally important as it is now. Where our government fails to reflect the moral beacon our country has always endeavored to be to the world, then Americans, particularly so Christians, must insist that right makes might, and not vice versa. Prior to World War II, one may marvel that Hitler and Mussolini were permitted to rise to power, but this occurred "…not because the truth had not been made known. It was rather because (a) not enough people recognized the truth (b) those who did recognize it did not exert themselves sufficiently in its behalf, and (c) many people saw the truth, but were indifferent to it."[13] American Christians, as followers of the greatest Teacher of Truth, must recognize the truth, exert ourselves strenuously in its behalf, and we will suffer great remorse should we treat it with indifference. We must always seek to influence government toward a

---

[12] George Orwell, 1984, p. 228.
[13] William F. Buckley, Jr., God & Man at Yale, p. 142.

reflection of Christian mores, but where those who govern us represent themselves to be devout Christians, and where they govern the mightiest, most influential nation in history during times which appear amazingly end-like, then those leaders have a much greater responsibility to truth and integrity than mere representatives of nations. For Jesus tells us

> Beware of false prophets, which come to you in sheep's clothing, but inwardly they are ravening wolves. Ye shall know them by their fruits. Do men gather grapes of thorns, or figs of thistles? Even so every good tree bringeth forth good fruit; but a corrupt tree bringeth forth evil fruit. A good tree cannot bring forth evil fruit, neither can a corrupt tree bring forth good fruit.[14]

Christians must demand Christian fruits of elected representatives who proclaim to wear the Christian mantle.

The Christian Duty to Challenge Government Leaders

American government was designed with recognition that government was patently untrustworthy, yet was a necessary evil to assist man to organize his worldly affairs. American colonists like Thomas Paine believed that if individuals possess natural rights, "…the

---

[14] Holy Bible, King James Version, Matthew 7:15-18. And Paul teaches "My friends, if someone is caught in any kind of wrongdoing, you who are spiritual should set him right; but you must do it in a gentle way." (Galatians 6:1, TEV) and "Rebuke publicly all those who commit sins…." (1 Timothy 5:20, TEV)

legitimacy of society can be discussed, and illegitimate societies reformed, in accordance with these rights."[15] To Thomas Jefferson, "…the system of democracy included the right, even the obligation, to revolt."[16] Of the United States, Ronald Reagan observed: "The eyes of all people are upon us. So that if we shall deal falsely with our God in this task we have undertaken, and so cause Him to withdraw His present help from us, we shall be made a story and a byword throughout the world."[17]

Modern American government has been heavily influenced by a liberal moral trend which swept through America as we placed more and more faith in the promises of technology and "Progress." Modern psychology explained human desires from the cold calculus of evolutionary/sexual analysis, ignoring the soul and inviting moral relativism and its abandonment of moral truths. "Permissiveness and lack of discipline are becoming the order of the day."[18] The growing spirit of anarchy and lawlessness in our society "…is closely related to the rejection of moral absolutes. Man is becoming progressively irritated with external restraints being placed upon his conduct….Since man is rejecting God and his Biblical revelation, he is concluding that such things as government, marriage, and the church are nothing more than institutions devised by men of another age."[19] Efforts toward world government echo the

---

[15] Thomas Paine, <u>Rights of Man</u>, introduction by Derek Matravers, p. X.
[16] Richard N. Goodwin, <u>The American Condition</u>, p. 268.
[17] David Aikman, <u>A Man of Faith: The Spiritual Journey of George W. Bush</u>, p.190.
[18] Renald E. Showers, <u>What On Earth Is God Doing</u>?, p. 96.
[19] Ibid., p. 96.

modern liberal sentiment that the goal of man should be unity, that "If man is to save himself from suffering and destruction, he must unite into a common, human community."[20]

With confidence in our ability to shape our own destiny with ever-improving technological innovations, modern Americans have ceased to rely on spiritual protection in their worldly movements. The American Left, particularly, has gone so far in its confidence of its own moral perspective that it too often is (ironically) intolerant and disdainful of those who would differ, especially Christians. Prior to the American backlash against liberal domination that embraced the traditionalism of Ronald Reagan (and echoed now, in the beginning of the twenty-first century), the Left's "…confidence in the rectitude of their own intentions, in their moral standing as protectors of beleaguered minorities, verged on self-righteousness. Their faith in administrative expertise offended those who put their faith in common sense."[21]

Withstanding this onslaught upon the Christian tenets which once bound American society together, Christians are compelled by their pure faith to both fight the moral decay in our government and to resist its influence when that battle is lost: "…moral law was not intended to be adapted to every new political trend. Moral law is, by definition, not infinitely malleable. Instead, the moral law stands implacably against arrogant

---

[20] Ibid., p. 97.
[21] Christopher Lasch, <u>The True and Only Heaven: Progress and its Critics</u>, p.38.

ideological claims."[22] However, resistance to the pressures of the moral relativism of the Left does not forgive the turning of a blind eye to the transgressions of the Right, for Jesus is not a lesser of two evils–obedience to a lesser evil in this world is still obedience to darkness instead of light.

One Christian writer has observed that:

> If we Christians care about those around us–and Jesus' message is that we must love our neighbors if we are to follow Him–we must concern ourselves with institutions that have such an important impact on people's lives. It is not enough that we act righteously; are the institutions that operate in our name also acting justly?....Christians should never forget that personal salvation will come through the efforts of the Holy Spirit, not Uncle Sam…. Christians….should insist that the state live up to its Biblical role as a just and righteous institution ordained by God, a bulwark against repression and a defender of the poor.[23]

Speaking of his native England, C. S. Lewis noted that citizens condemned the lying and dishonesty of politicians in private but would fail to rebuke them publicly, that "People will even go out of their way to meet them....It may be asked whether that state of society in which rascality undergoes no social penalty is a healthy one; whether we should not be a happier country if certain important people were pariahs as

---

[22] Frank Shakespeare, in epilogue to Russell Kirk's The Roots of American Order, at p. 481.
[23] Doug Bandow, Beyond Good Intentions: A Biblical View of Politics, pp.17, 227, 231.

the hangman once was…."[24] Politicians who represent themselves to be followers of Jesus must be held accountable to Christian standards in a healthy society, even more so in an unhealthy society in moral decline. And whether those leaders are Republican or Democrat is utterly irrelevant.

"The Christian fulfills all his duties to the state, offering no resistance to its decrees, except in one possible contingency: if the state commands him to worship false gods, and to act as if he were a creature of Satan rather than of God, then the Christian must disobey, and follow instead the law of God."[25] A "creature of Satan" elevates self to highest, supports unjust wars and unjust actions like torture, and amasses the wealth of this world at the expense of the less fortunate. However, to stand by and wait in inaction for the state to compel complicity before voicing Christ's teachings in opposition to corrupt state action would be to fail to stand for Christ. Standing for Jesus is not standing by. And if the American religious right, self-appointed guardians of the Christian influence in U.S. politics, influence government action in unchristian directions, then their status as Christians does not make them immune from scrutiny, but demands more earnestly that they be reminded of Scripture: "It is, of course, always fair game to criticize a political party for standing for the wrong causes, and many of the positions of the religious right are both morally and theologically objectionable…."[26]

---

[24] C. S. Lewis, <u>Reflections on the Psalms</u>, p. 67.
[25] Russell Kirk, <u>The Roots of American Order</u>, p.164.
[26] Stephen L. Carter, <u>The Culture of Disbelief: How American Law and Politics Trivialize Religious Devotion</u>, p.48.

The same Christian requirement of integrity to Christ in government which formed the motive for and foundation of the American political structure is in full effect today. "For if there is an authority higher than the authority of any particular state, then no state can demand our absolute obedience or attempt to control every aspect of our lives....That recognition has its roots, when it is recognized, in the teachings of the Christian religion."[27]

Non-Christians often misunderstand the Christian motivation to influence politics. But no one can fail to see why Christians would desire to influence, or hold accountable, Christian-tongued politicians. Yet in both cases the pure Christian heart seeks the same goal–to spread the true word of Christ and His Way to the joyful liberation from the illusions, fears, and worries of this world. Christians are called upon to criticize immoral behavior, but their motivation must always be to help even those they criticize. This is often termed "hate the sin but love the sinner." C. S. Lewis explains this with characteristic flavor when he says that "...the very reason why I hated the things was that I loved the man.... Christianity....want[s] us to hate [sins] in the same way in which we hate things in ourselves: being sorry that the man should have done such things, and hoping, if it is anyway possible, that somehow, sometime, somewhere, he can be cured and made human again."[28] Notwithstanding the title of this book, it is this spirit which

---

[27] John Hollowell, quoted by Russell Kirk in <u>The Roots of American Order</u>, at pp. 174-175.
[28] C.S. Lewis, <u>Mere Christianity</u>, p. 106.

animates this effort—toward George W. Bush, but also toward those who follow him with optimism and trust. I judge no one, but it is painful to see well-intentioned people misguided.

But perhaps the focus should not be on a Christian writer's right to criticize religious or political leaders, but on all Christians' strong Biblically-based obligation to do so, especially in America. After all, our system is based on the freedom of peaceful criticism, if only to keep government in line. Thomas Paine emphasized the importance of informed opinion in democracy, crediting freedom from the bonds of ignorance for prompting both the American and French Revolutions: "Ignorance is of a peculiar nature: once dispelled, it is impossible to re-establish it. It is not originally a thing of itself, but is only the absence of knowledge; and though a man be kept ignorant, he cannot be made ignorant."[29]

John Adams was particularly outspoken about the civic obligation:

> The steady management of a good government is the most anxious, arduous and hazardous vocation on this side of the grave. It becomes necessary to every subject to be in some degree a statesman, and to examine and judge for himself of the tendency of political principles and measures....Let us neglect all party virulence and adhere to facts. Let us believe no man to be infallible or impeccable in government, any more than in religion; take no man's word against evidence, nor implicitly adopt the sentiments

---

[29] Thomas Paine, <u>Rights of Man</u>, p.80.

of others who may be deceived themselves, or may be interested in deceiving us.[30]

And George W. Bush reminds us that "…free peoples might be tempted to take for granted the orderly societies we have come to know."[31]

We Americans have indeed taken our freedoms for granted, allowing our government to steer our country's policies relatively unsupervised for decades. We've benefited from cheap oil without truly trying to influence the Middle East toward democracy, and we've benefited from national security without regard for the sentiments or freedoms of the populations in Nicaragua, the Philippines, Iran, Afghanistan or Iraq, amongst others. Meanwhile, our fealty to Christ has waned in the glow of technological progress and an increased reliance on self in lieu of surrender to God. Recent studies reveal America to be a nation of religious illiterates, "…a nation that believes God speaks in Scripture but that can't be bothered to read what he has to say.…Such ignorance imperils our public life, putting citizens in the thrall of talking heads."[32] Of course, the Bible foretells of just such a mass turning away from God in the end times.[33]

---

[30] Catherine Drinker Bowen, <u>John Adams and the American Revolution</u>, pp. 265, 266.
[31] George W. Bush, quoted in Thomas A. Freiling, <u>George W. Bush on God and Country</u>, p.225
[32] Stephen Prothero, "A Nation of Religious Illiterates," *The Christian Science Monitor* January 20, 2005, p.9.
[33] Paul warns in II Thessolonians 2:3: "Let no man deceive you by any means: for that day shall not come, except there come a falling away first, and that man of sin be revealed, the son of perdition." (KJV)

This moral decline is not recent, (though recently it has become increasingly undeniable), for really this decay has been steady since the advent of the Industrial Revolution and the marvels of science and their influences on man's perception of his relationship to the universe. Darwinian selection, Freudian analysis, physics and chemistry dramatically altered how people viewed existence. Medicine largely conquered (until recently) disease, and innovations in agriculture and transportation elevated the standard of living for all, reducing the need for reliance on God. A. W. Tozer railed in 1949 that "...for millions of Christians,...God is no more real than He is to the non-Christian. They go through life trying to love an ideal and be loyal to a mere principle."[34] Of Christian writers, Tozer was similarly critical: "Christian literature, to be accepted and approved by evangelical leaders of our times, must follow very closely the same train of thought, a kind of "party line" from which it is scarcely safe to depart. A half-century of this in America has made us smug and content. We imitate each other with slavish devotion."[35] This is echoed today where so many Christians are taught not to read the Book of Revelation, or in the stellar rise of "feel-good" congregations that promote the promises of salvation without sufficiently emphasizing repentance, accountability, or good works. It is also echoed in those who accept all of George W. Bush's actions as acceptable without Christian scrutiny, based solely on a trust of his initial Christian "words."

---

[34] A. W. Tozer, <u>The Pursuit of God: The Human Thirst for the Divine</u>, p. 48
[35] Ibid., p. 86.

Of course, this condition of this world is all about to change. When surrounding culture has placed its faith in man and his machinations, when evolution is accepted as scientific fact without subjecting it to the rigors of science, when Americans assume that the greenback will be the first paper currency in history not to collapse, when we cannot supply the world's population with food without destroying ourselves with destructive, unsustainable agricultural methods, then man's faith in himself will surely run aground. Unpleasant though these thoughts be, reality will descend whether we choose or no. Richard N. Goodwin points out that the increasing gap between our physical capacity to ease hardship and the actual condition of modern man, will eventually lead to an enlarged awareness that may yield change: "It is difficult to glimpse the possibilities of an enlarged awareness from within the society. Indeed, almost by definition, one cannot know that his awareness is artificially constrained. One can only suspect it."[36] Because of the artificial constraints imposed in our country by advertising, corporate influence, unbridled capitalism, and the American myth-making machine, Americans do not seem to perceive the huge disparity between the potential of our country for greatness and the glaring shortcomings of our wealth disparity and our government's failure to act with integrity toward the world or toward its own citizenry. Christians are generally more alert to these problems, but theirs is the greatest responsibility because only God and His Son hold the answers to these problems.

---

[36] Richard N. Goodwin, <u>The American Condition</u>, p. 410.

In fact, Christians have been given a powerful mandate to improve worldly government. Paul tells us "See then that ye walk circumspectly, not as fools, but as wise, Redeeming the time, because the days are evil. Wherefore be ye not unwise, but understanding what the will of the Lord is."[37] This is an admonition to Christians that "ignorance is no excuse" where heavenly matters are concerned, and the wisdom referenced is not worldly street-smarts, but Christian discernment.

Every day we choose between God and self. "There is a choice before us—one that we express through a host of minor choices related to friends, activities, thoughts, attitudes, prayer. These everyday decisions put us on one of two paths. On one, God's image in us will be dimmed, blurred, eventually obscured. On the other, we are revealed as shining images of God...."[38] Tozer reminds us that "Complacency is a deadly foe of all spiritual growth."[39]

According to Doug Bandow, "[b]elievers have a Biblical responsibility to apply their beliefs in their civic as well as private lives....a Christian must never forget that his political activities, no less than any other aspect of his life, are to be subject to the Lordship of Christ."[40] Although this makes obvious sense, the strong emotional ties one can develop with political parties or

---

[37] Holy Bible, King James Version, Ephesians 5:15-17.
[38] Louise Perrotta, All You Really Need to Know About Prayer You Can Learn From the Poor, p. 11.
[39] A. W. Tozer, The Pursuit of God: the Human Thirst for the Divine, p. 17.
[40] Doug Bandow, Beyond Good Intentions: A Biblical View of Politics, pp. 23, 221.

positions can cloud Christian judgment. But, "[a]s the sailor locates his position on the sea by "shooting" the sun, so we may get our moral bearings by looking at God. We must begin with God. We are right when, and only when, we stand in a right position relative to God, and we are wrong so far and so long as we stand in any other position."[41] Christians must never let worldly affairs cloud our Lord's visage. And to keep the way clear, we must be forever on guard in this world. As Stephen L. Carter explains:

> ...there is a vital difference between a political inspiration that is fired by one's deepest religious beliefs and a claim of religious belief that is fired by a preexisting political commitment. It is the job of the religiously devout citizen to understand this distinction....
> By calling upon the word of God in service of every known cause, our society diminishes the weight and the force of religious belief. Indeed, by readily supposing that the word of God is so malleable that it can (by coincidence) support every cause that one's politics also happen to support, we undermine the idea of faith as a source of moral guidance.
> This is the essence of political preaching, as I have named the effort to use God's name to bend one's flock to the correct political view. It is the problem with George Bush's effort to link God to America's victory in the Cold War, and it is the problem with much that passes for liberation theology....

---

[41] A.W. Tozer, <u>The Pursuit of God: the Human Thirst for the Divine</u>, p. 95.

> God, it seems, not only roots for the right ideologies, but for the right basketball team as well. But if religion is to be a prop to support secular social and political movements, one cannot sensibly speak of it as an independent force in the world. If the role of the religionist is first to make up his or her mind about which political position to take and next to search for religious arguments to support the already selected view, the idea of faith as the source of moral inspiration is trivialized.[42]

Jesus does not ever suggest that we should pay such obedience to worldly political views, only that we should give Caesar what is Caesar's—implicitly we are not to dabble or engage in politics as worldly people, let alone as politicians. Yet, we must always be "politicians" for Christ, and we must never falter in that party loyalty: "...[p]rimary loyalty for the Christian is not to any nation, but to the kingdom of God."[43]

Loyalty to Jesus is never popular in this world, for Satan has been given permission to establish his dominion here. But wayward American Christians have allowed their faith to grow lukewarm, and it's time that political differences didn't divide the Christian community the way it is fractured in 2006 America. Whether it's civil unions, wealth distribution, capital punishment or euthanasia, God's word does not permit two interpretations—in other words, the two sides cannot

---

[42] Stephen L. Carter, <u>The Culture of Disbelief: How American Law and Politics Trivialize Religious Devotion</u>, pp. 80-81.
[43] "The Politics of the People of God," *Christianity Today*, September, 2005.

both be right. And it's not enough to "think" you're right. The entrance fee to heaven is that, even if we're mistaken, that we truly searched our souls and engaged in repentance and Christian remorse in our effort to serve God His way.

Richard N. Goodwin addresses at length the devolution of America's social structure in the face of the alienating effects of unbridled capitalism, bureaucratization and the influence of our mammoth military-industrial complex. Mr. Goodwin notes that individuals in a society associate their own identities with that of the culture in which they live, and that "[t]hrough this dependent identity individuals are induced to believe or fear that their integrity and being are at issue when the system is menaced."[44] Americans are thus conditioned to overlook shortcomings in their nation's current and historical moral conduct because to admit that their culture had failed morally would be a very uncomfortable personal condemnation. Materialism does not foster healthy spiritual development. Free market capitalism, embraced as American holy mantra, has always occasioned huge inequities and contains no restraints to protect the ecosystem, the disabled, the third-world impoverished, the moral fiber of the family, etc. "But," Goodwin tells us, "any fundamental attack on the nature or structure of economic demand is experienced as a threat to the individual's value, well-being, and identity. It is made to seem that the act of choice will destroy the power to choose, that to choose freedom is to receive slavery. In this fashion we are persuaded and coerced to

---
[44] Richard N. Goodwin, <u>The American Condition</u>, p.259.

tyrannize ourselves."[45] Modern examples of this include the withdrawal of public support for environmentalism because it is dismissed by the example of the extremists; or the refusal of many Americans to acknowledge global warming because to do so would impugn their past and present consumption habits; or the failure to address acid rain and heavy metal pollution because to do so would require that we take inventory of the damage we have done in pursuit of comfort; or the dismissal of those who would attack our capitalist system for the (predominantly non-white) downtrodden it leaves in the trenches rather than admit that the American dream is for the few at the expense of the "underclass;" or the defense to criticism that America is stingy for not doing more to relieve third-world famine, that the United States gives more in international aid than any country in the world, ignoring that, by percentage measures, we give less than almost all other developed nations.

No matter how many Americans are killed by our own government through deliberate experimentation or neglect, no matter how many scandals of greed or perversion shake our capitol, Americans still persist in faith in their institutions, a faith grounded in something they were taught in grade-school history about the sanctity of American government institutions. Or perhaps not by faith, but by a desperate hope driven by a lack of any alternatives. But perhaps the condition in which we find ourselves is not beyond our control except to the extent that we relinquish it: that is, it is by the very fact that we perceive that we are powerless that we become

---

[45] Ibid., p. 393.

powerless, and in the process we abdicate moral responsibility for the society to which we have actually quite willingly surrendered. Goodwin observes:

> ...the conditions we have described, the denials of freedom and the barriers to human fulfillment, have persevered and increased alongside the ceaseless accretions of government. The commanding institutions of our economy have increased their ascendancy through every administration. Yet no experience or analysis, no frustration or visible event, seems able to dispel our faith that the remedy for our afflictions is concealed within the tumescent labyrinth called politics.
>
> We persist in believing that the advent of some new leader, the coming of a wiser government, will reverse the process of modern life and take arms against the sources of oppression; that the fault is not in ourselves but in our political stars. An expectation so at odds with historical experience must be false.[46]

In a similar vein, Allan Bloom holds that "Nonphilosophic men love the truth only as long as it does not conflict with what they cherish–self, family, country, fame, love. When it does conflict, they hate the truth and regard as a monster the man who does not care for these noble things, who proves they are ephemeral and treats them as such."[47] But if truth conflicts with one's view of country or self, then improvement in either comes from critical reflection and introspection, not

---

[46] Ibid., p. 324.
[47] Allan Bloom, <u>The Closing of the American Mind</u>, p. 277.

from denial. This is the painful yet rewarding aspect of Christian life.... "Examine yourselves, whether ye be in the faith; prove your own selves....For we can do nothing against the truth, but for the truth."[48] C. S. Lewis talks of man's growing attachment to the cares of this world in <u>The Screwtape Letters</u>, of how affluence or success particularly can corrupt people:

> Prosperity knits man to the world. He feels that he is 'finding his place in it,' while really it is finding its place in him. His increasing reputation, his widening circle of acquaintances, his sense of importance, the growing pressure of absorbing and agreeable work, build up in him a sense of being really at home on Earth.... [49]

In criticizing the current administration, this book has no political agenda. Bill Clinton would make an easy target, but he never courted the Religious Right or trumpeted his Christian humility the way George W. Bush has. And George has already been elected to a second term. So, unlike his "religious" book, <u>A Charge to Keep</u>, and the umpteen other religiously-fashioned books which appeared so conveniently pre-election in 1999-2000 and 2004 to support his election and re-election, there is no effort here to use religion to influence politics. The world of politics is increasingly inimical to the spiritual condition of today's America, and so will not likely serve as the means for its spiritual betterment. As our society wanes despite our efforts at denial–while

---

[48] <u>Holy Bible</u>, KJV, II Corinthians 13:5,8.
[49] C. S. Lewis, <u>The Screwtape Letters</u>, p.83.

a whole nation medicates itself and its children with anti-depressants even as it exports to the world the consumptive culture which created the conditions in response to which it mass-medicates–we are forced to confront the failures of technology and of the pursuit of self. To deny our government's moral failures, or those of George W., requires a devotion to ideology which is not Christian, which in fact eclipses and corrupts Christ's teachings, and which is reminiscent of Orwell's <u>1984</u>, requiring "…a sort of athleticism of mind, an ability at one moment to make the most delicate use of logic and at the next to be unconscious of the crudest logical errors."[50]

Many Christians have allowed the cares of the world to distract them from watching closely what their government officials are doing, and many Americans voted for George W. Bush out of religious conviction. But a "lesser of evils" method of voting does not absolve the lesser evil from accountability, and this must be especially so for Christians. Many on the Religious Right believe that "Abortion…trumps all other issues:"[51] abortion and gay marriage have been deliberately employed to garner the Christian vote, while Christians have cast an uncritical eye on a myriad of other government actions under the Bush W. stewardship which have had a devastating impact on our world image (and therefore Christianity's image), and upon our future.

The invasion of Iraq does not comply with the Christian doctrine of just war, nor can any of the justifications

---

[50] George Orwell, <u>1984</u>, p. 229
[51] Ron Suskind, <u>The Price of Loyalty</u>, p. 311, quoting Bishop Michael J. Sheridan.

for the invasion be supported with Christ's teachings, nor has George W. ever even attempted to justify that war with either. The world holds its breath to see if George W. was "right" or not, ignoring the foundation of civilized man, of democratic forms of government, and of Christianity–the ends do not justify the means; might does not make right. If President Bush stabilizes Iraq, does that make his actions "right"? Without Christian justification for a war (i.e. just war theory, or self defense), winning that war does not make it just. And if George W. is proven "wrong" by increased deterioration in Iraq, and as a result world sentiment is turned against America and the ranks of the Islamic extremist terrorists are swollen, how will this have reflected on Jesus? How has America represented Jesus in the Iraq War, versus its worldly "national interests"?

The shear magnitude of torture, in geographic area and degree of barbarity, employed by Americans after the invasion of Iraq, logically can be explained only by one of two possibilities: either several generations of American soldiers, crossing race and gender lines, are fundamentally corrupt and chose to endanger themselves in wartime by inviting retaliatory treatment, ignoring our country's whole history of compassion in war as well as peace, all at the same time in many different locations; or, the United States government instructed that torture be employed to extract information in the service of the cause of fighting terrorists. White House memos support the latter theory. But neither scenario is acceptable to Christian doctrine.

Compassionate conservatism pretends to be faith-based but has yielded nothing but empty words and an excuse to cut government programs and "help" the poor by reducing their liberal-induced dependency on social programs. Is it really true that the poor are impoverished because of moral decay, as the conservatives currently assert? Redistributing wealth in reverse-Christian fashion while hiding behind the failed concept of trickle-down economics was greedy and patently unchristian, and now our economy is irrevocably crippled by debt from the double-barrel effect of tax refunds and a massive military build-up and nation-building investment. This unconservative and unchristian conduct is given a pass because the president prays humbly. Christians must not ignore unchristian actions in their leaders because those leaders spout pretty Christian prayers. Bill Clinton was a professed Baptist, but his pathetic oval office immorality was surpassed by his embarrassing public criminal perjuries, and it was well to call him on it, albeit with no success.

America's foreign policy has been hypocritical, short-sighted, and undemocratic for decades. Those policies are coming home to roost, and we are not being targeted "because we're free." Christians must take stock that their nationalism and fear do not eclipse Christ and His teachings in these most vital of times. This book seeks to prove, without political rhetoric but with facts and Scripture, that the American public has been misled—has perhaps allowed itself to be misled—about a number of important government actions under President George W. Bush. This book's heavy use of quotations for support of arguments is an effort to make a strong case, not a long book. As Ron Suskind writes: "when the latest innovations in public combat include unflinching denial of what is clearly true, a compelling document—there for the reader to see—can provide the indisputable facts to anchor meaningful debate."[52] Americans are alarmingly willing to dismiss factual evidence where it undermines or threatens previously held ideological views. Many have thus too willingly dismissed the Abu Ghraib abuses as the actions of a few errant soldiers, or swallowed a replacement justification for the Iraq War when it was finally admitted that there were no WMD. And criticisms of George W. are too often dismissed without reflection, based on "faith" in his integrity and Christian sincerity, but based on words only, without further inquiry.

For the secular conservative, perhaps this is forgivable....but Christians are supposed to know better. Galatians 6:1 instructs us "Brethren, if a man be overtaken in a fault, ye which are spiritual, restore such an one in the spirit of meekness; considering thyself, lest thou also be tempted."[53] In 1 Timothy 5, Paul declares "Them that sin rebuke before all, that others also may fear. I charge thee before God, and the Lord Jesus Christ, and the elect angels, that thou observe these things without preferring one before another, doing nothing by partiality."[54] In Matthew, Jesus encourages us to "Let your light so shine before men, that they may see your good works, and glorify your Father which is in heaven"

---

[52] Ron Suskind, The Price of Loyalty, p. 339
[53] Holy Bible, KJV, Galatians 6:1.
[54] Ibid., KJV, 1 Timothy 5:20-21.

and rejects the idea of human worldly leaders when he tells us "Neither be ye called masters: for one is your Master, even Christ. But he that is greatest among you shall be your servant. And whoever shall exalt himself shall be abased; and he that shall humble himself shall be exalted."[55]

A. W. Tozer observed of religious leaders in 1940s America that "[t]he grosser manifestations of these sins–egotism, exhibitionism, self-promotion–are strongly tolerated in Christian leaders, even in circles of impeccable orthodoxy....Promoting self under the guise of promoting Christ is currently so common as to excite little notice."[56] If such piggy-backing on Jesus is unacceptable in religious leaders, surely it is similarly objectionable in politicians, and we must hold them to comparable standards of integrity, not give them unquestioning support: "We must place our faith in Jesus, not the President, as high priest."[57]

Thomas Paine wrote that

[i]n the representative system, the reason for everything must publicly appear. Every man is a proprietor in Government, and.... [a]bove all, he does not adopt the slavish custom of following what in other Governments are called LEADERS....Government is not a trade which any man, or any body of men,

---

[55] Ibid., KJV, Matthew 5:16, 23:11.
[56] A. W. Tozer, <u>The Pursuit of God: the Human Thirst for the Divine</u>, pp.42-43.
[57] Doug Bandow, <u>Beyond Good Intentions, A Biblical View of Politics</u>, p. 230.

has a right to set up and exercise for his own emolument....It has of itself no rights; they are altogether duties.[58]

These are words of which George W. Bush would no doubt approve; holding leaders accountable, demanding transparency in government, questioning leaders to ensure they are responsive to their duties. And when it comes to faith, surely they should be questioned all the more: as George has proclaimed, "I believe it is important to live my faith, not flaunt it."[59] And after experience with previous Republican administrations and two years in the inner circle of the Bush Jr. team, Paul O'Neill stressed that "...the American people need to demand more of people who would be their leaders."[60]

Of course, since the birth of our nation the power of the government has grown at the expense of individual citizens: "The flight of political power to the federal executive has dispersed the citizenry's authority over the function of government. This fragmentation of influence diminishes the reality of control, by the individual voter and by the body of voters."[61] Additionally, the secular nature of our government subjects us to the potential for great risks to our freedom, for

...Catholic shrine seeking, Protestant poverty pounding and Puritan witch crushing were only previews of the spectacular modern mysticisms of racism, fascism, imperialism and the infinitely durable

---

[58] Thomas Paine, <u>Rights of Man</u>, pp.140, 144.
[59] George W. Bush, <u>A Charge To Keep</u>, p. 138.
[60] quoted in Ron Suskind, <u>The Price of Loyalty</u>, p. 341.
[61] Richard N. Goodwin, <u>The American Condition</u>, p. 349.

National Mission-Greatness-Destiny....Some forms of mysticism...contain...unparalleled possibilities for repression and control. Earlier leaders–popes, priests and kings–were compelled to justify their deeds by obedience to a divine will and nature as set forth in holy books....[62]

Men without moral codes or integrity are potentially more dangerous than religious zealots–no moral codes hampered Hitler's faith in science above divine will. America has a history of using "manifest destiny" to justify domestic and foreign expansions, including the genocide committed against the American Indians; now it is our stated national obligation to spread democracy (and of course the 'freedoms' of free markets) through the world, whether or not those we influence "know what's good for them."

Of particular danger is the religious zealot in the secularist government seat, for often what pretends to be orthodoxy contains doctrines tainted by unchristian influences. "Thus, although neo-orthodoxy opposed numerous liberal tendencies, it also contained several other of those tendencies. The fact that it used Biblical language to express unbiblical concepts made some of its teachings an even more deceptive tool than liberalism in Satan's war against the kingdom of God."[63] Similarly, the conservatives under George W. Bush have imbued their ideological platform with a smattering of liberal concepts like compassion (though an illusory compassion), increased federal government control and dependency,

---

[62] Ibid., pp. 47, 49.
[63] Renald E. Showers, <u>What On Earth is God Doing?</u>, p. 92.

and big spending. On the eve of the 2004 election, George W. Bush even said he'd support civil unions in an effort to garner votes. The greater sin, though, is that George W. Bush has brought a truckload of insidious, unchristian policies to government, masquerading as Christian. Giving wealth to the rich is not Jesus' bag, not even to trickle down some sustenance to some poor leper (Jesus was a more direct philanthropist). There is no Biblical support for this gimmick, even if there were economic support (there overwhelmingly is not, even from right-wingers). The war in Iraq is not a just war, and the Pope's plea not to invade was ignored by George W. Bush. (Have there been any "just" preemptive wars since Christ came to us?) The torture at Abu Ghraib and elsewhere, for which America will always be remembered, occurred with moral approbation from the top, or at least on their undisciplined watch, not to mention that this never would have been possible had we avoided an unjust, unchristian invasion. Our environment is being sacrificed to our demand for economic growth and for the benefit of corporate America's corpulent expansion. (God gave us the Earth to caretake, not desecrate.)

George W. Bush is due for a moral accounting, by his own standards and by the Bible he says he reveres. Just as Clinton should have been held to the laws of the land, George W. must be held to the laws of God so that others will see where he leads, and not follow: "Madness in great ones must not unwatched go."[64]

---

[64] William Shakespeare, <u>Hamlet</u>, Act III, Scene I, line 198.

Words Versus Deeds

> Beware of false prophets, which come to you in sheep's clothing, but inwardly they are ravenous wolves. Ye shall know them by their fruits....Not every one that saith unto me, Lord, Lord, shall enter into the kingdom of heaven; but he that doeth the will of my Father which is in heaven. Many will say to me in that day, Lord, Lord, have we not prophesied in thy name? and in thy name have cast out devils? and in thy name done many powerful works? And then will I profess unto them, I never knew you; depart from me, ye that work. iniquity. [65]

Repeatedly the New Testament emphasizes that Christian action is the measure of Christian devotion, not words or ceremony. Jesus says again in Matthew that "...the tree is known by his fruit,"[66] and these words are also recounted in the book of Luke.[67] Romans 2:6 instructs us that "...God will reward each of us according to what we have done."[68] In John 14:11-12, Jesus implores "Believe me that I am in the father, and the father in me: or else believe me for the very works' sake. Verily, verily, I say unto you, He that believeth on me, the works that I do shall he do also; and greater works than these shall he do; because I go unto my Father."[69] James 2:14 asks: "What doth it profit, my brethren, though a man say he hath faith, and have not

---

[65] Holy Bible, KJV, Matthew 7:15-23.
[66] Ibid., KJV, Matthew 12:33.
[67] Ibid., KJV, Luke 6:43-44.
[68] KJV
[69] KJV

works?"[70] and then answers (in verse 26) "For as the body without the spirit is dead, so faith without works is dead also."[71] And in Galatians, Paul admonishes "If we live in the Spirit, let us also walk in the Spirit."[72]

George W. Bush has often cited the scriptural premise that "faith without works is dead."[73] He is quoted as saying "…I'm mindful of walking that walk…That's the best thing I can do as president. And when you walk the walk, people of faith will walk right with you."[74] Actually, people of faith have walked with George W. Bush based almost solely on his words, for he is largely "works-less". Attending Ivy League schools, operating oil companies at a loss with rich cronies' money, accruing personal wealth in the millions of dollars at public expense, and building a baseball stadium just don't tally high with Jesus Christ. But he talks the talk and looks pensive really well, kind of like the way Ronald Reagan waved the flag.

Even non-Christians who learned their Christian theology from "Davy and Goliath" can readily recognize the Bushian disparity between words and proper Christian conduct. In <u>Shrub: The Short but Happy Political Life of George W. Bush,</u> the obviously liberal authors opine: "In the end, the Christian right gets more sermons than blood, sweat or policy out of Bush. He talks the talk but rarely walks the walk—and still gets

---

[70] KJV
[71] KJV
[72] KJV, Galatians 5:25.
[73] *See* <u>God and George W. Bush: a spiritual life</u>, Paul Kengor, p.89; Thomas Freiling, <u>George W. Bush on God & Country</u>, pp.82, 96.
[74] David Aikman, <u>George W. Bush: Man of Faith</u>, p. 130.

the support of the Christian right. Among other things, it's very shrewd politics....[T]he Christian right will settle for the talk instead of the walk in order to be a winner."[75] Christians might be inclined to dismiss such criticism from non-Christians, but non-Christians are Jesus' target audience, and their alienation by Christians causes Christ sorrow. Non-Christians have a sharp eye for hypocrisy in Christians, but only because of their own doubts about their non-belief, and their inner desire that there be a Greater Truth.

We fail Christ's opportunity with non-Christians when we mis-communicate His message, and we most powerfully do this when our actions fall short of our flowery proclamations.

And so I wish to serve my Christ by clarifying to as many who will listen that George W. Bush does not speak for Jesus Christ, notwithstanding his thinly-veiled appropriation of that function. Neither does the Religious Right speak for Jesus Christ. Neither do I speak for Jesus Christ. For He speaks clearly enough on His own, and He should be sought as the primary source always. Americans must no longer accept capitalistic sound-bite blurbs or snippets of Christian doctrine, but must breathe in deeply the truth of Christ's message in the Oswald Chambers tradition. Devotion to Jesus is not restricted to Sundays, and the political lectern is not His pulpit. Christians must be careful who they follow, for "…good intentions are not enough….believers who declare their support for worthy ends but then back ineffective–or even counterproductive–means do little

---

[75] At pp. 82, 83.

more than salve their own consciences."[76] George W. Bush, intentionally or through ignorance, has created counterproductive means for his own stated lofty goals: a war in Iraq that has bolstered the membership of terrorist groups and undermined international support for America; No Child Left Behind, an experiment doomed to failure which usurped local autonomy; a leniency toward business which has encouraged corporate fraud and postponed resolution of air and water pollution crises; tax refunds in the face of war and rising deficits, a drag—not boost—to the economy; an alienation of millions from Christianity instead of a modeling of Christ's peaceful promise of hope.

This list of complaints is not simply rhetoric, open to debate. For unlike political "science" disputes or partisan wrangling, Christianity looks to a universal moral code. God doesn't both support and reject capital punishment, gay marriage, pollution, war, wealth and gluttony in the face of poverty, etc. The concepts, then, of liberal versus conservative Christians require sincere reflection, not obeisance to an ideological platform–Jesus Christ's teachings are not an ideology. A. W. Tozer stressed that "[t]here must be somewhere a fixed center against which everything else is measured, where the law of relativity does not enter and we can say "IS" and make no allowances."[77] (Bill Clinton should have read Tozer.)

---

[76] Doug Bandow, <u>Beyond Good Intentions: A Biblical View of Politics</u>, p. XII.
[77] A.W. Tozer, <u>The Pursuit of God: the Human Thirst for the Divine</u>, p. 94.

The same rule of God's law applies to us all, and is not malleable to our earthly imaginings. Thomas Merton wrote:

> The Law can only be understood when it is kept. It cannot be kept unless God drives out the contrary law, the law of selfishness, of cupidity, and infuses into our hearts His selfless charity. Without grace, the "letter" of the Law, the truth of the Law, serves only to condemn us, because even though we understand it we don't keep it....Loving the truth, we are able to live by the truth. When we live by the truth our lives themselves become true. We become what we ought to be. We not only exist, we live. We not only hear the word, we keep it, and therefore we fulfill it. We live in God. God lives in us. His will is done in us. He is manifested in us. He is glorified in us.[78]

This rule of God's Law rules us all, and George W.'s soul is important, but each and every soul is equally important to our Lord. Therefore, the answers to the questions raised herein need to be sought by every individual Christian, independent of any assessment of George W. Bush as a Christian, just as each of us has our own relationship with and accountability to the Son of God. I do not judge George W. Bush, though I harshly judge many of his actions and urge him to repent.

It is astonishing that people, Christians included, can look at identical facts and draw opposite conclusions. As to George W.'s moral leadership, time has sufficiently lapsed that we can take stock of this administration's

---

[78] Thomas Merton, <u>Bread In the Wilderness</u>, p. 168.

actions. Paul Kengor, author of <u>God and George W. Bush: a Spiritual Life,</u> observes of George W.:

> His supporters and those of a conservative religious stripe have expressed a sense that God has dropped Bush into this grand moment to undertake this purpose. For every evangelical who proffers such an assertion, a liberal Christian or agnostic begs to differ....Such questioning of Bush's faith was popular among antiwar Christians. Therein lay an irony: liberal Christians chastised Bush for allegedly believing that he knew God's will, and being convinced that God was on his side. And yet they themselves claimed that Bush was not following Christ's teachings. In so doing, of course, they too were presuming to know God's will—and that God was on their side.[79]

These words are reminiscent of Thomas Paine's explanation of the importance of separation of church and state:

> Mind thine own concerns. If he believes not as thou believest, it is a proof that thou believest not as he believeth, and there is no earthly power can determine between you.

> With respect to what are called denominations of religion, if every one is left to judge his own religion, there is no such thing as a religion that is wrong; but if they are to judge of each other's religion, there is no such thing as a religion that is right; and therefore all the world is right, or all the world is wrong.[80]

---

[79] Paul Kengor, <u>God and George W. Bush, a spiritual life</u>, pp. x-xi, 229.
[80] Thomas Paine, <u>Rights of Man</u>, p.50.

The problem with both of these arguments is that they constitute moral relativism, and they could both be used to dismiss murder, adultery, incest, etc. God most certainly did drop George W. into modern America, but was this as savior or destroyer, for both serve God's purposes. Mr. Kengor's defense of President Bush dismisses those who would recite Christ's words, instead of responding to the doctrinal challenges that have been raised to specific Bush administration policies: he essentially claims that George W.'s "works" in this world, as Christian representative of the United States of America, are beyond judgment because both sides assert that theirs is the morally superior perspective.

Additionally, Mr. Kengor is disingenuous when he characterizes all those who disagree with the concept of George's divine insertion into our lives as "liberal Christian or agnostic." This implies that those asserting that Iraq is an unjust war, or that to distribute public funds to the wealthy while the poor grow poorer and more desperate is not what Jesus instructed, are automatically "liberal Christian or agnostic," implicitly denying the applicability, or even the existence, of universal or crystal-clear Christ-based truths which exist independent of party, church or ideological affiliation. And when Mr. Kengor writes that "…such questioning of Bush's faith was popular among antiwar Christians" he equates Christian doctrine with populism, trivializing people's devout Christian faith even though a majority of Christians worldwide are (understandably) pacifist arising from their yearning understanding of Jesus Christ and not because of their political belief system, and even though "antiwar Christian" is the only label relative to war that one could assign to Jesus–what war did he lead, propose, or approve of, aside from the war for peace and love of His Father? Did Jesus not say "...if my kingdom were of this world, then would my servants fight, that I should not be delivered to the Jews: but now is my kingdom not from hence."[81] Perhaps the Gospels are the actual inspiration for the opposition to war which is "popular among antiwar Christians." Perhaps those Gospels ought not so lightly be dismissed in this deceptive way, for perhaps Bush simply wasn't following Christ's teachings and that's what made many Christians oppose the War, rather than "antiwar" Christians creating doctrine–again, Jesus' words are there for all of us.

The Republican Party and the Religious Right believe they act with a God-given purpose. Yet self-righteousness is not of God, and this very attitude has carried a political and (worldly) ideological division into the church pews of America's Christian community. This is surely why "[t]he National Council of Churches (of which Bush[Sr.]'s own Episcopal Church is a member) issued a strong denunciation of the attempt to cast the GOP as God's Own Party, warning that the Republicans stood on the threshold of blasphemy."[82]

We must not cloud Jesus' words with absurd party loyalties–this is Satan's goal, and he is succeeding too well. We let him, through our material attachments and

---

[81] Holy Bible, KJV, John 18:36.
[82] Stephen L. Carter, The Culture of Disbelief: How American Law and Politics Trivializes Religious Devotion, p. 47.

our fears, through the busyness of this world which leads us to put Jesus and God on hold, allowing politicians to steer our religious views and our moral code instead of constantly searching, in each day's actions, for Christ. A. W. Tozer describes well the clarity of Christ's teachings, not allowing for easy dismissal on grounds of "antiwar" or "liberal" or even "conservative" biases: "His words are the essence of truth. He is not offering an opinion; Jesus never uttered opinions. He never guessed; He knew, and He knows.... He spoke out of the fullness of His Godhead, and His words are very Truth itself.... It is wisdom for us to listen."[83]

So to Mr. Kengor's assertion that no one can question our president because they just lay a competing claim to truth, I say there are great religious teachers who say differently, most importantly my Lord Jesus Christ. Allan Bloom writes: "The philosopher wants to know things as they are. He loves the truth. That is an intellectual virtue. He does not love to tell the truth (because that would threaten his survival). That is a moral virtue."[84] Jesus was the ultimate demonstrator of moral virtue in the risks he ignored to spread the Word of the Father. We are called to similarly not just speak but also to spread His Truth, fearless of reprisal where we act for His sake. In the American liberal revolution of the last half century, conservative Allan Bloom complained that "[i]t became almost impossible to question the radical orthodoxy without risking vilification....[A]ll parties in

---

[83] A. W. Tozer, The Pursuit of God: the Human Thirst for the Divine, pp. 104, 105.
[84] Allan Bloom, The Closing of the American Mind, p. 279.

a democracy are jeopardized when passion can sweep the facts before it."[85] Are we now riding the pendulum back with recent similar intolerance toward dissent, now from the Right?

Richard N. Goodwin, in <u>The American Condition,</u> addressed at length the gradual decay of the American dream at the hands of an ever-growing and amoral corporate and governmental bureaucracy, which has caused the dissolution of individual democratic power and freedom, practically eliminating accountability from these institutions: "...it is the citizenry, the American community, the "public good," which has become fragmented and made incapable of effective assertion."[86] Reviewing our nation's involvement in Vietnam, Goodwin addressed the ideological failures which led to our stubborn continuation of the war. He observed:

> A logical structure built on faulty premises can be rational. It can even be brilliant....But when premises themselves are contradicted or ignored when found contrary to desired conclusions, then reason becomes something else....But when a person purports to reason on the basis of information he knows to be inadequate, then he moves toward nonrational or mystical thought. It is a question of degree.[87]

History is being repeated in Iraq, as our military-industrial complex and huge business interests push us into debt-and war-driven growth without adequate

---

[85] Ibid., p. 355.
[86] Richard N. Goodwin, <u>The American Condition</u>, p. 338.
[87] Ibid., pp. 52, 53.

moral reflection. Americans have been led into war on inadequate information, hindsight rationalizations are being procured, and the deception and misinformation extends beyond the Iraq War. I do not seek to influence the decision to go to war–it's too late for that, we own the situation now. And as I've noted, George W. Bush is not up for another term. I seek to alert Christians and non-Christians to the benign watchfulness of a benevolent God, and that "Since believing is looking it can be done at any time."[88] Americans need to be attentive in these end times. As George Orwell observed of the 'proles' in 1984: "Until they become conscious they will never rebel, and until after they have rebelled they cannot become conscious."[89]

The Bible is a gift to us. Its wisdom and God's Word are being diminished by modern American culture and the advent of man's faith in, and dependence upon, science. Bloom describes the death of the studious appreciation of the Greek Classics in a way which echoes the loss of faith in God's truth: "…no one even tries to read them as they were once read–for the sake of finding out whether they are true."[90]

Not only must Christians study the Bible to discern truth, but "…believers should be dedicated to making people confront fundamental Biblical values in their political activities as well as all other aspects of their lives."[91]

---

[88] A.W. Tozer, The Pursuit of God: the Human Thirst for the Divine, p. 88.
[89] George Orwell, 1984, p. 61.
[90] Allan Bloom, The Closing of the American Mind, p. 373.
[91] Doug Bandow, Beyond Good Intentions: A Biblical View of Politics, p. 230.

And this peaceful confrontation has never been as important as it is now. As Tozer notes, for Christians

> [t]he 'other world,' which is the object of this world's disdain and the subject of the drunkard's mocking song, is our carefully chosen goal and the object of our holiest longing....But we must avoid the common fault of pushing the 'other world' into the future. It is not future, but present. It parallels our familiar physical world, and the doors between the two worlds are open.[92]

And so I call upon those who support this unholy war in Iraq to account to Jesus Christ for their actions, not to national security interests or megalomaniacal hallucinations about God choosing America to export its materialism and failed culture to the Middle East. Does George W. Bush ever, in proper Christian fashion, admit a mistake? Any mistake? Ever?

Again, Tozer: "Any man who by repentance and a sincere return to God will break himself out of the mold in which he has been held, and will go to the Bible itself for his spiritual standards, will be delighted with what he finds there."[93] I call upon Christians to review the facts of modern America's (and Americans') conduct in light of these spiritual standards, and to seek common Christian truth. Jesus says: "to this end was I born, and for this cause came I into the world, that I should bear witness unto the truth. Every one that is of the truth

---

[92] A. W. Tozer, <u>The Pursuit of God: the Human Thirst for the Divine</u>, p. 55.
[93] Ibid., p. 66.

heareth my voice."[94] Pray to Jesus for guidance. "Ask, and it shall be given you; seek, and you shall find; knock, and it shall be opened unto you."[95]

Paul was particularly strident in his repeated cautions in this regard:

> Take heed therefore unto yourselves, and to all the flock, over the which the Holy Ghost hath made you overseers, to feed the Church of God, which he hath purchased with his own blood.
> For I know this, that after my departing shall grievous wolves enter in among you, not sparing the flock.
> Also of your own selves shall men arise, speaking perverse things, to draw away disciples after them.
> Therefore watch, and remember, that by the space of three years I ceased not to warn every one night and day with tears.[96]

Over and over in Revelation, a key message is conveyed from our Savior: "behold, I come as a thief. Blessed is he that watcheth, and keepeth his garments, lest he walk naked, and they see his shame."[97] ; "Behold, I come quickly: blessed is he that keepeth the sayings of the prophecy of this book….And, behold, I come quickly; and my reward is with me, to give every man according as his work shall be. I am Alpha and Omega, the beginning and the end, the first and the last."[98] The last words of the Bible reflect this same message: "He

---

[94] <u>Holy Bible</u>, KJV, John 18: 37
[95] Ibid., Luke 11: 9.
[96] Ibid., Acts 20: 28-31. (KJV)
[97] Ibid., Revelation 16: 15.
[98] Ibid., Revelation 22;7, 12, 13.

which testifieth these things saith, Surely I come quickly. Amen. Even so, come, Lord Jesus. The grace of our Lord Jesus Christ be with you all. Amen.'[99]

---

[99] Ibid., Revelation 22:20, 21.

Chapter 2

ACCOUNTABILITY AND TORT REFORM

"I'm very firm on seeing to it that this government hold people to account."[100]

It is curious that our culture has devolved so quickly under the pressures of the most rapid technological modernization ever experienced by any society. Most Americans, and most industrialized peoples, have adapted their lives to the conveniences but also the burdens of modern life, where cell phones, satellites and computers make our lives, our brains and our spirits whir at unprecedented levels of activity and stimulation. Amongst the negative effects of this growing techno-codependency is that Americans by and large have too much stress and too little time to absorb information not required for that daily free-market grind. Television replaces, more than contributes to, informed insight.

---

[100] George W. Bush, from "Bush Downplays Bailout Prospects For GM and Ford," *The Wall Street Journal*, January 26, 2006, p. A4.

Americans are escaping into their alienating technologies, and that very escape is blinding them to the consequences of that abandonment to dehumanization. For Americans don't just blame lawyers for the lawsuits filed by non-lawyers, and for the cases decided by non-lawyers. Americans also blame politicians for the corruption, mismanagement and lack of accountability in government, while not only are Americans the ones who elected them, but they also demand a lack of integrity from their candidates by penalizing politicians for minor slip-ups or forthright statements: Americans want to hear happy talk and promises, celebrity-style polish, not honesty; and that's what they reward at the polls. John Kenneth Galbraith observes that American criticism of government is superficial because a majority of Americans elect our leaders: "We attribute to politicians what should be attributed to the community they serve."[101]

But let's not stop there. Americans complain about the ubiquitous availability of pornography, while we are the world's largest producers *and* consumers of the stuff. (Would the Internet ever have existed without it?) We want pills or 20$ gimmicks to erase our waistlines instead of facing up to the biological requirement of regular exercise and a healthy, balanced diet. We are hopelessly dependent on oil, which for Americans, the world leaders of oil exploration and refining technologies, has always been cheap. Low cost oil has yielded inefficient use–we have bigger cars and houses than anyone in the world–yet we still insist on gluttonous consumption of the stuff,

---

[101] John Kenneth Galbraith, <u>The Culture of Contentment</u>, p. 18.

and Vice President Cheney has pronounced that the administration is not about to tell Americans what cars to drive, i.e. tell them to reduce their gluttony.

Americans continue to borrow at mathematically-unrepayable rates; personally, but also nationally. Our trade imbalance is sucking the wealth from our country in direct exchange for our consumption, and our federal debt is so large it has lost the ability to be comprehended by mortal man's feeble intellect. No nation has borrowed anywhere near so much money, in dollar terms, ever. Ironically, the only reason we have been allowed to borrow so much is our historic innovativeness and work ethic, the very things which are presently in decline. Our oblivion to our collective indebtedness is only rivaled by our misplaced faith in the dollar, the mighty greenback, a false idol which we foolishly believe can never fall, but which is already nearly worthless, vapid paper kept alive by that very faith, materialism.

Or perhaps Americans should turn their blind eye back to poverty, within our own glorified nation, and world-wide, which we could have eliminated with our unprecedented though quickly-waning wealth. How do we rate as a "Christian" nation? Are we really so entitled to impose our "system" of government-corporate collaboration on the rest of the world when we're so obviously messed up? But wait, we have that handy (though decidedly unchristian) denial thing to call upon, our reverse-accountability pathology. This has been offered up so conveniently by the modern conservative movement of compassionate conservatism, which was founded largely upon the works of Myron Magnet and Marvin Olasky, both of whom George W. Bush has gushingly praised as visionaries. Both Messrs. Magnet and Olasky hold that the (predominantly black and Hispanic) poor, the "underclass," are in that condition because of a hopeless dependency created by the liberal welfare programs of the 1960s.[102] (Never mind that those programs, like the programs born of the Great Depression, arose in direct response to dramatic wealth disparities that threatened social unrest if not anarchy).[103]

The deceptive beauty of the compassionate conservatism dogma is that it dismisses both the poor and minorities in one fell swoop. Let us borrow from Myron Magnet to glimpse the Bush worldview of the impoverished:

> Yes, injustice and victimization long kept blacks poor, but the injustice was racism, not some recondite economic inequity....The crucial barriers have fallen. They fell years ago, giving way before the force of the civil rights movement and the 1964 Civil Rights Act....Not by any means has racism been expunged from the fabric of American life—and possibly the increasing rancorous tone of racial politics has pushed that goal further off into the future. But institutionalized racism has dramatically abated....[104]

---

[102] Magnet opines that "...welfare shields its recipients from the demands and obligations of the ordinary world." The Dream and the Nightmare: The Sixties' Legacy to the Underclass, p. 142.

[103] "Testifying before a Senate committee, the American banker J.P. Morgan warned, "If you destroy the leisure class, you destroy civilization." Asked later by reporters to identify the leisure class, he said, "All those who can afford to hire a maid." " John Kenneth Galbraith, The Culture of Contentment, pp. 5-6.

[104] Myron Magnet, The Dream and the Nightmare: the Sixties' Legacy to the Underclass, p.140.

After citing poll statistics of white attitudes as his sole support, Magnet concludes:

> It's a huge shift from the majority white view in the forties that whites should get job preference to the 1972 poll data showing that almost all whites support equality of economic opportunity for blacks. All this has meant that for years blacks have not been barred from the economic mainstream....Though doors still remain to be unlocked, as a general principle opportunity is open for whoever wishes to seek it.... But the idea of the victimized poor didn't allow the Haves to rest content with overturning the barrier of institutionalized discrimination....Mere equality wasn't justice enough for such victims; it wasn't adequate to solve their problem....[105]

How comforting for black Americans to know that white people don't believe they're racist any longer.... The only (glaring) fault with Mr. Magnet's (and by extension, Mr. Bush's) view, aside from its laughable absurdity, is that blacks made deplorable economic progress in the trickle-down years of Ronald Reagan, when jobs were created and incomes rose (albeit on borrowed funds that we have yet to start repaying): "In 1987 the income of the typical black family...equaled just 56.1 percent of the typical white family's income, the lowest comparative percentage since the 1960s."[106]

---

[105] Ibid., pp. 140-141.
[106] Kevin Phillips, <u>The Politics of Rich and Poor: Wealth and the American Electorate in the Reagan Aftermath</u>, p. 207.

And who do Americans blame for their pollution of the planet? Even if one chooses to deny the overwhelming factual evidence supporting global (ocean) warming concerns, the acid rain, solid waste, lawn fertilizer, mercury, lead, dioxin, and carbon dioxide we create is unparalleled by any people in the world, or in the history of the world, on a per capita basis. We're too busy to distract from our consumptive delirium to address the fact that we hold individual pound-by-pound responsibility for this problem.

While Americans enjoy their worldly comforts, barking at the lawyers they hire and politicians they elect, they ignore other countries and their cultures. No wonder America's wide-eyed ignorance that the Arab world resents us for eighty years of intrusion into their culture and religion in pursuit of oil and its control, and for one-sided military, economic and political support for Israel in the face of Palestinian home(land)lessness and suffering. But isn't it easier to live in ignorance of government policies and the individual accountability that that would require, and instead believe that the terrorists from Saudi Arabia attacked the world trade center "because we're free."

And while we're exporting our supposedly Christian-based culture to the rest of the world whether they like it or not, perhaps we should reflect upon the virtual extinction of marriage as an institution in our country, and the resulting collapse of the family unit and the society on which it rests. Are we shipping billions of doses of Xanax and Prozac to the countries we "liberate" to give them a head start absorbing our marvelous "culture"?

Are we forwarding copies of our modern sitcoms as well? Where gay men routinely engage in conduct that would be prurient and sexist if between heterosexuals? (Those silly Arabs need to get over thousands of years of homophobia, so let's help them revise their Koran the way we've liberalized our Bible). America with these incongruities must heed Christ's admonition: "Woe unto you, scribes and Pharisees, hypocrites! For ye are like unto whited sepulchers, which indeed appear beautiful outward, but are within full of dead men's bones, and of all uncleanness. Even so ye also outwardly appear righteous unto men, but within ye are full of hypocrisy and iniquity."[107]

Despite all this, Americans still repose faith in their government, and in their President. Yet again, denial serves, as we allow our leaders and our corporations to determine the world's future. Americans control the whole world's economic, environmental and perhaps moral future in their votes and in their daily consumptive choices. Christian Americans should know better, or have they too been lulled away from Scripture by the consumption conundrum? First Corinthians 7:22 tells us "For he that is called in the Lord, being a servant, is the Lord's freeman: likewise also he that is called, being free, is Christ's servant. Ye are bought with a price; be not ye the servants of men."[108]

In following Christ instead of our government we quickly see America's position in the world not as an opportunity for hedonistic wealth accumulation or its

---

[107] KJV, Matthew 23:27-28.
[108] KJV, 1 Corinthians 7:22.

exportation but for exemplary national conduct fostering peace through example. Nuclear bunker busters revive the nuclear arms race, expand the use of nuclear weapons to the battlefield (have we learned nothing from the mustard gas of World War I?), escalate tensions with countries like North Korea and Iran, and contribute to pollution without producing real long-term economic growth, all in the name of self-defense against an endless pressure from foreign foes who do not even begin to rival our military strength. Our government could have thrown its diplomatic might behind a resolution of the Israel-Palestine dilemma, but the current administration has been flagrantly pro-Israel. A fraction of our wealth could transform nations, but we don't even feed our own homeless....

Christ instructs us sharply: "For unto whomsoever much is given, of him shall be much required: and to whom men have committed much, of him they will ask the more....Ye hypocrites, ye can discern the face of the sky and of the earth; but how is it that ye do not discern this time? Yea, and why even of yourselves judge ye not what is right?"[109]

Is it un-American to speak so sharply of the United States Government and Americans? What would Jesus say to us? We must hold ourselves accountable for our government: if we Americans are to stand for good, if we are to carry the banner of justice and equality, then we must be capable of introspection. If God blessed Americans with providential opportunities, do we desecrate His gift of this nation if we fall so far short?

---

[109] KJV, Luke 12:48, 56-57.

Jesus in the temple said: "Is it not written, MY HOUSE SHALL BE CALLED OF ALL NATIONS THE HOUSE OF PRAYER? But ye have made it a DEN OF THIEVES."[110] America desecrates Christ when it proclaims itself to be a Christian nation and then exports capitalism and the pursuit of wealth as the panacea for the world's socio-economic ills.

Americans' hypocrisy extends also to its litigiousness. There is much confusion about tort law and litigiousness in modern America. Although the idea of recovering monetary damages in compensation against someone who had committed negligence originated in British common law, negligence recoveries, including medical malpractice claims, have exploded in America over the last several decades. Americans have become disgusted with the perceived excesses of our legal system, particularly since the O. J. Simpson trial and the infamous McDonald's coffee-burn case. In response, they blame lawyers. One commentator asserts that "[t]oo much of the nation's current overabundance of lawyers, legalism, and litigation is the product of a two-century evolution. Moreover, reversing the situation faces a slight technical hitch: the lawyers in the White House, Congress, the courts, and the state legislatures are the people who make the laws."[111]

First of all, the excesses are largely imagined–anecdotal cases are highly publicized, but the vast majority of cases litigated, usually overseen by (non-lawyer) juries,

---

[110] KJV, Mark 11:17.
[111] Kevin Phillips, <u>Arrogant Capital: Washington, Wall Street, and the Frustration of American Politics</u>, p. 198.

result in reasonable or even prejudicially low recoveries, and most unmeritorious cases are sniffed out by lay juries and fail. Many lawyers refuse to take cases that lack merit, for they invest large amounts of time, staff, and their reputations in every case.

Second, these large awards and bizarre verdicts are always rendered by juries, not lawyers. In our legal system, two sides are always each represented by legal counsel advocating opposite positions, and the non-lawyer jury members then decide which party is victor. So in every case tried to a jury (e.g., McDonald's coffee-burn and O.J.), no lawyers decided who won or what they got—members of the general public did.

Personal injury suits for medical malpractice are often cited as representative of the abuses of a hyper-litigious society. Here too there is general misunderstanding of the machinations of the legal system. For one thing, though much attention is drawn to jury awards as a cause of the high cost of medical malpractice insurance, another very high cost is the legal fees incurred in the bad-faith defense of meritorious cases. There are factors which contribute to make this problem complex.

In an effort to prevent doctors with a history of confirmed malpractice from relocating to other states to avoid professional expulsion and high insurance rates, a national data registry is maintained for U. S. physicians: not only judgments but also settlements are required to be reported. The intent of this legislation was to protect patients, but the unintended effect was that the large majority of American physicians defend and refuse to settle even meritorious claims. The general rule of thumb in the insurance industry is 'pay as little as possible, as far in the future as possible,' and the terms of medical malpractice insurance contracts provide that the insurer may defend a suit even where a physician wishes to settle. Add to this: the burdensome expenses of medical experts which plaintiffs' counsel must procure prior to and through trial; the laws of most jurisdictions which require plaintiffs to reimburse defense expert fees and other expenses in the event of a defense verdict; experienced, highly specialized defense attorneys who earn hundreds of dollars hourly to wear down plaintiffs; and the relatively short and strict statutes of limitation which apply to medical malpractice lawsuits, and one can understand why personal injury attorneys generally decline medical malpractice cases that are not "valued" at a minimum of $300,000.

Against this backdrop we view efforts at "tort reform," a disingenuous title. An emphasis on mandatory mediation would be a genuine benefit to lowering costs, but capping damages for pain and suffering is not equitable. A penalty on physicians who wrongly or frivolously defend against legitimate claims, or a limitation on the rate to be paid defense counsel, might well be of greater effect in reducing medical malpractice insurance expenses, but the bias is toward the insurance industry and their influential clientele: pain and suffering limitations disproportionately disadvantage the very young, the poor, and the very old.

Noticeably absent from recent tort reform efforts is limitation on economic loss. In wrongful death cases, permanent disability cases, and cases where medical malpractice results in an extended work or business absence, one aspect of damages is loss of income. People of greater earning potential, i.e. wealthier people, are more likely to have a substantial claim for economic losses than people of modest means. Thus, tort reform, as repeatedly advocated by President Bush, disadvantages young children (who have larger economic losses for "pain and suffering" when their lives are destroyed by unreasonable negligence, for they face many, many long years of pain and suffering) while not limiting awards which would restrict the economic loss claims of the wealthy.[112] One recalls Jesus' caution in Matthew 25:40: "Verily I say unto you, Inasmuch as ye have done it unto one of the least of these my brethren, ye have done it unto me."[113]

George W. Bush proudly proclaims his "achievement" of tort reform in Texas, but those "reforms" have favored powerful defendants at the expense of individuals and the public. After a protracted and emotional legal battle in Texas over birth defects caused by environmental pollution by General Motors and others across the U.S.-Mexico border, GM was prompted

---

[112] "One of the most common types [of limits on medical malpractice suits]–caps on damages for pain and suffering, or so-called noneconomic caps–is turning out to have the unpublicized effect of creating two tiers of malpractice victims. Cases involving high earners or big medical bills move ahead. Lawyers can still seek economic damages for the wages these patients lost or to pay for continuing medical bills. But lawyers are turning away cases involving victims that don't represent big economic losses–most notably retired people, children and housewives...." "As Malpractice Caps Spread, Lawyers Turn Away Some Cases," *The Wall Street Journal*, October 8, 2004, p. 1.

[113] KJV, Matthew 25: 40.

to start cleaning up its hitherto ignored toxic waste, to track birth defects,[114] and to a settlement for the benefit of affected children with birth defects. This led to "...a broad tort reform movement that has made it very difficult for injured or wronged individuals to sue business or corporate interests....Tort reform–insulating corporate interests from lawsuits filed by consumers, workers, injured parties, and the survivors of those killed through malice or negligence–has been at the top of the big business agenda since the 1980's."[115] Molly Ivins and Lou Dubose note that "...[b]y pushing tort reform through the [Texas] Lege in 1995, Bush helped make large, multiple-defendant torts almost impossible to try...."The bigger picture of tort reform is that industry and corporate America have been emboldened. They know we have to be lucky to get past the trial court." [quoting Brownsville attorney Tony Martinez]....Bush has acted to make sure that poor folks have even less access to justice in the system."[116]

George acted on tort reform purportedly to curb greedy plaintiffs, but the reforms don't distinguish, and legitimate complainants suffer hardships from this legislation–overall recoveries are reduced to a much greater degree than the perceived "benefit" of reduced fraudulent claims. But George W. had no objection to receiving "$138, 900 from individual lawyers with Vinson & Elkins, the law firm that represents Enron...."[117]

---

[114] Molly Ivins and Lou Dubose, Shrub: The Short But Happy Political Life of George W. Bush, p. 176-177.
[115] Ibid., pp. 76, 88.
[116] Ibid., pp. 176, 177, 143.
[117] Ibid., pp. 160-161.

and he has not addressed complaints that the changes caused legitimate claimants hardship:

> Asked to respond to a New York Times story that found plaintiffs had little success after tort reform, Bush said the old system "was bad for business and bad for the economy in Texas." Pressed about the rights of workers and consumers, he said, "Government should create an environment that encourages entrepreneurs to create wealth." That "good-forbidness" litmus test is Dubya's real measure of the value of public policy. The Times found the lower insurance rates–promised by tort reformers to consumers once those outrageous lawsuits were out of the way–never materialized, even though insurance-company profits are way up.[118]

A *Wall Street Journal* article in 2004 similarly concluded that tort reform in California had had inequitable results:

> A study of a 1975 California law capping malpractice awards for noneconomic damages, such as pain and suffering, at $250,000 found that:
>
> [] The law reduced the overall liability of defendants by 30%
> [] The median reduction in awards for noneconomic damages was $366,000.
> [] Injured babies under one year old had reductions imposed in 71% of their cases
> [] The median reduction for this group was $1.5 million.

---

[118] Ibid., p. 89.

- [] Plaintiffs 65 years of age and older had their awards reduced 67% of the time
- [] Female plaintiffs had larger cuts to their total verdicts than did men: 34% vs. 25%

Source: Rand Institute for Civil Justice[119]

Accountability of Christians and Their Leaders: Individual Christians' Accountability for Actions by Christian Leaders in Government:

The Bible makes very clear that God does not excuse us for ignorance. In the First Epistle of John we read that "He that saith, I know him, and keepeth not his commandments, is a liar, and the truth is not in him. But whoso keepeth his word, in him verily is the love of God perfected: hereby know we that we are in him. He that saith he abideth in him ought himself also to walk, even as he walked."[120] In Second Peter we are forewarned of our current situation: "Ye therefore, beloved, seeing ye know these things before, beware lest ye also, being led with the error of the wicked, and fall from your own stedfastness."[121] By "ye know these things before," Peter refers to promises to Christians of the second coming of Christ, of which there are ample

---

[119] "As Malpractice Caps Spread, Lawyers Turn Away Some Cases," *The Wall Street Journal*, October 8, 2004, p. 1. (emphasis in original) Also, " "When you put a cap on non-economic damages," says NOW President Kim Gandy, "quite literally [women's] lives are valued lower." "
[120] KJV, 1 John 2:4-6
[121] KJV, 2 Peter 3: 17.

predictions in the Bible.[122] Whether Christ is returning in ten thousand years or in ten minutes, the standard set for us is identical.

George Bush is President of the United States because of the support of Christian voters. Thus, Christians directly influenced not just a national election but elevated a supposedly devout Christian to the most prominent, highly visible human post of worldly Caesars, to the leadership of the most wealthy and militarily powerful nation in the history of the world. But this was accomplished against the backdrop of an America in moral decline, where moral relativism, materialism, and liberalism are culturally engrained. Generally speaking, Americans have abdicated moral decision-making in broad swaths of their lives, surrendering to "the cares of this world," and to devotion to the pursuit of wealth. Concurrent with our growing dependency on technology has come an abandonment of our collective historic faith in a higher power. Richard N. Goodwin cites loss of individual influence to growing self-guided bureaucracies as a chief cause of American discontent and social decline. He also implies that commercial "market" forces and technology further push us into alienation. Writes Goodwin:

---

[122] Tim LaHaye and Jerry B. Jenkins, <u>Are We Living in the End Times?</u>, p. 3: "...the Old Testament features more than one hundred prophecies regarding the coming of the Messiah to the earth. Through these prophecies we know that Jesus was truly the Messiah, for He fulfilled every one of them. That is how believers can be so confident that He will return physically to this earth to set up His kingdom, because He promised He would–five times more frequently than He promised to come the first time! Since His first coming is a fact of history, we can be at least five times as certain that He will come the second time."

There are growing numbers who do not apply their personal moral standards to their actions or occupations. Many would be surprised at the charge that they were responsible for the social impact of the organization which employed them. Their self-evaluation excludes this moral dimension....Our loss of power, the growth of alienation, is the consequence of...changes which are enforced and accelerated by an increasingly coercive and lawless economic bureaucracy....In non-socialist countries commercial enterprise had its most expansive years after the decline of that hierarchical religious faith once considered its principal support. People can work harder, want more and buy with greater intensity without the opiate of sacred beliefs.[123]

But America's Christians should not be going along for this ride, allowing affluence, convenience or recreation to eclipse their duty of loyalty to God. If people vote for a candidate in error (like those who voted for Bill Clinton), then admitting they were deceived and demanding their money back, so to speak, is quite understandable. Should that candidate profess loyalty to Christ, this is all the more the case. And for those who see the deception of the religious right that carried George Bush to the White House for what it is, we must band together to correct our country's moral course. As Ann Coulture opined of the Clinton escapades: "You can vote for a knave and a clown, but then you have to take some responsibility to correct your mistakes. And those who didn't vote for the clown have a responsibility to rescue

---

[123] Richard N. Goodwin, The American Condition, pp. 159, 160.

the country from its foolishness....The governed may be expected to abide a certain amount of evil for the sake of continuity and stability, but there's a limit."[124]

But again, this is especially true for representatives of Christ. Bishop Michael J. Sheridan said of John Kerry: "Anyone who professes the Catholic faith with his lips while at the same time publicly supporting legislation or candidates that defy God's law makes a mockery of that faith and belies his identity as a Catholic...."[125] Doug Bandow writes: "Politics is often a rough and dirty game, but if Christians really have been transformed by the Holy Spirit, we need to act differently. In all that we do we are personal witnesses for Christ, especially where we seek to put ourselves on display before the local community or nation through political involvement."[126] And George W. Bush has said: "I believe everybody should be held responsible for their individual behavior. All public policy should revolve around the principle that individuals are responsible for what they say and do.... our leaders should be judged by results, not by entertaining personalities or clever sound bites."[127] What are the "results" in this president's case, where he has tapped into Americans' political and religious trust in the Iraq journey he has embarked upon as our country's leader, in creating a torture loophole, and in incurring massive, fiscally-irresponsible debt? The disappointment of

---

[124] Ann Coulture, <u>High Crimes and Misdemeanors: The Case Against Bill Clinton</u>, p. 19.
[125] Paul Kengor, <u>God and George W. Bush, a spiritual life</u>, p. 311.
[126] Doug Bandow, <u>Beyond Good Intentions: A Biblical View of Politics</u>, p. 229.
[127] George W. Bush, <u>A Charge To Keep</u>, p. 30.

Christian trust is particularly galling, because "[p]eople sometimes put their trust in a spiritual leader and are terribly betrayed if that person then fails to live up to ideals."[128]

A review is thus in order of Mr. Bush's actions–because he carries Christ's name on his tongue; because all Christians should work to influence their leaders (of any party) to adhere to Christ's wisdom, and because George W. Bush claims to be the "accountability president." He named a plane "Accountability One,"[129] and once said: "My dream is to usher in what I call the "responsibility era"–an era in which each and every Texan understands that we're responsible for the decisions we make in life...."[130]

Mr. Bush would surely volunteer then to be the exemplary leader of the responsibility era, and be held publicly responsible in the democratic and Christian traditions for his words and actions. (I'm sure he won't mind....)

1) Mr. Bush has expressed great faith in the American free market system to advance the world. He has appealed to corporate and religious charity to help the disadvantaged, even as unprecedented numbers of corporate scandals rock our nation and charitable giving is down because of a slowing economy and public apprehension about the future. He wrote:

---

[128] Thomas Moore, Care of the Soul: A Guide for Cultivating Depth and Sacredness in Everyday Life, p. 254.
[129] Bill Minutaglio, First Son: George W. Bush and the Bush Family Dynasty, p. 276.
[130] David Aikman, A Man of Faith: the Spiritual Journey of George W. Bush, p. 210.

88 CHRISTIAN WORDS, UNCHRISTIAN ACTIONS

> We all have a role and a responsibility. Corporate America has a responsibility to treat its workers with respect and to give back to the communities in which it does business. Corporate America has a responsibility to work for cleaner air and cleaner water by cleaning up old plants that pollute and by developing new technologies to manufacture and produce in a more environmentally friendly way.[131]

But corporations have no souls, and no moral conscience to guide or even motivate such beneficence. Corporate directors and executive management are legally bound to maximize economic return for shareholders, and the stock markets demand the same. Also, directors and corporate executives increasingly rely on stock options or stock-price-indexed bonuses for compensation, so profit again rules the day. Government exists in part to protect citizens from unbridled corporate domination, to impose the very laws regarding pollution, wage and labor equity, and community protection that George in this statement wants to delegate trustingly back from government to the hallowed corporate forces of the market.[132] This was the excuse he used in Texas to delay requirements for corporate compliance with pollution control standards, and the same rationale he repeatedly employs to protect large business interests.

---

[131] George W. Bush, <u>A Charge To Keep</u>, p. 230.

[132] A student of history such as President Bush should have learned from the Depression: "There was no single cause of the crash and the ensuing depression, but much of the responsibility for both falls on the foolhardy assumption that the special interests of business and the national interest were identical." William E. Leuchtenburg, <u>The Perils of Prosperity</u>, 1914-1932, p. 245.

2) George has alluded to Pope John Paul II to support his accountability talk. In one speech he said: "The Pope reminds us that while freedom defines our nation, responsibility must define our lives."[133] But George must be reminded that he declined that same Pope's counsel on the capital punishment case of Karla Faye Tucker,[134] and again when the Pope dispatched an envoy to dissuade Mr. Bush from his intended foray into Iraq.[135] In fact, George Bush has never followed the Pope's advice against his own wishes, but he has done an expert political job of piggybacking on Pope John Paul II's popularity, even after the poor soul's demise.

3) Of the No Child Left Behind legislation, George said:

> We need to know in America whether or not our children can read and write and add and subtract. That's what an accountability system is for....Starting this September,...students across America who attend failing schools will have different options, of transferring to another public school. It's part of being an accountable society. It's part of strengthening public education....we've got to strengthen the public education system, by encouraging different opportunities if there's failure....Low income students, as a result of the new bill, in chronically failing

---

[133] George W. Bush, as quoted in Thomas A. Freiling, <u>George W. Bush on God and Country</u>, p. 157.

[134] Paul Kengor, <u>God and George W. Bush: a spiritual life</u>, p. 38: "An emissary from Pope John Paul II delivered a plea to spare the woman."

[135] Paul Kengor, in <u>God and George W. Bush: a spiritual life</u>, reports that "...on March 5, 2003, Bush met with a cardinal representing John Paul II, who said that the Pope believed that invading Iraq without UN approval would be "illegal." " (p. 109.)

schools will now have access to after-school tutoring....I believe in local control of schools....I think that by continuing to focus on high standards and results and local control of schools, we can all work together to make sure no child is left behind.[136]

Once again we see the pitch for accountability used to avoid any.

First, national testing is antithetical to the autonomy of local schools, so the plug for "local control" elevates words above substance: why isn't George held accountable in his accountability society for promising respect for local control with one hand while taking it away with the other? Second, accountability would presumably require some action addressing the "chronically failing schools," but the legislation's only response is to pull children out of those schools (if they are low-income and perform poorly enough) and relocate them, something apparently borrowed from the leadership of the Catholic Church (and don't tell me not to talk about that subject, because the greatest failing in the whole matter was the Church's avoidance of dealing with the problem openly—and all leaders must be accountable: who in the Catholic Church has been charged or penalized for covering up pedophilic offenses and relocating offenders to unsuspecting congregations, where they were thus enabled to reoffend? How will the Church regain trust without modeling Christian integrity, responsibility, and accountability?)

---

[136] Thomas A. Freiling, <u>George W. Bush on God & Country</u>, pp.170-171, 172.

Third, the expense of testing our entire nation's children is tremendous, and the burden on teachers' valuable time (were they consulted about this plan, or do they not merit that respect?) is substantial, but the relative federal funding for tutoring for those "low income students" from "chronically failing schools" is essentially nil. And the educational disruption, local intrusion, and adverse social and emotional risks for the affected children attendant on mandatory transfers as a solution for poor test performance reveal that this is hardly a sensible solution, and may well do more harm than good. Such poor responsiveness to the problem would be akin to testing a whole barn full of cows for mastitis and then not spending any money on medication or other treatment. Or as a local teacher said: "You don't fatten a hog by weighin' it!"[137] No Child Left Behind was an ill-considered but flashy-sounding and expensive experiment on our nation's children, and it's high time someone said so. Soon the whole nation will have learned how to cheat on tests "real good," like they scandalously do down in Texas, as a direct response to increased emphasis on testing.

4) George W. Bush deliberately chose not to disclose his DWI arrest to the American people prior to the 2000 election, and in fact dismissed as politically motivated the disclosure of that information just before the election. His stated reason for lying, that he didn't want his daughters to know he had been an irresponsible drinker, holds as much moral water as a sieve made of

---

[137] Karen Devereaux, Grade School Teacher, Barton Academy Graded School, Barton, Vermont.

92   CHRISTIAN WORDS, UNCHRISTIAN ACTIONS

tissue paper. Consider: instead, he modeled how to lie, intentionally, to the American people, and how to deflect an accountable response by dismissing the revelation as politically-motivated, suggesting one need not therefore explain or apologize for the drinking or the deception (sound like Clinton?); he lied while professing to be a Christian, without ever apologizing for that dishonesty, modeling that unchristian hypocrisy, without repentance, as acceptable Christian conduct for the world to marvel at. The Christian Right only gave that impression legitimacy when it gave Bush a free pass on the issues both of his drunk driving and his very unchristian deception about it.

5) George has been similarly unaccountable on his illegal drug use. While his biographers are free to extol his supposedly virtuous behaviors pre-drunken-binge period, even including his ancestors and their noble fortune-amassing and maid-employing largesse, his activities before he quit drinking (this brings us to his early forties) are beyond investigation as "youthful indiscretions." In one interview, "...the Houston Chronicle had decided to openly grill him about whether he had experimented with illegal drugs: "Maybe I did, maybe I didn't. What's the difference?" he had told the reporter."[138] And once again, Christian voters looked the other way. The Office of United States President would be expected to require thoroughness in the job interview process, but no, drug testing is not employed for this position, though you are free to admonish athletes and

---

[138] Bill Minutaglio, First Son: George W. Bush and the Bush Family Dynasty, p. 281.

young people about drug use with obvious hypocrisy, and you're free to ignore the accountability standards of which you proselytize. We are to believe that God chose George W. Bush to teach and model for us all how to be moral and pure–and although past drug use is of little relevance to the state of one's soul, it is quite relevant when running for office, and the correct Christian response is "I repent of that conduct," not "What difference does it make?"

6) Paul Kengor praises Bush for modesty, noting that after the China crisis was favorably resolved, "[t]here would be no gloating, he made clear."[139] But this contrasts sharply with the gloating of Bush's "Mission Accomplished" proclamation after the invasion of Iraq: although Bush supporters don't like to be reminded of this revealing moment, it requires mentioning in reviewing what the world sees as the representative face of Christianity and American hubris. The Muslim World saw the images on Al Jazeera, and have not been as quick to dismiss criticisms of this incident as mere political hooey. Ann Coulter identifies the Presidency as "…the nation's image of itself, the symbol of the nation."[140] Did Mr. Bush and America appear as Liberators to the world in that image, or as Conquerors?

Kengor also writes that in May 2001 George W. "…boasted that his administration would increase funding for "major social welfare and poverty programs" by 8 percent,"[141] hollow words in view of the

---

[139] Paul Kengor, God & George W. Bush: a spiritual journey, p. 92.
[140] Ann Coulter, High Crimes and Misdemeanors: The Case Against Bill Clinton, p. 306.
[141] Paul Kengor, God and George W. Bush: a spiritual life, p. 101.

displacement of federal dollars from those programs by "defense" spending and tax refunds to the wealthy. "They claim that they know God, but their actions deny it" (Titus 1:16 TEV).

7) Karl Rove's and Scooter Libby's disclosure that Joseph Wilson's wife was a CIA agent in retaliation for her husband's criticisms of the administration's flawed Iraq WMD intelligence was a serious violation of federal national security laws, and to date no one has been held accountable. It is known that Karl Rove and Scooter Libby disclosed Valerie Plame's secret CIA status. Since George W. Bush believes in accountability, loyalty, and Christian integrity, a) did George W. direct or just permit this unchristian, retaliatory action? b) if he actually didn't know who the offenders were (fat chance!), he has allowed them to continue in their positions with no consequence; no one has been held accountable; George W. didn't have either the influence or the desire to discover their identity, and his cabinet is not trustworthy. Guidance might be sought from the words of Ann Coulter, who wrote: "Surely the president is responsible for any bad acts that he has encouraged implicitly or explicitly."[142] Ms. Coulter advocates imposing more direct accountability on the presidency:

> Placing all the executive power in a single man would lodge all the responsibility in a single man. The president would not be able to hide behind the decisions of others. All the blame for any wrongdoing within

---

[142] Ann Coulter, <u>High Crimes and Misdemeanors: The Case Against Bill Clinton</u>, p. 290.

the executive branch would necessarily fall on the president....He would not be able to pass off his bad acts as the work of his subordinates because he would be held accountable for their misdeeds. And if the president did not orchestrate their misconduct, but merely failed to root out corrupt subordinates,[143] he would still be held accountable for their actions.[144]

8) Abu Ghraib has been dismissed as the work of a few deviants since its disclosure. But clearly there was an atmosphere and culture which created the routine, widespread employment of barbaric, un-American methods of physical and psychological torture right from the pages of George Orwell and Aleksandr Solzhenitsyn, employed in the name of freedom by a nation which dares to call itself Christian even while it sidesteps the laws of man (e.g., The Geneva Convention, the European Convention on Human Rights) with legal niceties concocted by White House chief counsel. No wonder President Bush refused to allow the United States to be signatory to the International Court of Human Rights, at a time when he already was planning to invade and occupy Iraq. Are Americans, and American Christians, really willing to permit the grunt military pawns being paraded as perpetrators to take the fall for Abu Ghraib when they were obviously following orders to employ extreme methods in the "cause" of good versus evil?

---

[143] Like Dick Cheney and his fabrications about Iraq; or Scooter Libby and Karl Rove and their immoral and illegal backstabbing of Joseph Wilson's wife?

[144] Ann Coulter, <u>High Crimes and Misdemeanors: The Case Against Bill Clinton</u>, pp. 290, 264.

Lynndie England did not have psychological problems (or did she?[145]) but was following orders in full view of fellow soldiers, all on duty. Dismissal of American torture based on the extremes of Islamic behavior is immoral relativism: since when does the conduct of America's enemies determine America's moral code? (Oh yeah, since the Iraq War....)

9) George Tenet was the key player supporting the assertion that Saddam Hussein possessed weapons of mass destruction. Bob Woodward writes in <u>Plan of Attack</u>:[146]

> The WMD issue pulsed in the background for 10 months until Kay's resignation and declaration that they had all been wrong. This put Tenet in a bind. He and the CIA took pride in their hard-nosed analysis and conclusions. The bar was very high, and being wrong was not acceptable. Tenet had been privately very critical of news stories that had been wrong or overreaching about a possible quagmire in the Afghanistan war in late 2001. 'There's never any price,' he had said, when the media is wrong. He said that if the CIA director had given out equivalent bad information the president 'should fire your ass.'
>
> But no one at the CIA was paying a price or being held accountable for what seemed to be a mistake,

---

[145] "Private Found Guilty in Abu Ghraib Abuse," *The New York Times*, September 27, 2005. England's defense argued that her "...history of depression and learning disabilities contributed to her willingness to join in." The jury was unconvinced. Perhaps all of the U.S. personnel who committed torture were just suffering from "mass concurrent depression and learning disability syndrome," a.k.a. "a few bad apples."

[146] Bob Woodward, <u>Plan of Attack</u>, p. 438.

and Tenet was the one who had assured Bush that the case on WMD was 'a slam dunk.'[147]

And yet, not only was Tenet not fired, but President Bush awarded him the Presidential Medal of Freedom, considered "America's highest honor."

This rewarding of the loyal soldier who fell on his sword contrasts sharply with the discharge of Paul O'Neill, who correctly and honestly differed with the White House on the risks and effects of large budget deficits. Rewards for liars, firing for truth-tellers....

Ann Coulter observed that:

> ...the misconduct in Bill Clinton's administration almost always benefits Bill Clinton. Second, the president has never routed out or punished malfeasance in his administration on his own....Third, the president's accomplices generally end up with promotions....Finally, though, the sheer number of mishaps the Clinton administration has stumbled into starts to make it look like it's not an accident.... Whatever the scandal, Clinton's defense is the same; POTUS is not responsible. It was a bureaucratic snafu, and he knows only what he reads in the papers. But he is responsible–it's his administration. And the fact that it is his administration is the one recurring factor in the never-ending series of bureaucratic snafus.[148]

---

[147] Paul Kengor, <u>God and George W. Bush: a spiritual life</u>, p. 109.
[148] Ann Coulter, <u>High Crimes and Misdemeanors: The Case Against Bill Clinton</u>, p. 291. Rumsfeld, Brown at FEMA, George Tenet, Scooter Libby...."the sheer number"....

Funny, recent commentators have leveled similar charges against the Bush administration, complaining that W. remains "...'inside the bubble' where no one can get at him—the dirty work is done by others; our boy is always hurt, surprised, and indignant when others attack him."[149] George Bush has criticized this lack of accountability in modern America, lamenting that "We went from accepting responsibility to assigning blame."[150] And he is a master at it: Christian words, unchristian actions.

John Kenneth Galbraith described the increased reliance on the delegation of tasks or decision-making in large bureaucracies, "[e]specially in the higher levels of an organization..., diminishing the role of thought itself....The culture of organization runs strongly to the shifting of problems to others—to an escape from personal mental effort and responsibility....The delegation process...adds ineluctably to the layers of command and to the prestige associated with command."[151] These words would not surprise George W. Bush, who has said of the conflict between the CIA and the military that "You can design a system so that nobody is held accountable."[152] This seems to have been successfully utilized as a methodology in the case of WMD and George Tenet, and of the illegal disclosure that Valerie Plame was a CIA agent by Karl Rove and Scooter Libby. Many have criticized Tenet, who George W. has loyally stood behind,

---

[149] Molly Ivins and Lou Dubose, <u>Shrub: The Short But Happy Political Life of George W. Bush</u>, p. 193.
[150] George W. Bush, <u>A Charge To Keep</u>, p. 229.
[151] John Kenneth Galbraith, <u>The Culture of Contentment</u>, p. 68, 69.
[152] Bob Woodward, <u>Bush at War</u>, p. 244.

making himself look good for supporting his underling, without taking responsibility for that person's errors. This pattern was also repeated with Alberto Gonzales and the torture memos: Gonzales was promoted for his loyal loophole creation, though America's reputation and credibility have been destroyed.

10) This is an administration that never questions itself or admits error or fault, ever. Besides Paul O'Neill's observations in this regard, Colin Powell was greatly frustrated by this tendency. In the case of the difficulties in Iraq immediately following the invasion,

> Powell thought that now that Bush and the administration had to live with the consequences of their Iraq decisions they were becoming dangerously protective of those decisions. There was no one in the White House who could break through to insist on a realistic reassessment….Powell believed it was the hardest of all tasks to go back to fundamentals and question your own judgment, and there was no sign it was going to happen.[153]

Three decisions for which George W. will be held accountable to God and the American people are the invasion of Iraq, the use of torture on prisoners, and the leveraging of our future for short-run economic return at the expense of the most poor. He may continue to employ deceptions like those just outlined to avoid or postpone his comeuppance, but he cannot hide from God. As Shakespeare creatively put it:

---

[153] Bob Woodward, Plan of Attack, pp. 415-416.

May one be pardoned and retain the offense?
In the corrupted currents of this world
Offense's guilded hand may shove by justice
And oft 'tis seen the wicked prize itself
Buys out the law; but 'tis not so above.
There is no shuffling; there the action lies
In his true nature, and we ourselves compelled,
Even to the teeth and forehead of our faults,
To give in evidence.[154]

---

[154] William Shakespeare, Hamlet, Act III, Scene III, lines 59-67.

Chapter 3

POLITICS AND CHRISTIANITY: DARKNESS AND LIGHT

> "Every kingdom divided against itself is brought to desolation; and every city or house divided against itself shall not stand:...He that is not with me is against me; and he that gathereth not with me scattereth abroad."
>
> —Matthew 12:25, 30[155]

Ideologies from whatever source are by definition in conflict with Christian doctrine. Americans easily identify certain ideological mindsets, such as communism, Nazi fascism, or the Ku Klux Klan, but most Americans cannot imagine that their commitment to their own nation or its belief system could be as threatening to world stability, to say nothing of our national image. Non-Christians may be forgiven for reposing faith in a government and the geographical area it controls, lacking

---

[155] KJV.

any alternative worldview: but Christ clearly instructed that we not eclipse our duty to God and fellow men with such worldly loyalties.

In The Roots of American Order, Russell Kirk defines "ideology" to mean "...servitude to political dogmas, abstract ideas not founded upon historical experience."[156] This seems to best describe our (delusional) national self-image, reflected in socio-schizoid contradictions such as: America as the defender of the underdog, epitomized by the Statue of Liberty and New York City's historic immigrant gateway, despite our genocidal elimination of indigenous peoples, for which we can never compensate with apologies, even if we did apologize; America as the advocate of the abolition of slavery, hypocritical at best for a nation that so heavily relied upon and indulged in the slave trade, which Thomas Jefferson called an "assemblage of horrors."[157] (John Adams protested long before the abolitionist movement that "freedom [was a] mere masquerade in a country that sold humans in chains."[158]); America's self-appointed role as defender of the world against communism, even as McCarthyism eroded the rights we said made our system superior, and even though that role placed us awkwardly before the world, telling others how they could be free, denying others the right to "choose" communism or socialism, for we knew our "system" to be "better."

Some would argue that it is unpatriotic to allege these things, but isn't it unpatriotic not to? That is,

---

[156] Russell Kirk, The Roots of American Order, p. 9.
[157] Catherine Drinker Bowen, John Adams and the American Revolution, p.601.
[158] Ibid., p. 601.

isn't our moral clarion call founded on a claim to integrity? Thus, if we've made mistakes, our admission of those mistakes and an effort not to repeat them is what makes us great as "Americans." But we don't admit our mistakes, especially those of our government: thus we perceive ourselves ideologically through "abstract ideas not founded upon historical experience," complying with Kirk's definition of ideological servitude.

As victims of such ideological imprisonment to the American myth-machine, our individual worldly identities are wedded from an early age to the "abstract ideas" of patriotism, of America always being on the side of right, of the superiority of our way of life, our form of government, our standard of living, never questioning the underlying values upon which those grandiose concepts are based. (Just like the Soviets, Chinese, Arabs, etc.) George Orwell saw more than fifty years ago that man was increasingly susceptible to the controlling influences of ideologies, and this constitutes the overriding theme of much of his work. Says Erich Fromm, in an essay on Orwell's 1984:

> "Doublethink means the power of holding two contradictory beliefs in one's mind simultaneously, and accepting both of them...This process has to be conscious, or it would not be carried out with sufficient precision. But it also has to be unconscious, or it would bring with it a feeling of falsity and hence of guilt." It is precisely the unconscious aspect of doublethink which will seduce many a reader of 1984 into believing that the method of

doublethink is employed by the Russians and the Chinese, while it is something quite foreign to himself. This, however, is an illusion….[t]he point which is essential for an understanding of Orwell's book [is that]…"doublethink" is already with us, and not merely something which will happen in the future, and in dictatorships….Specifically this applies to ideologies. Just as the Inquisitors who tortured their prisoners believed that they acted in the name of Christian love, the Party "rejects and vilifies every principle for which the socialist movement originally stood, and it chooses to do this in the name of socialism." Its content is reversed into its opposite, and yet people believe that the ideology means what it says. In this respect Orwell quite obviously refers to the falsification of socialism by Russian communism, but it must be added that the West is also guilty of a similar falsification. We present our society as being one of free initiative, individualism and idealism, when in reality these are mostly words. We are a centralized managerial industrial society, of an essentially bureaucratic nature, and motivated by a materialism which is only slightly mitigated by truly spiritual or religious concerns. Related to this is another example of "doublethink," namely that few writers, discussing atomic strategy, stumble over the fact that killing, from a Christian standpoint, is as evil or more evil than being killed. The reader will find many other features of our present Western society in Orwell's description in 1984, provided he can overcome enough of his own "doublethink."

Orwell…is simply implying that the new form of managerial industrialism, in which man builds machines which act like men and develops men who act like machines, is conducive to an era of dehumanization and complete alienation, in which men are transformed into things and become appendices to the process of production and consumption. [Orwell, Huxley, and Zamyatin] imply that this danger exists not only in the communism of the Russian or Chinese versions, but that it is a danger inherent in the modern mode of production and organization, and relatively independent of the various ideologies. Orwell, like the authors of the other negative utopias, is not a prophet of disaster. He wants to warn and to awaken us. He still hopes–but…his hope is a desperate one. The hope can be realized only by recognizing, so 1984 teaches us, the danger with which all men are confronted today, the danger of a society of automatons who will have lost every trace of individuality, of love, of critical thought, and yet who will not be aware because of "doublethink." Books like Orwell's are powerful warnings, and it would be most unfortunate if the reader smugly interpreted 1984 as another description of Stalinist barbarism, and if he does not see that it means us, too.[159]

Orwell as much as states this when he observes in 1984: "The citizen of Oceania is not allowed to know anything of the tenets of the other two philosophies, but he is taught to execrate them as barbarous outrages upon morality and common sense. Actually the three philosophies are barely distinguishable, and the social

---

[159] George Orwell, 1984, pp. 262, 264-267.

systems which they support are not distinguishable at all."[160]

As we in America assume we are somehow genetically immune to the weaknesses of government and human nature which infect other nations, we are by that cocky assumption condemned to learn the same lessons, to our national shame. Were it not for Jesus Christ, there would be no hope for the world at all, even with the almighty and morally infallible United States at the helm. This is particularly so in recent times, when Americans have endeavored to influence the political process with religion, a well-intentioned idea with two dramatically destructive consequences: firstly, expecting a worldly political system to comport with Christian doctrine naively risks mixing the two. While religious influences do belong in politics, political philosophies or doctrines have no bearing on Christ's words. And conversely, "[t]o inject religion into the political debate is to polarize and harden politics."[161] Secondly, almost all societies which have blended politics with religion have inexorably become totalitarian, and the writing is already on the wall for Americans, with fear (Satan's effective tool in this world) of terrorism and evil leading to the acceptance of Big Brother ID systems, torture, the slaughter of civilians abroad, and the whittling away of the freedoms our country once prided as our gift to the world. As Alvin Toffler has observed:

---

[160] Ibid., p. 162.
[161] David Aikman, quoting James O. Goldsborough, in <u>The Spiritual Journey of George W. Bush</u>, at p. 8.

Today, therefore, in country after country, secularism is in retreat. What do advocates of democracy have to put in its place? So far the new, high-tech democracies have renovated neither their outdated mass democratic political structures nor the philosophical assumptions that underlie them.

Religion is not the enemy of democracy....Yet within the giant religious revival, in every country, not just Iran, fanatics are breeding who are committed to theocratic control of the mind and behavior of the individual, and others lend them unwitting support....

Religions that are universalistic, that wish to spread all over the world and embrace every human being, may be compatible with democracy...[if they don't] try to impose their controls on non-members.... What is not compatible are those religions (and political ideologies as well) that combine totalitarianism with universalism. Such movements are at war with any possible definition of democracy....They are determined to seize power over the lives and minds of whole nations, continents, the planet itself. Determined to impose their own rule over every aspect of human life. Determined to seize state power wherever they can, and to roll back the freedoms that democracy makes possible. They are the agents of a new Dark Age.[162]

Although efforts have been made to obscure the religious undertones of the Iraq War, the Muslim world is well aware of the crusading nature of America's self-appointed role as world policeman and champion of democracy. Even if our government were sincere in its stated goals, the Muslim world will never believe it because of their historical experience with Americans (kind of like the American Indians, who finally caught on to our treaty-breaking duplicity) and because of their religion, which considers Christians to be polytheistic pagans. Is Christianity then being used to spread

---

[162] Alvin Toffler, Powershift: Knowledge, Wealth, and Violence at the Edge of the Twenty-First Century, p. 368. America assumes the "universalism" of democratic values, of "freedom," while ignoring the immoral downsides of capitalism and the empty spiritual death of materialism, both of which more accurately represent our contribution to the world. Anyone who dares to criticize the white-washed mythology of America in the interests of improvement or accountability is branded un-patriotic or "elitist." Michael Barone, of *US News & World Report*, regularly propagandizes the "American Way": "We Americans are lucky to live in a country with a history full of noble ideas, great leaders, and awe-inspiring accomplishments. Sadly, many of our elites want no part of it." "Spurning America," *US News & World Report*, October 24, 2005, p. 28. Mr. Barone concludes that those who criticize corrupt or mistaken federal policies, or America's actions in the past, "want no part of" its better qualities, when it is those better qualities critics often seek to preserve: this is the Iraq War translation of the Vietnam War slogan "America, Right or Wrong." This is idolatry to Christians, plain and simple. And Americans are not "lucky," they are *blessed*. Christ is truth, and His sheep know His voice. What are America's (worldly) "awe-inspiring accomplishments" that outweigh its current miserable shame, Mr. Barone? Is developing new technologies or freeing Europe a license to torture, imprison, and wage un-just war? The Emperor, and his Empire, have no clothes....

darkness through the world, the Christian label on the American Harlot?

Any ruling class becomes enamored with the structure of society which supports that class's position of influence, and any social, religious or political force which challenges this structure will be denied or ignored till the very last. John Kenneth Galbraith discusses this historical economic truth at length in <u>The Culture of Contentment</u>, in which he explains that the French aristocracy did not respond to the instability leading to the French Revolution because by definition they believed that their elevated position was best for the lower classes, and they were surrounded by yes-men who echoed that view. Galbraith explains that the only difference in the United States is that the aristocracy has been expanded to include the middle class, which then has a vested interest in the system which supports its socio-economic status. For this reason, the majority of Americans are committed to an economic belief system which leaves huge numbers of people in poverty, and despite the myriad moral failings outlined in Chapter One. In this aspect we are no different from the powerful ruling elite of the Soviet Communist Party, who clung to their positions and to the Party in the face of decline, "…protected in their fortunate position by the presumed power of socialist principles, adherence to which assured survival."[163] If Americans were to question the "presumed power" of their cult-like obsession with free market capitalism and wealth-accumulation, they would quickly realize that a) capitalism has failed

---

[163] John Kenneth Galbraith, <u>The Culture of Contentment</u>, p. 9.

humanity, and b) there is no worldly ideology available for acceptable replacement which will save or restore mankind. In other words, either the Bible is true and we should not worship wealth, in which case America's got some repentance to get started on; or, mankind has no God and has "evolved" into its own destruction, and there is nothing to be done to prevent that destruction, nor to comfort us as we face its inevitability. And American hegemony and nationalism are demonstrated unequivocally in either event to be failed ideological faiths—even our science and wealth have failed us.[164]

As we live in denial of America's implosion, we increase the dimensions of the impending calamity. Christ offers simple truths to live by that quickly release us from fear and worry, but instead Americans continue to rest their hopes for solutions in the very failed myths and governmental institutions that evade accountability for dismantling our society. Kevin Phillips writes in <u>Arrogant Capital</u> that

> as Washington has entrenched, the old two-party system, revitalized by once-a-generation bloodless revolutions at the ballot box, no longer works.... The American people, more or less aware of this loss, are grasping for a solution to what is clearly

---

[164] The conservative if cynical William E. Simon goes so far as to assert that our leaders are already aware of the intractable breakdown of our society. He writes in <u>A Time For Truth</u>, at p. 213: "There is tragically little awareness in the United States today that a guiding philosophy lies behind the destruction we are seeing....There is...a substantial awareness in our political leadership that our fiscal and economic policies have gone awry and that the multiple promises of cradle-to-grave security for our citizens can no longer be responsibly expanded, if indeed they can be fulfilled."

a larger, deeper problem....The electorate...is entitled to regard both parties as being crippled both ways–by ideology and even more by interest groups. In the matter of reversing America's slow decline, both parties have been so prominent a part of the problem that it is difficult to picture them as part of the solution.[165]

The same threats of social unrest and revolution that threatened our country in the Great Depression, and which gave rise to the American Revolution, are now tearing our nation apart. Phillips warns that "[t]here is... a danger in overromanticizing America's revolutionary past as the source of national renewal mechanisms" and that whether the United States can reclaim itself "may be the biggest test of American democratic institutions since the Civil War–and perhaps since the Revolution itself."[166] But Mr. Phillips, on cautioning Americans of a political breakdown, looks to the conventions of man for a solution, as opposed to Christians who see no solutions in man and recognize America's downfall as affirmation of God's love and the truths of the Bible, which tells us of all this. Sound extreme? Only if one's faith is in a nation instead of the Son of Man, in technology instead of God, in America the Beautiful and its leaders instead of Jesus Christ. To face the alternative–that civilization and society as we know them are nearing extinction–requires facing chaos for the rationalist, or facing God for the devout. Does the Bible not tell us that at Christ's Second

---

[165] Kevin Phillips, <u>Arrogant Capital: Washington, Wall Street, and the Frustration of American Politics</u>, pp. XV, 65.
[166] Ibid., p. XVIII.

Coming people will be filled either with terror or with tearful joy, both viewing the same events?[167]

But instead of America "reclaiming itself" through Jesus Christ and the special blessings God bestowed on this country, we look to our silly political institutions, our political "Parties," for deliverance, even as they become more and more alienated from reality, less and less responsive to the crises that face us. And politics in America has become ever more acrimonious and ugly, an embarrassment to our heritage and to our Christian pretense. Jesus teaches us that "if a kingdom be divided against itself, that kingdom cannot stand. And if a house be divided against itself, that house cannot stand."[168] Christians must pierce these party illusions for what they are, and cease to allow party loyalties to divide our Christian House, our loyalty to Christ. This is easily accomplished simply by revealing America's two-party political system for the failure that it is, which we shall now do.

Democrats Versus Republicans: The Party Illusion

Viewing modern American politics, one prays for the influence of the words of Paul: "For all the law is fulfilled in one word, even in this; Thou shalt love thy neighbour as thyself. But if ye bite and devour one another, take heed that ye be not consumed one of another."[169] In 1974, Richard N. Goodwin observed of the American presidential election process that "…every four years the

---

[167] *See*, e.g., Revelation 16.
[168] KJV, Mark 3:24-25.
[169] Galatians 5:14-15, KJV.

disbelief of millions is suspended while the course of the world seems to ride on the clash between champions.... Never has the nation been so politicized. Never have so many given so much attention to so few."[170] But if America was politicized in 1974, it is at political civil war today, with citizens so emotional about party affiliation and the gravity of modern decisions of state that the spirit of freedom of political speech is threatened by sheer bitterness. Unfortunately, Christians have been divided by these ideological rivalries, and their political (i.e. worldly) differences have influenced their spiritual/religious beliefs. It is largely as a consequence of this influence that the Christian community has splintered into "liberal" and "conservative" branches, though Jesus was neither. (Although it might be noted that Oswald Chambers said of Jesus that He "out-socialists the socialists"[171]) Of the liberal versus conservative approach to Christ, C. S. Lewis confessed:

> Most of us are not really approaching the subject in order to find out what Christianity says: we are approaching it in the hope of finding support from Christianity for the views of our own party....A

---

[170] Richard N. Goodwin, The American Condition, p. 355.
[171] Oswald Chambers, My Utmost For His Highest, February 25: "The ecclesiastical idea of a servant of God is not Jesus Christ's idea. His idea is that we serve Him by being the servants of other men. Jesus Christ out-socialists the socialists." *See also* C. S. Lewis, Mere Christianity, p. 80: "...the New Testament...gives us a pretty clear hint of what a fully Christian society would be like. Perhaps it gives us more than we can take....there will be no manufacture of silly luxuries and then of sillier advertisements to persuade us to buy them. And there is to be no "swank" or "side," no putting on airs. To that extent a Christian society would be what we now call Leftist."

> Christian society is not going to arrive until most of us really want it: and we are not going to want it until we become fully Christian....And so...we are driven on to something more inward–driven on from social matters to religious matters.[172]

Americans shall increasingly be driven toward religious matters as a response to the ever-more-undeniable failure of our morality, our political and economic systems, and our dependence on science and technology as panaceas.

What is first required is an acceptance of the simple fact that in the modern American political system, neither of the existing parties is capable of meaningful response to our condition. Whether to address this crisis requires the creation of a third party to effect real change is of secondary significance: until people acknowledge this failure, no change will come. In a spectacular display of faith, Americans continue in their democrat/republican loyalties despite the general acknowledgement by both the man on the street and academia that the system has been co-opted by the insidious reach of self interest.

Theodore Lowi writes in <u>The End of Liberalism:</u> "[t]he only difference between old school liberals and conservatives is that the former would destroy the market through public means and the latter through private means....The most important difference between liberals and conservatives...is to be found in the interest groups they identify with."[173] Paul Gottfried and Thomas

---

[172] C. S. Lewis, <u>Mere Christianity</u>, pp. 82-83.
[173] As quoted by Richard N. Goodwin, <u>The American Condition</u>, at p. 347.

Fleming posit that "Political differences between right and left have by now been largely reduced to disagreements over policies designed to achieve comparable moral goals."[174] And Kevin Phillips observes:

> In short, great power decline, and not simply the separate weaknesses of liberalism and conservatism, is responsible for the new force field that Americans must deal with, and the dilemma is always economic and cultural....To most Democrats and liberals, the critical American failure and deterioration of the late twentieth century has been economic. To many Republicans and conservatives, however, the emerging weakness has been moral and cultural. Although the line between the two alternatives is artificial, it may also be unbridgeable, because both sides have mutually hostile elites and interest groups on top of divergent philosophies.[175]

Christopher Lasch writes:

> We need to press the point more vigorously and to ask whether the left and right have not come to share so many of the same underlying convictions, including a belief in the desirability and inevitability of technical and economic development, that the conflict between them, shrill and acrimonious as it is, no longer speaks to the central issues of American politics.

---

[174] Quoted by Christopher Lasch, <u>The True and Only Heaven: Progress and its Critics</u>, at p. 22.
[175] Kevin Phillips, <u>Arrogant Capital: Washington, Wall Street, and the Frustration of American Politics</u>, pp. 66, 60.

Neither side has any use for "doomsayers." Neither wants to admit that our society has taken a wrong turn, lost its way, and needs to recover a sense of purpose and direction. Neither addresses the overriding issue of limits, so threatening to those who wish to appear optimistic at all times. The fact remains: the earth's finite resources will not support an indefinite expansion of industrial civilization. The right proposes, in effect, to maintain our riotous standard of living, as it has been maintained in the past, at the expense of the rest of the world (increasingly at the expense of our minorities as well). This program is self-defeating, not only because it will produce environmental effects from which even the rich cannot escape but because it will widen the gap between rich and poor nations, generate more and more violent movements of insurrection and terrorism against the West, and bring about a deterioration of the world's political climate as threatening as the deterioration of its physical climate.

But the historical program of the left has become equally self-defeating. The attempt to extend Western standards of living to the rest of the world will lead even more quickly to the exhaustion of nonrenewable resources, the irreversible pollution of the earth's atmosphere, and the destruction of the ecological system, in short, on which human life depends.

These considerations refute conventional optimism (though the real despair lies in a refusal to confront them at all), and both the right and left therefore prefer to talk about something else—for example, to exchange accusations of both fascism and socialism....Not only have these words lost their meaning through reckless expansion, but they no longer describe historical alternatives at the end of the twentieth century.[176]

Speaking of current policies favoring big business in the shadow of record budget and trade deficits, Harvard Law School professor Elizabeth Warren has called the dismal unresponsiveness of the political parties a war on the middle class:

> Do we run the country for the people, or do we run it for nameless, faceless banks or international corporations?....That was the issue way back as far as the depression. The ultimate decision was we run it for the people....And now we have made a complete turnabout: We not only don't invest in the middle class, we drain away from the middle class.... It's war on the middle class....It's now a war being prosecuted by both political parties. Neither party in Congress is looking out for the interests of the middle class."[177]

John Kenneth Galbraith reveals that the two parties hold no allure for the substantial numbers of our citizens who are long-term poor, noting that voting "is an idle exercise for the eligible poverty-ridden citizen. It is rightly

---

[176] Christopher Lasch, The True and Only Heaven: Progress and its Critics, pp.23-24.
[177] As quoted by Lou Dobbs in "Lonely in the Middle," *U.S. News & World Report*, May 2, 2005, p. 55.

perceived that the difference between the two parties on the immediately affecting issues is inconsequential."[178]

Still, each side to the American political divide contributes further to the problem by vilifying the other side, all the more effective a tool as we grow disgusted with our political system and vote for candidates based on a lesser-of-evils analysis. John Lukacs dismisses (accurately) the leftists as out of circulation, calling them "possibly more remote from the people than they have ever been."[179] Christopher Lasch criticizes the new right (accurately) for its failure to deliver on promises to improve our condition.[180] Satan loves to turn us against one another.[181]

Alvin Toffler and Richard N. Goodwin share the same conclusion with regard to the modern political system: that "[n]o matter how many parties run against one another in elections, and no matter who gets the most votes, a single party always wins. It is the Invisible party of bureaucracy"[182] and "[t]he concentration and

---

[178] John Kenneth Galbraith, The Culture of Contentment, p. 151.

[179] John Lukacs, The End of the Twentieth Century and the End of the Modern Age, p. 213.

[180] The True and Only Heaven: Progress and its Critics, p. 22: "Ritual deference to 'traditional values' cannot hide the right's commitment to progress, unlimited economic growth, and acquisitive individualism."

[181] C. S. Lewis alludes to this in The Screwtape Letters, in which one demonic spirit exhorts another in his efforts to lead a human soul astray: "...whenever all men are really hastening to be slaves or tyrants we make Liberalism the prime bogey....We direct the fashionable outcry of each generation against those vices of which it is least in danger and fix its approval on the virtue which is nearest to the vice which we are trying to make endemic." p. 74. This parallels our country's current swing to the right even as we become dangerously intolerant in our conservatism.

[182] Alvin Toffler, Powershift: Knowledge, Wealth, and Violence at the Edge of the Twenty-First Century, p. 251.

bureaucratization of economic power, and the consequent centralization of public authority continued undisturbed under 'conservative' and 'liberal' guidance alike."[183] Again, government only grows larger, and it inexorably requires more aspects of our lives to control in order to justify that expansion: the political parties lend the semblance of legitimacy or choice to a system that essentially has only one Orwellian Party, for these parties trip over one another to pander to the same interests, while each offers identical palliatives about the economy, race, compassion for the poor, etc., etc. Thus the populace is distracted with the illusion of an electoral choice, while both major political parties in America are bought and paid for by essentially identical corporate interests.

Our country's founders were quite aware of the risks of party affiliation in republican forms of government. "The framers of the Constitution did not mention political parties in it and were strongly suspicious of them as forces that would dissolve the unity of the nation and lessen the importance of the individual in the process."[184] Presently the unity of the nation is dissolved indeed, at a time when Americans need to stand together more than ever before. And obviously individual influence on government has indeed waned with the steady increase of party (and corporate) dominance.

So America has come full circle, having been created with a distrust for government and partisan politics,

---

[183] Richard N. Goodwin, The American Condition, p. 359-360.
[184] William Ebenstein, Today's Isms: Communism Fascism Capitalism Socialism, p. 167.

only to be slowly self-immolated by those very forces. But Christians are not surprised (and are in fact bolstered in their faith) when the wisdom of the Bible is affirmed in the experiences of this world. Our Christian concept of service is constructed not of government or of some larger societal 'good,' but of Jesus Christ and His sacrifice so that others could be freed from evil. Reminded of this, Christians must not allow themselves to despair when their worldly governments (no matter how mighty) fail them, nor allow cynicism and political disagreement to distance them from their Christian or non-Christian Brethren. For "…God has anointed no political philosophy as his own….[O]n many issues there simply is no single "Christian" position."[185] And as John McCain has said: "The politics of division and slander are not our values….They are corrupting influences on religion and politics, and those who practice them in the name of religion or in the name of the Republican Party or in the name of America shame our faith, our party, and our country."[186] Christian Americans must answer to a higher authority. Abraham Lincoln said: "I know that the Lord is <u>always</u> on the side of the right. But it is my constant anxiety and prayer that I and the nation should be on the <u>Lord's</u> side."[187] And of the two sides of the slavery dispute, in words that ring sharply

---

[185] Doug Bandow, <u>Beyond Good Intentions: A Biblical View of Politics</u>, pp. XII, XIII. But contrast this with the teachings of St. Augustine, who held "that Christianity is one thing that can be gotten right and therefore can be universal—with all Christians reading from the same page." "What He Did Not Confess," *U.S. News & World Report*, May 23, 2005, p. 65.

[186] Quoted in Molly Ivins and Lou Dubose, <u>Shrub: The Short But Happy Political Life of George W. Bush</u>, at p. 185.

[187] David Aikman, <u>The Spiritual Journey of George W. Bush</u>, p. 187.

when applied to Iraq, Lincoln said, "The prayers of both could not be answered. That of neither has been answered fully. The Almighty has his own purposes. Woe unto the world because of offenses; for it must needs be that offenses come, but woe to that man by whom the offense cometh."[188]

Politics is surely not a science. And it is also not God's process.[189] The American political system, self-promoted democratic model for the world, is particularly harsh and "worldly." It should be of no surprise to Christians then that political parties are worthy of little trust.

John McCain has decried "the corruption of the American political system, the elephant-in-the living room of politics."[190] Goodwin tells us that "Survival and growth are the first prescripts of the political bureaucracy,"[191] hardly Christian tenets, and reflecting that governments possess an innate perniciousness, a blob-like demand to expand unhindered by human conscience. Phillips laments "the hugeness of the infrastructure involved, and how little the politicians can walk away from the structures that finance and support

---

[188] Ibid., p. 188.
[189] Allan Bloom notes this ignominious distinction for political science, though: economics exists only in peace, whereas political science addresses both war and peace: "…the market…requires the prior existence of the social contract….without which men are at war….Political science remains the only social science discipline which looks war in the face….politics is the authoritative arena of effective good and evil," The Closing of the American Mind, p. 364, 365. If so, politics must be where the action is in Satan's war to rule this world.
[190] Molly Ivins and Lou Dubose, Shrub: The Short But Happy Political Life of George W. Bush, p. 182.
[191] Richard N. Goodwin, The American Condition, p. 350.

them."[192] Kirk quotes St. Augustine for the proposition that "the state itself shares in the general corruption....The state is governed by man, subject to sinful appetites—enslaved especially by the lust for power.... Put no faith in salvation through the political order."[193] John Lukacs describes how republicanism devolved into "democratic popularity contests....But in the twentieth century there was a more insidious devolution. The popularity contests became publicity contests. A decline of taste and judgment, of truthfulness and reason, was inseparable from this devolution...."[194]

In <u>A Time For Truth</u>, William E. Simon writes:

> Our political leadership today, which is committed to the 'ideals' of the mixed economy, is required to articulate a coherent advocacy of individualism and collectivism, of the free market and a planned economy, of individual liberty from government coercion and of government control over individual life. The American political language has become paralyzed by these conflicting assignments. It is impossible to articulate such massively contradictory 'ideals.' And those politicians who attempt to resolve this problem end up speaking a mediocre kind of double talk so rife with self-contradiction that they are winning the contempt of millions of Americans....[195]

---

[192] Kevin Phillips, <u>Arrogant Capital: Washington, Wall Street, and the Frustration of American Politics</u>, p. 64. Russell Kirk also quotes Charles Norris Cochrane: "The advice of Augustine is therefore not to put your trust either in princes or in peoples, in kingdoms or in commonwealths...." <u>The Roots of American Order</u>, p. 164.

[193] Russell Kirk, <u>The Roots of American Order</u>, pp.161, 162.

[194] John Lukacs, <u>The End of the Twentieth Century and the End of the Modern Age</u>, p. 286.

[195] William E. Simon, <u>A Time for Truth</u>, p. 42.

Richard N. Goodwin refers to the Presidency as "the temple's high altar,"[196] reflecting the intensity of American faith in the political process of the founding fathers, which continues to imbue political offices with trust no matter how often our leaders fail us. He identifies those who have "lost faith" in "the institutions of democracy" as possessing "an intuitive realism grounded in the congenital incapacities of politics."[197] Drawing parallels to the failed leadership of the Church of the Middle Ages, Goodwin relates that:

> Today, too, the foundation has shifted. The possibilities of human freedom are so much larger than the reality, the gap between the two so great, that politics as faith seduces us to support the agents of our confinement, the mutilators of existence. Politics is not an opiate. It is speed; creating an illusion of command, causing an outpouring of energy and force for their own sake. But always it wears off, leaving the world and us as before. To the believer, politics is real war, summoning the commanding spirits of decisive battle. Yet, such struggles do not interrupt the purpose of material rulers, although their attention may occasionally be distracted.[198]

Some religious commentators are even more outspoken in their condemnation of politics. Stephen L. Carter explains that "...when secular political considerations become prior to, rather than subsequent to, religious considerations, the result is not cross-pollination but

---

[196] Richard N. Goodwin, The American Condition, pp. 357, 358.
[197] Ibid., The American Condition, p. 362.
[198] Ibid., The American Condition, pp. 363-364.

pollution....the political tail wagging the spiritual dog."[199] James 4:4 asks us: "...know ye not that the friendship of the world is enmity with God? Whosoever therefore will be a friend of the world is the enemy of God."[200] And Doug Bandow says emphatically:

> Unfortunately Christianity...has often allied itself with the governments of its day. At such times the transcendent gospel, a message of God's eternal love for man, inevitably suffered, ending up submerged in the world's values. Religion merely became another tool for those with political power to satisfy their own selfish desires, whether wealth, position, status, sensuality, or power. The closer the relationship of church and state, the more spiritually irrelevant and institutionally fractured the Body of Christ seemed to become....
>
> Despite the obvious dissimilarities between democratic humanism and totalitarian atheism, in both cases the state has taken over the role of God and the Body of Christ, providing the transcendent justification for life, to serve the general polity, and the material means to survive, government transfer payments....
>
> The average politician is mainly interested in reelection, and the average voter is primarily concerned about his paycheck; if believers won't call this nation to account for its moral failings, who will? The institutionalization of envy and materialism,

---

[199] Stephen Carter, <u>The Culture of Disbelief: How American Law and politics Trivialize Religious Devotion</u>, pp. 81, 69.
[200] KJV.

mistreatment of the poor, mass killings of the unborn, and acquiescence in the face of widespread domestic and foreign injustice–God will judge the nation for its actions in such matters. Christians need to focus attention on these issues....Today's political process is fundamentally corrupt....Christians should never forget that lobbying is secondary to evangelizing.[201]

It should thus not surprise Americans that those devoted to careers in politics may be something less than model Christians. Ronald Reagan professed faith in Christ, but his political aspirations were paramount—for instance, he exchanged 600 missiles (with terrorists) for one hostage to generate a political boost for his reelection campaign.[202] (If one dismisses the claim that this exchange was politically motivated, or that the Iran-Contra matter was immoral, on what Christian basis can such an exchange, providing terrorists the arms to kill thousands in exchange for one human life, be justified?) Bill Clinton called himself a Baptist, but his public dishonesty is a putrid legacy to our nation's image. And there has surely been vocal criticism of Clinton–in God and George W. Bush: a spiritual life, Paul Kengor alleges, of three speeches delivered by President Clinton, "When Scripture was mentioned, it was tied to politics."[203]

---

[201] Doug Bandow, Beyond Good Intentions: a Biblical View of Politics, pp.15, 16, 229, 231. This "Christian" distrust of politics contrasts with the Muslim perspective: "Islam makes no essential distinction between religion and politics." Gerald Segal, The World Affairs Companion: The Essential One-Volume Guide to Global Issues, p. 55.
[202] George Donelson Moss, Moving On: The American People Since 1945, p. 353.
[203] Paul Kengor, God and George W. Bush: a spiritual journey, p. 187.

Certainly George W. is not immune from Scriptural assessment. Just because his deliberate misrepresentation of his DWI arrest in the 2000 election was silently accepted by the religious right, ignoring George W. Bush's clear dishonesty about the arrest (similar moral ill-logic to Democrats dismissing Bill Clinton's perjury because his sex life was private), doesn't mean that Christians will indefinitely close their eyes to Christ being dragged into the political melee and employed as a tool in the political game. What of the impatience to advance a war against Iraq based on faulty (manipulated?) intelligence? What of the criminality of the disclosure of Valerie Plame's CIA status? Of illegal wiretaps? Of the torture or indefinite detention of thousands, all presumed guilty without evidence? What would Jesus say to all of this? Just because George W. Bush ignores consultation with Christ in these behaviors does not excuse truly devout Christians from their responsibility to do so.

George W. Bush is politician first, Christian second, and this is easy to see if one looks beyond the piety act, to actions and to the convenient timing of this man's conversion to Christianity.[204] Paul O'Neill, who served as assistant director of the Office of Management and Budget under Richard Nixon, who had engineered "a legendary turnaround" of Alcoa Corp., and who Dick Cheney regularly called "the smartest guy I know" prior to his joining George W. as Treasury Secretary for two years, said after working for the Bush W. administra-

---

[204] "...at the exact time his father was keenly interested in asserting his credentials with the evangelical community...Bush began a series of conversations with Billy Graham...." Bill Minutaglio, <u>First Son: George W. Bush and the Bush Family Dynasty</u>, p. 288.

tion that he is "troubled about the way the business of governance is being conducted."[205] O'Neill (and Colin Powell) felt that this Administration allowed ideology to steer policy decisions, often unwisely, without permitting the airing of opposing viewpoints or constructive criticism. O'Neill's perspective (and it got him fired) was that "...without shared, agreed-upon facts to anchor debate, what's left is...the food-fight model of public discourse."[206]

This book seeks to establish a foundation of facts which are "true:" if they are not "agreed-upon" or "shared," that may be the reader's denial–I challenge any reader who finds any factual discrepancy in this book to research the issue and inform me of the error, for I have no political agenda, except perhaps an admitted disgust with both political parties and for America's wasted opportunities to improve the condition of the world. Many of the "facts" about George W. are simply startling in their unchristianness. For instance, mustn't a Christian renounce and repent of belonging to an elitist, Satanic cult like Skull & Bones (see Chapter Ten)? Is there no remorse over affronting God? Are Christians sleeping, as the Bible foretells they will be in the End Times?

George W. Bush is a great politician, but this is no compliment....Bob Woodward, in his authorized study of the Bush Administration's launch of the Iraq War, <u>Plan of Attack</u> (which was based on hundreds of hours of face-to-face interviews with the President and his

---

[205] Ron Suskind, <u>The Price of Loyalty</u>, p. 350.
[206] Ibid., p. 347. The words quoted are Suskind's description of O'Neill's view.

cabinet members), described the Bush Administration's response to the proposal that a commission be appointed to investigate failures in intelligence relative to Iraq's non-existent weapons of mass destruction:

> Bush initially said no, but then he, Cheney, Rice and others in the White House quickly grasped the necessity–and the opportunity. So they decided to seize the initiative and proposed an independent bipartisan commission to be appointed by the president. They would include two conditions. First, the commission would look at WMD and intelligence problems more broadly, not just in Iraq but at proliferation in Iran, North Korea and Libya. Second, the commission would not report until some time after the presidential election....By acting quickly and getting ahead of the curve...the White House shaped the news. "Bush to Back Probe of Iraq Data, Officials Say," read the headline in The Washington Post....[207]

Mr. Woodward reports that on February 6, 2004, President Bush announced that he'd appoint a commission to look at intelligence for WMD worldwide: "Then the president added, "Members of the commission will issue their report by March 31st, 2005." "[208] By controlling the contours of the so-called investigation, Bush successfully deferred the Commission's report until after his re-election bid, by which point the Commission's conclusions became essentially purposeless. Again, this

---

[207] Bob Woodward, Plan of Attack, pp. 434-435.
[208] Ibid., p.442. Mr. Bush similarly hid behind the parole board he appointed in the Karla Faye Tucker case to shield him from responsibility (*see* A Charge to Keep, pp. 150-151).

may be good politics, but good Christians strive for integrity and accountability in their representation of Christ, not just the appearance thereof in more politics-as-usual–God's judgment will not be deferred past an election or other worldly function in the fashion that Mr. Bush manipulates bureaucracy to escape truth, again and again.

This account reflects politics in action, and though Christians and others tend to make excuses for this Administration's conduct (e.g., George has to conduct himself this way to 'play the game,' etc.), the above example is a simple case of seeking to avoid the accountability so often promised. This is not a Christian pattern–big words, opposite action. We have been promised accountability, which in the case of WMD would simply require an apology and an admission, finally, that they weren't there (kind of like Clinton showed his true colors and committed a greater wrong by persistent lying rather than just come clean about his moronic behavior in the oval office). Instead, we see a direct effort by the current administration to a) control the substance of the commission's investigation by creating it before Congress did, b) broaden the investigation beyond the issue of whether the public was misled, to include unrelated analysis of actual nuclear threats, (more unchristian fear-mongering) and c) ensure that the commission's findings were pushed out to a date where it could not harm the Accountability President politically, i.e. until after his re-election bid (when it did). Those who dismiss this artful politicking as defensible because they view our involvement in Iraq as justified mirror the Democrats' refusal to hold Clinton accountable for criminal perjury (that would land an ordinary citizen in jail) because they said his sex life was his own business. But two wrongs don't make a right, at least in God's world. Using a commission to cover up one's misdeeds, which commission purports to be seeking responsibility and explanations, adds insult to the injury done to integrity, and is an example of the art of obfuscation, of deception, not of Jesus' way. We are reminded of Luke 16:8: "the people of this world are much more shrewd in handling their affairs than the people who belong to the light."[209]

But whatever else this example from Mr. Bush's tenure at the White House reveals, it is that he is a consummate politician.[210] In fact, he surely would not have risen in party influence without demonstrating effectiveness at politicking, and fealty to the worldly political powers that be.[211] But the appointment of a

---

[209] TEV.

[210] Regarding his push for privatized social security accounts, "He is a seasoned political operator, going back to his father's presidency, and it is clear from the way he speaks that he knows how Washington works." Alexandra Marks, "Bush's Term II: a slow road," *The Christian Science Monitor*, June 3, 2005, p. 10.

[211] As with George's years-long effort to disassociate himself from the image of the rich fat-cat, he has worked hard to portray himself as *not* being a politician (this is what moving cedar brush on his ranch is for). In The Faith of George W. Bush, Stephen Mansfield said of W. Bush: "it seems at times that politics takes a back seat to the religious imprint he hopes to make on the nation." (p. 173) But the opposite is true, for Bush has repeatedly flaunted Christian values while instead practicing ideological devotion, and politics always gets front seat in his decisions, like when he backtracked when he took political flack for saying that Jesus was the one true path to heaven–and he has never publicly said this again! And the "religious imprint" he has made on the nation is the antagonism he has engendered in non-Christians against Christianity.

commission to avoid accountability instead of find it is just one of many examples which are disappointing to his representation in A Charge to Keep, where he writes that "I want to show that politics...can be higher and better."[212]

The dilemma which faces us in twenty-first century America has been with us since the birth of our nation–how much of our society's future should be determined by political forces, which we recognize as necessary but distrust, versus infusing our government and politics with religious faith. The colonists didn't place their faith in government. Thomas Paine ridiculed "the pomposity which has always been part of political life,"[213] saying "[i]t is by distortedly exalting some men, that others are distortedly debased, till the whole is out of nature. A vast mass of mankind are degradingly thrown into the background of the human picture, to bring forward, with greater glare, the puppet-show of State and Aristocracy."[214] Ben Franklin said "only a virtuous people are capable of freedom. As nations become corrupt and vicious, they have more need of masters."[215] Is that why Americans are yielding their freedoms to the federal government via the ironically-if-ludicrously-named USA PATRIOT Act, and excusing their presidents (from both parties) from accountability?

---

[212] George W. Bush, A Charge To Keep, p. 241.
[213] Derek Matravers, in the introduction to Thomas Paine's Rights of Man, p. XII.
[214] Paine, p. 25. What would Paine think of our modern political displays–the second Bush inaugural festivities cost some $40,000,000.00!
[215] David Aikman, The Spiritual Journey of George W. Bush, p. 184.

But our nation's designers also relied heavily on Christian faith in the formulation of our political structures. They held a "faith" in the importance of religious integrity to the foundations of a just, Godly society. George Washington, in his farewell address, commented that "[o]f all the dispositions and habits which lead to political prosperity, religion and morality are indispensable supports...."[216] Thomas Jefferson remarked "...no nation has ever yet existed or been governed without religion. Nor can be. The Christian religion is the best religion that has ever been given to man...."[217] And John Adams, who was of the "view that it would be very difficult for the United States to sustain free institutions unless the ethical behavior of its citizens was guided by Christian principles," said that "[o]ur Constitution was made only for a moral and religious people. It is wholly inadequate to the government of any other."[218] So has our Constitution become "wholly inadequate," unworkable in the hands of moral relativism and liberalism-gone-cuckoo? Can the United States "sustain free institutions" when corporate greed and devotion to material accumulation dominate "the ethical behavior of its citizens" instead of Jesus Christ? And shall we place hope in our man-created system of government when we see it usurped by a perversion of Christ's example, as now?

Thus, Christians must hold the American government to Christ's teachings if that system of government

---

[216] Ibid., p. 183.
[217] Ibid., p. 183.
[218] Ibid., p. 185.

is to survive. As Doug Bandow observes, "Indifference to politics is not an option for Christians...."[219] And David Aikman reports that 70 % of Americans want their president to be "strongly religious."[220]

Yet, influencing politics toward Christian ends is a different matter from a Christian becoming completely committed to politics or to a political party. As Stephen L. Carter points out, "...if the principal value of religion to a democratic polity is its ability to preach resistance, it is difficult to see any gain to religion from the unswerving effort to take control of the apparatus of the state."[221] For a Christian, controlling the apparatus of the state is akin to wielding J.R.R. Tolkien's Ring of Power: ultimately it corrupts the user. Christ's Kingdom is not yet of this world, and until that blessed time arrives, all governments of men are imperfect and ultimately corrupted. However well-intentioned, no Christian can move the levers of power without being tainted with the insidiously evil stench of the powers of this world. The very nature of politics, where illusion and appearance are routinely elevated above substance, is at odds with the Spirit of Christ. Richard N. Goodwin observed of modern America that

> [t]he modern rallying to politics is something more than an intensification of tradition....When we bestow upon politics the power to guide and alter

---

[219] Doug Bandow, <u>Beyond Good Intentions: A Biblical View of Politics</u>, p. 16.
[220] David Aikman, <u>The Spiritual Journey of George W. Bush</u>, p. 175.
[221] Stephen L. Carter, <u>The Culture of Disbelief: How American Law and Politics Trivialize Religion</u>, p. 68.

> society by acts of will or decision we are engaged in mystical creation....It is made transcendent, and that element of transcendence reveals that we are in the presence of faith; a structure of belief which, as the corporeal translations of passions and revelations, is resistant to the contradictions of experience and logic.[222]

This is the sort of collision of faiths that this world has set us in, as foretold in the Bible and brought about by Satan: the American commitment to its own mythological greatness leads to a denial of "the contradictions of experience and logic" which a truly Christian nation would choose to confront. Our mysticism, our devotion, our faith to this concept of "nation" eclipses our ability to be self-critical, for to do so would be not only to risk social disapprobation but to challenge our individual identities which are so tightly knitted to our culture. And the increasing alienation caused by materialism and industrialization pushes us further toward dependence, conformity and fear: fear of change, of conflict, and of death. But all of this failed vicious cycle of faith in government, faith in wealth, faith in science, faith in man, faith in self, faith in the future, faith in the U.S.A., is in direct rivalry to faith in God, faith in Jesus Christ, and faith in the Holy Spirit. There is no room for divided loyalties. Thomas Kempis attributed to Jesus the thought "My son, My grace is precious, and may not be mingled with worldly concerns and pleasures....For

---

[222] Richard N. Goodwin, <u>The American Condition</u>, p. 360.

you cannot attend on Me, and at the same time take pleasure in worldly things."[223]

America's Christians must recall the words of Oswald Chambers, that "[i]f we are born again it is the easiest thing to live in right relationship with God and the most difficult thing to go wrong, if only we heed God's warnings to keep in the light."[224] And as George W. cited in a speech, "As the book of James reminds us, fresh water and salt water cannot flow from the same spring."[225]

But does George W. follow the words he mouths? "[H]e says that he relies on his faith for guidance and forbearance in a battle against what he views, unequivocally, as pure evil."[226] Yet a study of George's past quickly reveals that he spent his whole life grooming for wealth, privilege, and political office, and that he invested very little energy in Jesus (except, conveniently, just in time to garner the essential religious right vote: see chapter Ten). Said Mark Owen, a close Bush friend: "Running again came up a lot. After '78, he consciously decided to concentrate on his business and family, but he was always a politician. When his dad was vice president, he didn't want to get in on that because the 'dad's

---

[223] Thomas A. Kempis, The Imitation of Christ, p. 167.
[224] Oswald Chambers, My Utmost For His Highest, December 24.
[225] Thomas A. Freiling, George W. Bush on God & Country, p. 200.
[226] Paul Kengor, God and George W. Bush: a spiritual life, p. XI. This whole "evil" rhetoric is highly suspect, and Christians should be on guard: Christ teaches that all men possess the capacity for good and for salvation, and that even our enemies (whom we characterize as evil) are to be loved as ourselves. And the talk of a war to "rid the world of evil" is theologically absurd, for this is an impossible task for man–only God can save us from ourselves.

coattails' thing would come up. He was waiting for the right time. It's in his blood...."[227] David Aikman, in <u>A Man of Faith: The Spiritual Journey of George W. Bush</u>, writes that "In <u>A Charge to Keep</u>, George W. made it plain that he regards political life as a whole to be a walk of faith."[228] Is that like considering investment banking or real estate investment as walks of faith? Or mafia hit man or crack dealer? What could be as worldly a walk as the political one?

It is of little surprise then that a man with such shallow concepts of even how to fake true faith would disappoint those who placed their trust and hope in his professed fealty to Jesus. John J. DiIulio, Jr. ran W.'s faith-based initiative, and "[a]fter eight months in the White House, DiIulio felt his initiative had been revised from Bush's campaign rhetoric about "compassionate conservatism"–a way to support those in need–into a political and financial prop for those evangelicals who were in "the base."" DiIulio said that "everything...[was] being run by the political arm. It's like the reign of the Mayberry Machiavellis."[229] There is a pattern of duplicitous conduct toward Christ in this administration, of which this is just one example. When will Christians hold this man to the walk he *says* he's on?

In John 12:35-36, Jesus advises us: "yet a little while is the light with you. Walk while ye have the light, lest darkness come upon you: for he that walketh in darkness knoweth not whither he goeth. While ye have

---

[227] Bill Minutaglio, <u>First Son: George W. Bush and the Bush Family Dynasty</u>, p. 200.
[228] David Aikman, <u>The Spiritual Journey of George W. Bush</u>, p. 135.
[229] Ron Suskind, <u>The Price of Loyalty</u>, p. 170.

light, believe in the light, that ye may be the children of light."[230] Are American Christians "children of the light" any longer, or has darkness come upon us?

---

[230] KJV.

Chapter 4

COMPASSIONATE CONSERVATISM, THE "UNDERCLASS," AND THE PRIVILEGED

"Listen….God chose the poor people of this world to be rich in faith….But you dishonor the poor! Who are the ones who oppress you and drag you before judges? The rich!"[231]

George Bush has repeatedly proclaimed his commitment to the concept of "compassionate conservatism," carrying on a tradition (and familiar emulation) of the Reagan Administration. President Bush has credited Myron Magnet, author of <u>The Tragedy of American Compassion</u>, and Marvin Olasky, known particularly for his book <u>The Dream and the Nightmare: The Sixties' Legacy to the Underclass</u>, as the mentors of his personal political philosophy of compassionate conservatism. George W. is quoted on the front cover of Magnet's book, gushing

---

[231] James 2:5, 6, TEV.

> The Dream and the Nightmare by Myron Magnet crystallized for me the impact the failed culture of the sixties had on our values and society. It helped create dependency on government, undermine family, and eroded values which had stood the test of time and which are critical if we want a decent and hopeful tomorrow for every single American.[232]

Both of these books, and Compassionate Conservatism as employed by Mr. Bush, Jr., essentially hold that the long-term poor in America are perpetuated in that condition by a 1960s liberal culture which poisoned them with dependency and an entitlement mentality. Mr. Magnet modestly confesses that his "was the first book to argue that culture, not racism or lack of jobs or the welfare system, was the cause of the underclass."[233]

In truth, "Compassionate Conservatism" as employed by the current Republican leadership is logically absurd, even by "worldly" measures; but more importantly, Compassionate Conservatism as employed by this Administration as a rationalization for the systemic failures of America to aid millions of her citizens falls quickly before Christ's explicit teachings. There has been much flowery talk by George W. Bush of his infatuation with this rhetorical nicety, but the pattern exhibited is once again of no action to back up the rosy promises.

Bush adopted Magnet's and Olasky's arguments to his own use, but he didn't follow their advice–while both

---

[232] Myron Magnet, <u>The Dream and the Nightmare: The Sixties' Legacy to the Underclass</u>, front cover 2000 edition (conveniently for national election-year exposure).
[233] Ibid., p. 1.

authors offer thoughtful, practical ideas to address the chronic condition of the inner-city poor, George hasn't used more than the language, the words, of Compassionate Conservatism to support his idea of shifting the financial burden of aid for the poor off of the federal government, to private eleemosynary interests, and little else of policy or substance toward reducing the fast-widening gap between wealthy and poor in America. Yet, both Magnet and Olasky stridently condemn empty words of compassion rhetoric not supported with sincere action. In <u>The Dream and the Nightmare</u>, Magnet writes:

> The only value that hadn't curdled in the new culture was "compassion" or "caring" or "sensitivity" toward the excluded of all varieties. This attitude, for many, became the touchstone of moral worth, displacing considerations of justice and responsibility. But "compassion" or "caring" proved a barren value, for no amount of it made the condition of the lowest of the excluded get better. On the contrary, throughout the eighties the number of homeless increased and the underclass sank deeper into disorder.[234]

In addition to this recognition of the failure of the Reagan Administration to deliver on promises of conservative compassion, Magnet specifically criticizes President Clinton for using words of compassion to avoid moral accountability, "with his exaggerated I-feel-your-pain display of "compassion" for the

---

[234] Ibid., pp. 233-234. So much for the success of trickle-down economics.

"victimized" and "oppressed".".[235] Clinton, says Magnet, "has behaved as if the moral authority that flows from his compassion—the value that trumps all else—cancels or justifies his unprincipled conduct in so many departments of life."[236]

Marvin Olasky exhorted in <u>The Tragedy of American Compassion</u> that "…we need to look at ourselves and our society more honestly….We need to be honest in our self-criticism. It is easy for conservatives to criticize government…."[237] Olasky then derides the "compassion fatigue" which was prevalent among the better-off by 1990, emphasizing that "…we need to realize that we do not increase compassion by expanding it to cover everything. Instead, we kill a good word by making it mean too much, and nothing."[238]

Another conservative author who revealed suspicion (if not disdain) for the motives behind the use of supposed compassion was Allan Bloom: "Certainly compassion and the idea of the vanguard were essentially democratic covers for elitist self-assertion. Rousseau, who first made compassion the foundation of democratic sentiment, was fully aware that a sense of superiority to the sufferer is a component of the human experience of compassion."[239] This "sense of superiority" infects the current Compassionate Conservative agenda, allowing wealthy Americans to justify turning a blind eye to those morally-failed inner city poor, to reduce funding for

---

[235] Ibid., p. 8
[236] Ibid., p. 8.
[237] Marvin Olasky, <u>The Tragedy of American Compassion</u>, p. 198.
[238] Ibid., p. 232.
[239] Allan Bloom, <u>The Closing of the American Mind</u>, p. 330.

programs geared toward the poor, and to force recipients off welfare while jobs of all kinds dwindle. It also relieves the more-fortunate of guilt or responsibility for their better circumstances.

This attitude of condemnation or superiority makes offensive some of the assertions of those who would dismiss America's impoverished as morally culpable for their plight, and is patently offensive to the foundation of Christ's power in humility to the least among us: "Remember those who are suffering, as though you were suffering as they are."[240] Consider these excerpts from Myron Magnet's book, so strongly endorsed by George W.:

> True, well-paid jobs needing more than basic skills did mushroom in the eighties and will keep proliferating in the nineties. But around two of five millions of jobs created between 1983 and 1990…were unskilled or low-skill….These developments in the labor market suggest no shortage of opportunity to find employment, despite low skills, and–with ambition and energy enough to get trained–to advance further[241]….Just as underclass nonwork springs not

---

[240] Hebrews 13:3, TEV
[241] But Magnet points out that even with this strong economy (though built on borrowed money that we still haven't repaid), "job creation failed to draw additional young black males into the labor force" (p. 46). Magnet attributes this to fault, e.g. dropouts, lack of motivation, etc. rather than consider the real effects of demographics (low or unskilled job creation in Utah or Vermont does nothing to aid blacks in Detroit), or the possibility that blacks get hired last, which easily explains his additional observation that in cities with extremely low unemployment in this period, "labor force participation increase[d] among young black males" (p. 46). (low unemployment compels employers to tap the minority labor force).

out of lack of opportunity but out of the lack of inner motivations, so underclass crime is impelled more by cultural than economic causes....[I]n late-twentieth-century American cities, increased crime spawned by the underclass surely represents a step backward in the development of civilization....In the ghettos it's more like two or three steps backward.... Like most underclass pathology, [crime]...is the fruit not of economic deprivation but of inner defect.... in today's America, cultural values make economic opportunities....cultural deformation is the worst affliction underclass kids suffer. That deformation prevents them from getting what is already available for them to get. Plenty of scholarship money and lots of low-cost public institutions, after all, are already available to qualified low-income applicants....What the homeless encamped in the streets, parks, and train stations in the heart of our cities really embody is the most extreme and catastrophic failure of the cultural revolution of the Haves and the social policies that resulted from it....Were it to stop being so easy to drop out into a truly dead-end life—were compassionate citizens to stop sympathetically viewing the alcoholic, the drug-addicted, and the idle as poor, downtrodden victims to whom giving handouts is a public necessity—this variety of homelessness would become far less attractive. And in an intact social order, where petty flawlessness and self-destructive irresponsibility are not suffered to flourish in the heart of the city, many fewer would feel tempted to fall into such a fate....It's time to stop kidding ourselves and clean up the mess that a specious liberation has made....The poor already have the strenuous but genuine opportunity for escaping poverty, but they lack the inner resources to embrace their chance….the Have-Nots lack the inner resources to seize their chance, and they pass on to their children a self-defeating set of values and attitudes….[242]

Not only does Mr. Magnet overlook the simple fact that welfare and the liberal policies of the 1960s were created in direct response to the socio-racial unrest that threatened civil order across the country (making it a logical strain to blame those programs for creating the conditions they were designed to combat), not only does it rely on the specious assertion that racial barriers have largely evaporated,[243] but there is an almost contemptuous but certainly judgmental "superior" tone to his commentary.[244] None of the complained-of behaviors of this abhorrent "underclass" are excused by the

---

[242] Myron Magnet, The Dream and the Nightmare: the Sixties' Legacy to the Underclass, pp. 45-46, 49, 50, 51, 66, 75, 83, 118, 237, 13.

[243] Even were such impediments removed, blacks and their communities are heavily concentrated in the urban centers to which they migrated after the Civil War, areas which are in historic decline and which simply don't generate jobs. Do those inner-city minorities have equal economic opportunity to relocate to improved job markets, or might they have trouble with the higher rents or other living expenses that keep them pinned down in the cities? Magnet reaches such broad conclusions repeatedly, based always on anecdotal tales or selected statistics: there is no political, statistical or social science involved in these theories which now form the basis of our nation's policies toward our most impoverished countrymen.

[244] One Christian writer questions: "Can we stand silent and indifferent to poverty? No, for it robs the poor of their pride as persons. Somehow we must support, inspire, or motivate the forces that can cause the poor to recover their dignity through development." Robert H. Schuller, Self-Esteem: The New Reformation, p. 139. This patently excludes dismissing the poor as sub-human, responsible for their own condition, thereby excusing us from action or compassion.

crushing adversity which is poverty; they are all dismissed as character flaws, as "lack of inner motivation,"[245] "a step backward in the development of civilization,"[246] an "inner defect"[247] ("like most underclass pathology"![248]), "cultural deformation," or a "lack of inner resources." Myron describes it as "easy to drop out into a truly dead-end life,"[249] but this would be "far less attractive"[250] if we stopped enabling them with our compassion. (This is reminiscent of the paternalistic attitude, "In order to succeed, the poor need most of all the spur of their poverty."[251]) If only the vicious cycle of inner city life, of poverty, of the constant threat of violence, of children of teenage mothers and high school dropouts becoming the same in turn, of childhood drug abuse, homelessness, and fatherless-ness could be reversed by such simplistic moralizing, we could all embrace Mr. Magnet's delusional panacea and not bother with those arduous Christian teachings that demand compassion and understanding toward those in lesser circumstances, whether those circumstances are the consequence of moral or of economic failing. Christ demands of us accountability and a vigilant eye for the suffering of others, but

---

[245] Myron Magnet, <u>The Dream and the Nightmare: the Sixties' Legacy to the Underclass</u>, p. 49.
[246] Ibid., p. 50.
[247] Ibid., p. 51.
[248] Ibid., p. 51.
[249] Ibid., p. 118 (Because citizens are so sympathetic.)
[250] Ibid., p. 118.
[251] George Gilder, quoted in John Kenneth Galbraith, <u>The Culture of Contentment</u>, p. 102. Galbraith also notes that "In what is the…indeed, only accepted view, the underclass is deemed the source of its own succor and well-being…and it will be damaged by any social assistance and support," at pp. 40-41.

Magnet and George W. Bush offer us a rationalization to leave the poor to their devices. Would they judge Jesus a beggar, and spurn Him in similar fashion? Jesus was meek, and didn't measure a soul's worth by whether or not he or she could climb the economic ladder like those morally superior Magnets we aspire to emulate.[252] James 2 tells us:

> For if there come into your assembly a man with a gold ring, in goodly apparel, and there come in also a poor man in vile raiment;
>
> And ye have respect to him that weareth the gay clothing, and say unto him, Sit thou here in a good place; and say to the poor, Stand thou here, or sit here under my footstool: "Are ye not then partial in yourselves, and are become judges of evil thoughts?"
>
> Hearken, my beloved brethren, Hath not God chosen the poor of this world rich in faith, and heirs of the kingdom which he hath promised to them that love him?
>
> But ye have despised the poor. Do not rich men oppress you, and draw you before the judgment seats?
>
> Do not they blaspheme that worthy name by the which ye are called?[253]

---

[252] Magnet belies his own arguments when he acknowledges on page 1 that the poor can't engage in self-indulgence because their "lives have less margin for error than the prosperous….," explicitly affirming that economic circumstances impose limits on conduct for the less privileged.
[253] James 2:2-7, KJV.

Marvin Olasky advocates a similar simplistic dismissal of the poor as cultural rather than economic victims. Mr. Olasky, a "Bush welfare advisor,"[254] recently wrote that "even those who seem the most hopeless really want a dad, a coach, or a teacher who will show them the difference between vice and virtue."[255] There is no doubt that our society's impoverished youth would benefit from such emotional succor and compassion, but this view leads to the conclusion that this is not a role that can be filled by government, so no government, i.e. societal, response in the form of financial resources is required—such a response would in fact, in the view of Olasky et al., be counter-productive by making the situation of the poor, their moral decline and de-evolution, worse.[256] We must be cruel to be kind, and if we model our luxurious excess for them they'll be motivated to crawl up from the trenches and join us. Interestingly, twistedly, this entire illogical construction rests on the premise that lack of money isn't the reason for the moral decay of the lower classes, but that if only they could overcome their moral failings, the "underclass" could reach the goal of material bliss and happiness: money. So money is the goal but not the cause, and everything will be OK once poor people have money, but their lack of it is no excuse to complain and misbehave. Haven't these guys seen "Trading Places"?

---

[254] Bill Minutaglio, <u>First Son: George W. Bush and the Bush Family Dynasty</u>, p. 289.
[255] *The Christian Science Monitor*, 1/27/05, p. 9.
[256] "It is an abysmal thought that charity is wrong and that you should never ease people's suffering lest you render them dependent." Crispin Sartwell, "As prosperous superpower, what does US owe the world?," *The Christian Science Monitor*, June 3, 2005, p.9.

But let us examine the deceptive nature of this logic further. Myron Magnet summarizes the Compassionate Conservative perspective: "the key to the mystery of why, despite opportunity, the poorest poor don't work is that their poverty is less an economic matter than a cultural one."[257] This argument stereotypes the poor as amoral or immoral–Compassionate Conservatism alleges that that lack of morality is the cause of their predicament. But this flies in the face of human experience. Louise Perrotta's <u>All You Really Need to Know About Prayer You Can Learn From the Poor</u> describes the inspiring spiritual devotion amongst deeply impoverished and physically devastated Christians. And Jesus certainly had faith that the poor and suffering were morally worthy of Him, without exception.

Magnet and Olasky (and thus George W. Bush) echo in their dismissiveness the callous ignorance of those who similarly dismissed the "Okies" in 1930s America as responsible for their poverty:

> H.L. Mencken…was outraged by pleas for help from sharecroppers and exodusters. "They are simply, by God's inscrutable will, inferior men," he wrote, "and inferior they will remain until, by a stupendous miracle, He gives them equality among His angels." The best solution, Mencken supposed, was to move the Dust Bowlers away from the plains, out of farming and even out of childbearing–bribe them to be sterilized, he urged….Prejudice, of course, never waits for the facts, especially when they are complex;

---

[257] Myron Magnet, <u>The Dream and the Nightmare: The Sixties' Legacy to the Underclass</u>, p. 13.

> to get to the truth of the difficult situation required an empathy with the Okies that neither Mencken nor many Californians had. It was easier, and perhaps more human, to feel hostility toward them than attempt to resolve the contradictions.[258]

Is the "Underclass" any less deserving than "Okies" of Christian comprehension? Does Christianity condone human hostility or apathy in place of Christ's compassion? Reducing funding for social programs without a thought-out alternative is not a Christian option, and this is the only mechanism offered by George W.'s "compassionate conservatism."

In ignoring the effects of poverty as causative of the plight of America's "Underclass," Magnet, Olasky, Bush et al. place the responsibility for America's failure to care for its poorest citizens with the liberals, the "Other Party" bogeyman.[259] Are these men trying to prove Karl Marx right, by compelling the poor into deeper poverty until they revolt against the industrial-capitalist

---

[258] Donald Worster, <u>Dust Bowl: The Southern Plains in the 1930s</u>, pp. 53-54.

[259] According to Magnet, this cultural shift was caused by the "Haves," the materialistic liberals who created the welfare and other social programs of the 1960s and 70s. (Magnet, pp. 14-15). Magnet holds that the Liberals essentially created a theory which faulted lack of economic access for the condition of the impoverished, "a theory that thereafter clung like a halo around the raw reality, transforming its meaning for literate observers. The result: today, for many people, the magic of ideology converts the drug users they see with their eyes into the Homeless that they see in their minds, trailing clouds of explanation about how economic injustice has forged their fate." p. 126. Did Mr. Magnet never meet any homeless people who were not drug addicts or alcoholics? He has characterized all homeless people as loser druggies: is this fair? And even if true, would Jesus not show them compassion and lead them to the light?

structures that forced them into techno-dependency and permanent privation of the fruits yielded by the very revolution (Industrial) that enslaved them? Communism has been proven to be a failed dream, but this doesn't mean Marx's criticisms of capitalism were unfounded. As explained by Marx, if free market forces are left unfettered, untempered by social/governmental oversight, then the increased concentration of wealth in the hands of the wealthy (the controllers of capital), becomes the inexorable force which we see shaping America today, just like in a game of "Monopoly," where eventually someone accumulates all the money. But the Right and not just the Left have an interest in social justice, in controlling capitalism's forces like a nuclear reaction, extracting the benefits without the huge energy involved exploding in our faces: for those with wealth have the most to lose (financially) should the backs of the underclass snap under the load.

But greed is a player in worldly affairs, and its grasp is not limited to the very wealthy. America has the resources to solve world hunger, but our "rags to riches" mythology favors the possession of vast fortunes by the few because the rest figure they'll catch up, however incongruous this creed may be with the teachings of Jesus. We say we're Christian, but we like our "stuff," and our culture is built on pursuing it.

"Poverty in America is not the consequence of scarce resources, the need to concentrate capital for future growth, or the economic inability to end it. The

American poor are oppressed, the victims of a material deprivation imposed by the relationships of society."[260]

To this Magnet would no doubt respond: "Wishing to think themselves people of humanitarian goodwill, the Haves entertain a cockeyed notion like the culture of poverty to get themselves out of a dilemma."[261] But Compassionate Conservatism offers us no solution to this dilemma, except to place our faith in the market which created the very inequities democratic government is supposed to address. Essentially, Magnet asserts here that the Left bought off the poor and their own consciences with money. He would have us instead ignore the poor and tell them to get some values, presumably with a nice economy-healthy tax refund of the welfare program savings to the Haves to reward their beneficial ethics and contribution to society. But one cannot deny the effects of poverty and accompanying despair on the human will, or the moral decline attending the economic demise of every great empire. "In short, great power decline, and not simply the separate weaknesses of liberalism and conservatism, is responsible for the new force field that Americans must deal with, and the dilemma is always economic and cultural."[262] It is disingenuous to use self-excusing rationalizations for the condition of our nation's long-term (predominantly black and Hispanic) poor while we exhort the world to follow our

---

[260] Richard N. Goodwin, <u>The American Condition</u>, p. 197. See also John Kenneth Galbraith, <u>The Culture of Contentment</u>.
[261] Myron Magnet, <u>The Dream and the Nightmare: the Sixties' Legacy to the Underclass</u>, p. 135.
[262] Kevin R. Phillips, <u>Arrogant Capital: Washington, Wall Street, and the Frustration of the Underclass</u>, p. 66.

lead to freedom and equality through economic growth patterned after our cultural and moral model. We preach to the world how economic opportunity frees the poor, then Compassionate Conservatism tells us not to "give away" money to those people denied that opportunity at home. Economics is "…a discipline whose entire function is to support…the existing economic process. To ignore values, ultimate ends, is always to accept those which have been built into the structure. Although the relationship between economic activity and the necessities of human freedom may be ignored, it cannot be denied."[263]

The motivating idea behind the American experiment was that there would be equality: that class structures should yield to individual freedom and merit. But the means was freedom of opportunity: the goal was the development of a society which eliminated poverty and suffering. One scholar determined of Thomas Paine that

> Paine was a disinterested idealist….He devoted all his energies together with most of the money he earned from his writing to the cause that dominated his life: the pursuit of social justice….Perhaps because of his background, he was keenly sensitive to the condition of the poor and underprivileged. He believed society could be run more sensibly so as to eliminate these misfortunes and thus, for him, the differing histories of America and France made no difference. Revolution in both countries was justified in the name of establishing a more rational order. Frequently, in

---
[263] Richard N. Goodwin, The American Condition, p. 374.

the Rights of Man, he is driven to exasperation as he endeavors to focus on the grounds anyone could have for opposing this. How could anyone with a clear head and in good conscience oppose the idea of running the country in a way that would enable more of the people to live satisfactory lives?[264]

Equalities of opportunity alone (as relied upon by Mssrs Magnet et al.) do not hold water in social justice, in democratic institutions,[265] or in Christian doctrine as being the end-all of our obligation to our brethren–the reduction of, and sympathy for, human suffering is the true measure of human worth, individually and as a society. As one political writer observed:

> If all men were endowed with the same talents and abilities, and were born into the same homes, and received the same schooling, giving all an equal opportunity would be a fair solution. Yet people differ in native talent and even more in background and education….In other words, equality of opportunity, if it allows ability alone to operate, quickly establishes and perpetuates a meritocracy of inequality. Need, too, must be considered…."[266]

---

[264] Derek Matravers, in introduction to Thomas Paine's Rights of Man, at pp. XII, XIII.
[265] Richard N. Goodwin, The American Condition : "Americans have often conceived of justice as equality of opportunity…[yet] the phrase itself is a vacancy….," pp. 197-198.
[266] William Ebenstein, Today's Isms: Communism Fascism Capitalism Socialism, p. 173. Of course, such a system seems perfectly fair to those who have natural abilities of intellect or athleticism, or who are born into wealth and the opportunities it provides. George W. Bush has said he was never one to feel guilty about his birth into good fortune–he feels "lucky."

Again, Jesus did not concern himself with equalities of opportunity, because selfless love for one's neighbor ensures more than equality, and is not dependent upon judgments about opportunity levels. The Bible tells us: "If we are rich and see others in need, yet close our hearts against them, how can we claim that we love God? My children, our love should not be just words and talk; it must be true love, which shows itself in action."[267]

It is particularly unscholarly to blame the Liberal response to poverty, social unrest, and suffering for the condition it sought to address–this is mislabeling the effort at cure (however deficient) as the cause. There is no question that long-term welfare dependency is dehumanizing and spiritually unhealthy, and that it creates dependency. But that dependency didn't develop spontaneously. As Molly Ivins and Lou Dubose, discussing Texas welfare programs, observe:

> The record is so wildly different from the rhetoric in this area, one can only conclude the rhetoric is pure political hooey. We point out again that poor people in Texas are overwhelmingly workers; $201 a month doesn't encourage welfare queens. Their values have not been corrupted by sixties leftists. They just don't make a living wage, and the programs designed to help them are all but hidden by the state.[268]

And that dependency on state programs was created as a response to social unrest, a social unrest justified by economic instability and historical racial prejudice

---
[267] 1 John 3:17, TEV.
[268] Molly Ivins and Lou Dubose, <u>Shrub: The Short But Happy Political Life of George W. Bush</u>, p.179.

which continues to fester. Without that dependency, where would our society be? Would the sixties have devolved instead into a race war in America? Without the protections of social security and unemployment benefits, liberal programs created as a direct response to the social crisis of the Great Depression, where would America be focusing its energies? Aren't those old folks and laid-off workers becoming morally corrupt while they collect, losing their "inner resources" to the ravages of dependency? Wouldn't we save them from that inevitable Liberal victim-mentality dependency if we terminated all their benefits immediately? And we'd balance the budget, too, and stop all that waste....

Obviously, welfare programs did not create the poverty which pre-existed them.[269] American government's response

> cannot be justly attributed to "liberalism," or any other form of political attitude. To do so is to participate in the illusion that social changes have political causes. Politics evolved to reflect the imperatives of new economic relationships, and no change of government defied or even retarded the movement....The most prominent social movements of the 1960s–the civil rights movement and protest against the war–were not initiated by government. Public action was possible only when concerned private groups had acquired dimension and force which could not be ignored.[270]

---

[269] This is apparently not obvious to Magnet, Olasky and other historical revisionists. Charles Adams rails against the socialist tax structure that he says created chronic unemployment and welfare in <u>Those Dirty Rotten Taxes: The Tax Revolts That Built America</u>, at p.183.

[270] Richard N. Goodwin, <u>The American Condition</u>, p. 359.

The systemic, enduring nature of the wealth-disparity crisis in America was demonstrated by its continuation, even exacerbation, despite the economic growth and "benign" conservative compassion of the Reagan era, when

> [t]he unskilled and uneducated underclass was coming undone....a much larger and growing underclass was beginning to provoke worried questions about the nation's future. The realignment of economic opportunity–the rich and well-educated grasped it, while the poor and uneducated could not–devastated the lives of many low-income Americans by removing the jobs and circumstances needed for homes and family cohesion.[271]

The irony is that the protestations of the wealthy against granting financial support to the impoverished masses existed in the New Deal era also. John Kenneth Galbraith recounts this history, noting that in 1932 "[t]he country was a simmering cauldron of discontent."[272] Democratic spending under Roosevelt didn't seem to spark economic growth, but because that money prevented total social and economic collapse, Roosevelt actually "saved the traditional capitalist economic system in the United States and the well-being of those whom capitalism most favored."[273] As it was, dozens of able-bodied, working-age men died in the first years of

---

[271] Kevin Phillips, The Politics of Rich and Poor: Wealth and the American Electorate in the Reagan Aftermath, pp. 207, 202.
[272] John Kenneth Galbraith, The Culture of Contentment, p. 4.
[273] Ibid., p. 6.

the Great Depression of starvation in New York City alone. The tractor displaced hundreds of thousands of farm workers, as other technological advances displaced millions more across industries and across the land. By 1932 there were an estimated 200,000 homeless children wandering the country.[274]

Yet throughout the debate over how to salve the nation's malaise, the wealthy protested that government relief of the poor was socialist, and procured economists with dour warnings of the harmful effects of government spending.[275] J.P. Morgan warned, in testimony before a Senate committee, "If you destroy the leisure class, you destroy civilization."[276] Analyzing similar mentalities through the Soviet elite, the French aristocracy and post World War I Britain (in which welfare and unemployment issues led to a Constitutional crisis, though it is "now widely agreed that the measures then so opposed by the fortunate saved British capitalism...."[277]), Galbraith concludes that the fortunate generally don't "respond to their own longer-term well-being. Rather, they respond, and powerfully, to immediate comfort and contentment."[278]

Mr. Galbraith argues compellingly in <u>The Culture of Contentment</u> that America is very much a class society,

---

[274] Frederick Lewis Allen, <u>Since Yesterday: The 1930s in America September 3, 1929-September 3, 1939</u>, p. 61.
[275] John Kenneth Galbraith, <u>The Culture of Contentment</u>, p. 4.
[276] Ibid., pp. 5-6. Morgan defined the leisure class as "All those who can afford to hire a maid." This would include, then, at least three generations of Bushes.
[277] Ibid., p. 4.
[278] Ibid., p. 7.

notwithstanding what he calls our "social mythology"[279] that we are not, and that the middle class cooperates in the protection of its position through the perpetuation of the circumstances of America's poor:

> The most nearly invariant is that individuals and communities that are favored in their economic, social and political condition attribute social virtue and political desirability to that which they themselves enjoy. That attribution, in turn, is made to apply even in the face of commanding evidence to the contrary. The beliefs of the fortunate are brought to serve the cause of continuing contentment....[As to the U.S., c]ould anyone be so dour, so pessimistic, as to suggest that lurking in the successful system and its larger and well-proclaimed democracy were grave flaws similarly [to the Soviets],...concealed by preferred belief? Alas, there are. But the power of contentment over belief is universal....What is new in the so-called capitalist countries–and this is a vital point–is that the controlling contentment and resulting belief is now that of the many, not just of the few. It operates under the compelling cover of democracy....the people responsible cannot be condemned; a whole community cannot usefully be blamed or excoriated....one does not effectively censure an established pattern of life....It is the nature of contentment that it resists that which invades it with vigor and often...with strongly voiced indignation. [Government programs rendering assistance to the poor are] seriously suspect as to need and effectiveness and because of their adverse effect on

---

[279] Ibid., p. 30.

morals and working morale. This, however, is not true of government support to comparative well-being. By Social Security pensions or their prospect no one is thought damaged, nor, as a depositor, by being rescued from a failed bank.[280] The comparatively affluent can withstand the adverse moral effect of being subsidized and supported by the government; not so the poor….[S]hort-run public inaction…is always preferred to protective long-run action…[because] the long run may not arrive; that is the frequent and comfortable belief. More decisively important, the cost of today's action falls or could fall on the favored community; taxes could be increased….[281]

Applying Galbraith's conclusions to the (subsequently-concocted) ideology of Compassionate

---

[280] Indeed, these benefits are viewed as entitlements. Renald E. Showers notes in <u>What On Earth Is God Doing?</u> (at p. 95), that "In response to their own despair [from a denial of God], the older generations have substituted their material accomplishments in place of God. Any threat to these accomplishments is viewed with alarm. Thus the present social order which enabled them to make these gains has become their security in an insecure world." Becoming dependent on this world, we abandon God. Social Security creates the same dependent pressures as welfare, even though there is a mindset of "I earned it" amongst recipients (though in the large majority of cases, recipients of Social Security recoup what they paid in after the first few years of benefits).

[281] John Kenneth Galbraith, <u>The Culture of Contentment</u>, pp. 2, 10, 11, 12, 14-15, 20. Thus the idea of a contented American middle class which resists any avoidable threat to its continued enjoyment of its comforts also explains quite logically (at least to the extent that human nature follows logic) the continued deferral of solutions to problems like global warming, nuclear waste cleanup, acid rain or the national debt–these have been left to future generations, who will face even more intractable difficulties. Anything rather than raise current taxes and threaten the almighty economic growth machine, which must be fed at all environmental, debt, or other costs.

Conservatism, it is easy to see the truth of Galbraith's observations in modern American political thought. Galbraith identifies three requirements for a doctrine to serve the American/Western culture of contentment: 1) it must presume that government is inadequate to address the subject problem, 2) it must offer social justification for "the untrammeled, uninhibited pursuit and possession of wealth," and 3) it must

> justify a reduced sense of public responsibility for the poor....the members of the...underclass must, in some very real way, be seen as the architects of their own fate. If not, they could be, however marginally, on the conscience of the comfortable....To serve these ends, it must be emphasized, the required doctrine need not be subject to serious empirical proof...It is the availability of an assertable doctrine that is important; it is that availability and not the substance that serves.[282]

But how could John Kenneth Galbraith have predicted Myron Magnet's subsequent book so accurately....?

As Galbraith reveals, this culture of contentment is a culture of the middle and upper classes, not distinguished by Party affiliation–Democrats and Republicans both perpetuate the conditions which leave America's inner-city in increasingly irrevocable decay. But Magnet says that "when the Haves ask what responsibility they bear for the plight of the poor, they ask because

---

[282] John Kenneth Galbraith, <u>The Culture of Contentment</u>, pp. 96-97, 97, 97-98.

they want to help."²⁸³ Democratic efforts at welfare and benefits for the poor, though less than ideal, at least were efforts at an action-oriented response to a problem for which all Americans bear some responsibility: the Republican/Bush Administration answer is inaction,²⁸⁴ lots of compassion-language borrowed from the Left and then scattered over every Republican policy that requires inaction or paternalism. Kevin Phillips calls Myron Magnet's answer to the problems of the underclass "one-dimensional,"²⁸⁵ for it denies the economic dimension of moral decay and chronic poverty. Says Phillips,

> Politically, this emphasis on cultural and moral causations serves a double purpose: first, upholding the priorities of the religious traditionalists and fundamentalists so important to Republicans and conservatives, and second, defending business and financial elites against arguments of

---

[283] Myron Magnet, The Dream and the Nightmare: the Sixties' Legacy to the Underclass, p. 21.

[284] "The centerpiece of Bush's faith-based proposal, mobilizing "Armies of Compassion" among religious and community service organizations, had begun with a huge $90 billion promise of giving charitable deductions to those who did not itemize tax returns. This was cut to $6 billion in late 2002 by an agreement between the White House and the Republican leadership of the House. Professor Robert Putnam of Harvard University, consulted by the White House, commented, "They talked a really good game, but in the end, the compassionate part of compassionate conservatism got omitted from the final calculation." Even religious constituencies started to discern the deception that left pledges unfilled." Kevin Phillips, American Dynasty: Aristocracy, Fortune, and the Politics of Deceit in the House of Bush, p. 146.

[285] Kevin Phillips, Arrogant Capital: Washington, Wall street, and the Frustration of American Politics, p. 62.

economic mismanagement….And looking ahead, for conservatives the culture-is-responsible thesis enables them to sidestep the speculative bubble of the 1980s and to insist that Reaganomics worked, so tax cuts and deregulation should be renewed, not abandoned, in the 1990s….Yet the historical evidence…is that the two threads of "decline" occur together…, and parties and ideologies with one-dimensional explanations can only feed the breakdown.[286]

Phillips then quotes Christopher Lasch: "Republicans may hate what is happening to our children, but their commitment to the culture of acquisitive individualism makes them reluctant to probe its source. They glorify the man on the make, the small operator who stops at nothing in the pursuit of wealth, and then wonder why ghetto children steal and hustle instead of applying themselves to homework."[287] One can endeavor to dismiss this criticism as partisan, and thereby ignore the moral iniquity attendant upon American conspicuous consumption in plain view of those we teach to aspire toward the same (though for most of them America will never deliver on her promise, and their morality is blamed for their poverty!). But such ignorance is not acceptable to God or Jesus, however passionately or intensely one denies the truth—the oppression of the poor can be justified, even praised, by some moral perspectives (Machiavelli, for one), but not from the Christian standard, for words of compassion without

---

[286] Ibid., pp. 61, 62, 63.
[287] Ibid., p. 63.

actions to relieve the suffering of others are worse than nothing to God.

Americans may continue in their contentment until the sky falls upon them. This is understandable for non-Christians, who have placed their faith in science, mankind, and his governments, but Christians must break free of such worldly illusions if they are to follow Christ and practice true compassion. The Bible tells us that most people will not heed Jesus' words,[288] that the gate to heaven is narrow–those who deny their own excesses at the expense of the less fortunate will be wide of that gate. This sin of lack of compassion for the poor, of complacency, is practiced by Americans on both sides of the political aisle:

> Makes no difference how obvious the unfairness is, those who have been favored over others by the system invariably feel entitled to that favoritism. It is theirs by right, by heritage, tradition, and divine providence, and if you try to take it away, you are in for the fight of your life. The underprivileged in this country can still raise a fair political stink on occasion, but it is nothing compared with the titanic stench that erupts when the overprivileged are invited onto a level playing field.[289]

---

[288] 2 Timothy 4:3-5: "The time will come when people will not listen to sound doctrine, but will collect for themselves more and more teachers who will tell them what they are itching to hear. They will turn away from listening to the truth and give their attention to legends. But you must keep control of yourself in all circumstances;...." (TEV) The King James Version, line 5, admonishes "But watch thou in all things....")

[289] Molly Ivins and Lou Dubose, <u>Shrub: The Short But Happy Political Life of George W. Bush</u>, p. 134.

Richard N. Goodwin identifies the motivation for middle class complacency as fear of loss of worldly position,[290] relating that:

> The poor are not free, but the non-poor have more to lose than chains. Their vulnerable economic position, their insecurities and fear of decline, influences them toward support rather than resistance. They lack the confidence of owners, the experience of the affluent, the desperation of the impoverished. Inevitably, they fear that fundamental change will dislodge their precarious gains, level the mild amenities of their lives. They are made reluctant to join any struggle to recapture their alienated existence and to halt the manifold devastations of social life.[291]

There is no dispute that the gap between America's wealthiest and poorest citizens has steadily increased with the advent of a market system based on capitalism and an ever-growing industrial society, a "new industrial dictatorship" in which "[t]hose who tilled the soil no longer reaped the rewards which were their right. The small measure of their gains was decreed by men in distant cities....For too many of us the political equality we once had won was meaningless in the face of economic inequality."[292] Eventually, such income disparities

---

[290] This and other worldly fears are in direct opposition to the will and specific instructions of Jesus Christ, and keep us from Him. Satan preys on fear, especially in End Times, when people will view the end of the world either with terror or joy. Jesus never tells us to be afraid of this world–he repeatedly tells us *not* to be.
[291] Richard N. Goodwin, The American Condition, p. 258.
[292] Nicholas A. Masters and Mary E. Baluss, The Growing Powers of the Presidency, pp. 239, 240.

breed social unrest and economic decline: "It is obvious by now that the decline in living standards in the Western world is associated with a widening gap between the haves and the have-nots."[293] America has gone from trying to reverse this trend to ignoring the poor and accelerating the rate of disparity, risking urban unrest unparalleled in history, ignoring Christ's teachings and trammeling our supposedly Christian heritage.

And so, the model of Compassionate Conservatism originated by Myron Magnet and incorporated by George W. Bush into the Republican agenda and current federal policy, is based not on the Bible (and can draw on no scriptural support) but on the idea (ology?) that the inner city poor, the "Underclass," remain in that condition because of moral and cultural, not economic, causes.[294] Perhaps the clearest and most honest assessment of this newest rationalization for the inordinate comfort of the economically comfortable majority of Americans coexisting with horrible poverty and its consequences, is reflected in the following excerpt from <u>Race, Class, & Gender in the United States</u>, by Paula Rothenberg:

> "Using notions that blame victims may help the blamers to feel better by blowing off the steam of

---

[293] J. Edward Griffin, <u>The Creature From Jekyll Island: A Second Look at the Federal Reserve</u>, p. 559.

[294] Also left out of this equation are those chronically impoverished by physical illness or other legitimate physical disability, by mental illness or impairment, by emotional trauma (often caused by poverty and its resultant abusive environment of crime, sexual and physical abuse, etc.), or because they were born with below-average intelligence. Dismiss this as Leftist, and dismiss Jesus.

righteous indignation, but it does not eliminate the problems very poor people have or make."[295].... People publicly described as members of the underclass may begin to feel that they <u>are</u> members of such a class and are therefore unworthy in a new way. At the least, they now have to fight against yet another threat to their self-respect, not to mention another reason for feeling that society would just as soon have them disappear....[Another] danger of the term is in its use as a racial codeword that subtly hides anti-black and anti-Hispanic feelings. A codeword of this kind fits in with the tolerant public discourse of our time, but it also submerges and may further repress racial–and class–antagonisms that continue to exist, yet are sometimes not expressed until socio-political boiling points are reached....[T]he citizenry may read codewords even though planners are writing analytical concepts....[Underclass] is a handy euphemism; while it seems inoffensively technical on the surface, it hides within it all the moral opprobrium Americans have long felt toward those poor who have been judged to be undeserving.[296]

Rothenberg goes on to criticize partisans of the Right for "...arguing that the underclass is a product of the unwillingness of the black poor to adhere to the American work ethic, among other cultural deficiencies....,"[297] and identifies the label "underclass" as a euphemism for rabble, paupers, or "the dangerous classes."[298] Presaging

---

[295] Quoting Herbert Gans, "Deconstructing the Underclass," in Paula S. Rothenberg, <u>Race, Class, & Gender in the United States</u>, p. 362
[296] Ibid., pp. 360, 359.
[297] Ibid., p. 359.
[298] Ibid., p. 358.

our present quandary, Rothenberg concludes "the issue always boils down to whether the fault of being poor and the responsibility for change should be assigned more to poor people or more to the economy and the state."[299]

Compassionate Conservatism as conceived and implemented by George W. Bush assigns responsibility for change entirely to poor people, with an appeal to individual and corporate charity to voluntarily contribute to compensate for federal welfare and other budget cuts that have adversely affected the poor. In doing so, he once again continues the Republican/Conservative tradition of Ronald Reagan, his political idol. Of the conservative "movement" represented by Ronald Reagan, Christopher Lasch writes:

> The unanticipated success of the right has not restored moral order and collective purpose to Western nations, least of all the United States. The new right came to power with a mandate not just to free the market from bureaucratic interference but to halt the slide into apathy, hedonism, and moral chaos. It has not lived up to expectations. Spiritual disrepair, the perception of which furnished much of the popular animus against liberalism, is just as evident today as it was in the seventies....The "crisis of modernity" remains unresolved, according to George Panichas, by a "sham conservatism" that merely sanctions the unbridled pursuit of worldly success. The "everyday virtues of honesty, loyalty, manners, work, and restraint," Clyde Wilson writes, are more "attenuated" than ever.[300]

---

[299] Ibid., p. 359.
[300] Christopher Lasch, <u>The True and Only Heaven: Progress and its Critics</u>, p. 22.

Most Americans will agree that American society has continued to deteriorate since Mr. Lasch wrote these words in 1991. And the abandonment of the values of hard work and integrity are nationwide, party-wide, and denomination-wide.

The loss of our nation's values is demonstrated by the irresponsible spending by our federal government under both democratic and republican stewardship. But the Republicans are particularly hypocritical, having in George W. Bush and Ronald Reagan the greatest peacetime spenders in our history, with Clinton's fiscal responsibility[301] sandwiched between them as an embarrassing contrast to unceasing Republican criticisms of democratic pork. And the Republicans have become unabashedly pro-business, trusting in soulless corporate America to guide our (materialistic and consumptive) future. As Lasch notes,

> Reagan played on the desire for order, continuity, responsibility, and discipline, but his program contained nothing that would satisfy that desire. On the contrary, his program aimed to promote economic growth and unregulated business enterprise, the very

---

[301] Alan Greenspan has tremendous respect for Clinton's economic sophistication, and the two worked closely together to bring down the deficit during Clinton's tenure: true, Clinton presided over (but did not create) the economic boom of the 1990s, allowing him the opportunity to reduce debt, but he took advantage of that opportunity to do so, bringing down interest rates and proving the benefits of fiscal conservatism. In contrast, President George W. Bush fought unyieldingly and successfully against the efforts of Paul J. O'Neill and Alan Greenspan to limit tax refunds with "automatic triggers" in the event of the failure to realize continuing government surpluses. If only George W. Bush were as fiscally conservative as Bill Clinton....

forces that have undermined tradition. A movement calling itself conservative might have been expected to associate itself with the demand for limits not only on economic growth but on the conquest of space, the technological conquest of the environment, and the ungodly ambition to acquire godlike powers over nature.[302] Reaganites, however, condemned the demand for limits as another counsel of doom.[303]

The consequence of this "faith in the free market," (which is tantamount to a faith in Darwinian survivalism, except applied to the accumulation of wealth), is an immoral indulgence in greed and big business as America's hope and future.[304] As Kevin Phillips (a former Republican[305]) has remarked:

> The Republicans, collectively, are simply not free to admit that serious economic declines–for

---

[302] Like bunker busters, Star Wars, and retinal scans and remote-read computer chips required with ID's?

[303] Christopher Lasch, <u>The True and Only Heaven: Progress and its Critics</u>, p. 39. This irresponsible excess was, distressingly, echoed by the Bush Administration through Dick Cheney's determined refusal to consider conservation as an energy-policy component, a short-sightedness which will become increasingly apparent as the world's oil reserves continue to diminish in the face of exploding industrial expansion worldwide. No Party can be forgiven, or permitted, such irresponsibility.

[304] Reagan and Bush are just recent players in our country's split personality with regard to morality: we have always sought to expand our nation's wealth in the Imperialist tradition, while believing we are Christian and just. Our nation has always walked in the dark as well as the light, a feat not praised by Christ–and the good things we have done as a nation (that were not motivated by self-interest) do not cancel this out, for "indulgences" are not Christ's creation, and repentance must be lived, not bought.

[305] And chief political analyst for the 1968 Republican presidential campaign.

the middle class and the American dream, in accelerating national indebtedness, and the eroded competitiveness of key industries–occurred during the Reagan-Bush period. Party economic policies are too closely linked to the interests...[of] multinational corporations, [etc.]...that profited from the recent era's speculative bubble, tax cuts, bailouts and trade liberalizations.[306]

This same faith in corporate America and economic growth as the one true American value has been even more zealously reflected in George W. Bush's administration. Corporate corruption has flourished, not abated, under the unwatchful, nurturing eye of the man who has brought Christian compassion to corporate America in word only–"We believe in private markets, humanized by compassionate government....We believe in free markets, tempered by compassion."[307] But President Bush, who "believes" in private markets (compatibly with God?), has also noted that "[t]he problem is government is not a very compassionate organization."[308] So has he "humanized" "compassionate" government?

George W. Bush has given corporate America free-market reign unfettered by the constraints of compassion, aided by his "Underclass" rhetoric and his false pretense to Christian influence. No substantive ethical restraints on corporations have even been considered

---

[306] Kevin Phillips, <u>Arrogant Capital: Washington, Wall Street, and the Frustration of American Politics</u>, p. 64.
[307] George W. Bush, quoted in Thomas A. Freiling, <u>George W. Bush on God & Country</u>, pp. 220, 246.
[308] Ibid., p. 27.

by this administration, let alone implemented as policy, notwithstanding the ongoing pall of "corporate morality" intimately linked to members of Bush's cabinet. Bush's (previously) very close relationship with Ken Lay (Enron CEO), of which no serious voices of inquiry or indignation have been raised, is illustrative of the problem. Because there is no Christian explanation to be provided, and because he was "never one to feel guilty"[309] about his privileged life, George W. has never addressed the corporate nepotism of his own Cabinet, family, and business history, that his life has been spent developing networks of wealthy and corporate donors (whether for political purposes, through numerous campaigns; or private, i.e. for his oil companies, a baseball stadium, more of his oil companies after the old ones failed, etc.). Perhaps owing to the gratitude he feels to corporate America for the material blessings it has bestowed upon him, George instead looks to those same worldly forces to bestow our nation's future happiness and prosperity, and to fill the gap in government spending for the poor left by his compassionate government conservatism, gushing hopefully that "corporate and foundation America can give more and give wiser [sic]."[310] As if private and corporate donations to the poor in place of government are somehow different in their moral influence on the recipient than those liberal programs that 'created' the underclass: this is classic buck-shifting, and the fact that "corporate and foundation America" or individual donors have failed

---

[309] Christopher Anderson, <u>George and Laura</u>, p. 141.v
[310] Thomas A. Freiling, <u>George W. Bush on God & Country</u>, p. 193.

to pick up the slack is proof again that actions do not follow words of compassionate government, and Bush is therefore doing just what the conservatives Olasky and Magnet criticized in Clinton and the democrats–feigning compassion. But it's now infinitely more offensive, because it's done in Christ's name.

Indeed, President Bush routinely employs language of compassion in his conservative agenda, but there is always that same "I-feel-your-pain" hollowness when there is no accompanying action. Once again promoting government as the answer to government's failings, he writes in his autobiography: "We must close the gap of hope, but the answer is not found in yet another government program….Our sense of personal responsibility has declined dramatically, just as the role and responsibility of the federal government have increased."[311] But then Mr. Bush proposes as a solution "…charity tax credits and a change in tax policy to allow even those who do not itemize to deduct their charitable contributions, because I want to encourage an outpouring of charitable giving in America."[312] But this simply shifts the tab back to American taxpayers through voluntary contributions–and again there is no qualitative difference or change in the nature of dependency of the poor

---

[311] George W. Bush, A Charge to Keep, pp. 228, 229.
[312] Ibid., pp. 231-232.

in need of economic assistance.[313] George used similar accounting illusions in his social security battle for privatization accounts, where that debate, which only concerned shifting the existing payment structures into private instead of government accounts, eclipsed the true issues of entitlement and who will bear the cost for the increasing shortfalls of the system.

Again, the words of George W. Bush:

> Compassionate conservatism outlines a new vision of the proper role for the American government.... Government is too often wasteful and overreaching[314]....Compassionate conservatism is neither soft nor fuzzy. It is clear and compelling. It focuses not on good intentions but on good results. Compassionate conservatism applies conservative, free-market principles to the real job of helping real people, all people, including the poor and the disadvantaged. My vision

---

[313] Though private charities may distribute assets more efficiently to the poor, there is less oversight of corruption in this system, and there is no measure or guarantee that sufficient resources are being allocated to appropriate geographic areas of need–this is the function of centralized government which is being abdicated by this administration under the guise of compassion. This seems incongruous in a government which has striven so greatly to increase its influence via police powers, most noticeably through the NCLB Act, the USAPATRIOT Act (what 'words,' for a law that dramatically strengthened Big Brother), and after Hurricane Katrina, when Bush sought greater federal military police powers–clearly he already possessed these powers, according to legal scholars, so seeking to broaden the federal government's police powers by George W. Bush is an effort to shirk responsibility for the laggard federal Katrina response, and to (unjustifiably) enlarge the power of the federal government and the military-industrial complex with which that government holds hands.

[314] Funny, this concern does not appear to imbue Mr. Bush's view of military defense, space exploration or homeland security–government is just "wasteful and overreaching" when it spends money on the poor.

of compassionate conservatism also requires America to assert its leadership in the world….and encourage the spread of freedom.[315]

Wow!…What are the "clear and compelling," "free-market," "good results" that this magical policy creation of Mr. Bush's vision has brought to "the poor and disadvantaged?" Perhaps the cuts in federal subsidies across-the-board for the low income, or the cuts to food stamp programs instituted to balance a budget crippled by tax refunds. Or the refusal to release federal emergency fuel oil stocks for heating fuel relief in the bitter Northeast winter of 2003-2004. Or the expenditure of huge sums for the No Child Left Behind testing requirements with grossly insufficient funding for substantive responsive action once underperforming, underprivileged students are identified. Even if these complaints are dismissed in denial, there is little if anything of substance in the Bush Jr. record benefiting the underclass. Clear and compelling words, soft and fuzzy action; insincere intentions, and bad results.

George knows this is just political rhetoric–compassionate conservatism is political catch-phrasing in a marketing world. Politicians, George W. not excluded, seek inspirational slogans to rally support. According to Christopher Anderson, "Laura pushed him to use the catchphrase "compassionate conservatism," believing it made her husband look more sympathetic and softened the public perception of hard-hearted fat-cat Republicans."[316] The concept was designed not to represent actual substantive policy toward the

---
[315] George W. Bush, A Charge To Keep, p. 236.
[316] Christopher Anderson, George and Laura, p. 382.

impoverished, but to shape the public's perception of the candidate.

If, as George W. Bush has said, "[t]he measure of compassion is more than good intentions; it is good results,"[317] then one is invited to measure his administration's compassion by results. John J. DiIulio, Jr. ran Bush's faith-based initiative until he quit because he said the initiative had become "a political and financial prop"[318] for political ends. As to the ballyhooed corporate compassion, the compassion has been toward corporate profits at the expense of workers and the environment. Of recent bankruptcy code revisions, Lou Dobbs wrote: "Compassionate conservatism? The new bankruptcy law was virtually written by the credit card companies and banks, making it far more difficult for American families to erase their debt. The credit card firms are not exactly struggling. Their profits, in fact, have risen steadily over the past decade."[319]

But nowhere is the gap between words and action greater for this president than in the area of welfare policy and welfare "reform." Acknowledging the desperate need for some response to the cyclic despair, violence, ignorance and dysfunction of America's inner city poor, the answer is not a cut in government economic support in the face of national economic decline, massive job losses and growing inflation. It is odd to link religious faith and money in the way that Mr. Bush has in his compassionate conservatism/personal responsibility

---

[317] Thomas A. Freiling, <u>George W. Bush on God & Country</u>, p.126.
[318] Ron Suskind, <u>The Price of Loyalty</u>, p. 170.
[319] Lou Dobbs, "Lonely in the Middle," *U.S. News & World Report*, May 2, 2005.

rhetoric. Jesus tells us lovingly "Do not be afraid, little flock, for your Father is pleased to give you the Kingdom. Sell all your belongings and give the money to the poor.... For your heart will always be where your riches are."[320] But George W. Bush time and again advocates a) shifting responsibility for caring for the poor to religious or other charities, and b) "helping" the poor by pushing people off welfare by denying benefits to them. Bill Minutaglio's investigations led him to report that Bush used

> welfare as the one policy initiative where he could openly talk about his personal belief system....By the end of the campaign and with Rove's guidance, Bush was beginning to craft a "personal responsibility" manifesto that suggested that Texans would be better served by turning to God, not government, to improve their social standing. His proposed welfare cuts would be wrapped in a velvet hammer called "Faith Based Programs"....[321]

"Personal belief system" well describes this bizarre perversion of Christ's repeated teachings. Nothing in Oswald Chambers, A.W. Tozer, or C. S. Lewis supports such a plan–just the opposite. In Jesus' words, "Verily I say unto you, Inasmuch as ye have done it unto one of the least of these my brethren, ye have done it unto me."[322] Can conservative Christians support either shifting government programs for the poor to private charities, or pushing the poor off welfare to "help" them ("un-welfare assistance?") with Scripture? Or have they

---
[320] Luke 12:32-33, 34, TEV.
[321] Bill Minutaglio, <u>First Son: George W. Bush and the Bush Family Dynasty</u>, p.289.
[322] Matthew 25:40, KJV.

adopted this view for political comfort, just as those liberal Christians who pervert Christ's purity and divide his church in support of "Christian" homosexual unions, with absolutely no Scriptural support. If Christians are to influence the government of a Christian nation toward Christian action, then that direction would not be to reduce the amount of money that government allocates to the most needful–quite the opposite, if one heeds Jesus Christ. At a minimum, a Christian conservative response would at least have a plan to assist the poor beyond simply cutting benefits.

George W. consistently cultivates appearance over substance, and welfare "reform" is no exception. Of his activities reforming welfare and Medicaid in Texas, Ivins and Dubose report:

> The dirty secret of Texas government is that we keep our "low tax, low services" tradition going by cheating the poor. According to a 1999 Census Bureau study, Texas has the highest rate of people with no health insurance in the country, 25 percent. In October 1999, Families USA found that the number of Texas children enrolled in Medicaid declined by 14 percent between 1996 and 1999, the largest decline in the twelve states studied.[323]

The authors then assert that George W., while governor of Texas, fought CHIP (Children's Health Insurance Program) eligibility levels, and that, although he could have enrolled more children in the program in 1997, Bush instead appointed a committee to study the

---

[323] Molly Ivins and Lou Dubose, <u>Shrub: The Short But Happy Political Life of George W. Bush</u>, p. 94. This was during George W. Bush's tenure as governor.

issue (classic political delay, employed in this instance to postpone benefits for children—yet no committee was appointed to discuss national testing mandates for children under NCLB, or whether Iraq might lead to a reconstruction quagmire). Say Ivins and Dubose:

> When Bush realized the legislators weren't going to let him deny 200,000 kids health insurance, his office began to fight for separate applications for CHIP and Medicaid. In other words, if CHIP recipients qualified for Medicaid, they would have to make an application at a Medicaid office and fill out another application. [Because of his presidential ambitions, Bush tried to]...discourage poor children from receiving free health care to which they are entitled under federal law. "They were terrified of the Medicaid spillover because they want to be able to say welfare rolls are dropping," [Glenn Maxey, Austin state representative] said.[324]

But we get a very different account of welfare reform in Texas in the late 1990s from President Bush, who

---

[324] Ibid., pp. 95-96. Those quick to dismiss partisan sources should be careful not to dismiss facts as well. Just because a liberal or conservative source is quoted leads a frightening number of our citizens, Christians included, to dismiss the underlying facts cited. But 2+2=4, and if welfare benefits for children dropped on Bush's watch in Texas, a liberal critic reporting it does not make it not so. Jesus spoke of truth, and He would be dismayed if Christians dismissed reality in favor of a false belief system, like many Americans' eagerness to dismiss the Koran-flushing report even after confirmation by the International Red Cross of numerous desecrations of the Koran by U.S. forces—we have tortured naked men with electrodes, but refuse to accept that we might have got some paper wet in a desecration of others' faith. This time the "few bad apples" lie would not serve, so we deny the probable truth of the story without investigation or real introspection and with no repentance on any level. Do we really believe we delude the rest of the world when we delude ourselves?

boasts "I worked to reform welfare because I believe it is far more compassionate to help individuals become independent than to trap them in a cycle of dependency and despair."[325] And then, as President, Bush continued with the same (un-committeed, unstudied) welfare "reform" policies at the federal level, and proselytized that "[a]s Congress takes up welfare reform…, we must strengthen the work requirements that prevent dependency and despair….And by helping people find work…we practice compassion….It is conservative to encourage work…."[326] Is it conservative to restrict and cut government benefits to "encourage work" in a declining economy experiencing massive layoffs, with no government-provided employment other than in Homeland Security or the military? Is it Christian? As one person has noted: "Kicking the poor off the welfare rolls when the job market is dead or dying is essentially inhumane. Expecting them to work and survive on an income less than welfare is similarly insane."[327]

The failure of compassionate conservatism or any other of George W. Bush's sweet-sounding words to achieve actual improvement for any sector of America's poor would be unsurprising in a cynically-viewed political context; but it is deeply disturbing in the context

---

[325] George W. Bush, A Charge to Keep, p. 236. But Elliot Naishtat, chairman of the Texas House Human Services Committee, has charged that Bush attempted to incorporate "draconian sanctions" into Texas welfare reform. Does denying poor children health benefits "help individuals become independent"?

[326] Thomas A. Freiling, George W. Bush on God & Country, pp. 123, 124.

[327] "Welfare programs won't work without a strong economy," *The Christian Science Monitor*, January 18, 2005, p. 8.

of a man who has, by suggesting that he believes God chose him to be President, and by associating his name with faith in God in numerous biographical books, held himself out to America and to the world as a pious, compassionate servant of Christian integrity. As such, George W. has a special obligation to the poor, as an emissary of Jesus, to use the great powers of the United States Presidency to alleviate and publicize their suffering: "There is clear Biblical perspective on welfare. Christians are commanded to help the needy. Indeed, believers should demonstrate the same passion as did Jesus in reaching out to the poor, the hungry, and the homeless."[328] Mr. Bush's passion has been in words only. Jesus humbled himself to wash his disciples' feet, to show that he who is lowest is highest, and to teach that it is more humbling to have your feet washed than it is to wash another's, and so appreciate what those feel like who must look to others for help: for foot washing. Jesus said, "I have set an example for you, so that you will do just what I have done for you."[329]

No wonder George has been charged with insensitivity: "Bush is so blind to the difficulties of life in the nation's underclass that he often seems callous."[330] He himself has observed of his advantages in this world: "I was never one to feel guilty. I feel lucky. People who feel guilty react like guilty people."[331] But the point of Christianity isn't to feel "lucky" or "guilty," but to be

---

[328] Doug Bandow, Beyond Good Intentions: A Biblical View of Politics, p.183.
[329] John 13:15, TEV.
[330] Molly Ivins and Lou Dubose, Shrub: The Short But Happy Political Life of George W. Bush, p. 10.
[331] David Aikman, The Spiritual Journey of George W. Bush, p. 46.

aware of others. Mr. Bush's exhortation to the wealthy not to feel guilty about their privilege is an exhortation not to feel bad for those in need (from where else would guilty feelings arise?). But not addressed is any proposed response to or sense of responsibility toward those not born "lucky." Of course, the whole idea of feeling lucky to be wealthy is hedonistic, not Christian–the Christian way is to give humble praise to God for amply providing for one's family, and to pray and have compassion for the less fortunate: "But the wisdom from above is pure first of all; it is also peaceful, gentle, and friendly; it is full of compassion and produces a harvest of good deeds; it is free from prejudice and hypocrisy. And goodness is the harvest that is produced from the seeds the peacemakers plant in peace."[332]

The irony is that following the ways of this world, of Darwinian survival morality (an ethically ugly affair), results in a self-oriented distraction in direct opposition to the wisdom of the Bible. Ultimately, any moral code which holds self or individual as paramount will induce societal deterioration, because without community, without compassion, man is in anarchy. The real consequence of this culture of self in the American experiment is the gradually increased strain placed on the backs of the poor,[333] aggravated dangerously by doctrines of contentment like compassionate conservatism. And the less the well-off feel awareness–feel "guilty" toward

---

[332] James 3:17-18, TEV.

[333] "The number of Americans living below the poverty line increased by more than a million last year, to roughly 37 million–up from 31.1 million in 2000. For a family of four, the official poverty rate is $19,300, and at this level, it is up from its recent low of 11.3 percent in 2000 to 12.7 percent last year." Mortimer Zuckerman, "A Debt To Ourselves," *U.S. News & World Report*, October 3, 2005, p. 60.

the relative circumstances of the disadvantaged–the more the dehumanizing effects of modern alienation corrode human fellowship. Jesus warned: "You put onto people's backs loads which are hard to carry, but you yourselves will not stretch out a finger to help them carry those loads. How terrible for you!"[334]

But placing faith in this world, forgetting the poor and growing comfortable and fat like so many Americans (many Christians included), is to invite worldly consequences and heavenly retribution. As wealth disparities increase in any society, pressures build until somehow released. The New Deal programs of the Great Depression and the welfare programs of the 1960s were both releases of socio-economic strains resulting from the steady capitalistic concentration of wealth in increasingly fewer hands.[335] But a deeply-indebted America cannot bail herself out of a social justice accounting this time. We are on the eve of a class revolution and economic collapse, the consequence of placing faith in self, science, and worldly comfort instead of the higher power who warned us to hold love paramount. Though dismissed as fantastical satirist or science fiction doomsayer, George Orwell described with captivating accuracy our current condition. And so does the Bible.

A neglected lower class festers until it obtains revenge, paying back lack of compassion with lack of

---

[334] Luke 11:46-47, TEV.
[335] After the 1929 stock market crash, "...it became clear that the business titans were not miracle workers but as fallible as other mortals....The policies of the federal government in the 1920s were disastrous. Its tax policies made the maldistribution of income and oversaving by the rich still more serious....The administration took the narrow interests of business groups to be the national interest, and the result was catastrophe." William E. Leuchtenburg, The Perils of Prosperity, pp. 259, 246.

184 CHRISTIAN WORDS, UNCHRISTIAN ACTIONS

compassion, wrong with wrong, the worldly, ungodly cycle. In America, this lesson of history and of Biblical truth is being repeated before our modern eyes. Because the low-paying jobs which (barely) support the "underclass" are moving out of the cities,[336] the "inner-city problem" is intractable, and "[t]he underclass has become a semipermanent rather than a generational phenomenon."[337] Of course, Jesus told us that there would always be poverty in This World. But in America we have contributed to the plight of our own nation's poor by promoting and reinforcing a socio-economic structure which continues, with ever greater acceleration, to increase disparities in wealth:

> The American Dream, at least on the economic side, is fading. Most people see the United States as a special place where there is plenty of opportunity for someone to work hard, play by the rules, and get ahead,—maybe even become wealthy....Today, though, nearly 1 in 5 American households has zero net worth or actually owes more than it owns.... What that means is that the US is becoming less of a meritocracy, where skill and intelligence determine success, and becoming more of a class-bound society, where economic background, including the better education money can provide, matters more. There are still many rags-to-riches stories. But there's stagnation in the underclass....Most Americans don't believe that to be true, surveys show.[338] But academic

---

[336] John Kenneth Galbraith, <u>The Culture of Contentment</u>, p.37.
[337] Ibid., p. 37.
[338] Note the demonstrable disparity between reality and our American mythological belief system.

studies suggest that income mobility in the US is no better than in France or Britain.[339] It's actually lower than in Canada and is approaching the rigidity of Brazil....That marks a change from the past. From 1950 to 1980, Americans were more and more likely to see their offspring move up–or down–the income ladder....The picture is worse for most minorities and women: 1 in 3 minority households has zero net worth or is in debt (compared with the average of 1 in 5). Black families have, on average, only one-sixteenth the net assets of white families....[340]

If one were to measure America's "freedom" by the opportunities we provide to the poor instead of our fancy proclamations (words!), we are as free as Brazil (not to knock Brazil). If our nation has ever in the past lived up to that boastful talk, we are failing now. Since approximately 1980, the rich have been more likely to stay that way and the poor likewise. But Myron Magnet (and George W. Bush, who embraces this "moral" view) proclaims that equal opportunity has triumphed in America, and blames this wealth disparity on moral decay, ignoring the glaring undeniability that the situation has been made markedly worse by conservative influences from Reagan through the Bushes.[341]

---

[339] Class societies.
[340] "The American Dream gains a harder edge," David R. Francis, *The Christian Science Monitor*, May 23, 2005, p. 17.
[341] This does not ignore Clinton, who could hardly roll tax rates back to pre-Reagan levels, and who didn't have to because of the good fortune of presiding over the unprecedented wealth generation, albeit in the few, of the dot-com boom. Hard choices were not required, but neither was fuel added to the flames of wealth disparity to the degree of Republican, pro-business policies.

186   CHRISTIAN WORDS, UNCHRISTIAN ACTIONS

But those Americans who ignore the obvious truth of increased wealth disparity in our country ignore also the threat to their own economic comfort, just as Marie Antoinette and the Soviet Politburo did, to their regret. John Kenneth Galbraith predicted, based on his studies of history and economics, that the present age of contentment in America will end when there is 1) a widespread economic disaster, 2) a disastrous outcome from a military action associated with an international misadventure, or 3) the eruption of discontent in an angry underclass.[342] Richard N. Goodwin applies Nietzsche to modern American capitalism and its effects on our society, observing:

> "Only the weak man wishes to hurt and to see the sign of suffering," writes Nietzsche. Twentieth-century man has validated this insight on a titanic scale. Nietzsche also preaches that although "the desire for destruction, change, and becoming can be an expression of overfull...strength, it can also be the hatred of the misdeveloped, needy, underprivileged who destroy, who must destroy, because the existing and even all existence, all being, outrages and provokes him." The violence which has traditionally attended American social conflict has usually been related to a purpose, directed at unidentifiable adversaries. Today, especially in large cities, we inhabit an ambience charged with random anger; frequented by violent acts which seem to have no purpose other than to express that anger. And public leaders are assaulted by the prototypes of impotent humanity.

---

[342] John Kenneth Galbraith, <u>The Culture of Contentment</u>, p. 155. George W. Bush is at the helm as we confront all three, now.

As individual power wanes, the desire for a renewal of confidence becomes more urgent. The effort to satisfy this desire only strengthens the sources of alienation as the individual first accepts the goals and values which are eroding his power, and then–having persuaded himself that these are his true needs–intensifies the pursuit. The process feeds on itself. Nietzsche wrote that "The means of the craving for power have changed, but the same volcano is still glowing…and what one did formerly 'for God's sake' one does now for the sake of money…which now gives the highest feeling of power." The "craving for power" is not the only motive for the pursuit of wealth or worldly success. And, except in rare instances, such success does not satisfy the need for power. Indeed, the pursuit of external goods increases alienation, even though achievement can confer the illusion of control and confirmation.

We can find further evidence of dwindling power in the decline of moral action, that sensed responsibility which links an individual's way of life to its impact on others.…[A]n individual who is not morally implicated in the ultimate consequences of his activity necessarily views himself as a component in some abstract and unreachable process. If he does not will the result, it can only mean he has submitted to another will.[343]

As better-off Americans turn a blind eye to the condition of others in their near midst, there is no conscious malice of action, or even of inaction–all Americans would desire all to be well if a clear solution were

---

[343] Richard N. Goodwin, The American Condition, pp. 158-159.

presented. Yet many of those who gain material comfort in the American status system are like priests in this Nietzschean culture which replaces God with money, and look upon the less-well-off as the unconverted, the unsaved. At the least, they throw their hands up in powerlessness against the system by which they themselves were empowered, while they enjoy the recreational or other comforts which are their booty. But this same feeling of powerlessness imbues the perspective of those who lack power. Those who are left out, whether through moral failing or not, feel oppressed by the same unfathomable "market" or government forces which offer them no real hope of change; but instead of recreation as diversion, their resentment at their powerlessness festers. Even for American atheist millionaires, one would expect a self-protective awareness of the warnings of Karl Marx about the consequences to a society of increased capital concentration—let alone Christians, who with scriptural reflection can clearly see that this state of mutual destruction and incapacity for action is a direct consequence of placing faith in material wealth instead of love and compassion, placing faith in This World in its ascendancy before Jesus rescues us from our blindness and self-torture. And if this world's ultimate allocation of resources leads to the aristocracy-clothed-as-democracy model that is modern America, leaving few with much and many with little, one can hardly feel much sympathy for the few and might agree with Orwell's fictitious mantra, "If there is hope…it lies in the proles."[344]

---

[344] George Orwell, <u>1984</u>, p. 60. Ironically, this also echoes Jesus' repeated promises that the meek would inherit the earth, that he who is greatest will be least, and least greatest.

George Orwell's premonitory depiction of the human condition enslaved by materialism is eerily alive in today's America, the Materialism Mecca, where people live in densely-packed suburban and urban clusters designed to satisfy their individual comforts: neighbors on one-acre lots crammed in labyrinthine sprawls labeled deceivingly as "Juniper Heights" or "Highland Ridge" or such. Yet these neighbors don't share the traditional community bonds lost to America's less-materialistic past, for their lives are busy, their neighbors change often, and the cell phone, television, automobile and Internet, amongst other technologies, have dissolved that interdependency which once served as human society. To place trust in either political party in modern America is to trust (blindly) in technology, business/free market guidance, the economic and military power of America, and that the American political system is going to solve the world's problems. It is to pursue material comfort at the expense of introspection and compassion for others. But to abandon compassion is to become less human. More than 60 years ago, Orwell insightfully described this ideological/industrial enslavement, where people are led to think they are better off, and in the right, even while suffering the oppression of a system which we instantly recognize as toxic to humanity. This realization dawns on the main character of <u>1984</u>, himself a member of the "Party," called by his conscience and by faded memories of a more human existence to reject his situation of relative comfort in favor of the chance at feeling life, even at the risk of death. Trying to remember his own mother, Winston Smith thinks:

> When once you were in the grip of the Party, what you felt or did not feel, what you did or refrained from doing, made literally no difference. Whatever happened you vanished, and neither you nor your actions were ever heard from again. You were lifted clean out of the stream of history. And yet to the people of only two generations ago, this would not have seemed all-important, because they were not attempting to alter history. They were governed by private loyalties which they did not question. What mattered were individual relationships, and a completely helpless gesture, an embrace, a tear, a word spoken to a dying man, could have value in itself. The proles, it suddenly occurred to him, had remained in this condition. They were not loyal to a party or a country or an idea, they were loyal to one another. For the first time in his life he did not despise the proles or think of them merely as an inert force which would one day spring to life and regenerate the world. The proles had stayed human. They had not become hardened inside. They had held onto the primitive emotions which he himself had to relearn by conscious effort. And in thinking this he remembered, without apparent relevance, how a few weeks ago he had seen a severed hand lying on the pavement and had kicked it into the gutter as though it had been a cabbage stalk. "The proles are human beings," he said aloud. "We are not human."[345]

Replace the word "proles" with "underclass" and the hand in the street with Africa's starving and Iraqi children's shattered existence, and you have a modern

---

[345] George Orwell, <u>1984</u>, pp. 136-137.

American Democrat or Republican waking up to the fact that he or she has been had, and that America is about to finish the story that Orwell left for us to complete.

But Orwell's tale was an historic assessment of man's sociology and psychology, not just futuristic doom-saying or contemporary political satire (though it is these also). Creating a window into a vision of a future society, Orwell describes the cycle of worldly power in all human society, past, present and future:

> Throughout recorded time, and probably since the end of the Neolithic Age, there have been three kinds of people in the world, the High, the Middle, and the Low....The aims of these three groups are entirely irreconcilable. The aim of the High is to remain where they are. The aim of the Middle is to change places with the High. The aim of the Low, when they have an aim—for it is an abiding characteristic of the Low that they are too much crushed by drudgery to be more than intermittently conscious of anything outside their daily lives—is to abolish all distinctions and create a society in which all men shall be equal. Thus throughout history a struggle which is the same in its main outlines recurs over and over again. For long periods the High seem to be securely in power, but sooner or later there always comes a moment when they lose either their belief in themselves, or their capacity to govern efficiently, or both. They are then overthrown by the Middle, who enlist the low on their side by pretending to them that they are fighting for liberty and justice.[346] As soon as they have reached their objective, the Middle thrust the

---

[346] The Democrats?

> Low back into their old position of servitude, and themselves become the High. Presently a new Middle group splits off from one of the other groups, or from both of them, and the struggle begins over again. Of the three groups, only the Low are never even temporarily successful in achieving their aims. It would be an exaggeration to say that throughout history there had been no progress of a material kind. Even today, in a period of decline, the average human being is physically better off than he was a few centuries ago. But no advance in wealth, no softening of manners, no reform or revolution has ever brought human equality a millimeter nearer. From the point of view of the Low, no historic change has ever meant much more than a change in the name of their masters.[347]

This sentiment, long prevalent amongst America's underclass, will soon infect its middle class also. As national debt and spiraling health care and other expenses continue to squeeze more of the Middle into the Low even as more and more wealth is accumulated in the bankbooks and stock portfolios of a smaller and smaller percentage of Americans (the High), the middle class will realize that their plight is hopeless and dehumanizing. Add to this the irrevocable environmental damage that will pollute generations of our children and their food supply, a culture deteriorating in the logical progression of moral relativism, and the loss of America's image internationally, and one has an Orwellian recipe for either oppression or revolution (or extinction).

---

[347] George Orwell, 1984, pp. 166-167.

Galbraith summarizes America's the-more-you-have-the-more-you-want creed:

> Having enough, many wish for more. Being comfortable, many raise vigorous objection to that which invades comfort.[348] What is important is that there is no self-doubt in their present situation.... [Yet some] see the more distant dangers that will result from a short-run preoccupation with individual comfort.... A blockage in the movement upward and out of the underclass will not be accepted.[349]

America has not heeded Mr. Galbraith's warnings, nor those of God: "But if you treat people according to their outward appearance, you are guilty of sin, and the law condemns you as a lawbreaker....Speak and act as people who will be judged by the law that sets us free. For God will not show mercy when he judges the person who has not been merciful; but mercy triumphs over judgment."[350] Will we soon join other parts of the world in instability because we squandered our time of stability in self-absorption? Recent research "suggests that there may be a relationship between economic shock and fighting in unstable nations....'On average, a negative economic growth shock of 5 percentage points increases civil-war risks by about 50 percent,' according to the Millennium Project."[351]

---

[348] E.g. tax increases, wealth redistribution, restrictions on consumption.
[349] John Kenneth Galbraith, The Culture of Contentment, pp. 16, 17, 40.
[350] James 2:9, 12-13, TEV.
[351] "A blueprint to fight poverty around the world," *The Christian Science Monitor*, January 20, 2005, p. 2.

America cannot withstand a dramatic drop in wealth (e.g. the impending "pop" of the real estate bubble), in gross domestic product being tapped for debt service, because its underclass, long ignored, is festering miserably, waiting for a chance at a piece of the action, revenge, or both. The decline of real faith in God in the United States—the "pure" variety and not the accumulate-wealth-and-say-Christian-things-on-Sunday lukewarm creed prevalent in modern America—has led to an increase in the influence of evil. And as one Christian writer has chronicled, one of the consequences of a denial of God's existence is a cry for worldly revolution because of a deep sense of desperation.[352] America's economic inequity breeds resentment and worldly drudgery in a moral soup of relativism and liberalism, while the wealthy gluttonously enjoy the ride in the identical moral climate. Christ weeps for those lost to Satan's illusions. Jesus taught us to "give what is in your cups and plates to the poor, and everything will be ritually clean for you."[353] Christians must always look with compassion upon the poor, remembering that seeing God is within the reach of all of us, that "It would be like God to make the most vital thing easy and place it within the range of possibility for the weakest and poorest of us."[354] We must not avert our eyes from God for our own comfort and expect Him to bless America

---

[352] Renald E. Showers, <u>What on Earth is God Doing?</u>, p. 94.
[353] Luke 11:41, TEV.
[354] A.W. Tozer, <u>The Pursuit of God: the Human Thirst For the Divine</u>, p.87.

with anything but a sound rebuke: "Compassionate Conservatism" is devoid of any action furthering Christ's purpose. Christian words, unchristian actions....

Chapter 5

NO CHILD LEFT BETTER OFF

The Bush Administration's much-trumpeted No Child Left Behind (NCLB) legislation presents a clear demonstration of 'words' of encouragement followed by ineffective if not counterproductive 'actions.' The federal government needs to expand into local school systems about as much as gypsy moth caterpillars were needed to help our country's foliage. Testing by itself does little if anything to educate, and is at odds with our society's "liberal" egalitarian educational traditions. The NCLB Act provides essentially no funding to actually address problems, even if testing accurately identifies those problems. And the effect of NCLB testing on our nation's teachers' and students' morale has been destructive, not healthful, for America's education system. The industrialization, the dehumanization, of Americans is heightened under leaders like George W. Bush, who guinea-pig our children with experimental testing methods without foreknowledge that such testing will be beneficial—no pilot areas,[355] no preliminary studies, just a huge overnight national bureaucratic structure. But the government, assisted by Mr. Bush, does have most certain foreknowledge that this system will expand federal power over America's citizenry.

Generally, conservatives are supposed to be (and certainly proclaim themselves to be) associated with restraint in government, both fiscally and in its ever-lustful appropriation to itself of new areas of "jurisdiction." So what happened? President Bush praises Marvin Olasky, but Mr. Olasky insists that "Government programs need to be fought…because they are inevitably too stingy in what is really important, treating people as people and not animals."[356] In which direction is national testing? Is testing an effective tool to enhance moral fiber, spiritual growth, or learning? Both Left and Right agree that government is not the answer to social ills, is even perhaps not to be trusted as its bureaucratic self-preservation leads to gargantuan growth. So federal testing, a national system, is implicitly a dubious proposition. Back in 1974, Richard N. Goodwin observed:

> Central government has added more to its reach over the last few decades than during the previous century and a half of our history. In this respect, we are more distant from Herbert Hoover than he was from George Washington. The sovereignty withdrawn from states has gone to augment the immense, continual and unimpeded accumulation

---

[355] Unless one considers Texas a test project. If so, the results have been disastrous, and the test rat has taken very ill.
[356] Marvin Olasky, <u>The Tragedy of American Compassion</u>, p. 232-233.

of authority within the central government, especially its executive branch. The result is an Executive vested with almost exclusive power to take substantial initiatives....Many of the traditional constitutional divisions continue a formal existence, but they have lost their power to restrain.[357]

Thirty years later, this observation has been proven true, with federal influence affecting every facet of American life, almost always under the pretense of the interest of "commerce" (read "money"). George Bush wasted no time using the Presidency to "take substantial initiatives" toward expanding that power, through the NCLB Act, Homeland Security, the USA Patriot Act, new (federal) national driver's license documentation requirements, and in a dramatic increase in federal spending (even while pretending to be refunding money!). And storms in the Gulf of Mexico almost immediately were employed by George W. Bush to justify an expansion of military police powers.[358]

But wait. George W. Bush's words said he had no intention of doing any such thing. Unveiling the NCLB Act, he said

> The new education reforms we have passed in Washington give the federal government a new role in public education. Schools must meet new and

---

[357] Richard N. Goodwin, The American Condition, p. 348.
[358] Perhaps George W. has forgotten one of the grievances of the colonists against the King of Britain: "He has affected to render the military independent of and superior to the civil power." The Declaration of Independence, Samuel Eliot Morison, (ed.), Sources & Documents Illustrating the American Revolution, 1764-1788, p. 159.

high standards of performance in reading and math that will be proven in tests...And we're giving local schools and teachers unprecedented freedom and resources and training to meet these goals....It is conservative to let local communities chart their own path to excellence.[359]

Much like the tax refunds,[360] we see here in action the sleight of hand of giving with one hand while simultaneously taking back more with the other. What is "unprecedented" is not an increase in teacher freedom (where does that statement come from?!), but in the federal government's "new role in education:" local schools and teachers are given nothing by the NCLB Act, as the revolt against its provisions by a number of states has demonstrated. There are paltry resources to accomplish testing, let alone to implement real change. The Act's stated methods of response to "qualified" underperforming, underprivileged students are to get them tutors or move them to another school. But there is insufficient funding for tutors, teachers' resources are being distracted away from teaching and toward testing, and clearly this is the opposite of providing "unprecedented" autonomy and resources to those teachers and schools. And what happened to studying the issue or

---

[359] Thomas A. Freiling, <u>George W. Bush on God & Country</u>, pp. 122-123.

[360] Where Mr. Bush's cash basis refunds have been juggled with accrued liabilities which far exceed the moneys "refunded." (what good is it to refund $1000 per taxpayer if the government accrues $3000 per taxpayer in debt?) Ronald Reagan did the same thing, and we have yet to begin to repay the money he borrowed this way in the 1980s. Our children will figure it out....having been left behind.

maybe consulting with teachers before we revamp our nation's educational system to industrial/bureaucratic methodology: remember those CHIPS programs in Texas? Testing students and then moving them around for failure or underperformance places extraordinary stresses on children to pass, and compounds the problem by disrupting the student and his teachers in the event of failure. Solutions must address problems, not just expand government, and the NCLB legislation does nothing to address failing schools.

Mr. Bush nonetheless expounds many great words of "local autonomy" while he takes it away. He has said "I believe in the alignment of authority and responsibility away from the federal government[361] when it comes to issues of governance and schools…."[362] And in another typically oxymoronic speech, Mr. Bush advocated national testing while noting "But Washington shouldn't be telling Cleveland how to run its school system. See, that's up to you all to figure out how to run your school system."[363] If local communities' school systems aren't to be trusted to educate children and conduct their own old-time tests, what is President Bush suggesting is left to them to "run," janitorial and bussing operations? Frankly, Americans should be grateful to Mr. Bush for revealing with such clarity the inexorable, dishonest, blob-like expansion of the federal government under either political party. Now it's time to awaken to that revelation.

---

[361] That's for sure!
[362] Paul Kengor, God and George W. Bush: a spiritual life, p. 37.
[363] Thomas A. Freiling, George W. Bush on God & Country, p. 170.

Whatever government undertakes, and especially so with regard to such expensive and far-reaching legislation as the NCLB Act, there must be great care to avoid bureaucratic incompetence: meddling with changes in form, but with no real change in substance. Our children's futures and our country's international economic competitiveness depend on moving our education system forward and not toward further deterioration. As one conservative author has sternly remarked:

> Whatever form it may take, state intervention in the private and productive lives of the citizenry must be presumed to be a negative, uncreative, and dangerous act, to be adopted only when its proponents provide overwhelming and incontrovertible evidence that the benefits to society of such intervention far outweigh the costs.[364]

And Mr. W. Bush has said that "[t]he federal government should fund only what works in education, only those methods and ideas that prove their power to close the achievement gap."[365]

But what evidence established or "proved" that national testing would benefit students in learning or morale, or that they would "close the achievement gap"? There was none.

John Kenneth Galbraith was of the opinion that the only way to improve inner city America was "by better schools with better-paid teachers....,"[366] and criticized

---

[364] William E. Simon, A Time for Truth, p. 218.
[365] George W. Bush, A Charge to Keep, pp. 233-234.
[366] John Kenneth Galbraith, The Culture of Contentment, p. 180.

the first President Bush for calling himself "the Education President" but demonstrating an unwillingness to spend money for education, saying of Bush, Sr.: "Without this willingness no significant educational improvement can be expected."[367] In words with even greater resonance today, Galbraith also noted that "[t]he resources now going to the military establishment...would, if available, work a minor revolution in education and be a source of salvation and tranquility in the central cities."[368] George W. has allocated funds for NCLB testing that could have contributed toward the higher salaries (understandably) required to attract quality teachers to our inner cities. Words without action....Tests without substantive consequences for schools or students.... Bureaucracy at work for the citizens it taxes....No real money for those underclass kids because we'd ruin them and make them dependent...But plenty of money and resources for those impoverished military corporations and that malnourished group of loyal Americans in the Pentagon.

And testing is not only not proven to be helpful, it is well-proven to be the opposite. Typically for the federal government, especially under the Bush tiller, the ones making decisions about solutions have not studied the problems they're endeavoring to solve, and their motivations are always political or bureaucratic, either seeking votes, satisfying constituents, or expanding the government's influence and thus their own power. As Allan Bloom notes, "[t]he intellectual problems unresolved

---

[367] Ibid., p. 180.
[368] Ibid., pp.181-182.

at the top cannot be resolved administratively below."[369] President Bush, not qualified to teach, has created a bureaucratic response to a problem which is already most likely a consequence of bureaucracy. Perhaps the drive to learn and the quality of that learning have been compromised in American schools by an industrial, bureaucratic way of learning, compounded by government efforts to mandate and shape educational curricula, and by efforts to apply economies of scale to education, enlarging the scope of government bureaucracy instead of leaving education to local control. One political author noted that "[w]hat children learn formally in school is much less important than what they pick up unconsciously from the way in which the school in fact operates. Democratic educational theory requires that the teacher help the child learn how to think rather than what to think."[370] In other words, in a democracy children are taught freedom of thought, to think for themselves, a freedom being dumbed down by the industrialization, liberalization,[371] and bureaucratization of modern America. As to local autonomy over education in democratic countries, Ebenstein notes that "[w]hile this freedom has at times resulted in schools of poor quality in some regions of the country, it has been defended on the ground that local autonomy is a more fundamental value than a potentially better educational system run

---

[369] Allan Bloom, The Closing of the American Mind, p. 343.
[370] William Ebenstein, Today's Isms Communism Fascism Capitalism Socialism, p. 183.
[371] See Bloom, The Closing of the American Mind, for an incisive exposition on the demise of classical learning in the face of controlling liberal influences.

by the national government—as, for example, exists in France."³⁷² George Bush has paid lip service only to local autonomy, dramatically undermining that autonomy and alienating our nation's teachers for a system that is not likely to be "potentially better."³⁷³

In <u>Politics, Markets & America's Schools</u>, John E. Chubb and Terry M. Moe address in great detail the problems contributing to the decline in performance of America's schools. Acknowledging that private schools outperform public schools in teaching children in America, Chubb and Moe conclude that the chief cause of declining education quality is "the very institutions that are supposed to be solving the problem: the institutions of direct democratic control [which]…appear to be incompatible with effective schooling."³⁷⁴ In typical lack-of-government-accountability fashion reminiscent

---

³⁷² William Ebenstein, <u>Today's Isms Communism Fascism Capitalism Socialism</u>, p. 183.
³⁷³ Bush's NCLB creates red tape and resentment without printing a book or raising a salary. It's kind of like "studying" the effects of mercury or acid rain while we keep pumping the stuff into the air, or like Myron Magnet said of welfare, "holding basic beliefs in abeyance and using questionable means to try to achieve a worthy social end." (Magnet, p. 20.) But welfare programs (in the 30s and the 60s) probably prevented revolution in America, whereas NCLB will hasten social implosion by failing to address the underlying problems with America's education system and the poverty behind that system's eternal strain, and by increasing the dehumanizing and alienating pressures of government on the underclass–NCLB testing is more bureaucratic and less responsive than the welfare programs derided by Bush & Co. Maybe the government should send out questionnaires and ask inner city people how poor they are, and then move the really poor people to other cities, and thereby address poverty with the same logic as that employed by W. Bush in the NCLB legislation.
³⁷⁴ John E. Chubb and Terry M. Moe, <u>Politics, Markets & America's Schools</u>, p. 2.

of George W.'s hip-shooting solution to education decline, "[t]he notion that these institutions might themselves be undermining academic performance...was never seriously considered."[375] The authors determine that there are two reasons for this failure, the first being political/bureaucratic:

> ...the most powerful political groups by far are those with vested interests in the current institutional system....Current arrangements put them in charge of the system, and their jobs, revenues, and economic security depend on keeping the basic governance structure pretty much as it is. The educational system is hardly unusual in this regard. All social institutions are protected and stabilized in much the same way. Through their structures and the normal course of their operations, they generate all manner of benefits...and these beneficiaries naturally resist any fundamental change in the structural arrangements that are the source of their benefits.[376]

The second reason was that ideas for education reform have been shaped by social scientists who paid little attention to those influential educational structures and institutions. Later studies revealed that private schools outperformed public schools in educating children, and identified areas for improvement, but then the same

---

[375] Ibid., p. 11.
[376] Ibid., pp. 11-12, 12. I.e., government bureaucrats, or America's "comfortable" middle and upper classes. Richard Goodwin and John Kenneth Galbraith both express alarm at the manner in which such bureaucracy causes the same malaise in government and in our country's military-industrial complex.

bureaucratic structure was employed to implement supposed changes to the public school system. The authors conclude from their research that:

> One, schools do indeed perform better to the extent that they possess the effective school syndrome of organizational characteristics–to the extent, in other words, that they have such general qualities as clear goals, an ambitious academic program, strong educational leadership, and high levels of teacher professionalism.
>
> Two, the most important prerequisite for the emergence of effective school characteristics is school autonomy, especially from external bureaucratic influence.
>
> Three, America's existing system of public education inhibits the emergence of effective organizations. This occurs, most fundamentally, because its institutions of democratic control function naturally to limit and undermine school autonomy….we show that private schools are organized much more effectively than public schools are and that this is a reflection of their far greater autonomy from external (bureaucratic) control.[377]

Turning their attention to the efficacy of testing to improve performance, these authors conclude that government introduced competency tests

> to ensure that schools could not pass along students who had failed to meet certain minimum standards–

---
[377] Ibid., pp. 23, 24.

which many schools were clearly guilty of in the past. Schools would now be held accountable for really teaching these students something. Achievement tests served the more general purpose of indicating how well or poorly the schools were doing.[378]

These writers agree that there are benefits to testing, but conclude that "statewide testing of students can also be a misleading and counterproductive means of evaluating the performance of schools."[379] They discovered that testing requirements compel teachers to "teach to the test," and that the negative or "counterproductive" consequences outweigh the benefits (and this on a statewide, not federal analysis). In words that are now proved astutely accurate in view of the NCLB fiasco, these education scholars conclude that

> [i]n the end, testing requirements are a lot like certification requirements and many other traditional reforms. They seem to make good sense, and they do indeed offer certain benefits. But they are clearly deficient as solutions to the problems they are addressing, and they stand little chance of improving schools in any significant way. Worse, they create still more bureaucracy,[380] and they unleash new bureaucratic pathologies that divert people and resources from the pursuit of quality education. The

---

[378] Ibid., p. 197. As opposed to the current administration's use of tests on the students, instead of addressing the problem with the schools.
[379] Ibid., p. 198.
[380] The creation of more and more federal bureaucratic structure leveraged by stellar deficit spending is a signature un-Conservative hypocrisy of this administration. Larger government and corporate bureaucracies are Satan's tools to dehumanize and alienate people–especially Americans, who once counted themselves as God's children.

danger is not just that these reforms will fail to meet their lofty goals, but that they will actually hurt the schools more than help them over the long run.[381]

These "counterproductive...bureaucratic pathologies" have been demonstrated under President Bush's NCLB overhaul of our nation's education system, and for those children affected the damage cannot be reversed by more government efforts at bureaucratic solutions from above. Texas was the first jurisdiction to be subjected to this scientific methodology, and the consequences are evident. Despite Bush campaign boasts of improved education in Texas, these boasts were made based on corruptly doctored tests, as school districts and their bureaucratic masters were awarded bonuses not based on whether children actually learned but on test scores. Texans Molly Ivins and Lou Dubose opine that "[w]hat we have done is make a single annual test the most important event in every young Texan's life.... The message to Teacher is "Teach the test," and the message to kids is "Learn to pass the test." This is not education."[382] The consequences of this bureaucratic system which awards teachers (and, worse, administrators) for making our children into maze-running rats are now clear, with increasing incidence of teachers and students cheating even while the Bush administration supports the unconstitutional random searching of students via drug testing, and has been pushing to expand the NCLB

---

[381] John E. Chubb and Terry M. Moe, Politics, Markets & America's Schools, p. 198.
[382] Molly Ivins and Lou Dubose, Shrub: The Short But Happy Political Life of George W. Bush, p. 125.

testing structure to our nation's high schools.[383] In Texas, more money seems to have changed hands for slap-on-the-back salary bonuses for bureaucrats than went to children's tutoring, inner-city school improvement, or teachers' salaries:

> The "Texas Miracle" that helped launch the nationwide accountability movement in education[384] is facing new doubts as allegations surface about possible cheating on test scores. Last week the Houston Independent School District (HISD)–one of the nation's largest–announced an investigation of "suspicious" results on 2004 statewide tests....The wrangling is being closely watched by districts across the country that are bound by the federal No Child Left Behind Act of 2002, which was modeled in part after the success of Houston schools....[C]heating on standardized tests has been making the news with increasing frequency...."The No Child Left Behind Act, which has some very solid goals, when implemented creates an awful lot of trouble in the schools," says John Fremer, a testing expert with 40 years of experience. While he says cheating has been around for as long as there have been tests, the difference in the past few years is that teachers and administrators are heavily involved, "something that's so alien to

---

[383] "President Bush ....underscored his desire for senior high students to take the math and reading tests now required of younger students. Under the No Child Left Behind law, states are required to give fourth-and eighth-graders the National Assessment of Education Progress tests." *The Christian Science Monitor*, January 13, 2005, p. 20. What benefit will accrue to students by testing high school seniors? They are too old to tutor or to switch schools.

[384] There's that oxymoronic "accountability" again.

the concept of teaching."....The problem, say many education experts, is that the tests have been tied to teachers' job contacts [sic] and bonuses. "Once the outcome of these tests started to matter, was it any surprise that teachers began to cheat?" asks Steve Levitt, an economics professor at the University of Chicago. "And I think the other side is that the risk reward looks fairly good. The chances of being caught are tiny."[385]

This is what happens when policies are designed to win votes and attract publicity, not to actually address the problems they politically pretend to cure (like "compassionate conservatism").

Repeating a pattern of overconfidence seen also in Iraq and its rebuilding, in energy policy without conservation, in tax refunds and deficit recklessness with no real economic growth, George W. Bush pressed his NCLB agenda without researching the consequences, the potential downsides, of such a huge imposition on the education system of our country. His faith in government as the solution to every problem (except poverty, which he would leave to private interests and corporations to solve) extends to children's education, and he once again employs words without action:

> Listen, if you can teach a child to read, they can pass a test. You teach them to read, don't worry about

---

[385] "When tests' cheaters are the teachers," Kris Axtman, *The Christian Science Monitor*, January 11, 2005, p.1.

tests.[386]....We need to know in America whether or not our children can read and write and add and subtract.[387] That's what an accountability system is for[388]....Starting this September,...students across America who attend failing schools will have different options,[389] of transferring to another public

---

[386] It is absurd to tell teachers to teach children to read and not worry about the tests that will determine whether those teachers taught the children to read; to tell children not to worry about tests that could dramatically impact their life through school transfer or by requiring after-school tutoring; to tell people to ignore a test that you just passed a federal law mandating. Words without action—words don't change human emotions and the realities of the failures of bureaucracy to improve learning.

[387] We already know that too many of our country's children *cannot* read, write, add or subtract at an acceptable level—that's what the NCLB Act is supposedly addressing, just like it was obvious poor children were suffering in Texas from a lack of health insurance coverage when George W. postponed CHIP benefits pending a commission study. NCLB tracks, analyzes, numbers and assesses the nation's children for the federal databank, but does almost nothing to actually improve school conditions, or reading, writing or math skills amongst the nation's kids. Words without action....

[388] Where's the beef? Where's the accountability for schools or teachers if the consequence of failure is only to move or tutor the student? Is this like welfare and poverty, so it's the kids' fault they're all failing and cheating in our nation's schools? Perhaps the reason all those inner city black and Hispanic kids fail and drop out more than white rich kids is because they "lack the inner resources" to succeed, like the welfare moms who bred them....the precise view of Magnet, Olasky, Bush, and compassionate conservatism.

[389] This implies choice for students, but only *after* they've failed a test they were compelled by the federal government to take: Give with the left hand while you take away more with the right.....We are being overtaken in America by too many Left and Right hands.

school.[390] It's part of being an accountable society.[391] It's part of strengthening public education.

Listen, I think public education is one of the most important parts of democracy.[392] In order to make sure the American Dream[393] reaches every neighborhood, we've got to have good public schools all across America. We must.[394]

---

[390] Is a psychology or education degree required, or just common sense, to realize that changing schools is almost always disruptive and very stressful for children, that their grades and learning are often hurt by moving and by its disruption of the structure of their lives, and that such a dramatic decision should not be made based so heavily on standardized tests given their proven deficiencies, and should not be made by the Federal Government of Unprecedented Bureaucratic Magnitude?

[391] But society has failed our nation's children through NCLB. The fact that Bush and his supporters press on with this miserable Act is demonstration of this administration's refusal to recognize or admit its failures, the opposite of Christian repentance. The NCLB Act holds no one accountable–not the government, the "failing"schools, or the "society" (though the society will surely hold the bag in the end): only the students are held accountable, to line up like livestock or draftees for the federal government to faithfully step in and inspect, for our greater good and economic benefit, for progress, all with no new money for books, teachers or the poor, but with ample delay for all.

[392] So why make it less democratic, and more autocratic?

[393] Does this arrive on an ice cream truck? Is this more than words and marketing? Doesn't that "Dream" include equality of economic and educational opportunity, an equality denied the underclass by our "Dream's" increased concentration of wealth in the hands of the few, and denied their children because their inner-city schools are in chaos? Words....plenty of big worldly words.

[394] How emphatic! But what does NCLB do for schools? What changes does it mandate for schools? Absolutely none, except to conform to tests.

> So we've got to strengthen the public education system, by encouraging different opportunities if there's failure.[395]
>
> Low income students, as a result of the new bill, in chronically failing schools will now have access to after-school tutoring....[396] I believe in local control[397] of schools.[398]

It's bad enough that NCLB fails to achieve its lofty stated goals, may make the situation in our nation's schools worse, and increases federal control of Americans' lives at the expense of local freedom. But the methodology involved also serves to further the alienating bureaucratization of modern industrialized society, taking us closer to that Orwellian vision of people reduced to cubicle lives, watched constantly.

Allan Bloom, in The Closing of the American Mind, laments that America's colleges have become centers

---

[395] How does NCLB "strengthen the public education system"? Shuttling children around schools without subjecting those schools to testing or assessment? Words....

[396] So if a child a) fails the test and b) meets income guidelines, he or she *may* get tutoring. Apparently there is no interdiction necessary for rich kids, so if they're failing they don't get tutored or relocated–why is it again that we're testing them? And "having access" is different from compelled attendance, so a child *must* take the test, but does not *have* to attend tutoring. Perhaps all that testing money should have gone just to tutors, for anyone who wished to attend, rather than limiting the tutoring available to kids who might not go anyway–actions instead of words...testing is words only, with increased government control as a bonus.

[397] If George W. Bush believes in local control of schools, why has he invested such major effort to take it away? There is *nothing* in NCLB that increases local control over *anything*. Words with *opposite* actions.

[398] George W. Bush, from Thomas A. Freiling, George W. Bush on God & Country, pp. 170-171.

for grooming for the marketplace instead of centers for learning. And Richard N. Goodwin commented on the decline of quality in American education long before NCLB:

> Education has conformed to the imperatives of the modern economic process, just as it served the earlier industrial economy it was created to sustain.... Mass education was essential to the creation of an economy based on mass consumption....Education has been one of society's most effective instruments for securing a general acceptance of established values and ideology....The qualities rewarded in school are those valued by the economic bureaucracy–from good fellowship to achievement in a competition conducted along rather narrow and standardized lines which reward diligence.[399]

In other words, mankind is himself "industrialized" by modern industrial school systems. NCLB testing requirements do little if anything to make America more competitive globally, but they do indoctrinate our youth into a very early direct relationship with the United States government (not to be confused with the United States of America, a country in which decent human beings strive to live honestly). National testing requirements accustom children to be treated as numbers in a massive bureaucracy, as opposed to the American tradition of local community nurturing.

Consistent with this indoctrination and increased control, the NCLB legislation mandates that schools

---
[399] Richard N. Goodwin, The American Condition, pp. 325, 326, 327.

provide access to the military to recruit in high school. When challenged recently at some of the nation's high schools, the recruitment practices were defended by a US Army spokesman, who "pointed out the legality of military recruitment activity on campuses. "The No Child Left Behind Act requires schools to let us have access to these students," he says."[400] Exactly what educational opportunities, what improvements to schools, are generated by mandatory on-school military recruitment? How is local autonomy enhanced? Once again we see the ubiquitous, insidious hand of government taking what it's after while pretending to "help" us. And President George W. Bush is the leader of that government, and came up with this brilliant, socialist plan to nationalize education and testing.

George W. Bush has said of NCLB that "[I]t is compassionate to insist that every child learns, so that no child is left behind. By insisting on results, and challenging failure where we find it, we'll make an incredible difference in the lives of every child in America."[401] Mandatory military recruitment ensures that no child will be left behind when we go to war: no results are required by testing (there is no consequence to failure but being relocated or tutored), at least by schools, and therefore if we are to "challenge failure where we find it" then we ought to begin with the NCLB Act. There is no challenge presented to failing schools by the NCLB

---

[400] US Army spokesman Douglas Smith, quoted in "Rift over recruiting on school grounds," Dean Paton, *The Christian Science Monitor*, May 18, 2005, pp. 2, 3.
[401] Thomas A. Freiling, <u>George W. Bush on God & Country</u>, pp. 122-123.

Act, but surely the testing regimen, disruption of lesson plans and resentment by teachers, along with ongoing and future guaranteed military recruitment access, will ensure that the Act does indeed "make an incredible difference in the lives of every child in America," as Mr. Bush promised. It is therefore no surprise that there has been a "nationwide backlash"[402] against the NCLB Act, with several states going so far as to refuse to comply with the Act.

And yet, President Bush ignores this dissent, as he ignores dissent even in his own Cabinet or in the world community. He also ignores the teachers and education academics who have spent their lives studying children and the failings of our schools. He also ignores the mounting evidence that the supposed education gains in Texas, on which he based his national program, may be fabricated, and that similar dishonesty is most assuredly encouraged, now on a national level, by such high-stakes testing. Moreover, he continues to push to expand the use of such tests to high schools, even as all the evidence (though ignored) mounts of their inefficacy. One is reminded of Philippians 3:19: "They are proud of what they should be ashamed of, and they think only of things that belong to this world."[403]

Reflecting this pride in what should cause shame is the continued insistence that testing is the answer, with almost no evidence whatsoever to support such industrial experimentation. Jonathan Zimmerman, a proponent of

---

[402] Gail Russell Chadwick, *The Christian Science Monitor*, "In second term, a fight over direction of GOP," January 20, 2005, p. 4.
[403] TEV.

NCLB testing, reflected well the Olasky-Magnet-Bush compassionate view when he suggested that NCLB testing is desirable because African-Americans favor such standardized tests, that they "want classrooms that stress discipline, that follow a strict curriculum, and that children succeed on–gasp!–standardized tests."[404] But discipline and a strict curriculum can be achieved without federal standardized tests (and can be greatly wonting even with such testing), and popular opinion is hardly the best determinant of education policy–popular opinion leads Americans to destroy their bodies, spirits and self esteem by such habits/obsessions as high-fructose corn syrup beverages, nutritionless high-sugar cereal and other food consumptions, physical appearances, wealth accumulation, etc. Thus, parents' desire for discipline does not translate in any way to a support of standardized testing.

What this author fails to do is offer a shred of evidence or logic to support national standardized testing. Indeed, he says that he "share[s] many of the...concerns" of those opposed to standardized testing that it "ignores the interests of the individual student; it promotes needless competition and anxiety; it turns learning into a lock-step exercise, inhibiting exploration and imagination; and it measures students against an arbitrary standard, ignoring their idiosyncratic abilities and attitudes...."[405] But these concerns apparently carry no weight in the face of underclass popularity, for he waves

---

[404] Jonathan Zimmerman, "Minorities support 'racist' tests," *The Christian Science Monitor*, June 2, 2005, p. 9.
[405] Ibid.

them aside without intellectual response, moralizing that "Whatever we think of America's current testing craze, American racial minorities clearly endorse it. And if we dismiss their views out of hand, we'll be demeaning the very people whom we claim to defend."[406] This is logically ridiculous nonsense coming from a supposed college professor. First, Mr. Zimmerman in this statement dismisses "whatever we think" of testing in favor of racial minority endorsement.[407] Second, he suggests that those who oppose testing are "dismiss[ing] out of hand" the views of minorities, when there are ample reasons to oppose silly bubble sheets without dismissing anyone, and when testing makes no sense even when respecting those views. Third, he himself in the same article dismisses (out of hand, to boot) those who oppose testing, thus: "Many of these critics work at schools of education, where the standardized test serves as a symbol of everything that's wrong with American teaching."[408] But Mr. Zimmerman does not address why people trained in education view standardized testing so negatively, how he feels testing will improve American teaching when balanced against the legitimate criticisms of testing which he himself recounts, or what exactly is so untrustworthy about the opinions of people who study education for a career versus those of, say, politicians, when one is determining education policy. The Bush administration has not addressed these questions either....

---

[406] Ibid.
[407] Did they endorse NCLB's creation? Did they endorse George W. Bush for president? (Blacks overwhelmingly opposed Bush)
[408] Ibid.

Chapter 6

COMPASSION FOR GOD'S CREATION

George W. Bush's record on the environment, both in Texas and nationally, is abysmal. Recently Republicans (and George W.) have made the ridiculous assertion that our air is cleaner today than it was thirty years ago. Despite steadily increasing consumption at the highest level of any society in history, bar none, after thirty years of expanding coal-fired plants while doing very little to encourage pollution control technology, and while our automobiles became less fuel efficient (allowing consumer choice, that great unstoppable force, to dictate manufacturing rather than the lessons of the 1970s oil crisis), our air most certainly has not magically improved. In fact our air and water resources are being destroyed at an ever-increasing pace, owing to Americans' collective denial. This Administration has only set the United States of America backward environmentally while bolstering the interests of big business, leaving the economic, health, and environmental costs of such short-sightedness to be shouldered by future generations of Americans.

Is this too strongly worded? How do you get through to those for whom an admission of fault is not a Christian virtue but a worldly weakness? And this is America's culture now, if we didn't willfully ignore the overwhelming evidence staring us in the face. Six months after the Monica Lewinsky story broke, a majority of Americans polled still said they believed President Clinton's pathological lies–it took DNA evidence to clear up the confusion. Now we see the same psychosis settling over the Right, where party loyalty (worldly-belief-system loyalty) trumps fact. And we observe the same willful denial in the failure of compassionate conservatism to help the poor; in the failure of NCLB to improve education; in the failure to acknowledge that George W. intended to invade Iraq from the day he first took the oath of office (see Chapter Eight); in the failure to reverse the arrogant policies that are destroying America's international image, an image a hundred years or more in the making; in the failure to recognize that the Iraq debacle is like a U.S.-funded recruitment drive for terrorists; in the failure to confront the simple, undeniable fact that our country was attacked on 9/11 for a reason, not because of jealousy (an absurd rationalization concocted because of lack of a more credible deception); in the failure to realize what tax refunds, war in Iraq, huge military spending and a shrinking economy (despite the propaganda espousing how well the economy is expanding) have done to our nation's debt load and our national wealth, an irrevocable step into debtor land (the DNA evidence of which will very soon become 100% clear). As Richard N. Goodwin observed, "Within the bureaucracy a single large or dramatic failure can drown a lifetime of solid achievement, and not only in the bureaucracies of business but among those of government and politics...."[409]

But obviously none of this is at all surprising to devoted Christians, who look to Jesus Christ and not George W. and America for their salvation. Christians know that humans are all sinful, that God is where to place their faith, and that to be fearful of this world, of economic collapse, war or even death is Satan's influence. They also know from the repeated warnings in the Old and New Testaments that this world has a planned ending, and that in that ending the "world" fails, technology fails, reliance on and absorption with self fails, materialism and the "he who dies with the most toys wins" mentality fails, and that many will come who are false prophets and teachers. Those Christian clergy who embrace gay unions in Christ's church do so without scriptural support, ignoring the sacredness of marriage and the promiscuity of the gay lifestyle, and by so doing they are fulfilling God's word that the Church would be splintered by false teachers. And those Christian leaders, especially those oxymoronic "Christian politicians," who lead us into war or to turn our eyes from the poor or to treat God's Eden-like environment disrespectfully, are all false prophets telling us not to worry about God, not to keep our eyes on His promise, but to worry

---

[409] Richard N. Goodwin, <u>The American Condition</u>, p. 297.

ourselves with the cares of this world, with protecting our (soulless) Homeland, and with compelling other nations to adopt our definition of freedom, our economic way of life, and our culture.

But Jesus wants Americans to see Him without DNA evidence from a blue dress, and He wants us to *feel* His love and to trust Him and the clear words He left us. Christian readers, does Jesus not act as His own DNA test, or shall His warnings of these times be ignored as He said they would be, pushed aside for worldly fears? If Babylon is a physical location, Christians should avoid visiting: but if Babylon is a state of being, of sinful being, then American Christians live in the middle of it. No, we are not the Great Satan, but America has given Satan a cheap rental. The truth, if we care to look Jesus and ourselves in the eye, is that America, whatever she was in the past, has come to be the world's (and world history's) capital of individualism (selfishness), pornography, pedophilia, consumption, homosexuality, materialism, weapons manufacture, gluttony, pollution generation, waste, and destroyer of family values. What makes us most sinful, though, is our denial—even as the world looks upon us with open eyes and sees us for the "Empire Who Had No Clothes" that we are, we perceive of ourselves as the world's liberators, the beacon for freedom, peacemakers, generous, Christian. Usually the great Gomorrah-type civilizations of history who reveled in pleasure and absorption with self didn't simultaneously feign obedience to God or Christ. But the United States does so. This is what America has become.

America is polluting the planet, and the consequences to our environment are undeniable. People without faith may not care about such destruction, they may not care to avoid denial, but Christians who are thus care-less only betray Jesus Christ, who is Almighty and therefore quite aware of our deplorable stewardship of His Father's earth. Especially have we squandered America's opportunities, sacrificing our natural resources and our children's futures for our current consumptive comfort–and denial of this simple observation, or of personal responsibility for this sad, dire state of affairs, serves that comfort in direct opposition to service to Christ.

For God did not create the world for us to destroy, but as a gift that should be treated with respect and care as a reflection of Christian faith. One Christian writer has opined that when cast from the Garden of Eden,

> man's ability to exercise dominion over the earth was changed. He lost the ability to govern some things (Hebrews 2:5-8). The ability that he did retain became perverted. As a result, he became doomed to abuse the earth. Because of his attitude of enmity against God, man began to exercise his dominion in a manner contrary to what God had intended.[410]

American Christians must exercise dominion over their country's air, land, water, and scenic beauty in a manner which pleases God.

The increase in the size and number of corporations in America, and worldwide, over the last one hundred or

---

[410] Renald E. Showers, <u>What on Earth is God Doing?</u>, p. 15.

so years has resulted in a certain level of "corporate governance." Individual owners (shareholders) don't control corporate decision-making, and their moral responsibility is similarly removed from the consequences of corporate behavior. In "corporate" America, the wealthy need not come into contact or even awareness of the poor, for they may own the fruits of capital investment in the form of dividends or portfolio appreciation without any connection to, or even awareness of, the child labor, pollution, graft, or price-gouging that may have been a by-product of the production of that return.

Concurrent with this growth of corporate America has been a growth in American government, and its bureaucratic mass. Every year, new laws give new power to local, state and federal bureaucracy. Designed to protect its citizenry and foster prosperity, America's federal government has turned on its makers as it grows larger and larger, consuming more and more of Americans' tax dollars in the salaries and assets of the government bureaucracies, appropriating more and more money to spend on new areas to justify creating yet more new agencies. (The Department of Homeland Security was a recent whopper.[411])

---

[411] "Security at any price?," *US News & World Report*, May 30, 2005, pp. 22 et seq. "Investigators have repeatedly questioned whether the agency is spending its money wisely. Congress's Government Accountability Office, the DHS inspector general's office, and congressional investigators have issued reports that have repeatedly highlighted a pattern of troubling spending decisions." p.26. In one report, the government determined that the Department of Homeland Security had "$3,000 refrigerators, and a 4,200-square-foot fitness center complete with towel laundering service." *US News & World Report*, May 30, 2005, p. 22.

But Americans abandon their heritage of freedom if they yield to these modern bureaucratic creations of corporate and government control, increasingly augmented by the technologies that are likewise supposed to free us. Instead, America must take personal responsibility for the environment, and for ensuring that the U.S. government is not allowing corporate interests to determine what levels of toxins are to be permitted in the country's food, air, and water, and ensuring that businesses comply with measures intended to protect our health and environment. Doug Bandow has spoken out in <u>Beyond Good Intentions: A Biblical View of Politics</u>, explaining that, "…as the state has expanded, individuals have abandoned many of their responsibilities to other human beings. Controlling pollution is no longer seen as a matter of proper stewardship of God's resources….Christians should be at the forefront of efforts to protect both the health of Americans and the beauty of the outdoors."[412]

Americans have good reason to be concerned about the effects on their families' health of the pollution generated in the United States. As one physician summarized our plight in 1991:

> Humanity is in the midst of a world crisis. We are rendering ourselves toxic and malnourished while simultaneously destroying the ecological balance that supports life on earth. The rate of population growth has far outstripped the rate of ecologically

---

[412] Doug Bandow, <u>Beyond Good Intentions: A Biblical View of Politics</u>, pp.229, 202.

> sound production, geometrically complicating an already perilous world state.
>
> The many problems that now face the United States are symptoms of this basic planetary condition—manifestations of a global bioecological catastrophe that is finally coming home to roost....
>
> The chronic diseases—both social and medical—are really symptoms of a much more vast underlying problem. They are the culmination of years of inadequate nutrition, a toxic environment, sedentary lifestyles, familial and social disruptions, and dependence on artificial agents (from cigarettes to cocaine) for happiness. Every cell in our bodies—from the brain to the immune system—is affected by these abuses. The effects are particularly devastating in developing children—both in and out of the womb. The massive and irreversible loss of human potential in the children of this world is the most disturbing aspect of this planetary destruction. With each underweight, malnourished child born to a malnourished, poorly educated, drug-or alcohol-addicted mother another bit of the future is lost.[413]

Especially when Americans produce more waste and consume more fuel, food and water per capita than any other country, at any time in history, it is incumbent upon Christian Americans to call attention to the environmental consequences of an ever-increasing and toxic cycle of consumption and growth. Abandonment of this function to government is unchristian. Government is

---

[413] Joseph D. Beasley, M.D., <u>The Betrayal of Health: The Impact of Nutrition, Environment, and Lifestyle on Illness in America</u>, pp. 3, 4.

not our representative before the Throne of Christ, now or at Judgment, and government cannot be expected to be competent or trustworthy, being by nature worldly. Richard N. Goodwin notes that social movements like environmentalism have learned that government will yield to their demands

> ...until, and only until, the sources of dominant social power appear to be threatened. Government undertakes to heal social afflictions only when they are problems of administration, that is, when solution is possible without upsetting the existing social process or, more particularly, the dominant private relationships of society. It cannot act effectively if the source of discontent is fundamental, residing in the design of society.[414]

But Goodwin does not see a conspiracy threatening America, just the natural forces of bureaucratic existence growing beyond accountability:

> Most federal money, for example, goes just where private money goes–into the industrial bureaucracy. To a large extent, the middle class is taxed in order to sustain the rich–not rich individuals–but rich institutions. Not only does public spending lead to private revenue, but money goes to the same kind of products....Even more significant than spending is the labyrinth of laws, agencies and commissions with formal authority to fashion and regulate much of our economic life. Thousands of studies conducted over decades tell how this legal structure

---

[414] Richard N. Goodwin, <u>The American Condition</u>, p. 330.

serves the interest of dominant economic forces. A decade ago, for example, experts and commissions indignantly proclaimed that regulatory agencies were more dedicated to the health of their regulated clients than to the "public good." Since then, nothing has changed.[415]

Goodwin, writing in 1971, seems to echo the Bible: when it comes to corporations and government, "[t]hey take care only of themselves...."[416]

We can see government and corporate America working together more intimately in the Bush administration than in any American presidential administration this century. In addition to tort reform and bankruptcy rule changes which favored business interests, George W. Bush has at every turn hindered mandatory environmental compliance measures. Even though "Texas pollutes more than any other state or Canadian province....,"[417] George W. as Governor protected industry polluters (particularly the oil industry) from efforts at pollution control, pushing instead for "voluntary compliance."[418] But pressing for voluntary compliance for corporate America is like entrusting convicted pedophiles to operate a daycare facility, for nowhere has environmental stewardship been more compromised than by corporations.

---

[415] Ibid., pp. 344-345, 346.
[416] Letter from Jude, 1:16, TEV.
[417] Molly Ivins and Lou Dubose, <u>Shrub: The Short But Happy Political Life of George W. Bush</u>, p. 107. The authors discuss at length Mr. Bush's intense efforts to help the oil industry, notwithstanding the appalling condition of Texas' environment.
[418] Ibid., p. 115.

COMPASSION FOR GOD'S CREATION 231

The Bush Administration's EPA[419] has continued Mr. Bush's Texas solution. Recently, in the case of mercury emissions, "…the EPA concluded that nonmercury toxic emissions "posed no hazards to public health."…. But that statement is based on findings of a 1998 EPA study that specifically requested further risk analysis for many non-mercury toxins, says Martha Keating, a senior scientist with the Clean Air Task Force, an environmental advocacy group."[420] Perhaps as with acid rain in the Reagan administration (a problem which was deferred until huge areas were defoliated), when those other toxic metals attain high enough levels to prohibit fish consumption or to defoliate mountains, then the government can again announce that it will begin to study them, wait seven years to *not* do the study that was announced, then make a decision without any study at

---

[419] It is more appropriate to hold President Bush responsible for the current EPA's actions than most any administration of the past, for this is an administration that retains a very strong hand on policy in all branches of government. For clear examples, see Bob Woodward's Bush at War for an account of how Colin Powell's State Department was ignored and circumvented because it didn't toe the neoconservative party line on Iraq; and Ron Suskind's The Price of Loyalty, where clear evidence is presented documenting that Christie Todd Whitman (EPA) and Paul J. O'Neill (Treasury Secretary) were by-passed and ignored by Bush, Cheney & co. despite their efforts to address global warming (p. 60) (the account of this incident contained in Ms. Whitman's recent book comports exactly with Mr. O'Neill's account), that Paul O'Neill was dismissed for speaking out against fiscally-irresponsible deficit spending through tax cuts, and that Bush steered policy in the so-called Social Security Commission: "On May 2, the President announced the formation of the Social Security Commission. All of the members of the commission had been pre-approved by Larry Lindsey or Karl Rove as supporters of private accounts." (p.156)

[420] Mark Clayton, "In bid to cut mercury, US lets other toxins through," *The Christian Science Monitor*, March 31, 2005, pp. 13, 16.

all. This is *exactly* what has been done by the Bush W. administration regarding nonmercury toxins.

In this bureaucratic pattern is seen the balancing of our children's future against what John Kenneth Galbraith calls "the freedom from present cost."[421] While previous administrations and generations have also been guilty of such short-sightedness, the environmental noose is getting tighter under George W. Bush. In this political subterfuge, government procrastinates: "Notably, it proposes more research, which very often provides a comforting, intellectually reputable gloss over inaction. At worst, it suggests impaneling a commission, the purpose of which would be to discuss and recommend action or perhaps postponement thereof."[422] This is what the Bush EPA did with regard to non-mercury toxic metals, and what George W. has done repeatedly in many areas.

But just as putting money in the hands of the poor stimulates the economy more than putting it in the bank accounts of the well-to-do, investing in pollution control technology is not an expense with no return. In addition to preserving clean air and water and thereby protecting human health, and in addition to the common sense concept that it is less costly to prevent pollution than to clean it up, the purchase of pollution control technologies creates whole new industries of which America could be the leader, but is losing out to the Europeans: "The purchase of clean air for a city would stimulate the

---

[421] John Kenneth Galbraith, <u>The Culture of Contentment</u>, p. 21.
[422] Ibid.

COMPASSION FOR GOD'S CREATION   233

economy at least as much as the acquisition of a missile or a truck."[423]

Perhaps a greater failure of this administration, but surely an unchristian policy, is that the W. Bush administration has refused to support energy conservation as a component of its energy policy. Even after a dramatic spike in oil prices in late 2004 which demonstrated how sensitive the U.S. economy is to oil prices, Bush "policy" still focused on finding more oil to consume domestically and abroad rather than finding ways to consume less oil.[424] A Bush energy legislation package before Congress in April 2005 was reported as follows:

> [The measure]…contains much of what Bush wants. But critics say it's also filled with unnecessary subsidies, over-reliance on nonrenewable resources like oil and coal, and an overall philosophy that even Energy Department economic analysts say won't significantly reduce dependence on foreign oil or affect the price at the pump….There's a national security dimension to the debate as well. Bush and much of Congress stress the need for more domestic petroleum production to offset the growing dependence on overseas sources (now totaling nearly 60 percent). "The more oil we can produce at home in environmentally sensitive ways, the less dependent we are on foreign sources of energy," Mr.

---

[423] Richard N. Goodwin, The American Condition, p.189.
[424] W. Bush talks much about alternative energy technologies, but these are pie-in-the-sky: even if they could be developed in time, alternative energy sources can not be incorporated into our lives fast enough to prevent dramatic economic decline. Reducing consumption offers immediate relief, but requires sacrifice of comfort *and* of corporate profits, a tough sell in a culture of contentment.

> Bush said in a speech....Others—including some prominent conservatives—see a need to radically reduce US consumption as a quicker way to energy independence.[425]

There is no dispute, no opinion logically questioning, that reducing consumption is indeed the quickest way to energy independence—in fact, energy independence is absolutely impossible without reducing consumption, and we knew this thirty years ago. Further, there is absolutely no disputing that we "need" to reduce US consumption "radically."

Instead, we look for more places to pump smaller and smaller oilfields, which won't be available to commerce for years, and whose production by then will have been outpaced by steadily increasing US (and world) demand—we simply can't produce enough oil domestically to meet our current needs, let alone our future burning desire.[426] This search for domestic production as a distraction from our consumption crisis leads to the false hope offered by the Arctic National Wildlife Refuge (ANWR) in Alaska. Of course, the oil industry (Bush really does "believe" in the oil industry) has been pushing to open ANWR to drilling since the late 1970s.[427] Mortimer Zuckerman observes:

---

[425] Brad Knickerbocker, "Soft vs. hard energy path: the political lines harden," *The Christian Science Monitor*, April 22, 2005, p. 2.

[426] Nor will alternative sources of oil solve this problem, for extraction costs are enormously greater for these methods than for our passing age of "cheap" oil. The economic crisis approaching America is inescapable, and is worsened every day that we fail to reduce our dependence by reducing consumption. *See* "Twilight for Oil?," *Barron's*, January 2, 2006, p. 30.

[427] Ron Suskind, <u>The Price of Loyalty</u>, p. 144.

There is much talk these days about energy independence–a fantasy. Any program to reduce our 60 percent dependence on foreign oil will take anywhere from 5 to 10 years. And neither the Republican answer–more production–nor the Democratic answer–more conservation–will solve the problem. Any coherent energy program[428] will require us to do both. It is also fantasy to imagine that we can rely on alternative power sources from waves or windmills or solar panels. That kind of power is weak, intermittent, and expensive–costing roughly twice the cost of the electrical power produced by either coal or gas….Most Americans believe they're entitled[429] to cheap fuel, regardless of how much they consume….and now, with just 5 percent of the world's population, we use a quarter of the world's oil…. We are…going to have to look for places to drill, such as the Arctic National Wildlife Refuge, which has become a symbolic issue to environmentalists. The refuge is far from the picture postcard of green forests and snowcapped mountains its defenders would have us believe.[430] It's the Alaskan

---

[428] Would Mortimer Zuckerman therefore call Bush's energy plan incoherent?

[429] Must be the underclass….

[430] The relevance of this comment must be challenged–what value system does "picture postcard" represent to wildlife seeking refuge? Mortimer reveals his consumptive perspective, viewing the first and highest use of national forests to be their tourism value, and ignoring the preservation of species, undisturbed by man, as a goal. Further, who are "its defenders"? Do these people who defend wildlife areas have suspect motives? "Defenders" of wildlife should not be a derogatory moniker. And it is disingenuous to question their integrity by suggesting that they've misled people–Mortimer is the one who here uses the label "picture postcard" and then debunks this characterization as proof that "the environmentalists" are not to be believed: *this* is misleading.

tundra[431]...Drilling there makes sense....This isn't to say that we should overlook the environmental consequences of fuel consumption....an unimaginable threat to our environment and a surefire guarantee of global warming.[432]

So what Mr. Zuckerman has just said is that we should tear up a "miniscule portion"[433] of ANWR because it's just tundra, then when we burn the fuel we reap we'll threaten our environment and warm the globe. As he rightly says,

this is one of the great national issues facing the nation, and there is no justifiable excuse for avoiding the kind of informed debate that must take place if we're to put a coherent policy in place before too much more time passes. The failure of our elected officials in both parties[434] to come to grips with this vital issue long before now is a national disgrace. Continued failure is not an option.[435]

But notwithstanding American denial, continued failure is more than an option—it is certain. Even with

---

[431] He disdainfully remarks, with environmental ignorance....What of the indigenous peoples who live there and whose way of life will be irrevocably altered by drilling? It is typical for Americans to ignore the effects on other cultures in the quest for consumptive comfort.

[432] Mortimer Zuckerman, "Our Energy Conundrum," *US News & World Report*, April 25, 2005, p. 72.

[433] Ibid.

[434] It's those politicians' fault, not those of us who burn the stuff and elect the candidate who promises to further Americans' number one platform plank—boost the economy.

[435] Ibid.

conservation, it is too little, too late, and George W. did not even suggest any kind of reduction in our economy-fueling consumption until after two massive hurricanes crippled America's Gulf Coast.

But again, ANWR is a political red herring, held up for Americans to see that politicians are doing something to correct our impending crisis. But it is form only. The government is not actually doing anything if it is not reducing consumption:

> Geologists estimate that there could be several billion barrels of oil beneath the Refuge, perhaps enough to supply as much as 3 percent of U.S. oil consumption by 2025....For the relatively short-term gain–what may amount to only a few months of U.S. oil consumption–Congress would be allowing permanent, irreparable ecological damage and endangering an Alaska Native culture.[436]

Again, even if one ignores environmental concerns in ANWR, 3 % by 2025 is a fart against thunder–the only meaningful answer that more drilling (of a different kind) might provide is if the scientific/mathematical need, the vital nation-saving necessity, of decreased consumption could be drilled into the heads of Dick Cheney and George W. Bush, and thus be passed on to the American people who don't want to hear it. Lack of accountability is a national illness in America. Christianity is the only cure.

---

[436] Friends Committee on National Legislation, *Washington Newsletter No. 696*, April 2005, p. 5.

Perhaps Americans should consider giving up their lawns (it won't do if just the politicians who we blame for our problems abandon their lawns). Not only are lawns aesthetically dubious (tall grass is beautiful too), they generate pesticide and fertilizer pollution in (literally) sickening quantities. There are "800 million gallons of gas burned in lawnmowers every year....[and] Americans pour as much as 238 gallons of water per person, per day onto lawns during the growing season."[437] Perhaps Americans could simply mow less frequently as a compromise–Lord knows too many people mow their lawns altogether too often (perhaps as recreation or to avoid spousal conflict). Alas, America's collective inaction to address its energy dependency will kill all the lawns in the End.

Yet many Americans, many of those Christian, still contest the evidence for global warming. This is merely avoidance of responsibility, and of the need to change our consumptive behaviors. But also it's driven by fear of reality and a sense of powerlessness. But Christie Todd Whitman has stated: "There's no question but that global warming is a real phenomenon."[438] And there is no question that the USA is "responsible for more carbon dioxide emissions than any other country in the world."[439]

A lucid discussion of our modern imprisonment in pollution as a consequence of our consumptive-

---

[437] Thomas Hayden, "Could the Grass be Greener?," *US News & World Report*, May 16, 2005, p. 57.
[438] Ron Suskind, The Price of Loyalty, p. 99.
[439] Ibid., p. 101.

capitalist-materialist culture is found in Richard N. Goodwin:

> We buy pollution. Unlike a television set, this purchase is usually available to purchasers and non-purchasers alike, but it is paid for. Most people who buy a car or a ream of typing paper do not want to purchase pollution. They have no choice; it comes with the product. Their inability to choose is not an aspect of natural order, but an imposition of the economic structure and its political satellite. One cannot expect current economic bureaucracies to change this. Exhortations to "social responsibility" are equivalent to having advised the medieval Church to abandon the concept of salvation after death in order to encourage more vigorous pursuit of happiness in this world.[440]

We have turned the Christian spirit upside down in America, allowing commerce and comfort to rule us into our own physical deaths, and we're taking the planet with us.

Wendell Berry, in <u>The Unsettling of America</u>, observes that the American surrender to technology would result in a dependency much like that sought by Satan of Jesus on the Mountain:

> The technology of infinity (however that might be defined) would be vast and exclusive. It would be completely totalitarian, whether "publically" or "privately" owned. It would overthrow the whole

---

[440] Richard N. Goodwin, <u>The American Condition</u>, p. 394.

issue of control, for it would be the control. Since everyone would be totally dependent on it, it would necessarily be everyone's first consideration. [Even those who operated massive technological operations would more likely] be the absolute slaves of their machinery, no less dependent on it....The machine would become an anti-god–if not infinite, at least absolute. To have even the illusion of infinite quantity, we would have to debase both the finite and the infinite; we would have to sacrifice both flesh and spirit. It is an old story. Evil is offering us the world: "All these things will I give thee, if thou wilt fall down and worship me." And we have only the old paradox for an answer: If we accept all on that condition, we lose all.

What is new is the guise of the evil: a limitless technology, dependent upon a limitless morality, which is to say upon no morality at all. How did such a possibility become thinkable? It seems to me that it is implicit in the modern separation of life and work. It is implicit in the assumption that we can live entirely apart from our way of making a living....If human values are removed from production, how can they be preserved in consumption? How can we value our lives if we devalue them in making a living?[441]

Mr. Berry's insights are easily shrugged off by the amoral technological society, built on the "moral" precept of "Progress," which he condemns. But the moral decay he described in 1977 is more evident today: "'Consumers want muscle cars, manufacturers say they make

---

[441] Wendell Berry, <u>The Unsettling of America: Culture & Agriculture</u>, pp. 78-79.

what the consumer wants, and the government panders to both constituencies….It's a vicious cycle.'"[442]

And yet Americans, Christians amongst them, continue to leap faithfully into the newest technology, a great shift in social conscience since just 60 years ago, when many were suspicious of electricity and other startling innovations. And we continue to burn fuel thoughtlessly, mindless of God's sorrow at our failure as stewards. Like those who pursue other worldly pleasures without regard to moral consequence, those who ignore the effects of consumption and accompanying pollution are like those "Other people [who] are selfish and reject what is right, in order to follow what is wrong; on them God will pour out his anger and fury. There will be suffering and pain for all those who do what is evil…."[443]

> "Our environmental policy set high standards for stewardship…."[444]
> —"Words" of George W. Bush

Christian words, unchristian actions….

---

[442] Lee Schipper, head of transportation research at World Resources Institute, quoted in "Gas prices too high? Try Europe," Peter Ford, *The Christian Science Monitor*, August 26, 2005, p. 10.
[443] Romans 2:8-9, TEV.
[444] George W. Bush, from Thomas A. Freiling, George W. Bush on God & Country, p. 126.

Chapter 7

THE RICH, THE DEFICIT, AND WHAT TRICKLES DOWN

> "...[The] trickle down theory–...that if one feeds the horse enough oats, some will pass through to the road for the sparrows."[445]

George W. Bush proclaimed in loud words his belief in smaller federal government when he sought the nation's highest office. His actions have expanded government expense and government intrusion into American citizens' lives at a rate that would make Franklin Delano Roosevelt blush. And this increase in federal bureaucracy was not necessitated by 9/11–though 9/11 made it possible. The NCLB was not necessitated by terrorism; the Iraq War was independently planned prior to 9/11, and none of the 9/11 terrorists were Iraqis or linked to Iraq; the Homeland Security Department is more political pork and alarmism than it is actual defense; military

---
[445] John Kenneth Galbraith, <u>The Culture of Contentment</u>, p. 108.

expenditures have not made us safer, and have yet to be paid for; bunker-busters are not justified in Christ, common sense, or conventional war-planning assessment; and still *more* tax cuts, against financial experts' advice, were pushed through Congress *after* 9/11, at tremendous economic risk.

Myron Magnet quotes Thomas Paine for the proposition that "the animating principle of all societies remains nothing but the oppression of the poor and weak by the rich and powerful,"[446] and he cites Jean-Jacques Rousseau (with whom he does not disagree), who "once said that the rich, with feelings in every part of their possessions, would cease to feel happy if the poor ceased to feel miserable. Only the comparison allowed them to measure the magnitude of their own good fortune."[447] But the "animating principle" of Christian society is the opposite, for "…Hath not God chosen the poor of this world rich in faith, and heirs of the kingdom which he hath promised to them that love him?"[448] Faithful Christians aspire to make the poor less miserable, and are measured by their success or failure in this regard.

The wealthy are called by Christianity, and by any sense of conscience, to be responsible with their wealth so that it not be squandered and so that it be employed in buoying the poor in their hardship. Teddy Roosevelt once said that "a man of great wealth owes a particular obligation to the state because he derives special

---

[446] Myron Magnet, <u>The Dream and the Nightmare: the Sixties' Legacy to the Underclass</u>, pp. 161-162.
[447] Ibid., p. 126.
[448] James 2:5, KJV.

advantage from the mere existence of government."[449] And George W. has emphasized this theme in foreign aid: "To help developing nations achieve these goals, leaders of wealthy nations have a duty of conscience. We have a duty to share our wealth generously and wisely."[450] Hebrews 13:5 instructs Christians to "Keep your lives free from the love of money, and be satisfied with what you have. For God has said, "I will never leave you; I will never abandon you." "[451]

But the forces of this world, particularly capitalism and materialism, are directly in opposition to the Christian concept of sharing. Those liberals in the 1960s were well-intentioned: sharing–more equitably redistributing wealth–is what 1960s welfare programs were intended to accomplish (even if they often fall short), and is what compassionate conservatism essentially argues against (arguing that sharing by government makes the poor dependent,....but no one told this to Jesus). Discussing the philosophical aspects of the effect of industrialism and capitalism on mankind, one writer recalls of the philosopher Hegel, that "[n]ot only does Hegel fully acknowledge the emasculating effects…caused by the division of labor, but he is also aware of the social inequality that the wealth of nations necessarily creates: the antithesis emerges between great wealth and great

---

[449] Mortimer Zuckerman, "So the Rich Get Richer?," *US News & World Report*, May 2, 2005, p. 72.
[450] George W. Bush, from Thomas A. Freiling, George W. Bush on God & Country, p. 245.
[451] Hebrews 13:5, TEV.

poverty....to him who has, more is given."[452] We see these "market forces" at work in, e.g., the higher interest rates (for all lending) and insurance rates paid by those with poor or no credit, the unearned income of those with wealth (particularly tax-exempt municipal bonds), and exclusionary zoning which excludes the poor from even modest gains in the real estate market.

George W.'s oft-avowed devotion to free market forces means that these "natural" (i.e. untempered by government or morality) forces will continue to concentrate wealth in the hands of those who already possess wealth at the expense of those who do not. Of one of Bush's policies as Texas Governor, Ivins and Dubose (who chronicle endless Bush actions as Governor favoring the wealthy or disadvantaging the poor) observed: "As our economy keeps producing greater and greater distortions in income distribution—every study shows the rich have become vastly more rich while everybody else is stuck in place—Bush's proposal means the end of democracy and a direct leap into oligopoly, rule by the rich."[453] This degree of alarm by these authors may seem extreme, but it is hardly a whisper of warning when assessed against the impending and (now) inevitable collapse of America's financial structures, currency, and food distribution system occasioned by the over-reaching by the wealthy (as occurred with the Romans, French,

---

[452] Susan Buck-Morss, "Envisioning Capital: Political Economy on Display," from Lynne Cook and Peter Wollen, eds., <u>VISUAL DISPLAY: Culture Beyond Appearances</u>, p.132.
[453] Molly Ivins and Lou Dubose, <u>Shrub: The Short But Happy Political Life of George W. Bush</u>, p. 168.

and British, amongst others), unsupportable debt, and an ungodly dependency on oil.

In <u>The Politics of Rich and Poor: Wealth and the American Electorate in the Reagan Aftermath</u>, Kevin Phillips warns of the consequences to the privileged of ignoring, under any rationalization, the conditions in which the rest of America's citizens find themselves:

> Besides promoting speculation, past realignments of wealth to the rich…have hurt the bottom half of Americans by effects ranging from rural and small-town decay to urban crime, weakened families and lost opportunity for the unskilled. Indeed, previous American polarizations of wealth–combining easy money at the top with loss of hope and faith at the bottom–were also accompanied by the same conspicuous consumption and short-term "now" values that conservative spokesmen found themselves deploring in the last months of the 1980s.[454]

History repeats itself, with George W. employing the same hat tricks as the Reagan administration,[455] "[w]here Republican presidential cycles evolve into free-market excesses and the overconcentration of wealth…."[456] and

---

[454] At p. 217.
[455] "…the Great Divide between rich and poor in America is perhaps the most troubling legacy of the 1980s." Kevin Phillips, <u>The Politics of Rich and Poor: Wealth and the American Electorate in the Reagan Aftermath</u>, at page 211, quoting *BusinessWeek*, September 1989.
[456] Ibid., p. 38.

similarly we see consumption grow conspicuously[457] to absorb the surplus capital returned to the wealthy from tax refunds with no place to profitably invest it–if the economy has no new growth industries, placing money in the hands of the capitalists does not ensure economic growth, but only encourages spending, stock market investing, or saving.[458] The demise of the British (and most any other) Empire was attended by the ludicrous excesses of wealth and social pretense affected by the British nobility, but such spending not only failed to stimulate growth, it encouraged unrest because of the increasingly glaring contrast between the Haves and the Have-Nots. The American 1920s saw the same pattern of excess and ebullience created by surplus (and therefore unutilized) capital–spending and speculation combined to plunge the US economy into a flaming tailspin which only large-scale government spending programs could hold in abeyance, and which only war could extinguish.

---

[457] "As 1989 unfolded, so did a new wave of conspicuous consumption." Ibid., p. 210. This has been recently repeated, with a 2004-2005 balloon in sales of luxury goods across America in the face of declining sales in almost every other sector of the economy. The wealthy enjoy their sense of superior position all the way up to the end, which end hasn't already arrived in America because of the unprecedented and unanticipated explosion of wealth created by the dot-com technological explosion, and the run-up in residential real estate "values." (soon to pop!)

[458] "Historically, some of the greatest spurts of demand for luxury goods have occurred when the mantle of innovation passed from one economy to another. At such times, investors in the fading economy often have few productive opportunities to exploit....In such circumstances, spending money for personal luxury is a rational choice." James Dale Davidson and Sir William Rees-Mogg, Blood In the Streets: Investment Profits in a World Gone Mad, p. 250.

Richard N. Goodwin confronts the eclipse of genuine debate about issues of social justice by the pressures of commercialism and bureaucracy:

> The most traditional form of bondage is that imposed by material necessity. Hunger and deprivation are historical constants but the nature of poverty–its form and its relationship to the possibilities of freedom–depends upon the particular conditions of each society. American poverty and the barriers to its elimination are consequences of the same social process which dominates the life of every citizen…. The existence of economic "worth" is not a transcendent fact, but the expression of these social values which are enforced by the economic process….One invariably finds interests which command a share of wealth in excess of the concentrated accumulation needed for growth. The result is a surplus of poverty in excess of economic requirements. This power to command wealth–economic strength–is conferred by the ideology which sustains a particular social structure.[459]

In other words, social structures like government, class, remuneration for labor, etc., permit the accumulation of wealth beyond that necessary for capital investment, which invariably results in greater poverty than is necessary given that same society's resources. America, with the greatest collective natural and human (ingenuity) resources in the history of man, has proven the truth of this recurrent worldly failing, even while

---

[459] Richard N. Goodwin, <u>The American Condition</u>, pp. 195, 196.

pretending to look to Christ for guidance in government and society. Yet even our poorest are conditioned to parrot the party line that "America is the greatest nation in the world"—is that title earned? It often seems that other nations aren't even considered worthy of comparison, an arrogant attitude which prevents national self-analysis while alienating the world from America and its supposed greatness. Most Americans have never traveled abroad, yet that rarely dampens their conviction that they are the cat's meow of humanity.

Yet as Goodwin recounts, America was not borne into the industrial age by Jesus Christ, but by the advent of science and technology, by the influences of Darwin and Isaac Newton's Laws of Science:

> This age of secular systems was the transition from divine order to contemporary disorder....Time and corruption revealed that the market, like all economic institutions, was merely a social creation, bound and defined by custom and the legal structure, themselves sustained by the relationships of power and interest which emerged from early industrialism. The ideology of non-interference[460] disguised the fact that everyone involved in the market was struggling each day to distort and master its operation in their own interest; that power and wealth bred power and wealth independently of existing economic logic, law or system....The poor and impotent are rarely heard in defense of the freedom to be left alone.[461]

---

[460] I.e., Bush W.'s and Bush Sr.'s ideology, of "free" markets, of "private" capital flows.
[461] Richard N. Goodwin, <u>The American Condition</u>, p. 292.

Goodwin explains that the goal of liberal philosophy was to regulate and police markets to advance equal opportunity and social justice, to promote "the assertion of human needs adverse to the interests of dominant economic institutions."[462]

But, Goodwin concludes, liberalism was idealistic, and was thus impaled on the rocks of market forces. Liberalism failed in its quest because

> the effort to "perfect" the market turned toward the creation of a central government strong and resourceful enough to regulate and control powerful economic interests. This was the guiding faith of modern liberalism. We needed power to check power, public authority to prevent private abuses....It was not foreseen that economic and political power, instead of checking one another, might become leagued in pursuits and structures often hostile to the power of the individual citizen. Yet that has been the fate of the final liberal effort to perfect the market.[463]

The conservative alternative has generally been a hands-off approach—either option leaves corporate and wealthy America steering policy, influencing everything from health and diet to military growth and foreign policy.

Though it might entail some guilt or increased self-awareness, at least there would be some integrity in admitting that unbridled free market capitalism invariably improves the lot of the wealthy at the expense of

---

[462] Ibid., p. 293.
[463] Ibid., pp. 294-295.

the poor. Instead, those favored by this system create dogma that justifies their superior perch therein. John Kenneth Galbraith observes that wealthy people believe they deserve their wealth so strongly that the "normal response…is anger at anything infringing on what is so clearly deserved."[464] We thus gain insight into the indignant pretense by millionaire Republicans that they are neither responsible for the sorrows of others, nor do they owe them relief. Myron Magnet dismisses the obvious increase in wealth disparity caused by Reagan's trickle-down shenanigans as irrelevant: "So even if the economic developments of the eighties did increase the disparity in income between the rich and the poor,…those developments don't explain why we have an underclass or why the homeless haunt the streets."[465] Another conservative writer has the Galbraithian indignation to declare that "envy of the "rich" cannot be allowed to destroy a powerful economic system,"[466] which is nonsense when used as a defense of privilege, for surely "[t]he

---

[464] John Kenneth Galbraith, <u>The Culture of Contentment</u>, p. 19.

[465] Myron Magnet, <u>The Dream and the Nightmare: the Sixties' Legacy to the Underclass</u>, p. 13. But those developments easily explained the increase in the number of homeless that occurred during Reagan's tenure. And Magnet apparently ignores the chicken-and-egg logic which overlooks the poverty of the underclass which existed long before the welfare programs which he faults for its creation. He never answers his own question….why do we have an underclass? (Oh yeah, the liberals created them with government programs….) Frighteningly, this belief is what motivates President Bush's policy-making.

[466] William E. Simon, <u>A Time for Truth</u>, p. 219. Again, George W. ascribes strongly to this view, as reflected in his repeated statements that the privileged should not, and he in fact does not, feel guilty about their position, what he calls their "luck." But will failure to address the complaints of the poor, of their so-called "envy," itself be the cause which "destroy[s] a powerful economic system?"

elimination of poverty—an equivalent to the creation of consumers—would greatly expand the market [and].... would enhance the well-being of the entire nation...."[467] But Simons isn't content with discouraging jealousy—he refutes all history and human experience in his defense of the virtues of capitalism and in his condemnation of those who would challenge his right to have more toys than any of the other kids on the block:

> The crude linkage between wealth and evil, poverty and virtue is false, stupid, and of value only to demagogues, parasites, and criminals—indeed, the three groups that alone have profited from the linkage....The American citizen must be made aware that today a relatively small group of people is proclaiming its purposes to be the will of the People.[468] That elitist approach to government must be repudiated. There is no such thing as the People; it is a collectivist myth....There is only one social system that reflects this sovereignty of the individual: [the free-market capitalist system]....[T]he fundamental guiding principles of American life have, in fact, been reversed;...we are careening with frightening speed toward collectivism and away from individual sovereignty; toward coercive centralized planning and away from free individual choices, toward a statist-dictatorial system and away from a nation in which individual liberty is sacred.[469]

---

[467] Richard N. Goodwin, The American Condition, p. 197.
[468] George W. Bush has proclaimed such a mandate, despite his narrow wins in 2000 and 2004 and the intense division he has personally engendered in our nation.
[469] William E. Simon, A Time for Truth, pp. 220, 221, 222.

But Simon has just called Jesus "false, stupid" and a "demagogue, parasite, or criminal," for Christianity powerfully connects "poverty and virtue" and "wealth and evil." James 1:10 reminds us that "the rich will pass away like the flower of a wild plant."[470] And Jesus gives a camel better odds of squeezing through the eye of a needle than he does a rich person through the gates of heaven. (See Mark 10:25, Matthew 19:23, or Luke 18:23). What's more, Simon is elevating individualism as the motivating force in America, idolizing "individual liberty" as "sacred." Clearly, not only liberals and moral relativism worship self–some conservatives are open converts, under the auspices of free market economics. And self-worship is sinful, and the root of much of Americans' modern misery.

Non-Christian conservatives may understandably suffer from such warped belief systems, but Christian conservatives ignore Christ's teachings if they succumb to rationalizations which ignore the disparities in America's wealth:

> Scripture also challenges all people to follow Christ rather than money; wealthy believers face an especially stiff challenge in avoiding the temptations posed by riches....A poor person who turns to government to seize the possessions of his richer neighbors, no less than a wealthy man who devotes his life to making money in the marketplace, has fallen in love with this world....And there is no convincing prudential

---

[470] TEV.

reason to confiscate money from people simply because they have high incomes.[471]

Bandow clearly resents a government which seeks to "expropriate" the earnings of innovators "to satisfy the envy of a few."[472] There are certainly entitlement-mentality'd, lazy opportunists on the nation's welfare rolls, but that hardly makes all poor people guilty of "envy" and determined to "seize the possessions," "expropriate the earnings," or "confiscate the money" of the wealthy–many of them may just want to eat, without regard to envy or covetousness. The condition of those who are in genuine need cannot in clean Christian conscience be dismissed by the example of those who bilk the system, and there are many "convincing prudential reasons" for a progressive tax structure, including not just relief for those genuinely in need but the self-preservation of those in plenty–the State protects the wealthy when it provides for the poor, as does Christianity. To where have Simon and Bandow relegated those truly impoverished who humbly await each periodic welfare stipend because they haven't the training, opportunity, health or ability to do differently? Thomas A Kempis wrote that

> [Nature] desires recognition, and to do such things as win praise and admiration....Nature takes pleasure in a host of friends and relations; she boasts of noble rank and high birth; makes herself agreeable

---

[471] Doug Bandow, <u>Beyond Good Intentions: A Biblical View of Politics</u>, pp. 205, 206, 207.
[472] Ibid., p.206.

> to the powerful, flatters the rich, and acclaims those who are like herself. But Grace loves even her enemies, takes no pride in the number of her friends, and thinks little of high birth unless it be applied to the greater virtue. She favours the poor rather than the rich, and has more in common with the honourable than with the powerful. She takes pleasure in an honest man, not a deceiver….she is not arrogant and presumptuous. She does not argue and exalt her own opinions before others.[473]

There is only one Christ. Thus, gay marriage cannot be both OK and not OK with Jesus. Capital punishment is likewise not a multiple answer concern for Christians—either Christ is forgiving of capital punishment or he considers it sinful. Similarly, there is no split-personality, pick-your-issue Christ on whether the comfortable should assist the poor—Jesus was abundantly lucid on the subject. And whether or not liberal Christians have been true to Christ's teachings when devising welfare policies, it is clear that the Republican concept of compassionate conservatism has meant no actions, only steadily decreasing economic assistance for our nation's poorest under President Bush. Didn't Jesus praise the widow for giving the little money she had, or did he administer a stern lecture on the merits of hard labor and a flat tax? Jesus did not stomach laziness, but His compassion for the poor and unwell define Him. It's what being Christ, or Christian, is all about—help thy brother, thy neighbor…all the more so if his need

---

[473] Thomas A. Kempis, <u>The Imitation of Christ</u>, p. 170.

is great. Where are the Christian actions to match the words of compassionate conservatism?

But the widening of America's income disparities is not a recent development—it's been going on for decades, most notably during the Reagan presidency. Kevin Phillips recounts in <u>The Politics of Rich and Poor: Wealth and the American Electorate in the Reagan Aftermath</u>:

> For women, young people and minorities the effect of economic polarization during the 1980s was largely negative....Overall, a disproportionate number of women, young people, blacks and Hispanics were among the decade's casualties....And none of it augured well for the future skills level and competitiveness of the U.S. work force....[474]

> To Americans with long memories, the policy thrust of the Reagan years toward inequality had not been a coincidence. Simultaneous top-bracket gains and bottom-echelon stagnation represented a familiar politics. Other Republican political cycles and administrations had been there before....[D]uring the 1980s—and not for the first time in U.S. history—Reagan's GOP became a high-powered vehicle...for the accumulation of wealth by a relatively narrow elite.[475]

---

[474] This is not partisan statistic-twisting—it is irrefutable, acknowledged fact (as specifically recognized even by Myron Magnet) that wealth disparity increased dramatically under Reagan, and that minorities and women got the short end of the stick. Denying the truth of the effects of trickle-down economics may help the wealthy accumulate goodies, but it doesn't fly with Jesus Christ.

[475] Phillips, <u>The Politics of Rich and Poor: Wealth and the American Electorate in the Reagan Aftermath</u>, pp. 208, 202, 31, 33. And now history has been repeated again with the 2000-2006 Bush tenure.

Americans do not require "long memories" to realize that "the policy thrust" of the Bush presidency "toward inequality," so closely patterned after the failed policies of Reaganomics, is likewise not a coincidence. This is not a conspiracy theory, but simply a recognition that those who have wealth and capital (traditionally, the Republicans have been strongly associated with wealth, however much they try to shake off that justified perception) tend in free-market economies to influence government and government policies in a manner which will maximize their own reward. The French aristocracy truly believed that it did the poor a favor by ruling over them, the Soviet politburo was fanatically loyal to the Communist Party at the expense of human freedom, and America's wealthy have no doubt that they are the best ones to be trusted with decision-making regarding capital allocation. America's upper class has faith in the "free" market to win the day, even though history repeatedly teaches us that capitalism ruthlessly oppresses the bottom ladder rungs of industrial workers, in a worldly display of heartless Darwinism in direct opposition to the core meaning of Christianity. America's wealthy are contented in monetary assets, but discontented in soul: for Christian or non-Christian alike, and notwithstanding George W.'s salving talk about not feeling guilty, no one with any conscience in America can ignore the disparities between the Haves and the Have-Nots that grow shamefully larger every year.

Indeed, a recent Federal Reserve report, "…the most comprehensive survey of household wealth,…found a widening of the gap between households at the top and the bottom of the economic ladder. "While the typical American household basically ran in place, less affluent households actually lost ground [between 2001-2004]," said Stephen Brobeck, executive director of the Consumer Federation of America."[476]

For conservatives, tax policy goes hand in hand with free-market economics and government deregulation. Thus, Republican tax policy has tended toward "flat" taxation under the rationale that the rich should not be unfairly penalized, and that the capital of the "entrepreneurs" (even though they be sunbathing passive income earners) should be freed for reinvestment. The tragedy is that this rationalization is another example of the culture of contentment leading to its own destruction. If the wealthy promise rewards to the poor if they (the wealthy) are just trusted to allocate wealth where it will grow and produce rewards for all (the "trickle-down" theory), then they will surely bear the blame, in this world and the next, if those rewards fail to materialize. Those wealthy Americans who contentedly pursue self while blaming "society" and forces beyond their control for the suffering of others risk killing the proverbial golden goose.

The current Bush administration economic policy is déjà vu. As Kevin Phillips has written:

> …this same Republican values system becomes increasingly selfish, speculative and counterproductive as GOP cyclical dominance becomes entrenched….

---

[476] Christopher Conkey, "Typical U.S. Family's Net Worth Edged Up Only 1.5% in '01-'04," *The Wall Street Journal*, February 24, 2006, p. A4.

> Bush's[477] continued opposition to tax increases[478] reflected Republican support for business and financial activity at the cost of new money for education, the aging, the U.S. transportation infrastructure, housing, drug control and the rising number of children in poverty....[T]he commitment to market economics, the free flow of capital and the uninhibited accumulation of wealth were deeply held principles of Republican faith....Policies of sharp tax-bracket reductions, unprecedented federal deficits and borrowing at high real interest rates, along with deregulation, permissive finance, massive borrowing overseas and consequent sales of U.S. assets and companies, accelerated America's relative economic decline beyond what would have occurred in a less avaricious environment....Washington's excessive commitment to private wealth worked against the national interest.[479]

The current President Bush is surely accelerating "America's relative economic decline beyond what would have occurred" if we had stayed out of Iraq, not engaged in short-sighted tax refunds, and focused on contributing to real economic growth coupled with frugality. Our "national interest" is more gravely threatened by runaway debt than it is by terrorists.

The cumulative effect of these tax policy shifts has been not only an increasing wealth disparity in

---

[477] (Senior)
[478] Galbraith tells us that for those in positions of relative economic superiority, "...resentment to taxes for whatever reason is basic in their culture of contentment." (The Culture of Contentment, p. 86.)
[479] Kevin Phillips, The Politics of Rich and Poor: Wealth and the American Electorate in the Reagan Aftermath, pp. 215-216, 216, 217, 218.

America but also a de facto implementation of a flat tax system:

> Ever since the introduction of the modern income tax in 1913, US policy has been guided by the notion that the rich should pay a larger [sic] of their income in federal taxes, since they arguably owe something extra to a government that protects their greater wealth, and to a society that has helped them prosper....
>
> Chalk up President Bush as not just a tax cutter but also a tax flattener. Under Mr. Bush and a Republican Congress, big tax cuts since 2001 have given major tax reductions to those wealthy individuals presumed, up to now, to be able to afford paying a bigger chunk of their income in taxes. By one measure of the federal, state, and local tax burden, just 3.4 percentage points separate the effective tax rate paid by the top 1 percent of earners from the other 99 percent of American households....
>
> If the Bush tax cuts are made permanent by Congress, by 2010 billionaires and millionaires will be paying a smaller percentage of their income in federal taxes than those in the upper middle class, according to a calculation by Brian Roach, an economist at Tufts University, in Medford, Mass....
>
> All income tax brackets have got tax cuts under Bush. But the reductions for less affluent Americans are smaller, proportionally, than those for the millionaires and billionaires.[480]

---

[480] David R. Francis, "US already moving toward a flat tax," *The Christian Science Monitor*, April 14, 2005, p. 3.

Whether or not George W. intends or professes to implement a flat tax is irrelevant–he is implementing one. Actions speak louder than words....

Despite the apparent logical appeal of a flat tax (that everyone pay the same percentage), the concept encounters a number of obvious problems and is therefore rejected by almost all taxation scholars. Because of the various financial benefits that wealth provides, those with wealth always have an advantage. But the biggest problem with a flat tax is that it "...may have some economic merit in capital formation, but it strikes a negative chord for tax equity."[481] That negative chord is the payroll tax, which already burdens lower wage earners. The flat tax suffers from "the apparent injustice to the little guy, even the middle class. For example, besides the fact that wages are taxed, and capital income is not, payroll taxes continue for the wage earner. And a majority of working people pay more in payroll taxes than they do in income tax."[482] As even Marvin Olasky has acknowledged, "[t]he payroll tax is a flat tax, paid disproportionately by low and middle class workers."[483] Thus this administration favors, and in fact has effected, a tax policy shift which leaves the regressive payroll tax in place while further reducing tax rates on capital (dividends, interest, and capital gains, which are not "earned" or labor-related income). This is classic republican favor-the-rich tax policy at its greatest height in U.S. history. "These are

---

[481] Charles Adams, <u>Those Dirty Rotten Taxes: The Tax Revolts That Built America</u>, p. 218.
[482] Ibid., p. 220.
[483] Marvin Olasky, "No basketball player left behind," *The Christian Science Monitor*, January 27, 2005, p. 9.

the methods of the old elites, who time and again put their own self-interest above the interest of the people they claim to serve....They deserve true leaders."[484]

But George W. was no true leader by this measure while Governor of Texas. Ivins and Dubose write of their home state that, because of the lack of an income tax, "we have the third most regressive tax structure in the country; in fact, looked at as a financial entity, the state of Texas is a system of income redistribution that takes from the poor and gives to the rich."[485] John Kenneth Galbraith focused on the crux of the problem: without balancing against market forces some form of income redistribution by government, capitalism would focus wealth in the hands of the wealthy until the system collapsed: "the only effective design for diminishing the income inequality inherent in capitalism is the progressive income tax. Nothing in the age of contentment has contributed so strongly to income inequality as the reduction of taxes on the rich...."[486]

Essentially, if nothing else, progressive tax systems are a bulwark against the "natural" free market forces which invariably consume themselves in violent swings of fortune if left unchecked: the wealthy have the most to gain by paying an extra 10% or 20% more of their wealth in taxes if this prevents instability and a

---

[484] George W. Bush, from Thomas A. Freiling, <u>George W. Bush on God & Country</u>, p. 231. Actually George W. Bush is not guilty of hypocrisy here, for he has merely rewarded his base in the fashion for which he was installed. Thus, he has acted for the financial benefit of "the people [he] claim[s] to serve."

[485] Molly Ivins and Lou Dubose, <u>Shrub: The Short But Happy Political Life of George W. Bush</u>, p. 136.

[486] John Kenneth Galbraith, <u>The Culture of Contentment</u>, p. 179.

threat to the other 80%-90%. But neither George W. Bush nor wealthy American Christians should require appeals to their self interest in order to persuade them to embrace equitable tax structures and rates. An appeal to Jesus would presumably be sufficient. The New Testament warns that "...those who want to get rich fall into temptation and are caught in the trap of many foolish and harmful desires, which pull them down to ruin and destruction. For the love of money is a source of all kinds of evil. Some have been so eager to have it that they have wandered away from the faith and have broken their hearts with many sorrows."[487] Paul tells us in Romans: "Share your belongings with needy fellow Christians, and open your homes to strangers."[488] And Jesus teaches the wealthy man that "If thou wilt be perfect, go and sell that thou hast, and give to the poor, and thou shalt have treasure in heaven: and come and follow me."[489]

Which brings us to the next magical economic cure-all in the Republican bag of tricks of illusion, "trickle-down" economics. Although George W. "had little experience in economic analysis,"[490] and even though Christians are admonished to "Keep away from foolish and ignorant arguments,"[491] this has not discouraged George W. Bush from implementing

---

[487] 1 Timothy 6:9-10, TEV.
[488] Romans 12:13, TEV.
[489] Matthew 19:21, KJV.
[490] Ron Suskind, The Price of Loyalty, p. 35. Or in education, or in foreign policy–additional areas where George has instituted similar dramatic government policy shifts.
[491] 2 Timothy 2:23, TEV.

dramatic "supply-side" tax refunds, what his own father called "voodoo economics."[492] "Voodoo economics" is an apt catchphrase for the "faith" required to institute dynamic tax law changes which place government in massive debt, exposed to the risks of the future, when history and Reagan have demonstrated that trickle-down economics is like a perpetual motion machine—it exists only in theory, and will never work. Perhaps when we begin to pay off what Reagan incurred in national indebtedness for now-obsolete military arsenals, we may begin to realize that borrowing massive funds and then spending them, with little hope of return other than a small percentage in increased tax revenues, works no better for the national government than it would for a high school graduate who thinks he's rich because he got a big credit line on his Mastercard.

There is no uncertainty or "gray area" concerning trickle-down slopponomics. As Allan Bloom notes, economics is far from a science. Markets are driven more by psychology than capital, and they are more often irrational than sober. But trickle-down theory is easily dispelled by both common sense and experience.

With economics one can double count or explain away almost any figure, or allude to vague concepts that were only theories anyway, though now embraced as "laws." Goodwin explains that Keynes' logic led to the bureaucracy and technology logic embraced by America's markets, which in turn "stripp[ed] modern economic thought of any concern with the entire social

---

[492] Joseph Nocera, <u>A Piece of the Action: How the Middle Class Joined the Money Class</u>, p. 214.

process or ultimate human ends….[Economics is] a discipline whose entire function is to support…the existing economic process."[493] In other words, America's embrace of Keynesian economic theory and the goal of wealth maximization took hold so quickly and powerfully that it occluded considerations of social justice. As Alan Greenspan cautioned shortly after the Bush (Sr.)-Reagan deficit run-up, "The federal deficit was so high and cumulatively unstable, Greenspan said, that increased government spending to increase jobs–in accordance with the traditional model–no longer worked."[494] Thus, America broke the Keynesian economic model with debt, killing the golden goose of its own glory, a glory which is itself tarnished by the consistent failure of America to have ever set aside that small portion of her vast resources necessary to lift its poor citizenry out of poverty, though it possessed the wealth to feed and clothe the entire world many times over.

And this bureaucratic American economic system, which rewards returns only of a monetary kind, coupled its ethics with the culture of contentment, a rhetoric-generating, self-serving belief system that seeks to feel justified, even righteous, in its possession of more wealth than others (i.e., compassionate conservatism). The result was Ronald Reagan and trickle-down economics,

---

[493] Richard N. Goodwin, The American Condition, pp. 373, 374. Foreshadowing the stellar spike in executive pay, options, and stock market returns, Goodwin also saw that "the rewards bestowed by the large modern, economic bureaucracies bear an increasingly more tenuous relationship to economic productivity." (p. 197)

[494] Bob Woodward, Maestro: Greenspan's Fed and the American Boom, p. 96.

The Rich, the Deficit, and What Trickles Down

and now George W. Bush with the same nutritionless cure for the patient who is still ailing from the last quack remedy. John Kenneth Galbraith sums up the Reagan economic legacy, which almost all economists agree was proof positive that trickle-down economics is a failed economic fantasy:

> Ronald Reagan's single most celebrated economic action, the acceptance of the related budget deficit possibly apart, was his tax relief for the very affluent....In the 1980s, the percentage of very rich Americans...who derived their wealth from financial operations grew enormously. The share gaining great rewards from manufacturing...declined precipitously....The number of Americans living below the poverty line increased by 28 percent in just ten years, from...1978 to...1988. By then, nearly one in every five children was born in poverty in the United States, more than twice as high a proportion as in Canada or Germany....[David Stockman, OMB Director, said Reagan's] "newly espoused doctrines were simply a cover story; the actual and deeper purpose was to lower taxes on the affluent."[495]

The statistical evidence demonstrating the wealth disparity that resulted from trickle-down initiatives under Reagan is so strong that even conservatives like Myron Magnet acknowledge its effects:[496]

---

[495] John Kenneth Galbraith, The Culture of Contentment, pp.27, 102-103, 107, 108.
[496] Though Magnet, in words that ring all the more hollow to today's workers, suggests that jobs were lost in the 1980s because this was "necessary to keep American industry competitive"–on this economic rationale, if all jobs are eliminated, U.S. industry should win all contracts.

> Yet however necessary to keep American industry competitive, the restructuring [from 1980 to 1990] undeniably swept away jobs, including many unionized unskilled or semi-skilled jobs paying over ten dollars an hour....The result is that real earnings of unskilled young working men dropped: down 18.8 percent between 1979 and 1988 for white males aged twenty-five to thirty-four lacking a high school diploma....[497] [T]hroughout the eighties the number of homeless increased and the underclass sank deeper into disorder.[498]

Trickle-down efforts failed to stimulate the economy in the 1980s sufficiently to repay the debt incurred (it still hasn't been repaid, and remains a part of the country's current national debt), and caused the increasing wealth disparity that one might expect if increasing amounts of money were provided to the wealthy while giving assistance to the poor was decreased. More money for the wealthy, and less for the poor: what does Jesus think?

In true Reagan style, Bush has coupled tax refunds favoring the wealthy with massive federal spending, even though he has said that "America doesn't need more big government, and we've learned that more money is not always the answer."[499] But his words are empty when

---

[497] Myron neglects to mention that the statistics were markedly worse for blacks, presumably because their removal from the workforce was "necessary to keep American industry competitive," not because of some liberal social-worker-concocted lack of equality.

[498] Myron Magnet, <u>The Dream and the Nightmare: the Sixties' Legacy to the Underclass</u>, pp. 45, 234.

[499] George W. Bush, from Thomas A. Freiling, <u>George W. Bush on God & Country</u>, p. 121.

contrasted with the enlargement of government and siphoning of present and future funds that have been accomplished under his ambitious eye.

In more vapid pronouncements, George W. has endorsed trickle-down, voodoo economics despite the warnings of Alan Greenspan, Paul J. O'Neill and other economists and businesspeople, and in the same breath made more bait-and-switch promises that the federal government would not expand if money was refunded to American citizens:

> America will be prosperous if we cut taxes.[500] Reducing marginal tax rates will increase economic growth and create higher-paying jobs.[501] By returning money to the taxpayers,[502] we can also limit government.[503]

---

[500] Not without cutting spending….The left hand giveth, while the right hand taketh away.

[501] But Reagan's experience is still dragging on our growth, and resulted in a loss of higher-paying jobs, as recounted by Magnet. So where does Mr. Bush get these arguments? They are economic falsehoods, talk, justification for policies which benefit the well-off.

[502] How is anything returned when government is still spending more than it is "refunding?" Accepting $100 cash to permit someone else to charge $1000 on one's credit card account would be no different—what benefit is there if the government refunds $500 per taxpayer, if in the meantime it incurs $2,000 in per capita pork debt?

[503] Words…..How does cutting tax rates limit government if it just appropriates whatever it wants on the taxpayers' tab? Accrual versus cash basis accounting concepts are either lost on President Bush (Harvard MBA?), or he is counting on them being lost on the people whose money he's spending into the far-distant future. Tax refunds did not hinder his profligacy.

> Money returned to Americans will not be spent on new or expanded government programs.[504]
>
> In 2001, the federal government will take a bigger share of the U.S. economy in taxes than in any year since 1944. And I remind you, in 1944, we had 11.5 million people under arms....Our country is at peace, but our government is charging wartime prices. Enough is enough. The American people deserve tax relief[505]....You often hear it said, we cannot afford tax relief. But even after adjusting for inflation, the U.S. government will collect twice as much income tax revenue in 2001 as it did in

---

[504] No, they can print all the fresh new money they want from America's pockets while we spend the money they sent us that we actually still owe because we're in the red. It's the federal government equivalent of convenience checks sent with your 19.9% credit card that has a multi-thousand dollar balance already. And George W. has shown quite clearly that refunding taxes did not stop him from spending more money on "new or expanded government programs."

[505] "Deserve?" This sounds like an appeal to an entitlement mentality. But no one "deserves" a tax refund unless it is effected through considered social policy planning, and even then, balancing the budget is a little mathematical detail that cannot be ignored, and it cannot be simply ignored because someone decides that a tax refund is "deserved." Do the American people "deserve" economic collapse from too much debt?

1981.[506] Enough is enough, folks.[507] It's time to give our folks some tax relief in America.[508]

Federal discretionary spending rose 8 percent in 2001. The Senate has just voted to increase discretionary spending by another 8 percent in 2002.

I hope Americans will send a clear message: excessive federal spending threatens economic vitality. What

---

[506] But it now has more than twice as much debt, which means that that doubling of income tax revenue is insufficient to pay off the debt being incurred–one must match income with expenses, which this facile argument avoids. The government requires this revenue to finance the interest on the last big run-up in national debt under Reagan–we still have not paid off our 1980s spending binge, or the costs of the S&L crisis. Bush's argument is thus financially identical to telling the bank you don't want to increase your mortgage payments after incurring a massive second mortgage, just let it accrue. Sooner or later (and the more fiscally irresponsible our government is, the sooner it will be), we have to repay borrowed money. Again, George W. has an MBA from Harvard, which we're told means that despite his abysmal grades, he learned something about business–so when he spouts off with statements like these, is it because he's a liar and deliberate deceiver, or because he's incredibly unintelligent, for no third option exists, period. If a doctor were this incompetent, he or she would be banned from practice if our society cared at all for the public. Again, there is no legitimate economic debate about the efficacy of spending a dollar to create a quarter–Reagan proved this failing unequivocally, and the only reason the Republicans continue to push for tax refunds is that it feeds their wealthy base.

[507] If enough was enough when this statement was made in 2001, then spending by government since then must be substantially more than enough, and this after such words of frugality. Middle class Americans are usually not free to spend their mortgage payment money on going out to dinner–the federal government should not be able to, with citizens' money.

[508] True tax relief is only accomplished through reduced spending–otherwise, tax refunds in the face of increased government spending offer false promise, for larger debt service and spending mean citizens end up with larger government in even deeper debt, increasing the very problem Mr. B. is presuming to solve. And "our folks" are multi-millionaires; that's who received the lion's share of Bush tax "refunds."

we want is a stronger economy, not larger federal government.[509]

My plan...is a plan for real people,[510] and it will help produce real prosperity....My plan, when fully implemented, returns about $1,600 to the typical family of four[511].... For families with children to

---

[509] Marvelous words.... But what we have received is exactly the opposite of what Bush promised–larger government which is itself burdening a failing economy. His "cure" is more of the same problem, only worse, for we have *much more* debt and *much more* government in America today than we did in 1999. In December, 2005, Bush requested a *fourth* increase in the federal debt limit–there *is* no federal debt limit, only an illusion of one. Words versus actions....

[510] What are "real" people? This effort to appear to have I-feel-your-pain compassion for the little guy is quite a contrast to the clear effects of these very policies–to give to the rich at the expense of the poor, and leave the poor holding the tab for the trip. Intentions (though questionable) are irrelevant–trickle down economics is a proven sham, and any MBA knows it. And the promised benefits, that "it will help produce real prosperity..." (what is "real prosperity?") have not only failed to materialize, but the resultant unmanageable and unrepayable debt is devouring America's society from the inside, even without the additional pressure from terrorists, globalization, and spiraling oil prices.

[511] This is a gross manipulation of statistics, and again cannot be excused as innocent from the mouth of a supposed MBA grad. For a detailed and factually accurate analysis of the deceptions implicit in this $1,600 figure (so gleefully echoed by Limbaugh and co.), *see* Al Franken's Lies and the Lying Liars Who Tell Them, Chapter 35 (page 288) for an excellent analysis of how this administration grossly manipulated these numbers. Furthermore, and more importantly because it's the "real" ball to keep one's eye on, even were the $1,600 figure accurate, tax refunds are still financial suicide if revenues ultimately fall short to cover expenditures. In other words, without surplus there is nothing to refund, so all tax refunds are thus borrowed funds in addition to other government overruns. Yet Bush insisted on further rounds of such cuts subsequent to 9/11, and incredible spending that does not create a return–Homeland Security is mega-pork with no income, military equipment can be dumped in the sea upon production with as much impact on the economy as it's ever going to have, and the interest expense on America's national debt is an increasingly massive anchor on growth.

The Rich, the Deficit, and What Trickles Down

raise and debts to pay, tax relief will lift burdens and ease worries.[512]

Tax relief will create new jobs. Tax relief will generate new wealth[513]....You see, there are some who say,[514] $1,380, that's nothing, that's not enough money for anybody....It means a lot to a lot of folks in America: those who are struggling with higher energy bills,[515] because we hadn't had an energy policy....[516]

---

[512] Now we hear the salesman, peddling the culture of we-can-have-our-cake-and-spend-it-too contentment to gluttonous American consumers who are once again being told what they want to hear, and will blame the government afterwards for incompetence. Like consumers being sold overpriced furniture with the lure of no interest for six months and no payments for a year, Bush has continually deceived taxpayers about the inevitable though hidden costs of fiscal Fantasy Island.

[513] New wealth for whom? Is government-financed debt even "real" wealth? But since it's been six years since these failed policies were implemented, isn't it about time that the naked emperor, the accountability president, admitted his failure rather than keep saying "One more time on red," and had another roll at the dice with our children's now-overleveraged future? Where is Christian integrity, or even worldly accountability for worldly words of promise? If government revenues are up, do they even approach the price tag for the tax refunds?

[514] It is a common Bush practice to refer to "some" people who hold extreme views and don't exist, in order to present himself as reasonable and those who disagree with him as senseless. This is deceptive political tongue-wagging, not Christian truth. The truth is that the only people who would say that $1,380 is "nothing" are the extremely wealthy who got a lot more than nothing back from Bush's federal reign. Who are the people that say $1,380 is nothing? Certainly not those who got a $1,380 refund!

[515] Here we are with the compassion-for-the-little-guy routine again. Words are nice, but what about Bush's refusal, two years later, to increase funding for low-income fuel assistance. That would have directly benefited those "struggling" with higher energy bills rather than delay assistance until it trickled down to them from the wealthy hands to whom it was entrusted. And what of the impact of Bush-Cheney energy policy on the price of energy?

[516] If we have an energy policy now, it's an exponential increase in the oil-dependent, oil-company-driven nightmare of consumptive dependency, with no conservation initiative. As such, it is abysmal failure in the face of our own extinction–it hastens that extinction.

> Let me tell you some of the things $1.6 trillion could mean to the private economy. It could buy 10 million new middle income homes. It could pay the tuitions of 26 million young people at a private college or university for four years each. It could purchase 76 million new automobiles.[517]
>
> This is an important debate for our country. It's a debate about how to make sure our economy continues to grow. But it's really a debate about who do we trust....And we've always got to remember, the role of government is not to create wealth.[518]

---

[517] Salesmanship. The only thing these numbers reflect is the mind-boggling magnitude of the debt incurred on behalf of our grandchildren. This exposition by Bush is politicking made shameful by the fact that he must know better. The very list is multiple spending, like the binge wishes of a lottery-winning millionaire, who buys six yachts and four houses spending the same money over and over. Further, Bush's numbers are meaningless as economic policy because 1) the hypothetical allocation of spending in this manner is fantastical, because the money simply won't be spent there—again, the implication, the assumption, the argument, is that this money will encourage capital spending, when it could all just as easily sit idly in the investment accounts of the very wealthy (which is where most of it actually went); 2) You can hypothetically allocate money all you like, dreamily imagining your spending spree, but if the money is all borrowed, subject to interest (variable at that), and you lack an investment or business plan to repay that leverage, you are just another American consumer racking up your credit card. Maybe all those college educated kids will figure out how to repay that enormous millstone of debt with their free educations, while they drive back and forth to work (oops, no jobs...) in those 76 million free cars (three each!) to their ten million free middle income homes. It's all fantasy, Christians, so wake up to who's in control of this world, and what world leader is steering This World towards fear and catastrophe by furthering our dependence on man and his economics and technology instead of on God.

[518] But isn't that exactly what trickle-down policy seeks and claims to do, place government in the role of investor to stimulate growth? Didn't this man just say that his plan "will help produce real prosperity"? Give with one hand while taking with the other....Politics, not Christ. This is truly " a debate about who do we trust."

THE RICH, THE DEFICIT, AND WHAT TRICKLES DOWN   275

> You see, I think we've finally made the case that we can meet the obligations of the federal government, that we don't have to grow at 8 percent in order to meet obligations[519]....It's important for you to follow your government closely. It's important for you to not let the filter decide what's reality and not reality.[520] It's important to get the facts. And it's always important to realize that tax relief will stimulate creativity and enterprise[521] for individual Americans.[522]

Perhaps another Bush quote will best summarize the accountability to be expected from our "Christian" president for his fiscal mismanagement of our nation. In the weeks leading up to the U.S. incursion into Afghanistan, President Bush anxiously pressed for immediate action, clearly failing to perceive the military and support logistics involved in an operation of that magnitude and that far away. His advisers, particularly

---

[519] No, we can grow our government at much higher rates than that, blame it on terrorism while we reward our wealthy buddies, and defer the obligation to repay as long as possible. Indeed, this financial wizardry does require an MBA....

[520] Ironic, coming from the filter....But George is again speaking in doubletalk, for he has repeatedly demonstrated that the last thing he desires is for American citizens "to follow [their] government closely."

[521] Outrageous! Bush admonishes Americans to get the facts and then immediately presents as fact the mistruth that trickle-down tax relief will "stimulate creativity and enterprise" (there's government "creating wealth" again), for "individual Americans." (there's that little guy biz again, even though the bulk of refunds went to the wealthiest taxpayers, and as if economic growth doesn't redound first and foremost to the benefit of corporate America and its shareholders). And it's all borrowed money....

[522] George W. Bush, <u>A Charge to Keep</u>, p. 237; George W. Bush, in Thomas A. Freiling, <u>George W. Bush on God & Country</u>, pp. 175, 176, 177, 178, 179, 180.

Condoleeza Rice, Donald Rumsfeld and Colin Powell, squirmed between achieving the impossible militarily and telling the president that his demands for action were unrealistic and could not be met. When this became clear to Bush, he disingenuously said he'd been "testing" his staff. When Bob Woodward asked him whether he ever explained to Condoleeza Rice that he had been testing them, Bush replied:

> Of course not. I'm the commander–see, I don't need to explain–I do not need to explain why I say things. That's the interesting thing about being the president. Maybe somebody needs to explain to me why they say something, but I don't feel like I owe anybody an explanation.[523]

But George W. didn't wait for the presidency to be imperious. His mother never told him "no," his father was often away and missed his kid's ballgames, he was always aided by influence but never rebuked. Great leaders learn from their mistakes, while this one never admits them. And democratic concepts of freedom generally expect leaders to be responsive to the people who elect them, an accountability thing.... George W. owes the American people a lot of explanations, including how his words of fiscal restraint and taking care of the little guy transformed into crippling economic actions and steadily increasing wealth disparity. He also owes an explanation to Jesus Christ for blinding so many to the sufferings of others, for contributing to that

---

[523] Bob Woodward, <u>Bush at War</u>, pp. 145-146.

suffering, and for discouraging people from following Christ because of his poor example as a self-avowed Christian. "If the majesty and grace and power of God are not being manifested in us, God holds us responsible."[524] George W. *will* owe somebody an explanation, eventually.

The failure of tax refunds to stimulate the economy would be of little consequence if the success of such a gambit weren't so high-stakes—in the (now inevitable) event of failure, we will have nothing to show for a huge debt that shadows our future for as far as our longevity permits us to imagine. In fact, the debt created by the Bush shopping spree and the Bush tax cuts, when then compounded by the expense of the Iraq War, oil inflation (which is directly linked to dollar deflation), hurricane damage and then further tax (and food stamp program) cuts, is a financial burden which is unsupportable by our nation's economy. This is especially so with a dearth of new growth industries or technologies of sufficient scale to buoy American consumption, let alone pay down debt. Add steadily rising oil prices (in the face of certain increasing demand, increased costs of production, and certain decreasing production), the intractable financial legacy of Social Security, spiraling health care costs concurrent with spiraling health problems from poor environment and nutrition, and a hotbed of economic unrest in our major cities, and increasing our national deficit without significantly addressing any of these issues (making most of them worse) is an irreversible thrust of our nation into economic collapse.

---

[524] Oswald Chambers, <u>My Utmost for His Highest</u>, May 16.

The chief cause of our current condition is not just poor government, but poor citizenship. Americans have too often permitted the lust for gain to be the motivating force behind government action. This is an abdication of the God-given duty or obligation that accompanies the God-given right of freedom. Nothing is free, and by trusting, even looking to, government and the market to shape their futures, Americans have become a nation of soft, worldly, technology-dependent entitlement babies. The expectation of something for nothing is not limited to the poor, despite Olasky's and Magnet's moral assessments.

This relinquishing of freedom to the bedfellows of big business and government really became a critical mass in America following World War II: "[t]he fortunes of war made the government a wasteful and large-scale consumer, and that government spending precipitated the advent of the modern economy."[525] Government essentially became a consumer. This led to an economy increasingly driven by government. The problem is that such government intervention cannot actually grow the economy, only fuel debt and the consumption cycle, for "the only alternatives to an interventionist state [are: i]t can confiscate; it can redistribute what it has confiscated; it can spend more than it possesses by borrowing and by printing baseless money. There is only one thing it cannot do: produce wealth."[526]

---

[525] Richard N. Goodwin, The American Condition, p. 180.

[526] William E. Simon, A Time for Truth, p. 214. This is, of course, standard conservative ideology in opposition to large liberal government spending. These are the words echoed by George W. Bush when he said "the role of government is not to create wealth." But trickle-down economics, when leveraged (as now), constitutes the third alternative: spending more than it possesses.

Richard N. Goodwin discusses at length the failure of economic bureaucracy to offer sustained growth. Because of the inefficiencies found in even the purest of free markets, a capitalist economy like America's can only be maintained with steady growth–not merely the same GDP each year, but steadily growing production (supply) and demand (consumption, to absorb production). To avert recession, depression, or collapse, growth (and thus demand) must be constant. But sooner or later growth must slow, usually because of overproduction which leads to a downward spiral as the wind escapes the system's sails. The impossibility of indefinitely feeding an ever-increasing supply and demand is the conundrum of capitalism, an impasse. Goodwin explains that "[m]uch of the theory behind large-scale government spending or its Keynesian counterpart–the tax reduction–consists of the assumption that this impasse can be avoided if government prods a stagnating demand by increasing its own consumption or by placing more money in the hands of individuals and/or corporations."[527] If government lacks the revenue to stimulate the sagging economy, debt can be employed to "raise the total level of demand. (For example, one way to buy something without foregoing other purchases is to spend money one doesn't have by borrowing against future income)."[528]

And so America and its government, the new great consumer, gradually became dependent on debt to fuel, even increase, its standard of living. Although this was against the American way of self-reliance, this was

---
[527] Richard N. Goodwin, <u>The American Condition</u>, p. 181.
[528] Ibid., p. 182.

replaced by self-confidence, faith that Americans were destined to find fresh areas of prosperity through ingenuity and hard work. So Americans bought foreign goods and oil on faith. Faith in country. Faith in the future. Faith in the dollar. Faith in the economy. But that faith didn't reduce government debt or trade imbalances, which silently transformed America from the world's largest creditor to the world's greatest debtor:[529]

> When America's seventy-year status as a creditor nation came to an end, under Ronald Reagan, it was surprising how quickly U.S. indebtedness and foreign influence mounted to record levels....Still worse, late-nineteenth-century indebtedness had been undertaken to expand production, but much of what America borrowed in the 1980s was spent on consumption.[530]

The increased federal budget deficit under Reagan "was less of a threat to the contented than the taxes that would have reduced it,"[531] taxes which would have required a deferral or surrender of material comforts and in which a progressive tax structure would impact the most wealthy.

History has repeated itself in the second Bush administration, where Americans have accepted pie-in-the-sky-promises of an economic solution which is a

---

[529] *See*, e.g., John Kenneth Galbraith, The Culture of Contentment, p. 87: "Large and persistent public deficits...were accepted, if rhetorically regretted, during the 1980s, and they continue."

[530] Kevin Phillips, The Politics of Rich and Poor: Wealth and the American Electorate in the Reagan Aftermath, p. 124, 125.

[531] John Kenneth Galbraith, The Culture of Contentment, p. 179.

proven failed premise, but which offers hope, comfort, and the promise (the encouragement) of continued, increasing consumption, a debt-junky sociology. But this is no different from an acid-head jumping off a roof because he believes he can fly–but with more dire consequences, for Americans have taken their innocent children off the roof with them. The experience of twentieth century history, in which nations which collapsed economically repeatedly rose again (often on America's engine of growth and technological innovation), is no guarantee that if America becomes insolvent that she will rise again. America is in deeper debt at this very moment than any nation in history, even more so than war-ravaged nations. In post-World War II France, England, Italy, Poland, Russia, and other nations worldwide, whole industries had been decimated, infrastructures destroyed, populations eliminated. But those nations possessed more wealth than America does in 2005, for they still owned their soil and their labor. Facing a growing loss of global competitiveness, America's economic infrastructure is crumbling from a starvation, a lack of more business, more raw resources and labor, to feed the beast of the free-market economic equation. But as our industry and capital stand more and more idle (productivity gains, good for efficiency, also force more and more human capital into obsolescence), the situation is the more bleak because *America no longer owns her own factories, stock markets, bonds, dollars, land or national parks*. Our recent and current capitalist leaders, business and political, have sold out…. Oh, and most of the rest of the world hate us…not because we're free, or because of jealousy, but because we've been wasteful, greedy, boastful, arrogant and bullish for decades, we consume more than hogs (literally) and our refuse and consumption limit the future possibilities for others in the world. Plus, we back Israel at the expense of Arabs to secure our military influence (over oil) in the Gulf, just as we have most always backed whichever dictator or regime furthered our economic interests,[532] almost always at the expense of goodwill and the furtherance of democratic freedom.

But consumption breeds complacency (no news to Christians), and in the eighties, Americans (with the means) consumed. Attention to the national debt would entail not only questioning the faith, but detracting from the enjoyment, of the consumption culture: "For most American voters, talk of a national debt involved incomprehensible abstractions that did not seem to have any relevance to their daily lives or to have any obviously adverse impact on the national economy. Most voters in 1988 were not poor, were not minorities, and did not appear much concerned about people who were."[533] The explosion in national debt sent a message to Americans that "By borrowing against future growth we help to

---

[532] Marcos, Somoza, the Shah of Iran, the Taliban, Saddam Hussein, Noriega,.... (*See* Chapter Nine)
[533] George Donelson Moss, <u>Moving On: The American People Since 1945</u>, p. 364.

bring it about. The miracle of the loaves and fishes[534] has been transformed into an economic process."[535] So in the 1980s, Americans borrowed individually as well (rivaled only more recently, where now that they've spent their future income, Americans have been burning up their "home equity"–through refinancing, thereby increasing mortgage debt). By the end of the 1980s, "[t]he banking industry, in sum, had accomplished what it had set out to do some twenty-five years before: it had made credit cards indispensable....Of all the symbols of the American consumer society, credit cards had a hold on the subconscious that was matched–in a completely different way–only by the automobile."[536]

The foundation capitalist principle controlling modern debt is interest, the charging of which the Bible calls usury, and sinful. Like many worldly sins, usury in small doses may not corrupt or destroy. But America is on the threshold of proof of biblical teaching as it serves as large-scale worldly example of the excess of the sin of borrowing, of relying on worldly commerce, of planning fortunes far into the future, instead of praising God

---

[534] This allusion to Christianity is most instructive, for much of modern man's faith in technology, science and the future is even more mystical or irrational than believing in a bottomless basket of fish requires–for technology, despite all of its acclaimed successes, is an abysmal failure to help humanity, and there is no higher power in sight (having been dismissed, by definition, by that very belief system) in that "world"-view, to look to when that faith in technology is proven to have been misplaced, when the currency, economy, and environment collapse together despite science's promise and humanity's foolishly misplaced hopes.

[535] Richard N. Goodwin, The American Condition, p. 191. An economic process of boot-strapping.

[536] Joseph Nocera, A Piece of the Action: How the Middle Class Joined the Money Class, pp. 301, 300.

for today and not looking past tomorrow.[537] In 1987, in <u>Blood in the Streets: Investment Profits in a World Gone Mad</u>, James Dale Davidson and Sir William Rees-Mogg concluded based upon years of study of financial markets that terrorism's greatest threat to the West was as a disruption of commerce, and that America and its debt load threatened world stability:

> The battles against Western people, investments and influences are no longer confined to the remote fringes of the desert. Terrorists can use their modern weapons to shoot little girls in the capital cities of Europe. And they do.
>
> As menacing as terrorism is, however, what is at stake is not merely a matter of containing terrorists. It is a matter of economic stability. The shifting balance of power in the world is the most important hidden threat to the economy today.[538]

The authors then note that a global financial crisis could be caused by a number of different factors, including "Any striking evidence of U.S. weakness in the military, economic, or political spheres. For reasons already spelled out, weakening American hegemony

---

[537] "Boast not thyself of tomorrow; for thou knowest not what a day may bring forth." Proverbs 27:1, KJV; "Go to now, ye that say, Today or tomorrow we will go into such a city, and continue there a year, and buy and sell, and get gain: Whereas ye know not what shall be on the morrow. For what is your life? It is even a vapour, that appeared for a little time, and then vanisheth away. For that ye ought to say, If the Lord will, we shall live, and do this, or that." James 4:13-15, KJV.

[538] James Dale Davidson & Sir William Rees-Mogg, <u>Blood In The Streets: Investment Profits in a World Gone Mad</u>, p. 67.

is the fundamental cause of the debt crisis in the first place."[539]

What grammar-school students can calculate mathematically is that the wealth generated from non-oil-producing nations has steadily returned to the dunes of the Middle East in exchange for yet more oil, in a continuous cycle, like a game of Monopoly where one player holds all the rental properties. And just like in Monopoly, there is only a finite amount of wealth. Between the flow of wealth for oil, interest on debt, and trade imbalance with China, the only thing which has boot-strapped the United States along this far is that our confidence in technology is contagious, and that we buy lots and lots of (largely useless) stuff. It was therefore understatement when "Standard & Poor's predicted [in April, 2005] that unless we change course, our debt will be downgraded to junk bonds within 25 years."[540] Such a loss of confidence would reflect the financial/mathematical improbability of repayment, and would no doubt constitute "striking evidence of U.S. weakness in the…economic…sphere," precipitating the global financial crisis Davidson and Rees-Mogg describe. And if these international finance experts are correct (and many of the predictions in their book have so far proven remarkably accurate) when they argue that "weakening American hegemony" precipitated our reliance on debt, then surely continued economic decline from servicing

---

[539] Ibid, p. 129.
[540] David Gergen, *US News & World Report*, April 4, 2005, p. 60. It won't take anywhere near that long. More like 25 months, or less.

that debt is a vicious cycle which becomes increasingly less possible to control or escape.

This is perhaps the biggest danger of national debt–it drags on society's ability to respond to crisis. As Machiavelli shrewdly observed of government largesse centuries ago, once in power a (Machiavellian) ruler must resist rewarding his supporters with public funds as George W. has done (surprisingly, since George seems to borrow so many pages from Machiavelli's book) or else, "having harmed the many with his liberality, and rewarded the few, he will feel every mischance which first arises and he will be endangered by every danger which appears."[541] This is the real crisis, made exponentially worse by Bush II, that faces America–the country has almost no capacity to borrow money in the event of crisis. The nation would have collapsed in the Great Depression without the ability to borrow, and a much smaller blow to our economy today could lead to an economic collapse which without debt could have been averted. Modern financial guru Alan Greenspan is of this fiscally-prudent (and conservative) position:

> If the federal government were debt free, Greenspan said, that would not take away its ability to do expansive things. Without debt, the government could eventually reborrow trillions of dollars if necessary in a crisis or an emergency. It would be available for the right moment.[542] The surpluses and absence of deficits would also help keep long-term interest rates down, because the federal government would

---

[541] Niccolo Machiavelli, The Prince, p. 96.
[542] Note that Greenspan did not mean the "Right" moment.

not be borrowing, making more money available for business borrowing.[543]

Should all those financial experts and economists who condemned trickle-down economic theory (who were ignored by Bush) turn out to be correct (and unfortunately they will be, if history and economics are guides), then George W. Bush, despite all his show of humble piety, will have fueled the debt flames of our own economic conflagration, inducing the horrible poverty and suffering of so very many at home and worldwide. Jesus cautioned His followers:

> Beware of the scribes, which love to go in long clothing, and love salutations in the marketplaces, And the chief seats in the synagogues, and the uppermost rooms at feasts:
>
> Which devour widows' houses, and for a pretence make long prayers; these shall receive greater damnation.[544]

It is simply astounding for twenty-first century conservatives, employing sheer ideological determination, to overlook the failings of Reaganomics.[545] Paul Volcker was convinced (and has now been proved correct) that Reagan's supply-side tax rate reductions were fiscally

---

[543] Bob Woodward, Maestro: Greenspan's Fed and the American Boom, p. 223.
[544] Mark 12: 38-40, KJV.
[545] Almost equally amazing is the unquestioning acceptance of illogical reminiscences of the Reagan debacle, such as crediting Reagan for increasing military strength while ignoring the never-yet-paid-down budget deficits that he employed to finance that investment–what else was the money spent on, welfare?

unwise, that "such a tax cut was about the most irresponsible thing the government could do at such a moment."[546] One historian records that "Reagan's deep tax cuts that had favored the wealthy had also compounded the federal government's enormous debt problems."[547] And John Kenneth Galbraith observes that "[i]n the 1980s the preference for short-run advantage was dramatically evident…in the continued deficits in the budget of the United States and in the related and resulting deficits in the international trade accounts."[548]

Reagan used charismatic appeals to American nationalism to peddle a false hope of economic revival:

> But…the great things promised were not delivered. Reagan was unable to reconstruct the circumstances of prior capitalist heydays, when America was rising to world leadership. Reagan would seek less to cope with U.S. world decline than to deny it by reenacting past glories. In economic policy, this included the conspicuous accumulation and display of wealth, invocation of the late nineteenth century's overseas borrowing to build U.S. industry, and mimicry of the tax cuts and stock market boom of the 1920s. It resembled what the British historian Arnold Toynbee called a Shadow Empire—the reveries of a declining nation trying to revisit the counting-houses and parade grounds of its triumphant zenith.[549]

---

[546] Joseph Nocera, A Piece of the Action: How the Middle Class Joined the Money Class, p. 219.
[547] George Donelson Moss, Moving On: The American People Since 1945, p. 374.
[548] John Kenneth Galbraith, The Culture of Contentment, p. 22.
[549] Kevin Phillips, The Politics of Rich and Poor: Wealth and the American electorate in the Reagan Aftermath, p. 125.

Just as with words and actions, economic "theory" or "policy" is meaningless if there are no tangible, measurable results to its implementation.[550] The tangible, measurable results of "trickle-down" theory under Ronald Reagan are not proclaimed by this theory's advocates (including George W.) because they do not exist.[551] On the contrary, statistical evidence demonstrates clearly that "trickle-down" economics is even more wasteful and inefficient than communist-controlled or state-owned enterprises, in which at least the state determines the allocation of capital, can create productive jobs, and has a stake in the return on the investment. Stimulating debt to stimulate the economy is financial porkfoolery–it sounds good, but it just rewards those

---

[550] Like Bush's tax giveaway to corporate America, which allowed "…U.S. companies …to repatriate about $206 billion in foreign profits under a special one-year tax break….But it's far from clear whether the spending has spurred the job growth that backers of the break touted….A law signed by President Bush shortly before the 2004 election allows companies to transfer profit from overseas operations back to the U.S. this year at a special low tax rate of 5.25%….Direct job creation rarely appears on the list [of what companies intend to do with repatriated profits] Some companies are even bringing home piles of cash while continuing to downsize." "Tax Break Brings Billions to U.S., But Impact on Hiring is Unclear," *The Wall Street Journal*, October 5, 2005, p. 1. Tax breaks on dividend income have also been shown to have failed to produce their promised benefits, but Bush renewed them in 2005 nonetheless.

[551] As President Bush's Council of Economic Advisors put it in 2003: "Although the economy grows in response to tax reductions (because of higher consumption in the short run and improved incentives in the long run), it is unlikely to grow so much that lost tax revenue is completely recovered by the higher level of economic activity….If we are worried, and not everyone is, about the widening gap between incomes of best-off and worst-off Americans, then spending and taxes are part of the response." "Politicians Must Decide How to Raise Taxes," *The Wall Street Journal*, October 13, 2005, p. A2.

who receive the immediate economic benefit with the discretion to determine where to "invest" (read "spend") that "capital" (read "borrowed money"). Again, the Reagan era evidence (the gathering of which required an unprecedented trickle-down experiment on America the guinea pig) proved this truth dramatically:

> The total amount of dollars in salaries funneled to the rich soared in the 1980s—as did the number of rich themselves. Meanwhile, the total dollars in wages that went to the middle class increased an average of just 4 percent a year, or 44 percent over the decade. It was a phenomenon unlike any America had seen in the century.[552]

Though some have argued that "[d]eficit spending…was an Insiders' tool to precipitate America's internal decay,"[553] such cynicism is not prerequisite to understanding the effects of that national leveraging—the rich got (much) richer, the poor got poorer, the nation's infrastructure was neglected, and materialism gained more ground in America's culture. This didn't have to be planned to be self-destructive: Americans will pay the price for unrealistic hopes pinned on consumption and debt. The Republican Party which made us a

---

[552] Donald L. Bartlett and James B. Steele, <u>America: What Went Wrong?</u>, p. 1. The authors report, at page 2, that the salaries of people with incomes exceeding $1,000,000 increased 2,184 % in the 1980s, versus a 697% increase for those with incomes in the $200,000-$1,000,000 bracket. (contrasted with 44% for the middle class). This experience is being repeated again in the first decade of the twentieth century, under George W. Bush.

[553] Robert A. Goldberg, <u>Grassroots Resistance: Social Movements in Twentieth Century America</u>, pp. 138-139.

debtor nation has given us George W. Bush instead of accountability, but Jesus will judge not by the promise of their words but by the results of actions: "those who do not *do* what is right or do not love others are not God's children."[554]

There is surely irony in the Republicans constant harping (however justifiably) on Democratic overspending, while launching America's deficit into stellar orbit, never to return. As Lou Dobbs reported in the May 2, 2005 issue of *US News & World Report*:

> There is nothing conservative about our rising record budget and trade deficits....It's ironic that Congress approved the bankruptcy bill to impose fiscal discipline on the middle class when the federal government last year ran up a $412 billion budget deficit and a $617 billion trade deficit. President Bush's temerity in signing this legislation was the ultimate hypocrisy in a town already very well credentialed.[555]

Neither party really wants to stop spending, because government and private bureaucracy feed on spending; spending is fuel for the machine.....

Alan Greenspan's chief job is to foster and maintain market stability, not just market gain. To that end, Mr. Greenspan has been an outspoken critic of deficit spending (with no recognition of a supply-side exception), which threatens the economy with inflation: "For Greenspan, a big reduction in the federal deficit would

---

[554] 1 John 3:10, TEV. *Emphasis added.*
[555] "Lonely in the Middle," p. 55.

make his job immensely easier, because lower deficits would likely mean lower actual inflation."[556] When George W. pushed to re-implement the failed Reagan economic equation of trickle-down monkeynomics, Greenspan objected to tax cuts if they led to deficits (he and Paul O'Neill worked together unsuccessfully to include "triggers" in the tax refund legislation which would halt tax cuts if the budget went beyond certain pre-set limits). He warned that "[w]ith today's euphoria surrounding the surpluses, it is not difficult to imagine the hard-earned fiscal restraint developed in recent years rapidly dissipating. We need to resist those policies that could readily resurrect the deficits of the past and the fiscal imbalances that followed in their wake."[557] This last sentence is a direct (Greenspanian) reference to Reaganomics and the threat of economic instability from unreasonable spending. Alan Greenspan also dubbed the first rounds of George W.'s tax cuts "irresponsible fiscal policy."[558] The strength of Greenspan's aversion to deficits is revealed by his willingness to break with party ideology (Greenspan himself being a lifelong Republican) in order to prevent them:

> Part of Clinton's campaign promise included tax increases on the wealthy, a violation of Republican orthodoxy. But increasing taxes reduced the federal

---

[556] Bob Woodward, <u>Maestro: Greenspan's Fed and the American Boom</u>, p. 100. Woodward also notes that "Greenspan thought that Clinton had broken the gridlock on dealing with the deficit. He couldn't say it publicly, but he believed the president had displayed an element of political courage." p. 101.
[557] Ron Suskind, <u>The Price of Loyalty</u>, pp. 63, 64.
[558] Ibid., p. 162.

deficit[559]–and those deficits, Greenspan thought, were such a threat to the future of the economy that it might just be worth it to support Clinton's proposal....

One of the main paradoxes, Greenspan realized, was that by running up the federal budget deficits, Reagan had effectively borrowed from the period[560] that was now going to be the Clinton era....Reagan had bequeathed Bill Clinton his major problem....

Clinton was happy that Greenspan had not made the typical Republican plea against raising taxes on the rich.[561]

Also ironic is that Bush Jr. learned so little from his father. The elder Bush was not a "believer" in

---

[559] This brings to mind a new theory which ought to be implemented immediately without empirical evidentiary analysis, the trickle-up theory. This theory requires government to tax the very wealthy at unprecedented high rates, then reinvest the money in the economy by distributing the funds to the poor, and by paying off government debt–this will surely stimulate immediate economic growth and a more favorable investment climate from low inflation and interest expenses. Surely the wealthy will be the big winners in the boom created by this minor government wealth-creating intervention, and a new cycle of wealth will shine on America, allowing tax rates to be cut across the board. Isn't this the *exact* reverse of the trickle-down model? The argument that tax refunds pursuant to trickle-down theory "return" money to the wealthy ignores the reality that the poor finance those refunds even if they don't pay as much in taxes, because the resultant *deficits* are borne by *all* citizens, and because our tax system becomes more regressive in direct proportion to the reduction of top marginal rates.

[560] Luckily the dot-com boom saved America from the full burden of the Reagan-years deficits which had forced even Bush Sr. to raise taxes. But where is the next boom to rescue us this time?

[561] Bob Woodward, <u>Maestro: Greenspan's Fed and the American Boom</u>, p. 97.

supply-side theory, possessing instead an intellect. It was for this reason that Bush Sr.

> started the government on a path of fiscal prudence. That meant not just talking about the virtues of a balanced budget but taking a courageous, <u>rather-right-than-reelected</u> stand, especially after the irresistible promise of supply-side economics–that tax cuts would create economic growth that would boost tax revenues and eventually shrink deficits–was shown to be hollow....[<u>Under Bill Clinton, i</u>]nterest rates dropped and it became clear, year by year, that receding federal deficits were a prime reason.
>
> To be sure, some of this might have happened no matter who was in the White House. But, across a decade of often angry partisanship, an <u>answer</u> somehow took shape: Fiscal prudence works. A balanced budget means that the government won't be out borrowing billions and, thereby, driving up interest rates.[562]

---

[562] Ron Suskind, <u>The Price of Loyalty</u>, pp. 13, 14. Watch the interest-rate and inflation response to America's debt load in 2006 and beyond. An increase in the use of adjustable-rate mortgages "...means more people are stretching to keep up–and if rates rise quickly, buyers with relatively short adjustment periods may be forced to sell." Mortimer Zuckerman, "Home Sweet Home," *U.S. News & World Report*, May 16, 2005, p. 64. "Because the US has a massive deficit in trade and international financial flows and because this is being financed mostly by Asian central banks,...[i]f foreign lenders decide to shift their investments away from the dollar, its value could plunge and force the US to jack up interest rates to attract and keep foreign lenders and investors. Higher rates could damage the economy....What's needed, experts say, is a reduction in the huge federal budget deficit....The deficit under Bush has ballooned, although he has promised to crack down in his second term." David R. Francis, "The multilateralist at the White House," *The Christian Science Monitor*, March 31, 2005, p. 17.

The final irony is that the framers of the constitution knew that George W. Bush or those like him would inexorably whittle away at their effort to protect the citizenry from the greed of politicians and those in control of government, that common sense would be trumped by self-interest. (George Bush is a supposed student of history and business, but apparently his "youthful indiscretions," which plagued him into his 40s, obliterated whatever he learned of value in these disciplines.) "The framers realized that taxing and spending are inextricably tied together, so you have to control both sides of the public purse—the spenders and the taxers."[563] But George W. promised tax refunds from a one-legged economic platform, an asset-side-only balance sheet approach that ignores basic math, promising tax "refunds"[564] without any sort of business plan to make up the revenue shortfall or pay the money back in the future. As Michael Barone of *US News & World Report* remarked, "Bush talks of disciplining government, but in his first term he failed to cut spending nearly as much as taxes."[565] Yet here once again, words are padded when directed at the Bush White House: Bush did not "fail

---

[563] Charles Adams, Those Dirty Rotten Taxes: The Tax Revolts That Built America, p. 54.

[564] Again it is hardly "refunded" if that money, and then some, adds to our nation's indebtedness….. Tax dollars "returned" by a government which is in the red and which continues to overspend is no more "refunded" than money drawn down on a home mortgage line of credit.

[565] Michael Barone, "Eyes on the Future," *US News & World Report*, January 24, 2005, p. 36. Reagan did this also, always promising future spending cuts. But he never delivered—it was all talk without actions. Bush W. has acted somewhat in this regard—in the wake of Hurricane Katrina, he moved to cut farm subsidies and food stamp programs to pay for the relief effort.

to cut spending"–he increased it fantastically, except in programs that benefited the poor, and in ways not necessitated or excused by 9/11. Trickle-down economic promises have been employed by the W. White House to slip the bonds of fiscal prudence and binge-spend with America's checkbook.

And the effects of this fiscal irresponsibility are dramatically compounded by the economic strains incurred by the Iraq War.[566] Once committed to such an ideological venture, money becomes no object (as seen by how few congressional leaders oppose funding for the war–how dare they?), for freedom and democracy and America's image, etc., etc. are at stake…. However, money has a way of influencing reality in this world, and eventually debt related to war spending has to be repaid, like any other type of debt–the markets don't take sides or pity. The Vietnam War took its toll not only in human lives–"[t]he cost of the Vietnam War eventually cracked the system, and the deficits blew up in the 1970s….the magic bullet of any successful economic plan was to keep those long-term rates down."[567]

If only George W. put as much energy into economic policy as he did into Iraq or Social Security, our

---

[566] "…while annual defense spending is now as high as it ever was during the Reagan buildup, the US economy as a whole is much larger, making it easier, in economic terms, for the nation to shoulder the bill." Peter Grier, "The rising economic cost of the Iraq War," *The Christian Science Monitor*, May 19, 2005. But the federal deficit is *much* larger, making it *harder* to shoulder the same bill. America's larger size permits it to incur more debt, but size does not guarantee growth–economic decline will magnify the weight of all US debt, especially when compounded by spiraling interest rates and inflation.

[567] Bob Woodward, Maestro: Greenspan's Fed and the American Boom, p. 102.

country would perhaps not face the calamitous future she now undoubtedly must confront, like a debt junky gone cold turkey, with no one to call for aid with her last dime (is Britain going to bail us out, with its declining economy and popular distrust of the U.S. government?). In fact, George W. Bush has made matters worse on Social Security, ignoring Alan Greenspan's and Paul J. O'Neill's advice[568] to freeze the social security problem and divide the cost by determining a cut-off age (37, at the time) which would be employed to determine how and whose benefits would change. The consequence of this has been wasted government and other public resources, costly delay (deferral of a solution increases the difficulty and costs of forging one), and clouding of the true issues involved–private accounts solve nothing, only shift money between accounts:[569] the underlying gap in Social Security between promised benefits and anticipated receipts remains unbridged, and the problem grows and becomes more intractable, just like the deficit on which it piggy-backs.

Adding yet another drag on America's financial future was Mr. Bush's initiative to eliminate the inheritance tax. Even if tax equity merited eliminating this tax (which it frankly doesn't, as alluring as the "moral" arguments are) the cuts to American government's revenues occasioned by repeal of the estate tax must be compensated by other revenue increases or by spending cuts, neither of which has been undertaken by Bush. And

---

[568] Ron Suskind, <u>The Price of Loyalty</u>, pp. 152-153.
[569] *See*, e.g., Josh Bolten, "A Believer in Tax Cuts," *US News & World Report*, July 25, 2005, p. 36. (Mr. Bolten, budget director, dodges the question of whether supply-side economics works.)

such an extremely narrow initiative as estate tax relief can hardly be expected to promote economic stimulus. The dastardly part of this Bush policy was not just the additional drain on our future income, but that it was presented as relief for small family farms,[570] when in fact the lion's share of the money no longer collected would be left in the hands of America's very wealthiest families. This reverse-Christian pattern of Mr. Bush's favoritism toward those who possess great wealth and influence at the expense of the less fortunate extends throughout Bush administration actions. As Mortimer Zuckerman writes regarding Bush inheritance tax repeal efforts in *US News & World Report*:

> ....the gift to the super-rich is even bigger than it seems at first blush....How, in the face of our increasingly dire fiscal problems, can Congress[571] even think about giving away so much money to this handful

---

[570] Mortimer Zuckerman: "Of the 18,800 people [estimated to be subject to the Estate tax], only 440 will leave estates with assets primarily generated by farms or family-owned businesses. That's relevant because proponents of eliminating or further cutting the tax portray it as dismembering family businesses that have been built up over many years....If the exemption were set at [the anticipated] level, the Tax Policy Center of the Brookings Institution and the Urban Institute notes, only 50 estates would be those of owners of farms and family businesses. The notion that thousands would be forced out of family businesses is, in other words, preposterous...." "So the Rich Get Richer?," *U.S. News & World Report*, May 2, 2005, p. 72.

[571] Mr. Zuckerman never mentions the driving force behind this initiative–George W. Bush. Instead, the Congress is blamed for this repeal, and implicitly for the cutting of social programs, increased national debt and increased wealth disparity that have headlined Mr. Bush's agenda. Mr. Zuckerman has become an unquestioning W. supporter since the commencement of the Iraq War–in fact, his column has been devoted almost exclusively to pro-Israel and pro-Bush positions since the commencement of the War.

of wealthiest Americans? And how dare it add to our national debt in this way when it is cutting so many other vital social programs while forcing the middle class to pay still more in taxes!

Eliminating the estate tax would widen the gap between rich and poor and deepen the divide for generations to come, passing wealth on to those who never earned it, creating a plutocratic leisure class.[572]

Once again, the words of George W. Bush, when held up for Christian comparison (that is, accountability), fall remarkably short of having been followed by meaningful action. The man who has increased the debt of all Americans, cut welfare and repeatedly provided tax refunds to the very wealthy once "criticized his own party in Washington for trying to balance the federal budget "on the backs of the poor.""[573] (Not to be outdone, George has managed to *un*balance the federal budget on their backs). And the man who gave America the USA PATRIOT Act, the No Child Left Behind Act, the Department of Homeland Security, tax refunds and unprecedented debts which are stifling the country today and will stifle our children's futures, once proclaimed "we will work tirelessly to make sure that bureaucracies don't stifle the very reason you exist in the first place...."[574] Liberating words, stifling actions.

---

[572] Mortimer Zuckerman, "So the Rich Get Richer?," *US News & World Report*, May 2, 2005, p.72.
[573] Molly Ivins and Lou Dubose, Shrub: The Short But Happy Political Life of George W. Bush, p. 178.
[574] George W. Bush, in Thomas A. Freiling, George W. Bush on God & Country, p. 30.

If the United States were to discover that a huge meteor was hurtling toward the planet and would eliminate all life on Earth in 20 years, it is to be presumed that incredible resources would be allocated by America to address this threat and attempt to prevent disaster for the whole world, even if the effort was futile and hopeless. And yet, Americans sit like deer in front of headlights, staring blankly at re-runs of sit-coms, game shows, or reality TV with one hand in a bowl of micro-waved popcorn and the other holding a favorite commercial beverage, choosing comfort, recreation, and attendant denial and willful ignorance instead of addressing the meteor of destruction which is the US over-leveraged economy, which is of our own self-indulgent creation, which will strike much sooner than twenty years, and which we could have solved had our complacent reverie evaporated pre-W.

Chapter 8

"CHRISTIAN" LEADERSHIP INTO THE HORRORS OF WAR: IRAQ AND THE DOCTRINE OF PREEMPTIVE WAR

"My country, right or wrong" is like saying "My mother, drunk or sober."

–G.K. Chesterton

Not only does neither U.S. political party have claim to Jesus Christ or His teachings, but neither do "liberal" or "conservative" Christians, for Jesus Christ was not of two truths. Consequently, liberal and conservative Christians cannot both be right in their opposing positions on abortion, gay unions, or capital punishment. Truth in Christ crosses party lines, religious denominations, class, wealth and ideology. The search for that truth is what binds Christians, hopefully even when they disagree, for with God's Grace we are all on the same path.

There are not two positions acceptable to Jesus Christ with regard to America's invasion of Iraq–either He supports that venture as furthering His Father's plan for mankind through the spread of democracy and American ideals, or He weeps that children are being maimed and killed daily by horrible modern weaponry in a conflict purportedly undertaken in His name, which conflict is turning more eyes away from His Love than toward it. It is extraordinarily clear to any honest follower or student of Jesus Christ that He is weeping in the deep sorrow of watching His words left in the ditch while mankind forgets Him and the Father; while America abandons her promise even as God keeps His. The invasion of Iraq was a worldly venture, undertaken by worldly powers for worldly gain. But Satan rules this world, and the War in Iraq was undertaken under Christian pretense with Christian soldiers, some with Christian crosses on their helmets. Our Lord Christ is weeping....His Sorrow as infinite as His Love.

No reader of this book answers to this writer—we all answer to One. I speak not for Christ, for He spoke so clearly for Himself, and He prays that we listen and see. The end times were ordained by God to occur at a time when the world's human population will be greater than at any time in history (than at all times in history combined?) so that a great harvest of His children would occur, a time of affirmation and great joy, not the fear and terror Satan spreads through the world—such terror must drive Christians closer to Jesus and not further away. Jesus tells us again and again not to fear this world: "Fear not; I am the first and the last:"[575] Satan would have us live in this world in fear, and thus flee to him instead of to our Lord.

---

[575] Revelation 1:17, KJV.

Americans, do not fear terrorists, fear God; do not fear the loss of wealth or the loss even of your nation, fear the loss of your soul, loss of Christ's promise; fear the despair of allegiance to the false hope of this world. The Iraq War is an ungodly, horrific societal sin, and God's blessing on America will in righteousness be the stern, wrathful rebuke that might wake a wayward child to the harm caused by its selfish callousness. America's Christians must awake to follow Christ, awake to His words, and study Christ's teachings to determine whether America's course in Iraq and Abu Ghraib has been unchristian. "He that is of God heareth God's words"[576] To fail to assess the Christian moral truths of America's invasion of Iraq is perilous, willful ignorance for Christians worldwide–either Jesus is supportive of U.S. actions, or our nation must repent and pray for forgiveness.

George W. Bush professes that Christ guides his actions, that he prays and reads Oswald Chambers daily. This leads to two inescapable conclusions:

1) If George W. is to be held accountable to anything, it must be to his declared Christian faith, which includes that we all be judged by our actions and not just our Sunday words, and which holds Christian leaders and all Christians to a representative standard for Jesus. When scoffers would not accept Jesus' words, He said to them "you should at least believe my deeds."[577] George W.'s actions in deciding and embarking upon the Iraq War will be judged by Christ, and so will the support

---
[576] John 8:47, KJV.
[577] John 10:38, TEV.

or opposition of each individual Christian for that War and for the man who single-handedly manifested it (and ignorance is no excuse). Again, there are no two Christian sides to this issue—how will America's actions in Iraq be judged? And if those actions were unchristian, our Lord promises forgiveness and infinite love to the repentant.

2) The American incursion into Iraq cannot be supported by any words of Jesus Christ or the New Testament, by any Christian doctrines such as the "just war" doctrine, or by any reasonable interpretation or application thereof. This theological oversight has been neatly side-stepped by the vengeful, fear-mongering, worldly Mr. Bush. No Christian words of support for preemption, for none exist. Jesus gave His life for the worthless human race, praying to God that He forgive His tormenters, by His actions demonstrating the power of forgiveness. Jesus never advocated vengeance, let alone preemptive vengeance, let alone the overwhelming military might of the United States bearing down upon the battered civilians of Iraq, themselves victims of Saddam and having no connection to 9/11. George W. took a supposedly Christian nation to war without considering what Jesus would do. We must ask, as will Jesus, "You boast about having God's law—but do you bring shame on God by breaking his law?"[578]

The War in Iraq desecrates Jesus Christ because it has been undertaken by a president and nation who call themselves Christian, while the violence and injustice of that war are akin to the actions of Christ's oppressors—Je-

---

[578] Romans 2:23, TEV.

sus abhorred violence, and never endorsed its use, even in his own defense. The doctrine of just war is also violated by our country's actions in Iraq. President Bush's Iraq War smacks strongly of unchristian vengeance, was planned from before Bush came into office (the evidence is overwhelming to the willfully-informed), and had no supportable connection to 9/11, weapons of mass destruction, terrorism, or humanitarian liberation. This tremendous waste of life, resources, opportunity (to actually combat terrorism rather than incite it), and American goodwill is demonstrably unchristian, and need not await an outcome in Iraq to be judged accordingly. For under Christ's and God's law, the end does not justify the means. If things deteriorate completely out of control in Iraq, that would not make Christian effort sinful: neither does "success" (however that is measured) bestow God's blessings on an unchristian action.

Because America was born a Christian nation, Christ's goodness once influenced its policies and actions more heavily than current preemptive warmongering initiatives. Even the federal government's early budgets were influenced by Jesus, for "[l]imiting military expenditures for defense only was in keeping with the Christian view that there should be no taxes for offensive wars."[579] Alexander Hamilton argued in <u>The Federalist No. 34</u> in support of "tying up the hands of government from offensive wars founded upon reasons of state."[580] (But, "Hamilton's reasoning was not moral, but fiscal: America should stay out of wars because they cost too

---

[579] Charles Adams, <u>Those Dirty Rotten Taxes: The Tax Revolts That Built America</u>, p. 58.
[580] Ibid., p. 58.

much."[581]) Thus Al Gore and Ted Kennedy were actually accurate when they said that U.S. preemption could destabilize the Middle East "and overturn an American tradition of generally not striking first."[582]

The only possible Christian exception to the prohibition of violent action is the doctrine of just war, though many Christians are pacifistic and do not accept violence as permissible under any circumstances.[583] One author has remarked: "war is evil; but doctrinaire pacifism may be more evil, and a just war is conceivable. (If we apply no rules of justice to the conduct of wars, those wars become the more frightful and destructive.)"[584] Otherwise, as George W. has observed, "we can travel without an ethical compass into a world we could live to regret."[585]

If we are to apply an ethical compass to the situation in Iraq, Christianity would presumably be the ethicality of choice for this administration, unless President Bush excepts his actions in leading the nation to war in Iraq from Christian scrutiny, an absurd notion. Christianity never advocates war, but the Christian doctrine of just war, as developed by St. Augustine, St. Thomas Aquinas and others, would be the one doctrine or circumstance under which a Christian might with integrity use violent

---

[581] Ibid., p. 58.
[582] Bob Woodward, Bush at War, p. 351.
[583] "...it may be that pacifism is again, as at other times in the past, moving into the forefront of Christian consciousness." James F. Childress and John Macquarrie, eds., The Westminster Dictionary of Christian Ethics, p. 329.
[584] Russell Kirk, The Roots of American Order, p. 164.
[585] George W. Bush, quoted in Thomas A. Freiling, George W. Bush on God & Country, p.104.

force. Noteworthy is that George W. Bush has never claimed that the war in Iraq was justified by the just war doctrine, presumably because he is fully aware that it is not. In fact, George W. has specifically said that he will *not* justify the Iraq War based on God.

The just war doctrine arose from a perceived need for Christians to assist in the defense of the Roman Empire from invaders. Thus the just war doctrine "came into being as a product of a close relation between church and secular society, and it has ever since developed in dialogue with the requirements of statecraft as manifested in different eras."[586] (Under George W., man of many Christian words and long prayers, there has never even been a dialogue–statecraft has predominated, and no Christian justification for the Iraq war has been proffered.) Then, "[r]ight authority, just cause, and right intention, listed by Aquinas as the conditions for a just war, all derive from Augustine and entered medieval consciousness through Gratian...."[587] By the end of the Middle Ages, the doctrine "included as well the ideas that force should be a last resort, should be proportionate to the evil remedied..., should expect to succeed in its ends, and should contribute to a new state of peace....[B]oth religious and secular just war thought in this period concentrated on restraining the prosecution of war, a tendency marked in subsequent Western moral thought on war up until the present."[588]

---

[586] James F. Childress and John Macquarrie, eds., <u>The Westminster Dictionary of Christian Ethics</u>, p. 328.
[587] Ibid., p. 328.
[588] Ibid., pp. 328-329.

The Iraq War initiated by President George W. Bush does not make the cut. He does not have the "right authority," because he is neither educated nor ordained as a religious leader, did not seek counsel with those who are, and has never even pretended to consult the teachings of Jesus Christ in deciding whether to go to war–he therefore does not possess even the pretense of "right Christian authority." George W. did not use force as a last resort, being instead impatient with the U.N. (which was proved right in the lack of any weapons of mass destruction). The force employed by the U.S. is extremely disproportionate to the threat[589] that Saddam Hussein posed to the United States (Saddam's evil intentions were insufficient, or else one could argue Christian war was appropriate in limitless cases.) Success was expected without question, and affected post-invasion planning as well–"As the war planning had progressed over the nearly 16 months, Powell had felt that the easier the war looked, the less Rumsfeld, the Pentagon and Franks had

---

[589] President Bush's "belief" that Saddam posed a threat, even if genuine, would not serve as an exception or excuse under just war doctrine, nor should it. If thousands of lives are at stake (perhaps millions, should Middle East instability prevail), a leader *must be right*; and if wrong, a Christian leader must repent, and heal the victims of that error in Christian compassion. God does not condone a war simply because an errant Christian "thought" he should be afraid. Fear is sinful: "There is no fear in love; but perfect love casteth out fear; because fear hath torment. He that feareth is not made perfect in love.' (1 John 4:18); "All our fears are wicked, and we fear because we will not nourish ourselves in our faith. How can anyone who is identified with Jesus Christ suffer from doubt or fear!;" "This does not mean that I will not be tempted to fear, but I will remember God's say-so....Are you learning to say things after listening to God, or are you saying things and trying to make God's word fit in?" (Oswald Chambers, My Utmost For His Highest, November 13, June 5.) "Only fear of the Lord is allowed." Isaiah 33:6.

worried about the aftermath."[590] The assault on Iraq has not "contribute[d] to a new state of peace," but instead has (along with Abu Ghraib and Guantanamo) turned global post-9/11 empathy for the U.S. into resentment, and has contributed to a growing holy Muslim jihad against the United States and its interests. And just war theory is not served by George W. when it requires "restraining the prosecution of war," for Mr. Bush shows little restraint in this area.

To summarize, none of the foregoing components of just war theory have been met by George W. Bush's War in Iraq:

- Right authority
- Just cause
- Right intention
- Force employed as a last resort
- The force employed should be proportionate to the evil remedied
- The war should be reasonably expected to succeed in its ends
- The war should contribute to a new state of peace

In a faint effort to somehow postulate a half-baked just war rationalization for the Iraq invasion, author Paul Kengor in <u>God and George W. Bush: a spiritual journey</u> writes (in hindsight, for Christianity was not considered in the Bush war room) that "just-war theory is an explicitly Christian doctrine....[Oswald] Chambers wrote frequently of war, and much of what he said

---

[590] Bob Woodward, <u>Plan of Attack</u>, p. 414.

resonated naturally with the situation in Iraq."[591] This is an outrageous representation, backed with absolutely no quotes from the pious and utterly devoted Mr. Chambers–nothing in Oswald Chambers' devotion to Jesus Christ "resonates naturally" with warfare, except perhaps that he felt that we should not fear this world as we look to Jesus.[592]

Kengor attempts unpersuasively to gloss over Christian just war theory, but he never addresses just war doctrine meaningfully. And yet he goes on the offensive (very), chastising Christians who dared oppose the war: "Despite this liberation [of Muslims], many liberal Christians were unrepentant in their opposition to the war that enabled this freedom."[593] Well, how righteous for one who has still made no presentation as to how the war was a just war acceptable to Jesus Christ. Does the "liberation" of Iraqis include the little children we've bombed, shot, starved and orphaned? Does "liberation" of Muslims, even if long-lived, justify our means without further analysis? Does the label "liberal Christian" not just serve to dismiss Christ, Himself quite the liberal? And is there great risk to a Christian being "unrepentant in their opposition to…war?" How about those who are "unrepentant in their support of a bloody war against a man they armed?" Deceiving Christians into thinking this war was just or holy, and alienating non-Christians by enlisting Christianity in warfare, Mr. Kengor fulfills

---

[591] Paul Kengor, God and George W. Bush: a spiritual life, pp. 235, 239.
[592] Nor does Mr. Kengor cite any just war doctrine to support his bland assertion that the Iraq War is a just war, because *there isn't any*.
[593] Ibid., p. 272.

biblical prophecy, which warns repeatedly of the false prophets who will come in end times, leading good souls astray and discouraging many from following the way of Jesus. God showed purpose in warning Christians of the troubles they would face from false prophets, a purpose of love, that the true not be lost. God does not want His children to be deceived into believing that they should ever kill in His name, for He made no just war exception to the command "thou shalt not kill." Better arguments are required than Mr. Kengor's (or Mr. Bush's silence) to justify on Christian grounds the U.S. invasion of Iraq,[594] but such arguments are non-existent, or they would surely have been offered up to the American people in another of those timely, convenient books with the pious, godly Bush-photo covers that pretend to extol the faith he professes but which themselves contain nothing of substance to support that illusion.

And yet George W. Bush apparently has not suffered from reservations about the morality of this war. Bob Woodward reported that "[I]t was clear that the president was convinced [the war] was both 100 percent correct and moral."[595] Not surprising from a president whose beloved father was the target of an assassination attempt by Saddam Hussein, who began planning for a war with Iraq more than six months prior to the 9/11 attacks, who stretched WMD intelligence information, and who fabricated links between al Qaeda terrorists and Iraq–clearly George W. Bush is "convinced" that any-

---

[594] 2 John 1:9: "Anyone who does not stay with the teaching of Christ, but goes beyond it, does not have God." TEV.
[595] Bob Woodward, Plan of Attack, p. 272.

thing he does is "both 100 percent correct and moral," for he has never apologized to the American people for *anything*. Perhaps George W. is really a student of Machiavelli instead of Jesus, for his actions are more reminiscent of the advice of Machiavelli: "…those who have known best how to use the fox, have turned out best. But it is necessary to this nature to know how to color it, and to be a great hypocrite and deceiver, and men are so simple, and so obedient to present necessity, that he who deceives will always find one who will let himself be deceived."[596]

After issuing the lofty order "For the peace of the world and the benefit and freedom of the Iraqi people, I hereby give the order to execute Operation Iraqi Freedom. May God bless the troops,"[597] Bush subsequently said "I'm surely not going to justify war based upon God. Understand that."[598] So George W. Bush does not even attempt to justify the Iraq War in God's name, a patent acknowledgement of God's disfavor of war. So by what moral code does George W. Bush, who cautioned against America "travel[ing] with an ethical compass into a world we could live to regret," steer the nation into war? If he acknowledges he cannot "justify war based upon God," what is there to base it on? Are Christians not to strive to "base" everything on God? And is it not then incongruous, even heretical, to ask God to bless troops sent into a war which is not just by

---

[596] Niccolo Machiavelli, <u>The Prince</u>, p. 108.
[597] Bob Woodward, <u>Plan of Attack</u>, p. 379.
[598] Ibid., p. 379.

Christian standards, a war for which God and Scripture were not consulted?

George W. was similarly unresponsive to Pope John Paul II, though the President rarely missed an opportunity to use the Pope's popularity coattails, in classic politico expertise. President Bush has said of the now-former Pope:

> We remember his visit to a prison, comforting the man who shot him. By answering violence with forgiveness, the Pope became a symbol of reconciliation....And maybe the reason this man became Pope is that he bears the message our world needs to hear....To those with power, the Pope carries a message of justice and human rights. And that message has caused dictators to fear and fall. His is not the power of armies or technology or wealth....And we, in our country, must not ignore the words the Pope addresses to us.[599]

But George W.'s words fall hollow once again, for he failed to "answer violence with forgiveness" in Iraq or Abu Ghraib, and moreover, he failed to heed the Pope's words regarding Iraq–he ignored the words of Pope John Paul II addressed to him. Paul Kengor relates that George W. "differed" with "Rome" over Iraq, for "the

---

[599] Thomas A. Freiling, George W. Bush on God & Country, pp. 156, 157.

pope believed that invading Iraq without UN approval would be "illegal.""⁶⁰⁰

But more accurately, the Pope was vehemently against the war, with or without UN approval, and even worked diligently to persuade other nations to decline to join the U.S. "coalition." In fact, *most* Christian denominations opposed the war, vocally, before Bush invaded:

> On Iraq, Bush's pro-war view was opposed by most Christian religious leaders. The pope spoke out forcefully against the war, and so, too, did the leaders of most, though not all, American Christian denominations, as well as most leading Christian theologians. When the leaders of the National Council of Churches, and of Bush's own church, the United Methodists, asked for the opportunity to present their objections to the war, Bush refused to meet with them. On any reasonable interpretation of the Christan message, there was nothing especially Christian about his decision to go to war, and there is a strong case for saying that it was distinctly un-Christian.[601]

---

[600] Paul Kengor, God and George W. Bush: a spiritual life, pp. 108, 109. Bush also "ignore[d] the words the Pope addresse[d] to [him]" when the Holy See sent an envoy to the then-Governor to stay the execution of Karla Faye Tucker. President Bush just doesn't "ignore" the publicity which visiting or talking about popes attracts: though he ignored two moral "message[s] of justice and human rights" which the Pope brought to him as one of those "with power," Bush did find time to attend funeral services for the Pope.

[601] Peter Singer, The President of Good and Evil: Questioning the Ethics of George W. Bush, p. 207.

Politics ("statecraft") and true Christian devotion are not compatible. It is therefore unsurprising that a politician permitted to scale the heights of America's political edifice should be truer to politics and the power of the deal than to Christ's Church and the power of the Father. But Christians are reminded: "Do not let all kinds of strange teachings lead you from the right way."[602] The U.S. presence in Iraq does not comport with Christian doctrine or with America's history, and is making the world not more but less safe. And the preemption doctrine fabricated to fill in the unchristian cracks is a "strange teaching" that "goes beyond"[603] the teachings of Christ, that has been employed to "lead [Christians] from the right way."

The alternative to Christian guidance in war-making (to "justifying war based on God"), is to justify war on some worldly or morally relativistic ethics. Indeed, much of President Bush's cynical political maneuvering is quite reminiscent of Machiavelli, whose morality would well suit the Iraq war, Abu Ghraib torture, or raising the civil union debate as political fodder to rally the Religious Right (though even Machiavelli would see the current deficit spending extravaganza as self-destructive). Machiavelli, whose philosophy is generally equated with the maxim "the end justifies the means," wrote in words that reflected a sort of reverse-Christianity:

> And many have imagined republics and princicipates that have never been seen or known to be in truth;

---
[602] Hebrews 13:9, TEV.
[603] 2 John 1:9.

because there is such a distance between how one lives and how one should live that he who lets go that which is done for that which ought to be done learns his ruin rather than his preservation–for a man who wishes to profess the good in everything needs must fall amongst so many who are not good….Hence it is necessary for a prince, if he wishes to maintain himself, to learn to be able to be not good, and use it and not use it according to the necessity….for, if one will consider everything well, he will find something which will seem virtue itself, and his conforming to it would be his ruin; and something other which will seem vice itself, and his conforming to it would succeed in security and the good being his.[604]

This is the kind of moral logic which would lead a political candidate to attempt to conceal a drunk driving conviction, or to then say he did so to protect his daughters from knowledge of his drinking history (like the girls didn't know from an early age that their father had a serious drinking problem–*see* Anderson, George and Laura). Or that would lead to bait-and-switch logic in the rationale for an invasion of a perceived foreign (oil) goldmine. Or the use of torture to elicit information from prisoners held indefinitely with no constitutional or international protections, or the discrediting of honest Republican Americans like Paul J. O'Neill for speaking truth about the evils of deficit spending, or the exposure of a CIA agent's cover as political retaliation for her husband speaking the truth. When supporters of this president dismiss his actions as politically necessary to

---

[604] Niccolo Machiavelli, The Prince, pp. 93, 94.

counter the evil of the "other side," they are not echoing Christ but Machiavelli, who argued that a leader cannot be virtuous (e.g., Christian) "for human conditions do not allow it."[605]

The doctrine of preemption, as (vaguely) outlined and (irrationally) implemented by the Bush administration, is such a Machiavellian contrivance. No scripture is cited to support this newly-created (though Reagan-patterned) and economically-convenient "doctrine," because there is no scriptural support, and the doctrine runs afoul of historical Christian just war doctrine.[606] Jesus Christ absolutely does not condone attacking another nation in His name under pretense of defense, pretense of "liberation," for revenge, or under any other rationale. In fact, Jesus disapproves of using His name to justify any war or violence, ever. Preemption is Machiavellian, but not Christian:

> If any man teach otherwise, and consent not to wholesome words, even the words of our Lord Jesus

---

[605] Ibid., The Prince, p. 94. Ironically, if Bush had exercised forgiveness and peacemaking in his response to the 9/11 attacks, and had with Christian integrity declined to invade Iraq, this course of action would have been supported by the "liberals" and whiny left-wingers, who would be thus aligned with Christ. Strange that the Christian Right should elect a leader who turns liberals and non-Christians off to Christianity, even while those lefties cry out for the values of peace which Christ represents.

[606] On July 31, 2002, Bush stated "Our intent is serious. There are no war plans on my desk. I believe there is casus belli and that the doctrine of preemption applies." Bob Woodward, Plan of Attack, pp. 137-138. But what is the definition of the doctrine of preemption, which Bush says applies? This has never been disclosed, just employed as a vague, undefined conclusion, like his definition of "enemy combatant." And though the war plans were not "on his desk," they were clearly in his desk drawer….

Christ, and to the doctrine which is according to godliness;

He is proud, knowing nothing, but doting about questions and strifes of words, whereof cometh envy, strife, railings, evil surmisings,

Perverse disputing of men of corrupt minds, and destitute of the truth, supposing that gain is godliness: from such withdraw thyself.[607]

To Christians, George W. Bush's lack of fealty to Christ in deciding to wage war should be extremely disturbing, as Mr. Bush is an acknowledged member of Skull & Bones, an elite, secret society which unquestionably engages in grossly unchristian ceremonies and worship. President Bush has said Skull & Bones is "so secret I can't even talk about it,"[608] but he has never once disavowed his membership or repented publicly for participation in this Satanic group linked to the Illuminati. For the Illuminati, members are considered destined to rule, superior to others, and not bound to righteousness. As Texe Marrs has summarized, one of the "Five Central Beliefs of the Illuminized Brotherhood" is that "[t]he illumined person is considered one who is able to wield the spiritual energies of both sides of reality–the good and the evil, light and darkness. Such a man becomes superman. He becomes his own deity, a master magician, a prince among princes, and a king

---

[607] 1 Timothy 6:3-5, KJV.
[608] George W. Bush, A Charge To Keep, p. 47. Skull & Bones is "...the sin qua non of secret societies," Anderson, George & Laura, p. 130

over many."⁶⁰⁹ This is eerily close to the instruction of Machiavelli, and too close for Christian comfort to the decision-making process reflected in the actions of George W. Bush and his administration. Christian words, unchristian actions…..George W. Bush should publicly proclaim Jesus Christ Lord and renounce Satanic worship and Skull & Bones, and stop attempting to serve two masters, "light and darkness."

The deployment of preemptive force by American troops with a compass-less moral foundation for that action is sin enough if committed by a non-Christian, but is more heinous when that action is advanced with Christian words from the highly-visible tongue of an avowed Christian leader of an avowed Christian nation. Christ is clear that God has a moral code that we will be held to, whatever our intentions, and there is really not much vagueness in that code. President Bush has asserted that "our security will require all Americans to be forward-looking and resolute, to be ready for preemptive action when necessary to defend our liberty and to defend our lives."⁶¹⁰ But "preemptive action" has never been defined, nor has the vital issue of what is "necessary." (When the president decides it is so….) Jesus is more concerned with souls than lives, and probably has a different definition than the politician of what it is to "defend our liberty and defend our lives." President Bush's words sound patriotic, but they are morally without any paddle but his own, and he is on his own

---

⁶⁰⁹ Texe Marrs, <u>Dark Majesty: The Secret Brotherhood and the Magic of a Thousand Points of Light</u>, p. 213.
⁶¹⁰ Thomas A. Freiling, <u>George W. Bush on God & Country</u>, p. 262.

personal ad hoc joyride with the greatest (once-) Christian nation in history in the back of his canoe.

The ease with which such loose moral logic as that used by President Bush can be employed willy-nilly to avoid moral responsibility for America's aggression is everywhere in current American media and government bias. Every Iraqi who resists America is a "terrorist" or "insurgent," (when the Taliban fighters, including Osama bin Laden, resisted the Soviets, the United States armed them and dubbed them "freedom fighters"), and there is widespread national self-delusion that America's purpose in invading Iraq was liberation, in an Orwellian re-write of history. Left and Right are both guilty of viewing, and therefore painting, the conflict with a patriotic brush, but God's relationship to man is not through a nation. Mortimer Zuckerman, of *US News & World Report*, presents as "fact that, yes, these same Middle East oil producers have enmeshed us in two wars over the past two decades,"[611] performing in a major-selling magazine ("rated America's most credible print news source"[612]) the amazing moral logic somersault of blaming the Arabs for the wars prompted by America's quest for dominance in the Middle East to protect its oil addiction. (In the same "credible" issue, "[v]eteran foreign correspondent and New York Daily News op-ed columnist Richard Chesnoff" stated that "One of the major reasons we went to war was that Saddam thought

---

[611] "Our Energy Conundrum," *US News & World Report*, April 25, 2005, p. 72.
[612] per every cover.

the French would back him up."⁶¹³ Oh yeah, it's the French, they're at fault....)

Paul Kengor, in his spiritual retrofit of George W., goes to surreal (though short) lengths to justify the doctrine of preemption and George W.'s foray into Iraq:

> It can be argued that preemptive action against terrorists and the nations that harbor them is not really preemption, but rather the only response to a war begun by terrorists against the United States long ago....Yet the primary intent of a war in Iraq would be to head off a perceived possible disaster down the road, making it preemptive in the broadest sense.⁶¹⁴

But Iraq did not deliberately harbor terrorists, until America's presence drew them like flies to Imperialist manure, so Kengor has linked the Iraq War with terrorists when there simply was no connection prior to the U.S. invasion: he argues that the Iraq War was a "response to a war begun by terrorists." Actually, it was a detour from that war. And, George W.'s logic is echoed in Kengor's position: where Bush advocated "preemptive action when necessary to defend our liberty and to defend our lives," he foreshadowed the moral grayness of Kengor's "to head off a perceived possible disaster down the road...." But what does "perceived possible" do as a moral standard other than convey to the standard bearer

---

⁶¹³ "Frying the French," *US News & World Report*, April 25, 2005, p. 20.
⁶¹⁴ Paul Kengor, <u>God and George W. Bush: a spiritual life</u>, pp. 197-198, 198.

sole discretion to decide carte blanche when to attack another nation, and fill in the blanks later? And how far "down the road" does a threat have to be? "Preemptive in the broadest sense" says nothing of Jesus or the moral standards he bore to the world. Jesus sees disaster in unchristian action, not in nebulous anxiety about a worldly future. And the "perceived possible disaster" which was sold to Americans and the world was the supposed threat of WMD, a threat subsequently proved to be nonexistent, if not contrived.

Bush's doctrine of preemption is morally dubious, and the stakes could not be higher. Albert Einstein held that "[y]ou cannot simultaneously prevent and prepare for war. The very prevention of war requires more faith, courage and resolution than are needed to prepare for war."[615] Having ignored Christ and the Pope, George W. is hardly likely to heed Einstein, but the penalties for a misstep in international affairs have rarely been greater. If one takes on to oneself the sole, God-like power to determine when it is "necessary" to use offensive force to supposedly "defend" against unarticulated, vague future threats, one had better be correct. As Paul J. O'Neill stated: "It's not my view that says preemption is all wrong...it just gives to the appropriator such a weight of responsibility to really be right. And that's where it all breaks down, because politics, as it's now played, is not about being right. It's about doing whatever's necessary to win."[616] Politics, winning at all cost, "not about being

---

[615] quoted in Helen Caldicott, <u>The New Nuclear Danger: George W. Bush's Military-Industrial Complex</u>, p. 187.
[616] Ron Suskind, <u>The Price of Loyalty</u>, p. 314.

right"…sounds like Machiavelli, or our legal system, or the Illuminati and Skull & Bones. But it doesn't sound like Jesus Christ. Sounds like Christian words coupled with unchristian actions, the worst of all desecrations of God's only Son.

> Jesus said to his disciples: "Things that cause people to sin are bound to come, but woe to that person through whom they come. It would be better for him to be thrown into the sea with a millstone tied around his neck than for him to cause one of these little ones to sin. So watch yourselves.
> "If your brother sins, rebuke him, and if he repents, forgive him."
>
> —Luke 17:1-3, NIV

This is indeed "a weight of responsibility to really be right." But George W. knows this and therefore will have no objections to these honest, free-speech American Christian criticisms, for he himself has set the standard: "Some acts and choices in this world have eternal consequences. It is always, and everywhere, wrong to be cruel and hateful, to enslave and oppress. It is always, and everywhere, right to be kind and just, to protect the lives of others…."[617] "Always and everywhere" includes America, now.

If the "logic" of preemption is carried to its conclusion, it actually greatly increases international tension and distrust, wastes scarce resources, and increases the risk of war. Edward M. Kennedy called Bush's

---

[617] George W., quoted in Thomas A. Freiling, <u>George W. Bush on God & Country</u>, p. 36.

preemption doctrine "a call for 21st century American imperialism that no other nation can or should accept."[618] The roots of preemption are no doubt found in the so-called Reagan doctrine, the major elements of which included "an assertion of American rights under international law to use force unilaterally in self-defense...."[619] In direct contrast to Einstein's proposition that one cannot simultaneously prevent and prepare for war, the Reagan position, echoed today by Bush & co., is that "[i]f force is to remain our last resort, it follows that an important objective of diplomacy must be the preservation of this option....Clearly we cannot permit an opponent to lock us into diplomatic embrace while he exploits his military advantage."[620]

But the problem with such implicitly distrustful unilateralism is that it invites, understandably, a similar posture from other world powers, creating the very self-fulfilling circumstances employed as logic to support "preserving our option" of force. This circuitous logic is not only unchristian, it is even illogical by worldly standards, for it acts as a chip on America's shoulder, and invites others (as we do in most everything) to follow America's "lead," a lead into distrust and certain

---

[618] 10/10/02, per Bob Woodward, Plan of Attack, p. 203.
[619] William R. Bode, "The Reagan Doctrine in Outline," Central America and the Reagan Doctrine, p.249. The author, William R. Bode, writing in 1987, goes on to stress that "It needs to be noted that the right to unilateral action in self-defense is also becoming a conspicuous element in the Reagan Administration's evolving counterterrorist policy....the battle against terrorism may well add impetus to the Reagan Doctrine." p. 249.
[620] Ibid., p. 256.

conflict.[621] Christianity builds trust based on surrender, the kind of trust Jesus showed when He surrendered His worldly form to the cross, the trust Christians showed when they were burned in oil or fed to lions rather than betray an unseen Truth. And this is the kind of trust he asks of Christian nations, for how is the world to live in peace until Christian nations take Christ-like risks of faith, and invite other nations to lay down their arms by first laying down their own—for Jesus' unilateralism is one of disarmament, not of aggression.

Thus is President Bush's outspoken aggressiveness so incongruous coming from a supposed Christian, and just like the liberal versus conservative Christian rift, George W. Bush is either right or wrong in his unilateral military enthusiasm—judged not by himself, but by Jesus Christ, and regardless of outcome. As with NCLB, sweeping reversals of U.S. policy are being rapidly and irrevocably effected by one man, who never appears to look critically back at his own decisions. Years of effort over numerous administrations to slow, stop, or even reverse the proliferation of nuclear weapons are being

---

[621] This has been demonstrated by world public opinion polls, which show some nations supporting America's unilateralism because such unilateralism is desirable to further their own nationalistic agendas: "Today, as India aspires to be a global power itself–based on its huge consumer economy, advanced technological prowess, and nuclear weapons–many Indians now see the US as a partner with common goals. 'George Bush has done a lot to rehabilitate the language of pure national self-interest [here],' says Pratap Bhanu Mehta, president of the Center for Policy Research, an independent think tank in New Dehli. He says, 'Let's not beat around with a lot of talk on humanitarian norms or multilateralism. Rather it's national interest that is most important.' And that allows India to do the same. It's a *realpolitik* scenario." Scott Baldauf, "Most Indians say 'thumbs up' to second Bush term," *The Christian Science Monitor*, January 21, 2005, p.7.

reversed by this administration, where "we have seen confirmation of President Bush's commitment to a new generation of nuclear weapons, with clear indications that such weapons will no longer be regarded as deterrence but for pre-emptive use against nuclear and non-nuclear powers alike. We have entered an era in which the United States, the lone superpower, has assumed the role of world policeman...."[622]

The ease with which this newfound preemption doctrine can be employed without thorough analysis, democratic consensus, or Christian doctrinal support is evidenced by the Iraq War, in which this doctrine was brought into play immediately after 9/11 to rationalize a war planned long before. Donald Rumsfeld raised Iraq as a military target on September 12, 2001:

> Why shouldn't we go against Iraq, not just al Qaeda? he asked. Rumsfeld was speaking not only for himself when he raised the question. His deputy, Paul D. Wolfowitz, was committed to a policy that would make Iraq a principal target of the first round in the war on terrorism.
>
> Rumsfeld was raising the possibility that they could take advantage of the opportunity offered by the terrorist attacks to go after Saddam immediately.[623]

---

[622] John Cornwell, <u>Hitler's Scientists: Science, War and the Devil's Pact</u>, p. 460. The fact that Bush has finally dropped his effort to secure these weapons does not make this issue moot, because it a) reveals his unchristian, hawkish ambition, b) an attempt to commit a criminal act is equally punishable under American jurisprudential doctrine as the act itself, and c) he's probably just having these weapons developed anyway, in secret....
[623] Bob Woodward, <u>Bush at War</u>, p.49.

The term "preemption" serves simply to mask the more disturbing connotations raised by "aggression" or "offensive" or "invasion." But whatever else characterizes the U.S. invasion of Iraq, "defensive" does not apply–there were no nuclear or biological weapons (though the artful conjuring of their imagined existence stirred the nation to fear, making all too many complacent lest they be faulted in the event of "the next terrorist attack"), and even were Saddam to have possessed such weapons, he had no means to deliver them to U.S. soil, and no known ties to terrorists in any capacity. Viewing the Iraq War as an offensive action, it is not surprising that there has been consistent grassroots resistance in Iraq, elections notwithstanding. The situation is reminiscent not just of Vietnam (where our government similarly contrived (Tonkin Gulf) to "liberate" a people who hadn't invited us), but also of the Russian incursion into Afghanistan in the 1980s. In "The Reagan Doctrine in Outline," from <u>Central America and the Reagan Doctrine</u>, the conservative author notes that for the Soviets,

> The basic vulnerability lies in the incompatibility of Marxism with fundamental popular expectations and aspirations....[which] renders the Soviet leadership, and its local conflict managers, prone to serious miscalculations of popular attitudes in the target countries. Thus, the Soviet leaders as well as their invading forces apparently were genuinely surprised by the determined resistance mounted by the population of Afghanistan to the Soviet invasion. It was a case of ideological misperception leading to a

> major military miscalculation....clearly Moscow can ill afford additional engagements on the model, let alone scale, of the Afghanistan conflict. [624]

But in the case of Iraq, an engagement of much larger scale than Afghanistan (which America concurrently controls), the same vulnerability of "ideological misperception" led neo-conservatives, including if not primarily led by George W. Bush, to "miscalculate popular attitudes in the target country." America, having preempted a non-existent WMD threat, dealt a blow against a government with no interest in terrorists, and now faces a Soviet-like situation in that its "liberation" is viewed widely with skepticism. Standing on extremely thin moral ice, having alienated much of the world, America stands "holding the bag" which is Iraq. The Soviet Union's doomed effort to occupy Afghanistan was driven by a decades-long jostling for dominance in the oil-rich Middle East, and an effort to rejuvenate its waning economy. The drain of resources and morale in Afghanistan sapped a fundamentally-flawed economic system, and contributed greatly to the collapse of the Soviet Union. American conservatives watched with glee as the Soviet Union slammed its massive military might impotently into the bleak hills of Afghanistan, only to incur steady losses from American-armed Taliban fighters, including bin Laden. The economic toll on the Soviet Union was obvious to the objective observer, as

---

[624] William R. Bode, "The Reagan Doctrine in Outline," <u>Central America and the Reagan Doctrine</u>, pp. 251-252.

was the degenerative cycle of hearts and minds when there was no stability from which to rebuild:

> A third vulnerability is economic. The Soviets are endeavoring to defray the costs of their expanding empire by imposing on their clients a major share of the latter's own military outlays. Angola, for example, is paying for Cuban troops from oil revenues…. Impoverished Soviet clients, however, shoulder this burden indefinitely. They are forced, in effect, to "eat their own seed corn"—diverting into the military resources and investments critically needed for basic economic infrastructure and, thereby, for the consolidation of political power. Trade and investment drawn from Western sources can help to stave off disaster, but the steady economic drainage eventually must cut debilitatingly into the provision of even basic services, while combat is continued against insurgent forces which further disrupt those services. As that predicament deepens, the Soviet Union faces the choice of assuming increasingly heavy economic burdens or countenancing the economic and military collapse of its clients.
>
> These ideological, political and economic liabilities of the Soviet empire translate into conspicuous military vulnerability….This spontaneous combustion not only threatens every new Soviet expansionist venture, but it also holds the potential of spilling back into the core of the Soviet empire.[625]

Iraq is presently in an identical though larger-scale vicious cycle of deterioration than the Soviet failure in

---
[625] Ibid., p. 252.

Afghanistan, and the Bush administration, which was expecting a hero's welcome in Iraq and was ill-prepared for the "reconstruction" (occupation?) process, is hardly likely to acknowledge this inevitable deterioration until the U.S. economy is tapped out. America similarly suffers "conspicuous military vulnerability" which could "spill back into the [(American)] empire," but just as later proved true of the Soviets, America's greatest vulnerability is economic.

The disconnect between military reality and (until recently) American public opinion about the Iraq War is a direct product of the government propaganda and patriotic optimism/denial that is interposed by the ideological spin-doctors of modern America–the government, the military, and the media. Of course, a great deal of corporate money greases all of these wheels.... Despite Americans' ardent though unchristian faith in their country's mythology, the United States Government has a proven and consistent history of lying to its citizenry. In this we are become George Orwell's vision of a future bureaucratic, dehumanizing society. Americans have blind faith in their nation and their technology, and America's continued though waning military edge has been driving the nation's economy for at least 65 years.

And George W. Bush's preemption logic, (though no truly logical manifestation of this concept has been presented) fits perfectly with George Orwell's description of doublethink:

> Doublethink means the power of holding two contradictory beliefs in one's mind simultaneously,

and accepting both of them....The process has to be conscious, or it would not be carried out with sufficient precision, but it also has to be unconscious, or it would bring with it a feeling of falsity and hence of guilt. Doublethink lies at the very heart of Ingsoc, since the essential act of the Party is to use conscious deception while retaining the firmness of purpose that goes with complete honesty. To tell deliberate lies while genuinely believing in them, to forget any fact that has become inconvenient, and then, when it becomes necessary again, to draw it back from oblivion for just so long as it is needed, to deny the existence of objective reality which one denies–all this is indispensably necessary.[626]

Orwell was not a Christian, or he perhaps would have seen doublethink as willful ignorance, which is assisted by Satan the deceiver, whose favorite deception is the cloak of Christianity. Orwellian doublethink is reflected in current policies such as: NCLB testing, which "believes" in testing even though most educators see it as deleterious to learning, more harmful than good; trickle down economics, which though no doubt "believed in" by many of its proponents, has been clearly established (and is soon to be proven unequivocally) as failed, fantastical economic theory; environmental policy, where clean air and water are proclaimed while pollution increases by all measures and big business writes environmental legislation; the denial of the clear evidence establishing the dramatic threats of global warming; Americans placing faith in politicians and government

---

[626] George Orwell, <u>1984</u>, pp. 176-177.

despite decades of lies and uncontrolled bureaucratic growth; belief that the oil will run out sometime in the distant future, when that future is imminent; arguing that torture is justified, or that war is Christian; faith in technology despite its obvious failures which threaten all life; the war in Iraq, which will devolve into modern hell and world economic collapse no matter how sincere President Bush's deluded "belief" that he is the great Arab liberator. Doublethink....

Examples of doublethink abound in the modern world–many Arabs, Germans and neo-Nazis dismiss the holocaust, many Jews ignore the unfairness of the Palestinians being denied a homeland, and most Americans prefer not to think or talk about their country's history of systemic slavery and the widespread rape of American slaves, the genocide of the American Indians, or Vietnam. A fine example of this worldly human condition, where mankind routinely substitutes belief in place of truth, is found in Serbia: "In fact, a new poll released [June 14, 2005] shows that at least one-third of the Serbian public say [a video graphically depicting Serbian paramilitaries killing Muslim civilians] is fake. That sentiment, observers say, reflects cognitive dissonance–the human capacity to hold contradictory beliefs simultaneously."[627]

A majority of Americans in their perceived cultural, financial, and religious superiority profess disdain for those ignorant enough to deny the holocaust or Serbian genocide. But Americans are equally human and fallible,

---

[627] Beth Kampschror, "Serbs divided over grim video," *The Christian Science Monitor*, June 15, 2005, p. 6.

as Christians understand. And Jesus Christ is truth whose love cuts through cognitive dissonance/doublethink/willful ignorance, which is what is controlling America and its actions today.

Horrible, Soviet-style torture has been routinely employed by hundreds or thousands of civilian and military personnel at Abu Ghraib, Guantanamo Bay, and other American "detention" facilities. Americans by and large choose to dismiss this systemic barbarity as a "few bad apples," but the rest of the world knows or believes differently. Can Americans' cognitive dissonance trump world opinion, or will unilateralism bend to reality? And the tortures committed by the United States government under George W. Bush are morally more heinous than the slaughters in Serbia or the gulags of the Soviet Union, because America holds itself out as a Christian nation doing Christian work. America can deny truth, but the country's world dominance has made it the greatest purveyor of culture, faith, etc., in human history, and its dominance is currently doing more widespread and intense damage to the body of Christ than the Medieval Crusades. At least Hitler did not pretend to be Christian while he attempted to dominate Europe–Bush W. believes that God selected him to impose the (morally decaying) American way of life on the entire world: whether one is imposing their superior race or their superior culture/economy/"democracy" is of little consequence to those whose families, cultures and economies are devastated by the imposition.

President Bush W. has demonstrated marvelous mastery of cognitive dissonance in his repeated declarations that Muslim terrorists hate America "because we're free." This statement is a complete rationalization, a fiction with utterly no factual or logical support. (See Chapter Nine)

A "world" picture of the current America-Iraq War would take into consideration the simple global truths that: 1) If a global election were held today, with strict adherence to voting integrity, and there were only two candidates for world leader, George W. Bush or Osama bin Laden, then Osama would most likely soon be out of hiding, sending out the UN troops to find George W. the war crimes fugitive, hiding in a cave somewhere in Crawford, Texas. This is the case not just because of the huge numbers of Muslims in the world, but because of the ill will felt toward America's (George W.'s) aggression and the fear which that belligerence engenders. What message to the world is America presenting from Jesus?

2) America is not "defending itself" from Iraq. On the contrary, the Iraqi people, and the Muslim Middle East, are much like the American Indians. The American capitalists sought the resources of their lands for material gain at the expense of their indigenous culture, of which the Christian Americans thought little. After a time, resentment grew, and isolated groups resisted American power, dared to resist "progress." The huge technological and logistical Goliath, ignoring the legitimacy and human value of the culture it is eclipsing with its own, then cried foul and embarked on a righteous "manifest destiny" of justification to pacify and liberate the dysfunctional savages who don't treat their women right.

A substantial majority of American colonists who were abducted by American Indians did not wish to return to their former "civilized" lives, and a large number of Arabs who live in America choose to return to what Americans view as a backward culture, but our society does not address this–America is "the greatest country in the world." Well, do look now but, "the greatest country in the world" is on a global genocidal torture quest in righteous outrage, believing God to be on its side again, like it did while it slaughtered Indian children and women. And Jesus is stamped on America's military helmets. (And He doesn't approve.)

Again, the contrast between what is Christian and what is done by the current White House is glaringly evident to those not blinded either by false ideology about America or by fruitlessly-placed trust in the Christian integrity of a fraud. In a worldly twist on the dual nature of Christ, Machiavelli proposed that a successful ruler would be half man and half beast:

> There are two kinds of fighting: one with the laws, the other with force. The first one is proper to man; the second to beasts; but because the first proves many times to be insufficient, one needs must resort to the second. Therefore it is necessary for a prince to know well how to use the beast and the man.... To say this is simply to say that one has to have as a preceptor one who is half-beast and half-man, that it is needful for a prince to know how to use the one and the other nature, and that the one without the other is not durable.[628]

---

[628] Niccolo Machiavelli, The Prince, p. 107.

But Christ was not of the beastly nature, and He taught His followers not to attempt to walk in the dark and in the light, for such is not possible if one is to follow Him. Unlike Machiavelli, Jesus taught to play by the rules: "An athlete who runs in a race cannot win the prize unless he obeys the rules."[629]

The rules for a Christian, to be understood and modeled all the more by Christian leaders, are those laid down by Christ and Christian doctrine such as just war, which is itself debatable as justified in Christ but which is the minimum moral standard to be met by any Christian individual or nation who launches or supports a war. The truth is that George W. Bush has pointedly and explicitly avoided defending the doctrine of preemption in Christian logic, because *it is indefensible in Christ*. Further, George W. refuses to be held accountable to any Christian standard in answering to any of the various charges against him regarding Iraq–non-existent weapons of mass destruction, but also Abu Ghraib, or the lack of any connections between Saddam Hussein and terrorists. George would prefer to sweep such accountability aside, with unchallenged yet indefensible assertions like "[t]here were good-faith disagreements…over the course and timing of military action in Iraq. Whatever has come before, we now have only two options: to keep our word, or to break our word."[630] This statement is patently unchristian and is not reconcilable with Jesus Christ: "whatever has come before" avoids the issue of whether the "course and

---

[629] 2 Timothy 2:3, TEV.
[630] Thomas A. Freiling, <u>George W. Bush on God & Country</u>, p. 229.

timing" of that original action were Christian, instead focusing on ends. But to do this is Machiavellian, where ends justify means, and where means can never be immoral if they lead to desirable ends. Also, W. employs simplistic grade school logic which is deceptive when he states that "we have only two options," for there is an obvious third option excluded by his position–to admit that the Iraq War was a mistake.

Truly, to reduce the Iraq situation to a decision about whether or not America keeps her word employs patriotic pride in place of Christ, and avoids accountability. For if the U.S. incursion into Iraq is not defensible before Christ, then both the outcome and America's word are completely irrelevant. If America has no Christian or legal right to invade Iraq, imprison Arabs, or torture those prisoners (which it surely does not have before Christ), then America is an Imperialist lout rapist, and saying that America has to finish the job is then to continue that rape without remorse after realizing that the victim is resistant–keeping one's word is not Christian if that word was corrupt or unchristian. And using a Christian moral precept like 'keeping one's word' as logic to continue in unchristian conduct is itself another layer of deception and desecration of Christ's integrity. Christian words, unchristian actions….

And yet we hear religiously righteous declarations from this man like: "Others killed in the name of racial purity or the class struggle. These enemies kill in the name of a false religious purity, perverting the faith they claim to hold. In this war…we are defending civilization itself."[631] This is really twisted, for in one breath George W. Bush alludes to Hitler and the Soviets, ignoring that America kills all-too-well using its own ideology. Then he ignores his own "false religious purity, perverting the faith [he] claim[s] to hold," while he masks his preemption embarrassment as a defense of "civilization itself." No greater threat has ever existed to world peace and the welfare of mankind than George W. Bush at the helm of a crumbling nation of frightened, misinformed, insular, materialistic consumers. Nationalism led the Soviets, Nazis and now America in their killing, and the defenders of the Middle East hold legitimate, religiously pure complaints in their desire to keep western values and corruption from destroying their culture, family, and way of life. The Iraqi insurgents had nothing to do with 9/11, and are defending their homeland–it is thus fantasy logic or outright deception to call America's invasion of Iraq under such circumstances "defending civilization itself."

The Bush administration's creation of the doctrine of preemption to justify its unchristian aggression against Iraq recalls Alan Bloom's observations that "[r]ationality is only the activity of providing good reasons for what has no reason or what is unreasonable"[632] and that "[t]he mixture of unwise power and powerless wisdom…would always end up with power strengthened and wisdom compromised…."[633] But whatever dubious rationalizations George W. Bush hides behind in his unrepentant

---

[631] Ibid., p. 243.
[632] Allan Bloom, <u>The Closing of the American Mind</u>, p. 206.
[633] Ibid., p. 285.

push forward in Iraq, he will ultimately be held to Christian clarity–"Goodness is the harvest that is produced from the seeds that peacemakers plant in peace."[634] What then is the harvest of the seeds that warmakers plant in war, or preemptors in preemption? Jesus is wonderful, almighty, and fully aware of worldly events.

In addition to ignoring Christ in fashioning the doctrine of preemption, George W. has failed to address Christ's vital teachings regarding the implicit evil of vengeance. For Americans, too, explanations like WMD or terrorist links serve as rationalizations for a war which quite naturally has engendered powerful desire for revenge–these rationalizations serve to mask vengeance as justice.

For non-Christians, revenge may be acceptable to their world-view. But more powerful evidence of the truth of Christ than any proof that Jesus walked on water or healed the sick, is the power of His words that we must "love our enemies." This tenet is central to Jesus' message and follows as a direct corollary to what He said was the most important commandment in the law–

> THOU SHALT LOVE THE LORD THY GOD WITH ALL THY HEART, AND WITH ALL THY SOUL, AND WITH ALL THY MIND. This is the first and great commandment. And the second is like unto it, THOU SHALT LOVE THY NEIGHBOUR AS THYSELF. On these two commandments hang all the law and the prophets.[635]

---

[634] James 3:18, TEV.
[635] Matthew 22:37-40, KJV.

In reversing the pattern of evil that Satan preys upon, Christianity teaches that evil be returned with good, breaking what otherwise is an ever-escalating cycle of pain and retaliation; this is true on both the individual (marriage and all interpersonal relationships) and societal levels. Thus Christians are taught "Do not pay back evil with evil or cursing with cursing; instead, pay back with a blessing...."[636] George W. Bush has more reason to hate and therefore seek revenge on Saddam Hussein than perhaps any other American on earth, yet he has not discounted or convincingly disavowed his personal enmity for Saddam Hussein as an underlying motive for the depositing of hundreds of thousands of committed, trusting, loyal U.S. troops into an inhospitable desert filled with bitter hatred fueled by religious fury. And this in an administration that is the most tightly secret and loyal in American history, and in which George W. was raring to go after Saddam Hussein since day one, and has employed his very powerful personality and frightening over-confidence to dominate all those who work under him. Not a little suspect?

In April of 1993, the Iraqi government (headed by Saddam Hussein) attempted to assassinate the senior George Bush (Herbert Walker).[637] On September 28, 2001, George W. said to King Abdullah of Jordan of the 9/11 attacks: "There's a certain level of blood lust, but we won't let it drive our reaction."[638] Further, Americans' anger at the September 11 attacks put pressure on the

---

[636] 1 Peter 3:9, TEV.
[637] Gerald Posner, Why America Slept: the Failure to Prevent 9/11, p. 61.
[638] Bob Woodward, Bush at War, p. 168.

White House to demonstrate American resolve and to come up with results.[639] Now four years after 9/11, we've captured Saddam Hussein and dangerously stretched our military and economic resources occupying Iraq. This is classic bureaucratic scapegoating: Saddam didn't attack America on 9/11, nor did the Iraqi soldiers or the civilian population of Iraq, nor did any of them torture American soldiers or civilians (or other categories of Americans). How can liberation be touted, let alone accepted, as the justification for the Iraq venture when that supposed liberation effort was launched immediately after, and as a direct response to, an attack on our nation by totally unrelated parties? What will Jesus say?

"Al Qaeda and the Taliban have made a serious mistake. And…they will pay a serious price."[640] These words of George W. Bush do not even pretend to be Christian, though they may have served political utility.[641] But the

---

[639] Roger Ailes, "former media guru for Bush's father," conveyed a message to President Bush that Americans would be patient in their support of his response to the 9/11 attacks, but that "[s]upport would dissipate if the public did not see Bush acting harshly." Bob Woodward, Bush at War, p. 207. Not only was this counsel unchristian, it was of dubious ethicality–Woodward reports that the message from Ailes to Bush "had to be confidential because Ailes, a flamboyant and irreverent media executive, was currently the head of Fox News, the conservative-leaning television cable network that was enjoying high ratings. In that position, Ailes was not supposed to be giving political advice." (p. 207).

[640] George W. Bush, from Thomas A. Freiling, George W. Bush on God & Country, p. 56.

[641] Which raises the interesting ethical question about just war—if Jesus would have us forgive those who do us evil, as He modeled with His own life, then it seems difficult for Christians to countenance even a counterattack against an enemy (as opposed to simple defense), let alone a preemptive strike on distant foreign soil, against an enemy that has only attacked us with fiery, impotent words.

serious price has been paid by Saddam Hussein and the Iraqi people, while al Qaeda grows and gains more international membership, and American soldiers guard desert pipelines and roadwork with their lives. The proof of the Gospels is reflected in this failure, because the cycle of revenge always ends in horror, whereas Christ's way offers healing and the possibility of reconciliation. Whatever alternatives were available in the fight to disband al Qaeda, invading Iraq was a dead-end from any angle, and has drawn resources, attention, and international support away from the war on terror.

What would Jesus have counseled to President Bush and the American people, had His opinion been solicited? For He has said "But now I tell you: do not take revenge on someone who wrongs you….love your enemies and pray for those who persecute you."[642] Paul drew from his devotion to Jesus the lesson that:

> If someone has done you wrong, do not repay him with a wrong. Try to do what everyone considers to be good. Do everything possible on your part to live in peace with everybody. Never take revenge, my friends, but instead let God's anger do it….Do not let evil defeat you; instead, conquer evil with good.[643]

America will not conquer the "evil" of al Qaeda with the "good" of the Iraq invasion, and unilaterally jumping the gun on the United Nations may be defended by neo-conservatism, but it was not doing

---

[642] Matthew 5:39, 44, TEV.
[643] Romans 12:17-19, 21, TEV.

"everything possible on [George W.'s] part to live in peace with everybody."

So Mr. Bush's words of retaliation have been unchristian, as well as his actions in the Iraq response. The New Testament instructs that "if we hate others, we are in the darkness; we walk in it and do not know where we are going, because the darkness has made us blind."[644] The darkness of 9/11 has blinded too many Americans, including Christians, to the wisdom of this simple yet difficult logic. By panicking in fear and retaliation, America walks into al Qaeda's (and Satan's) hands:

> We love because God first loved us. If we say we love God, but hate others, we are liars. For we cannot love God, whom we have not seen, if we do not love others, whom we have seen. The command that Christ has given us is this: whoever loves God must love others also.[645]

C.S. Lewis devoted much attention to the temptations of vengeance, noting that indignation at a wrong (like 9/11?):

> [leads] to a more terrible sin. For it encourages a man to think that his own worst passions are holy. It encourages him to add, explicitly or implicitly, "Thus saith the Lord" to the expression of his own emotions or even his own opinions; as…some politicians…so horribly do. (It is this, by the way, rather than mere idle "profane swearing" that we ought to mean by "taking God's name in vain"…)….For

---

[644] 1 John 2:11, TEV.
[645] 1 John 4:19-21, TEV.

the Supernatural, entering a human soul, opens to it new possibilities both of good and evil. From that point the road branches: one way to sanctity, love, humility, the other to spiritual pride, self-righteousness, persecuting zeal. And no way back to the mere human virtues and vices of the unawakened soul. If the Divine call does not make us better, it will make us very much worse. Of all bad men religious bad men are the worst.[646]

Lewis posits that when a person harbors bitterness and resentment toward one who has wronged them, then two evils have been created and two injuries inflicted: "Such hatreds are the kind of thing that cruelty and injustice, by a sort of natural law, produce....The reaction...to injury, though profoundly natural, is profoundly wrong."[647] For those who succumb to bitterness and resentment, "...of course the fatal confusion between being in the right and being righteous soon falls upon them....There is also in many of the Psalms a still more fatal confusion—that between the desire for justice and the desire for revenge."[648] In words that ring ominously next to Bush's "Mission Accomplished" overconfidence, Lewis concludes that "obviously all this—taking upon oneself to hate those whom one thinks God's enemies...–is an extremely dangerous, almost fatal, game. It leads straight to "Pharisaism" in the sense which

---

[646] C.S. Lewis, Reflections on the Psalms, pp. 31, 31-32.
[647] Ibid., pp. 25, 26. Lewis quotes Leviticus 19:17-18 in support: "Thou shalt not hate thy brother in thine heart...but thou shalt love thy neighbor as thyself," at p. 26.
[648] Ibid., p. 18.

our Lord's own teaching has given to that word....But we must not be Pharisaical even to the Pharisees."[649]

George W. Bush has preached that "instead of directing hatred and resentment against others, successful societies appeal to the hopes of their own people."[650] But this president has acted as a lightning rod for post-9/11 hawkish sentiment, linked with a pre-9/11 Iraq invasion agenda hardly motivated by a desire to liberate. In keeping with the pattern: Christian words, unchristian actions…. But the stakes for God's Kingdom are high, for "…our nonjudgmental love of the other remains the condition of God's love for us. For, knowing how little we merit his love, our best opening to the faith that he does, lies not in the hope of being better than others, but in the security that his love encompasses even the least deserving among us."[651]

The surreal effects of cognitive dissonance are seen in Americans waiting for news of WMD or to see whether the Iraqi people will succeed in implementing democratic reforms, while the clear evidence of Bush's false intentions and deliberate deception in invading Iraq are everywhere. George W. Bush and the clutch of neo-conservatives he assembled were itching to invade Iraq well before 9/11, but the twin towers attack gave them the casus belli they sought to unfurl their already-prepared war plans. Dick Cheney was actually

---

[649] Ibid., pp. 66, 67.
[650] George W. Bush, quoted in Thomas A. Freiling, <u>George W. Bush on God & Country</u>, p. 149.
[651] Elizabeth Fox-Genovese, "A Conversion Story," <u>The Best Christian Writing 2001</u>, John Wilson (ed.), p. 112. And so His love encompasses even those we deem our enemies, those on whom we desire revenge.

pressing for action against Iraq before George W. was inaugurated—he felt that "Topic A should be Iraq," and "he harbored a deep sense of unfinished business about Iraq,"[652] having served in the federal government under President George H. W. Bush during the first Gulf War. (There's that powerful, unchristian revenge influence in the highest levels of U.S. government again.)

Bob Woodward, whose political affiliation may be questioned but whose journalistic integrity is legendary (and who George W. invited in to do the interviews for *two* books), discovered that when George W. first came into office in January 2001, George Tenet gave a security briefing which focused on the three major threats to U.S. security, number one of which was "Osama bin Laden and his al Qaeda terrorist network, [who was]…a "tremendous threat" which had to be considered "immediate"….There was no doubt that bin Laden was going to strike at United States interests in some form."[653] Woodward concluded from his interviews with most of the parties present that "Iraq was barely mentioned. Tenet did not have an agenda for Iraq as he did for bin Laden and al Qaeda."[654]

And yet on February 5, 2001, the 17th day of the Bush presidency, a meeting was called in which George W. Bush relates that "I instructed the secretary of defense to go back and develop a more robust option in case we really needed to put some serious weapons on Iraq in order to free a pilot."[655] (Mobilizing the Pentagon for

---

[652] Bob Woodward, <u>Plan of Attack</u>, p. 9.
[653] Ibid., p. 12.
[654] Ibid., p. 12.
[655] Ibid., p. 14.

months to completely redraft its Iraq war plans in case a pilot was downed alive in Iraq, while ignoring al Qaeda–how patently contrived.) On February 16, 2001, the U.S. executed the "largest strike in two years"[656] against Iraq, and on March 1, 2001 Donald Rumsfeld presented "evidence" that the Iraqis were buying dump trucks and that the dump cylinders could possibly be removed and used to construct a rocket. In typical fashion, Rumsfeld pushed the issue until Powell finally spoke up: "For Christ's sake, Powell said, if somebody wants a cylinder to erect a rocket, they don't have to buy a $200,000 dump truck to get one!"[657] In May and July 2001, Paul Wolfowitz, who was "[t]he intellectual godfather and fiercest advocate for toppling Saddam,"[658] proposed invasion plans for Iraq which were called the "enclave strategy" and which contemplated the seizure of southern Iraqi oil wells.[659] Powell thought Wolfowitz' plan "was one of the most absurd, strategically unsound proposals he had ever heard."[660] But that proposal, based

---

[656] Ibid., p. 14. Rumsfeld was "furious" that he was not informed prior to the strike, having his own vengeance axe to grind–he brokered the sale of weapons to Saddam Hussein (even posed for pictures shaking Saddam's hand), then also participated in the U.S. government's Bush I Gulf War.
[657] Ibid., p. 15.
[658] Ibid., p. 21.
[659] Ibid., p. 22. Wolfowitz advocated invading Iraq because "It was necessary and it would be relatively easy." (p. 21). There's that handy if amorphous word "necessary" again….Powell is reputed by Mr. Woodward (at p. 79) to have an opinion about hasty military decisions: "He had found too many who were willing to pull the trigger without making sure it was done with decisive force for a political objective that was necessary, and one that was supported by the Congress and the public." Now he had found another such person, in G.W. Bush.
[660] Ibid., p. 22.

not on Christianity, actual need, or a viable threat, is exactly what became America's actual invasion mindset and plan after the September 11 attacks some months later.

Rumsfeld and the neo-conservatives wasted no time to seize on the 9/11 attacks as a justification to invade Iraq: "At 2:40 that day, [September 11, 2001]...Rumsfeld raised with his staff the possibility of going after Iraq as a response to the terrorist attacks, according to an aide's notes."[661] Rumsfeld asked a lawyer to talk with Wolfowitz about the Iraq connection with bin Laden,[662] and then "[t]he next day in the inner circle of Bush's war cabinet, Rumsfeld asked if the terrorist attacks did not present an "opportunity" to launch against Iraq."[663] And according to Woodward's information, Bush approached Rumsfeld to frame war plans against Iraq on November 21, 2001.

But Ron Suskind's research for The Price of Loyalty strongly suggests that Bob Woodward was lied to about this November 21 date.[664] Suskind's account is based on inside information provided chiefly by Paul J. O'Neill, a lifelong Republican who actively participated in Bush cabinet meetings for two years, and whose chief motive to blow the whistle on the Bush administration was his (conservative) conviction that the country was being

---

[661] Ibid., pp. 24-25.
[662] Gosh but they knew awfully quickly who blew up those towers, even though Condoleeza Rice initially issued a (deceitful) public statement that no one could have foreseen terrorists using planes as weapons!
[663] Ron Suskind, The Price of Loyalty, p. 25. And Bush himself said "we're not going to miss this opportunity to make the world more peaceful and more free...." p. 83. Which manifestation of preemption is this?
[664] Ibid., at p. 336.

steered into dangerous fiscal waters. Suskind too reports that Wolfowitz was a long-time advocate of invading Iraq, having pressed for a U.S. ground force presence in Iraq since 1999.[665] Not surprisingly, Suskind learned from Paul J. O'Neill and "several other senior officials" that the Iraq War was decided "by the time Bush arrived in office."[666] And O'Neill was somewhat astonished to learn on January 10, 2001 (the first Bush II administration cabinet meeting) that the Bush administration embraced a hands-off approach to the Israel-Palestinian conflict, that "[a] major shift in U.S. policy was under way. After more than thirty years of intense engagement—from Kissinger and Nixon to Clinton's last stand—America was washing its hands of the conflict in Israel. Now, we'd focus on Iraq."[667] Again, at this very first Bush W. administration cabinet meeting on January 10, 2001, eight months prior to the terrorist attacks on the World Trade Center, the administration was already focused on Iraq, with Condoleeza Rice commenting that "Iraq might be the key to reshaping the entire region," and Cheney and others scrutinizing a map of Iraq that showed a building that "might" be a WMD plant.[668]

Unknown to, and thus unreported by, Bob Woodward,[669] war plans for Iraq began to take shape on February 1, 2001. According to Paul J. O'Neill (who was there),

---

[665] Ibid., p. 97.
[666] Ibid., p. 335.
[667] Ibid., p. 74.
[668] Ibid., p. 74.
[669] One wonders whether Woodward's credibility was sought by the White House to whitewash the pre-9/11 Iraq War machinery—for clearly Woodward was misled, and the Iraq War intentions existed *ab initio*.

Iraq was the focus of that meeting, at which Rumsfeld remarked "[I]magine what the region would look like without Saddam and with a regime that's aligned with U.S. interests...."[670] According to O'Neill:

> From the start, we were building the case against Hussein and looking at how we could take him out and change Iraq into a new country. And, if we did that, it would solve everything. It was all about finding a way to do it. That was the tone of it. The President saying, 'Fine. Go find me a way to do this.'[671]

O'Neill also foresaw a battle brewing between Colin Powell and right-wing hardliners "who were already planning the next war in Iraq and the shape of a post-Saddam country" in January 2001.[672] One of those warplanners (not peacemakers) was Donald Rumsfeld, who in January 2001 was already busy through the Defense Intelligence Agency preparing documents "mapping Iraq's oil fields and exploration areas and listing companies that might be interested in leveraging the precious asset."[673]

Despite pretending to seek U.N. approval, pretending to be preparing to possibly recover a downed pilot, pretending that there were WMD or terrorist

---

[670] Ibid., p. 83. A true snapshot of American nation-building: Rumsfeld said "regime," not democratically-elected government. And "aligned with U.S. interests" is the paramount goal, not liberating Iraqis.

[671] Ibid., p. 96. The ends justify the means, as with torture....

[672] Ibid., p. 96.

[673] Ibid., p. 96. The government was even working on designating areas of Iraq for future oil exploration.

connections for which no evidence existed, and pretending to liberate the Iraqi people, Bush W. had actually been working behind the scenes from the first day of his administration to create a justification for an Iraq invasion:

> Already by February, the talk was mostly about logistics. Not the <u>why</u>, but the <u>how</u> and <u>how quickly</u>. Rumsfeld, O'Neill recalled, was focused on how an incident might cause escalated tensions–like the shooting down of an American plane in the regular engagements between U.S. fighters and Iraqi antiaircraft batteries–and what the U.S. responses to such an occurrence might be. [<u>By mid-March, 2001, a</u>]ctual plans, to O'Neill's astonishment, were already being discussed to take over Iraq and occupy it–complete with disposition of oil fields, peacekeeping forces, and war crimes tribunals–carrying forward an unspoken doctrine of preemptive war. [<u>By September 11, 2001, t</u>]he Pentagon had been working for months on a military plan for the overthrow of Saddam Hussein.[674]

And Richard A. Clarke, who was also closely involved with the Bush administration during this period, writes:[675]

> Former Treasury Secretary Paul O'Neill has written that the Administration planned early on to

---

[674] Ibid., pp. 96, 129, 184,.
[675] Richard A. Clarke, <u>Against All Enemies</u>, pp. 264-265, 30. Clarke also relates (at p. 32) that President Bush personally asked him to see if he could find any links between the attacks and Iraq.

eliminate Saddam Hussein. From everything I saw and heard, he is right....

The administration of the second George Bush did begin with Iraq on its agenda. So many of those who had made the decisions in the first Iraq War were back: Cheney, Powell, Wolfowitz. Some of them had made clear in writings and speeches while out of office that they believed the United States should unseat Saddam, finish what they failed to do the first time. In the new administration's discussions of terrorism, Paul Wolfowitz had urged a focus on Iraqi-sponsored terrorism against the U.S. even though there was no such thing. In 2001 more and more the talk was of Iraq, of CENTCOM being asked to plan to invade. It disturbed me greatly.

President Bush has said that September 11 was a turning point in his thinking about Iraq. There was also a supposed decision point when the President decided to go to the U.N. and another when he decided not to wait further for the U.N., but all along it seemed inevitable that we would invade. Iraq was portrayed as the most dangerous thing in national security. It was an idée fixe, a rigid belief, received wisdom, a decision already made and one that no fact or event could derail.

[On the morning after the September 11 attacks, Clarke] expected to go back to a round of meetings examining what the next attacks could be, what our vulnerabilities were, what we could do about them in the short term. Instead, I walked into a series of discussions about Iraq. At first I was incredulous that we were talking about something other than getting al Qaeda. Then I realized with almost a sharp physical pain that Rumsfeld and Wolfowitz were going to try to take advantage of this national tragedy to promote their agenda about Iraq. Since the beginning of the administration, indeed well before, they had been pressing for a war with Iraq. My friends in the Pentagon had been telling me that the word was we would be invading Iraq sometime in 2002.

It would appear from George W.'s hell-bent fixation with Saddam Hussein that W. acted once again according to the moral precepts of the likes of Machiavelli rather than Jesus, for Machiavelli would no doubt approve of orchestrating a war to increase wealth through plunder, improve advantage, or seek revenge: "A prince, then, ought to have no other object nor any other thought, nor take anything else for his art, but war, its orders and its discipline; for this is the only art awaiting one who commands."[676] Hardly Christian words, but consistent with Bush's actions….

But George W., in his oft-repeated unchristian pattern of lying to the American people while he says he worships Jesus Christ, said on March 21, 2006, "I didn't want war. To assume I wanted war is just flat wrong."[677] Actually, Mr. President, what is 'flat wrong' is to lie blatantly to the world and not own up to your personal responsibility for this War and those who have been killed in its violence. It was 'flat wrong' to ignore Colin Powell, who tried to talk you out of this War and told you you'd 'own it.' It was 'flat wrong' to ignore

---

[676] Niccolo Machiavelli, <u>The Prince</u>, p. 88.
[677] *The Christian Science Monitor,* March 22, 2006, p. 3.

Richard Clarke, who tried to direct your attention to al Qaeda and away from your pathological fixation with Iraq.[678] It is 'flat wrong' to assume the American people will continue to tolerate your endless, incredible lies. It was 'flat wrong' to ignore Jesus Christ in your decision-making, and to ignore Him as you lie to the world and try to avoid 'owning' the War you gave birth to.

The only possible moral defense of the Iraq invasion would be a just cause argument based on WMD. But in the case of Iraq, the Bush administration's single-minded focus on dubious information smacks of bad faith, especially when coupled with the foregoing evidence of a premeditated plan to invade Iraq. In this case, such false pretense under the guise of defense will be reckoned to Christ, whose name was implicitly employed in the venture, with higher standards because the actors spoke as Christian emissaries, with well-advertised group prayers in the war room (Christian words, unchristian actions). The stakes also escalate daily, in both this world and the next, as the death toll visited upon Iraqis (most of them civilian; and not to forget infant mortalities and deaths from malnutrition, lack of medical care, lack of basic services and potable water, etc.) begins to rival the much-propagandized mass executions by Saddam Hussein. The higher the stakes (i.e., the death toll), the

---

[678] Clarke writes in <u>Against All Enemies</u> (at p. x) that "George Bush…failed to act prior to September 11 on the threat from al Qaeda despite repeated warnings and then harvested a political windfall for taking obvious yet insufficient steps after the attacks; and…launched an unnecessary and costly war in Iraq that strengthened the fundamentalist, radical Islamic terrorist movement worldwide." Perhaps Mr. Bush would lie, and call Richard Clarke a liar.

more inexcusable the war, especially when U.S. credibility, and consequently international political capital, has been shattered on the tissued fabrication of a case for WMD, not to mention (but let's, as Christians holding our Christian nation accountable to Jesus Christ) the effects of Abu Ghraib et al. on the world's view of America and Jesus Christ.

And all the time, the huge Imperialistic vessel which is America moves across the globe militarily and culturally like a colossal glacial plate, unilaterally grinding over most everything in its path, with Christ strapped unwillingly to the mast. If America possessed a manifest destiny from God, it would be a peaceful, non-materialistic, compassionate, poverty-liberating movement which America would lead, not this ideological perversion of Christ's mission–He came to share God's forgiveness and mercy, sacrificing Himself to blunt and defeat the evil of others. America's current open-ended venture is the reverse, killing others lest Americans' comforts and materialism be threatened (hardly sacrificial), under pretense of sharing "liberation," whatever that means and whatever business America has being the self-appointed delivery boy and enforcer of said liberation. And America's military might (not exactly Christian raiment for a nation, though it served the Crusaders well in their embarrassing foray which similarly desecrated Christ's message) lays waste to the comparatively "meek" Iraqi rag-tags in their Toyota pickups brandishing outdated rocket-propelled grenades. America's military superiority over Iraq (as in the first Gulf war) is far from a demonstration of mercy, but is instead a shameful display of brute worldly technological force that makes Hitler's blitzkrieg look like flintlocks on chariots, and wherein far fewer casualties are suffered by the aggressor than were incurred by the Germans in comparable military exercises in World War II.

In reviewing the clear evidence of the Bush administration's massaging of the WMD issue and its refusal to even consider the possibility that such weapons had been destroyed (apparently they had), or that such weapons had not been used in years, and could not be delivered to the territorial United States,[679] the words of Allan Bloom, criticizing the liberal influences which dumbed down America, are apposite. Bloom complained of those who would "make the facts fit their agenda and influence the public...It became almost impossible to question the radical orthodoxy without risking vilification.... all parties in a democracy are jeopardized when passion can sweep the facts before it."[680] But Bloom's extremely intelligent insights seem prescient today, for he rightly summarized America's cultural and moral direction:

---

[679] If Iraq is any indication of what the Bush administration envisions when it advocates preemption based on "necessity," then clearly the hurdle to the use by America of preemptive force is low and grey indeed. But *de facto* actions are how preemption and necessity are being defined by this administration, for it has been no easier to nail down what these terms mean than on how moving money from one account to another will fix Social Security, or how the budget will be balanced within four years with runaway spending, tax refunds, a declining economy, international resentment and a nasty, interminable war. *De facto* inaction will assuredly be the result of this administration's budget-balancing and privatized accounts talk. In war and torture, there is no talk and much action–in NCLB, economics, the environment, and welfare cuts, there is much high-brow talk and only counterproductive actions. Where is Jesus in this picture? "Lord, why hath we forsaken thee?"

[680] Allan Bloom, The Closing of the American Mind, 354, 355, 356. See also Orwell, 1984, p. 354.

"our way of life is utterly dependent on the natural scientists."[681] But the social scientists deny spirituality without offering an alternative spiritual or ethical foundation for human existence,[682] so America's morality has become Lockian: "Life, liberty and the pursuit of property are the fundamental natural rights, and the social contract is made to protect these rights."[683] Bloom correctly reveals economics as " 'the science of man's proper activity,' and the free market as the natural and rational order (a natural order unlike other recognized natural orders in that it requires establishment by men, and they…almost always get it wrong)."[684] Economics is seen by Bloom as a product of liberal democracy, embraced by the Conservative Right (like compassion?), but as a spiritually fruitless way of life: "Civilization, practically identical to the free market and its results, threatens happiness and dissolves community."[685]

So instead of liberals as seen by Bloom, it is now the Bush administration with WMD which attempted to "make the facts fit their agenda and influence the public," in pursuit of those (spiritually empty) economic bounties which Bush believes are the solution for mankind's ills.

Having been informed in advance as to what subjects and order of presentation would be required for a May 16, 2001, cabinet meeting about Iraq, "…George Tenet

---

[681] Ibid., p. 356.
[682] Ibid., p. 360.
[683] Ibid., p. 362.
[684] Ibid., p. 362. "Undeveloped, bad; developing, better; developed, good–for man and for the science of economics." Bloom complains that economists "have substantial influence on public policy," p. 363.
[685] Ibid., p. 362, quoting Rousseau.

gave his report on intelligence–it was still only speculation, he told Bush, whether Hussein had weapons of mass destruction or was starting any weapons-building programs...."[686] This pre-9/11 assessment somehow mysteriously morphed into a "slam dunk" assurance that Saddam had WMD, which was the chief justification employed to persuade Americans to support President Bush's spectacular campaign. The tipping point, at least in rhetoric, arose from unauthorized comments by Dick Cheney, whose overconfidence and reality-defying zeal transformed the administration's position overnight from one of "we think Saddam Hussein has WMD's" to "we know without question that Saddam has WMD's." In August, 2002, Cheney

> issued his own personal National Intelligence Estimate of Saddam: "Simply stated, there is no doubt that Saddam Hussein now has weapons of mass destruction [and] there is no doubt that he is amassing them to use against our friends, against our allies and against us." Ten days earlier the president himself had said only that Saddam "desires" these weapons. Neither Bush nor the CIA had made any assertion comparable to Cheney's.[687]

---

[686] Ron Suskind, The Price of Loyalty, p. 160.

[687] Bob Woodward, Plan of Attack, p. 164. This snowball quickly gathered mass, as Cheney's close ally Ken Adelman wrote in an op-ed piece two days later in *The Wall Street Journal* that Saddam was a bigger threat than al Qaeda because he had "scores of scientific laboratories and myriad manufacturing plants cranking out weapons of mass destruction." (Bob Woodward, Plan of Attack, p. 165.) The Bush administration could hardly retract Cheney's position, without seriously harming their credibility and chances to get their war. And of course there was no evidence to support these false claims: this agenda was built on lies, which were presented as "no doubt" by Mr. Cheney. Where is the accountability?

The fact that there was never any evidence to support this assertion, and that no such evidence has been found, has not required accountability of Mr. Cheney any more than the rest of the unrepentant Bush clique.

Instead, George W. carried this position forward officially (and irresponsibly, for the stakes were much too high to be wrong), in keeping with the goal of ousting Hussein that he and his cabinet brought into the White House with them. Even before approaching the United Nations about the matter, George W. proclaimed "Saddam Hussein possesses weapons of mass destruction."[688] On December 2, 2002, Ari Fleischer announced "[W]e have intelligence information about what Saddam Hussein possesses."[689] After Saddam provided a weapons declaration on December 7, 2002, Cheney continued to push for war, without reading it—obviously the Bush administration's apparent outreach to the UN was form to mask the substance of a war already in motion.

When the U.S. case for Iraq's possession of WMD was placed before the UN, it was clear that persuading the international community to support war was more important than truth. Bush employed lawyers "to make the best possible case" for WMD from CIA information[690]—but shouldn't this be scientists' work? Colin Powell was selected to present the scant evidence for WMD because he was 1) credible; 2) everyone knew he was soft on Iraq; and 3) when he was prepared he was

---

[688] Ibid., p. 178.
[689] Ibid., p. 234. This vague assertion was accepted by Americans, but no evidence has ever been procured to substantiate it.
[690] Ibid., p. 288.

very persuasive.[691] The administration wanted Powell to deliver his presentation over three days (instead of one—form over substance): "They wanted it as long, detailed and boring as possible to demonstrate the depth of the case…."[692]—just as you'd expect lawyers to do, in the troublesome absence of actual facts.

But as the UN procured evidence that there were not in fact any such WMD, the Bush administration's consternation revealed its lack of true interest in any peaceful solution—with typical unilateralism, the catch-22 logic was that either the UN would back America's military plans, or the UN was corrupt and not to be trusted. This was disingenuous political posturing to mask true intent. After Hans Blix submitted a report to the UN Security Council covering the first two months of inspections (on January 27, 2003), Bush pronounced to the American people that there were 38,000 liters of butulinum toxin unaccounted for, "enough to subject millions of people to death by respiratory failure….The British government has learned that Saddam Hussein recently sought significant quantities of uranium from Africa…."[693] This was the infamous Nigerian uranium connection that caused Joseph Wilson to blow the intelligence whistle and the Bush administration (with accustomed impunity) to disclose the CIA cover of Wilson's wife. Of course, it is now irrefutable that this scare-tactic intelligence was never more than rumor. Yet,

---

[691] Ibid., p. 291.
[692] Ibid., p. 291.
[693] Ibid., p. 294. This is the negative reverse of the positive hyperbole Bush used to overcount the myriad ways one could spend the tax refunds—it's all fantastical smoke and mirrors, the province of politicians.

"less than four months earlier, Tenet and the CIA had excised the sentence [regarding African uranium] from the president's speech in Cincinnati because the assertion could not be confirmed and was thought to be shaky. Tenet had not reviewed the State of the Union speech, and Hadley had forgotten the earlier CIA warning."[694]

But the UN, lacking the biased intelligence-fabricating and spinning apparatus that the Bush administration created, had to rely on conventional on-the-ground means of inspection to gauge Saddam's capabilities. In January 2003,

> Mohamed ElBaradei, director general of the International Atomic Energy Agency, said "We have to date found no evidence that Iraq has revived its nuclear weapons program since its elimination of the program in the 1990's....We should be able within the next few months to provide credible assurance that Iraq has no nuclear program...." All this only made Bush more determined on war. All of Cheney's predictions about the U.N. were coming true.[695]

---

[694] Ibid., pp. 294-295. Does the president not review his own speeches? (He rehearses thoroughly). Is he aware of the content and ramifications of his words as he speaks them? Is he accountable for clear errors of fact when they utter from his supposedly Christian mouth, or does he dismiss the truth as "good faith disagreements that we must move past to keep our word," or dismiss the error as that of an underling (in this case Hadley) without addressing his misrepresentation to the American people on a pivotal, vital issue determining our nation's course to war. Perhaps an apology for a mistake would be appropriate at minimum, but instead there is retaliation at the man who told the world the emperor had no clothes. Christian words, actions without accountability.... Fortunately, every day more and more Christians are seeing Bush's spiritual nakedness.
[695] Ibid., p. 294.

362   Christian Words, Unchristian Actions

But how does any investigator meet the United States' burden of proving that there is not a smoking gun, when there is no evidence that a shot has even been fired? The burden and situation deliberately contrived by the Bush administration led to a bureaucratic comedy in which the whole world knew George W. Bush was invading Iraq no matter what the UN did. On February 14, 2003, Blix reported that UN inspectors had conducted over 400 inspections covering 300 sites without finding *any* weapons.[696] But George W. still feigned magical insight, alluding to secret knowledge to which he was privy but which ordinary Americans could not be informed for purposes of national security,[697] suggesting "trust me and the American intelligence network."

And trust him they did. And notwithstanding the hundreds of inspections performed by Hans Blix and other inspectors with specialized professional expertise, George Bush continued to maintain with crystal clear certainty, based on undisclosed, nonexistent, or spurious intelligence, that Saddam actually possessed such weapons and was preparing to use them. On March 17, 2003, Bush declared in a speech that "[t]he Iraqi regime continues to possess and conceal some of the most lethal weapons ever devised."[698] The cogs of war were by that point in motion, and truth would not be permitted to

---

[696] Ibid., p. 315.
[697] Much like the mysterious empowerment created by his refusal to disavow his involvement with an unchristian elitist cult like Skull & Bones, while alluding to how "secret" that cult is. He can have his cake and sacrifice it in Satanic ritual too, in America's new blind Christianity.
[698] Ibid., p. 362. Again, this was presented as irrefutable fact–who could oppose war facing such "evidence"?

"CHRISTIAN" LEADERSHIP INTO THE HORRORS OF
WAR: IRAQ AND THE DOCTRINE OF PREEMPTIVE WAR   363

interfere with George W's unshakeable resolve to subdue Saddam Hussein.

"Two days before a 2003 White House announcement that captured Iraqi trailers were "biological laboratories," a Pentagon-sponsored mission concluded they had no connection to production of weapons of mass destruction, The Washington Post reported...." This President lied to the world, in this case blatantly announcing the opposite conclusion of a Pentagon report to serve his "mission" of war.[699]

The rest is history (of which George W. is a big fan): "White House Press Secretary Scott McClellan admitted[700] that the search for weapons of mass destruction had officially ended–and that no[701] WMD had been found. Bush says the war was still worth fighting[702] because Iraq posed a threat in other ways[703] and Saddam Hussein was a brutal dictator.[704]"[705] But this was

---

[699] The Christian Science Monitor, April 13, 2006, p. 3.
[700] In January, 2005–in keeping with the bureaucratic Bush pattern of postponing bad reports until after elections.
[701] Notice that absolutely "no" weapons were found, contrasted with the thousands of liters that President Bush assured Americans with absolute certainty existed. Time will demonstrate similar results for his tax refund promises, when a net sum of "no" new houses, college educations or jobs will be created.
[702] Fill in excuse here–apologies are not a component of the Bush brand of Christian humility, ever.
[703] Will this vague allusion be substantiated in the same way as WMD, using mere words with zero untainted evidence? No, this assertion is, in yet another layer of American cognitive dissonance, accepted on faith though never factually established.
[704] So is Kim Song Il. This rationalization avoids Christian, or any other, moral accountability, and is a bait-and-switch replacement morality, equally deficient, for the failed WMD/preemption pitch.
[705] "Bush 2.0," US News & World Report, January 24, 2005, p. 20.

not news to Paul J. O'Neill. Having sat in on the first two years of Bush administration cabinet and top-secret national security council meetings, Paul J. O'Neill stated (with no apparent self-interest or unpatriotic desire to undermine his government, just a commitment to truth and integrity) that he "never saw anything that [he] would characterize as evidence of weapons of mass destruction...."[706] O'Neill actually took personal risk to speak out in such a fashion, but his words have fallen largely on ears deafened by cognitive dissonance, by doublespeak, by willful ignorance.

Of course, Machiavelli and many non-Christians would perfectly well accept oil as a legitimate justification for the seizure of Iraq. It's just the Christians who couldn't be told the truth, if that were the case. And the old denial-coupled-with-cognitive-doublespeak can be employed so that any theories suggesting oil as a justification for war can be dismissed out of hand as cynical conspiratorial speculation, just as America would never see itself becoming gulag-like or Hitler-like no matter how extreme its conduct, because the comparison is simply not allowed–minds have been conditioned via nationalism to exclude the possibility of evil action or motive by the homeland. America is always the good guy...the end, happily ever after–other endings are unthinkable, even (generally) in Hollywood, because movies that make Americans uncomfortable with their culture (or worse, confront it) are as popular as double anchovy pizza.

---

[706] Ron Suskind, The Price of Loyalty, p. 334.

Oil is more than just a commodity. In the modern world, especially in America, oil is the staple upon which all other staples depend. Any government, especially America's, that did not pay especial attention to this reality would be derelict in serving its citizenry. And after fifty years of international jockeying to control or own this resource, to deny the importance of oil in geopolitical decision-making is more than just naïve....

Richard N. Goodwin observed that "[o]ne of the classic ways to increase national wealth was to acquire a new supply of natural resources either by discovery or conquest."[707] Myron Magnet decried the elitist Western tradition which "aimed to exploit economically a non-white population dismissed as inferior."[708] The most prominent imperialist tradition of the West has been the exploitation of local populations to control indigenous resources. And the most important natural resource in the history of man's earthly habitation has been black gold–oil.[709] More amazingly, oil's tenure as super-currency is just begun, for its future value will only escalate as depletion collides with increasing world consumption: "...the U.S. economy is at present dependent...on supplies of oil from the Middle East, and thus the defense of the American Way of Life requires that the United

---

[707] Richard N. Goodwin, The American Condition, p. 184.
[708] Myron Magnet, The Dream and the Nightmare: the Sixties' Legacy to the Underclass, p. 214. Magnet avoids, though, addressing the American tradition in this vein, in such countries as Nicaragua, the Philippines, Iran, Iraq, Panama, etc.
[709] "One of the most enduring currencies of power in the post-war world has been oil." Gerald Segal, The World Affairs Companion: The Essential One-Volume Guide to Global Issues, p. 44.

States must have the ability to ensure its own continued access to those supplies."[710]

As a consequence, America faces increasing, not decreasing, dependence on primarily Middle Eastern sources for its oil consumption. "Any interruption in the flow of gulf oil would generate a major Western economic crisis that would carry over into the military."[711] But the truth is that this dependency is a direct consequence of gluttonous American consumption in the free-market tradition instead of Christian temperance, stewardship, and ethics. Writing in 1971, Goodwin observed that "[e]xisting institutions are not likely to market or create new products in a way which might imperil the source or magnitude of their present earnings....For example, to the extent there is an "energy crisis," it is a result of the failure to pursue technological alternatives whose possibilities have been known for a quarter century."[712] Now that thirty-plus years have intervened with Goodwin proved right and the situation unaddressed,

---

[710] Jeff McMahan, Reagan and the World: Imperial Policy in the New Cold War, p. 12. One history text notes that "By 1970, the United States, with only 6 percent of the world's population, used over one-third of the world's energy." Moss, p. 271. Having reduced that to one-quarter by 2006 is not enough to stave off disaster, since the world's consumption continues to expand exponentially.

[711] Sandra Mackey, The Saudis: Inside the Desert Kingdom, p. 339. George W. Bush reveals his awareness of this connection when he refers to "nations of the Middle East" as "countries of great strategic importance" Thomas A. Freiling, George W. Bush on God and Country, p. 143. *See also* www.lifeaftertheoilshock.net for a discussion of the coming global military confrontation over oil resources, which is unavoidable due to steadily rising world oil consumption.

[712] Richard N. Goodwin, The American Condition, p. 314.

the crisis is become reality.⁷¹³ Because of the sheer scale of energy consumption now involved and the consequent increased shock and cost of any large-scale conversion to a new energy source, the technological alternatives offer fewer possibilities than in 1971. As Mortimer Zuckerman of *US News & World Report* recently declared:

> There is much talk these days about energy independence–a fantasy. Any program to reduce our 60 percent dependence on foreign oil will take anywhere from five to 10 years….It is also fantasy to imagine that we can rely on alternative power sources from waves or windmills or solar panels. That kind of power is weak, intermittent, and expensive–costing roughly twice the electrical power produced by either coal or gas.⁷¹⁴

Again, America's oil dependency is not lost on our president, a man who was born and raised in an oil family in Midland, Texas, "the administrative center of the petroleum-producing region called the Permian Basin, which holds some 20 percent of all of America's oil and gas reserves,…the apotheosis of American middle-class boosterism…From 1973 to 1981 the price of oil

---

[713] "Cars and trucks are more technologically adept than ever, but Americans aren't using less gasoline. Instead, they're buying vehicles that are heavier and faster, and they're driving them farther. That's a major reason that the U.S., with 4% of the world's population, burns 25% of the world's oil." "In Texas Suburbs, Conserving Energy Doesn't Come Easy," *The Wall Street Journal*, October 20, 2005, p.1.
[714] "Our Energy Conundrum," *US News & World Report*, April 25, 2005, p. 72.

rose 800 percent, creating a thick crust of Midland millionaires."[715] So George W. was quite aware that the October 1973 energy crisis was caused by an OPEC embargo of oil shipments to the United States,[716] that the Iran-Iraq War threatened U.S. oil supplies,[717] that Saddam threatened to control the world's oil in the first Iraq War,[718] that America's and the world's modern armies march more on their gas tanks than on their stomachs, and that whichever nation(s) control(s) the world's oil reserves (i.e., the Middle East) will control the world and its future. So important is oil that one Bush biographer has suggested that George W. advocated granting

---

[715] David Aikman, A Man of Faith: The Spiritual Journey of George W. Bush, pp. 66, 68. Bill Minutaglio quotes a Bush childhood friend who calls Midland "the ugliest place on the face of the earth. The only reason to be there was because they had oil under the ground...." (at p. 28) George W. idolizes Midland as the epitome of the American dream. Paul Kengor writes in God and George W. Bush: a spiritual life, that "To know Texas—and Midland in particular—is to know Bush." (at p. 6.)

[716] "The oil cutoff was initiated by Saudi Arabia and other Arab members of OPEC to protest U.S. support of Israel in its recent war with Egypt and Syria, and to force a settlement of the war favoring the Arabs." Moss, Moving On: The American People Since 1945, p. 271. It is strange that, knowing this, Bush would allow U.S. peace brokering efforts in the Israeli-Palestinian division to lapse. And Bush's favoritism toward Israel has only heightened Arab resentments of America.

[717] George Donelson Moss, Moving On: The American People Since 1945, p. 349.

[718] Bill Minutaglio, First Son: George W. Bush and the Bush Family Dynasty, at p. 206: Saddam went into Kuwait, and "In the process, he moved his troops to the border of Saudi Arabia, suggesting that he was going there next. Had he been successful in the enterprise, he would have single-handedly controlled the majority of the world's oil supplies—his grand objective."

recognition to illegal immigrants to gain more favorable terms in the future for access to Mexican petroleum.[719]

It cannot be proven with certainty that oil was the primary motivation for U.S. entry into Iraq, but it is folly to ignore that oil was very much on the "front burner" in American war planning and rebuilding for Iraq. In a meeting between Colin Powell and George W. Bush on August 5, 2002, Powell had set out to dissuade the president from invading Iraq:

> Powell's notes filled three or four pages. War could destabilize friendly regimes in Saudi Arabia, Egypt and Jordan, he said. It could divert energy from almost everything else, not just the war on terrorism, and dramatically affect the supply and price of oil....War would take down Saddam and "You will become the government until you get a new government."[720]

In a National Security Presidential Directive regarding Iraq, a stated objective was "to minimize disruption in international oil markets."[721] And in one pre-invasion meeting, Bush said: " "We will take over the oilfields early–and mitigate the oil shock," interrupting himself to issue the stern warning–"Nobody needs to be telling anybody this!" "[722]

---

[719] David Aikman, <u>A Man of Faith: The Spiritual Journey of George W. Bush</u>, at p. 151.
[720] Bob Woodward, <u>Plan of Attack</u>, p. 150. Sixteen months later Bush confirmed that Powell had in fact warned him he'd own Iraq if he went to War: "He sure did," Bush replied. "He did say that." (p. 152).
[721] Ibid., p. 154-155.
[722] Ibid., p. 186.

Bush W.'s knowledge of the oil business stems from his own (failed) business ventures in oil, which were intimately tied to dozens of prominent names in the oil business, and also from his family's longstanding and extremely close friendship with Saudi royals, including the bin Laden Group. In <u>Forbidden Truth: U.S.-Taliban Secret Oil Diplomacy and the Failed Hunt for Bin Laden</u>, the authors follow the money trail to connect Osama bin Laden to

> ....U.S. oil tycoons, defense contractors like the Carlyle Group. The links even extend into the very heart of the administration and include President George W. Bush (a prior recipient of bin Laden investment money), his father (an advisor to Carlyle and its major client, the Binladen Group), and Vice President Dick Cheney, (a beneficiary of Saudi monetary largesse as the head of the oil services company Haliburton).[723]

This intimate familiarity with America's vital dependency on Middle East oil is what naturally makes many in the world suspicious of Mr. Bush's and America's motives in establishing so substantial and unprecedented a military presence in the heart of the world's most oil-rich region on the eve of maturing global oil supplies. In <u>Blood in the Streets: Investment Profits in a World Gone Mad</u>, James Dale Davidson and Sir William Rees-

---

[723] Jean-Charles Brisard & Guillaume Dasquie, <u>Forbidden Truth: U.S.-Taliban Secret Oil Diplomacy and the Failed Hunt for Bin Laden</u>, p. xvi-xvii. The authors also chronicle "the close economic ties between the Bush and Clinton administrations, U.S. Big Oil, and the Taliban and their Saudi patrons." (p. xiv)

Mogg explain the cycle of military technology which shapes world events:

> Unless whoever first attains a new weapon can use it immediately to conquer the entire world, and that has never yet happened, other groups will come into possession of similar weapons and use them as well. Before long, they will turn the new weapon against the power that first possessed it, neutralizing the advantage.[724]

This occurred with the American Indians and the rifle, and with the Taliban and SAM missiles. But two aspects of modern warfare change this equation: nuclear weapons have upped the ante as never before, such that world domination or destruction is quite possible; and, almost all modern conventional weapons are powered with fossil fuels, so that increasingly, holding the power source (oil) will be more strategically and militarily important than holding the actual weapons (which cannot be transported, manufactured or in many cases deployed (tanks, jets, non-nuclear ships) without that oil).

Perhaps the oil does have something to do with America's presence in Iraq after all…. In February 2003, Egypt, Jordan, Saudi Arabia and Turkey were involved in exile negotiations for the peaceful exit of Saddam Hussein, which negotiations if successful would have averted war. On February 7, 2003, Egypt approached Bush W. regarding this idea, which George promptly

---

[724] James Dale Davidson and Sir William Rees-Mogg, <u>Blood in the Streets: Investment Profits in a World Gone Mad</u>, p. 52.

rebuffed.[725] And if Saddam were to have been deposed in a coup, the president and National Security Council agreed "the U.S. would immediately call on the new leader to turn over authority to a duly constituted, publicly supported Iraqi authority appointed by the U.S. There had to be some movement toward democracy."[726] But where, on the brink of war, is mention of weapons of mass destruction or connections to terrorists, neither of which actually existed? What of all the Saddam-specific rhetoric deflated by the removal of Saddam via coup or voluntary exile? The only remaining rationale in the bait-and-switch bag of moral tricks was nation-building, in a country with no connections to 9/11 but possessing the world's second-largest oil reserves, in a nation on which George W. Bush had had his eye since at least January 2001. G. W. Bush would not take "no" from anyone in his zeal to possess Iraq, not even the Pope. Clearly his interest extended past Saddam....

And the promised rebuilding of Iraq, leveraged with its own oil, has not materialized. The oil is still there, being pumped and sold, but "[t]he U.S. authority itself has not been able to properly account for up to $9 billion in funds earned from sale of Iraqi oil."[727] Nor is the administration interested in accountability in this area: "Despite audits showing missing rebuilding funds and likely fraud under lax U.S. supervision early in the

---

[725] Bob Woodward, <u>Plan of Attack</u>, p. 314.
[726] Ibid., p. 315. If Saddam was the threat, on what basis does the United States demand the right to appoint a new government in the event of a coup?
[727] *Friends Committee on National Legislation Washington Newsletter*, No. 696, April 2005, p. 7.

occupation, Washington appears in no hurry to trace or recover any of it." *The Wall Street Journal*, January 17, 2006, p. 1.

But what of that other Bush administration ground justifying hasty war with Iraq, the oft-repeated connection alleged between Saddam Hussein and al Qaeda or other terrorist groups? Ignoring conspiracy theories that Bush & co. orchestrated 9/11, it is still painfully clear that this administration has capitalized on that event to launch its planned invasion of Iraq, to greatly expand federal governmental power through the USA Patriot Act, the Department of Homeland Security, and other such enlargements, and to win carte blanche political power domestically because no one dared challenge the President at war "defending" against terrorism.

The Westminster Dictionary of Christian Ethics relates in its definition of terrorism that

> [w]hile difficult to define, terrorism in practice is often a smear word applied indiscriminately to military opponents, especially nongovernmental ones. [When the definition is narrowed to nongovernmental opponents only, t]he trouble is that it suggests one standard for states and another for rebels, contrary to the spirit of the just war idea, as applied to resistance and revolution....In common parlance, "terrorism" is such a lazily deployed pejorative that one needs to ask for a clear explanation of what is meant whenever the word is used.[728]

---

[728] pp. 621-622. What a perfect word, then, for liars.

A clear explanation has never been proffered by the Bush administration of how it defines terrorism, (or, for that matter, how it defines the "evil" that we are supposedly in a war to eradicate). If terrorism is defined to refer to the deliberate killing of civilians, it immediately becomes morally indistinguishable from killing large numbers of civilians tangentially to a conventional war—is intent the only distinguishing factor between killing civilians as terrorists and killing civilians as "casualties of war," a sort of "Oops, sorry…" American criminal jurisprudence does not traditionally accept this distinction, for shooting into an empty house is called reckless malice, and is most comparable to the children, wedding parties and other civilians bombed or shot by American troops and armaments in Iraq—Americans can ignore or deny these deaths (like a third of Serbs deny Serbian genocide) all they want, but the evidence is overwhelming and everywhere, and the rest of the world knows that the Emperor and his Empire have killed tens of thousands of civilians in the Iraq War. And Americans attend their Christian churches regularly, an embarrassing number of them praying for U.S. troops without any prayers for the innocent victims of America's purportedly Christian action, without any begging for forgiveness from God if our nation and leader have erred, without repentance for the evil that America's war, as all wars, undoubtedly has unleashed: "Jesus might say to George W. Bush and others who claim to be followers of Jesus: "And right now, your final judgment test is going to be how you treat my beloved Iraqi children." "[729]

Also, as the Westminster Dictionary of Christian Ethics explains, a "non-governmental" narrowing of the definition of terrorism is "contrary to the spirit of the just war idea." And this is exactly the definition that the Bush administration has persisted in presenting to the American people in its "war on terror," at their and America's peril–that al Qaeda and their supporters are neither State nor revolutionaries, but an in-between animal, "terrorists."[730] (and that governments at war are consequently outside the purview of the definition of "terrorist," much like Bush would have the United States be permanently beyond the reach of the international war crimes and human rights courts that Americans like to employ against other nations). But Bush did not restrict his definition in this manner when Iraq was at issue–Iraq was labeled a terrorist "state," as were Iran and North Korea. As one book has observed:

> Aside from bureaucratic obstacles, political or analytical blindness, the principal factor that explains America's poor response to the fundamentalist

---
[729] Paul Kengor, <u>God and George W. Bush: A Spiritual Life</u>, quoting Gary Kohls, at p. 229. No Christian should balk at expressing Christ's love and compassion toward Arab or Muslim children–Christ loves all equally and without reservation, and all are free to follow Him.

[730] Much like the convenience of the term "enemy combatant" was contrived by Bush, Alberto Gonzales and others to create a new animal that was neither American (and entitled to constitutional protection) nor prisoner of war (and entitled to Geneva Convention and other international protections). But these "animals" are human, and deserve always Christian treatment and understanding if Americans are to hold themselves to their own standard.

phenomenon is cultural...[T]he myth of state terrorism, of which Al Qaeda is precisely the counterexample, continues to enjoy favor in American government circles. Operationally we know it is on its way out, yet it continues to hold sway as a political argument—as if nothing had changed since the Cold War, as if bin Laden had never breached the narrow frontiers of the United States. It's as if the United States were incapable of taking into account the considerable mutation of terrorism in the past twenty years, or rather, as if certain people were looking for useful political scapegoats to justify a planetary war against "the axis of evil."[731]

Colin Powell generally has been considered a man of integrity, notwithstanding his UN testimony regarding weapons of mass destruction (which he now says he regrets). But General Powell was not ever taken in by the Bush administration rhetoric[732] linking Saddam Hussein and al Qaeda:

Colin Powell was adamantly opposed to attacking Iraq as a response to September 11....Powell thought that Cheney had the fever. The vice president and Wolfowitz kept looking for the connection between

---

[731] Jean-Charles Brisard & Guillaume Dasquie, Forbidden Truth: U.S.-Taliban Secret Oil Diplomacy and the Failed Hunt for Bin Laden, p. 52.
[732] Actually, more fabrication than rhetoric. Truly, this link was created by sheer political propaganda and the bully pulpit. George W. Bush created the supposed link between Saddam Hussein and terrorists out of thin air—evidence couldn't be found which was this stretchable, so the conclusion was simply repeated over and over and over in Presidential speeches, until it became linked, became "truth," to a substantial number of Americans. Christ is Truth, sees truth, and will demand and receive truth.

Saddam and 9/11. [Powell thought Cheney had] an unhealthy fixation. Nearly every conversation or reference came back to al Qaeda and trying to nail the connection with Iraq. He would often have an obscure piece of intelligence. Powell thought that Cheney took intelligence and converted uncertainty and ambiguity into fact. It was about the worst charge that Powell could make about the vice president. But there it was.[733]

Powell was also made uncomfortable by the intensity, even just two days after the September 11 attacks, of Paul Wolfowitz's interest in invading Iraq. Powell and Army General Hugh Shelton (chairman of the Joint Chiefs of Staff)

> firmly opposed bringing Iraq into the military equation at this early stage. In his analysis, the only justification for going after Iraq would be clear evidence linking the Iraqis to the September 11 attacks. Short of that, targeting Iraq was not worth the risk of angering moderate Arab states whose support was crucial not only to any campaign in Afghanistan, but to reviving the Middle East peace process.[734]

---

[733] Bob Woodward, Plan of Attack, p. 25, 292.
[734] Bob Woodward, Bush at War, p. 61. There has been no evidence linking Saddam Hussein to the September 11 attacks. See Helen Caldicott, The New Nuclear Danger: George W. bush's Military-Industrial Complex, p. XVII. Of course, there is ample common-sense evidence demonstrating the clear links between al Qaeda and those attacks, including the fact that al Qaeda has repeatedly claimed responsibility, and that the majority of the hijackers were Saudi Arabian, as is Osama bin Laden.

Brent Scowcroft, President George H. W. Bush's national security adviser, has also been a vocal critic of Bush administration efforts to equate Saddam with al Qaeda:

> He was baffled that Cheney and Rumsfeld were so focused on Iraq. He had remarked, "The only thing that Osama and Saddam Hussein have in common is they hate the United States. Saddam is an anti-clerical socialist." He wrote an op-ed piece which stated "There is scant evidence to tie Saddam to terrorist organizations, and even less to the September 11 attacks. Indeed, Saddam's goals have little in common with the terrorists who threaten us, and there is little incentive for him to make common cause with them."[735]

But truth does not get in the way of George W. Bush's determination to have his way, and having his way in this case required fabricating the perception that Saddam had worked with the terrorists to attack the World Trade Center buildings as a rationale for invading Iraq. After the September 11 attacks, Bush's speechwriter, Michael Gerson (a theology major!) believed the administration had "an occasion to educate and explain. The world had changed....It was an optimum time to mold and rally public opinion...."[736] And mold and rally public opinion they did, in an Orwellian hate-chant against a made-up enemy (at least as regards 9/11). Bush alleged

---

[735] Bob Woodward, <u>Plan of Attack</u>, p. 159.
[736] Ibid., p. 85.

that Hussein was "teaming up with al Qaeda,"[737] and said "War is my last choice. Saddam Hussein is using his money to train and equip al Qaeda with chemicals, he's harboring terrorists."[738] And at the commencement of the war, Bush stated that Iraq "has aided, trained and harbored terrorists, including operations of al Qaeda."[739] This was a blatant lie. (Even if it had connections with al Qaeda, Iraq would be only one of dozens of countries in which al Qaeda operates, and Bush has no evidence that Iraq or Saddam Hussein had any involvement in the 9/11 attacks–so why Iraq ?) Is this what Gerson means by "an occasion to educate and explain"?

The Bush administration can connect any regime or foreign government to terrorism if the Iraq model is precedent–no evidence of any connection between Saddam Hussein and the 9/11 hijackers has ever been provided or required, but fear was employed to waive the need for proof, just as Satan works….In working U.S. public opinion (through fear) into support for an attack on a foreign nation in retaliation for 9/11–even though that nation had no established connection thereto–the administration conjured a horrible scenario of terrorist links to Saddam and WMD that just didn't exist. But it didn't matter, because truth is not requisite to manipulating citizens' emotions. In working people up to support the Iraq war,

---

[737] Ibid., p. 188, on September 26, 2002.
[738] Ibid., pp. 240-241. To US troops Bush has said "You are defeating the terrorists here in Iraq, so that we don't have to face them in our own country." Thomas A. Freiling, George W. Bush on God & Country, p. 214.
[739] Ron Suskind, The Price of Loyalty, p. 325, March 17, 2003.

> Gerson remembered that...[in summer 2000] Cheney...had raised the connection between weapons of mass destruction and terrorism in internal campaign discussions....[s]o he changed [the] phrase "axis of hatred" to an "axis of evil,"broadening the notion, making it more sinister, even wicked. It was almost as if Saddam was an agent of the devil. The connection between his regime with weapons of mass destruction and international terrorism could put the world on the road to Armageddon.[740]

But that "connection" has never been established because it didn't exist, so this vilification of Saddam Hussein, evil though he be, was an Orwellian creation by the Party and its spin-doctors, in the absence of real solutions against al Qaeda, to rally public support via 9/11 for a cause that the administration had been pursuing since January of 2001. The battle against terrorists was sacrificed, used instead to further the Iraq agenda.

The failure of the Iraq War to combat al Qaeda and other terrorist organizations is evident from the post-invasion insurgency, which many Middle East experts and academics predicted prior to the U.S. attack but which the Bush administration failed to anticipate[741]–ideology often trumps reality for GWB. In yet more boot-strapping, George W. Bush and his administration have blamed terrorists for the Iraq insurgency, yet the increased terrorist presence in Iraq is undoubtedly (the Bush administration would not

---
[740] Bob Woodward, <u>Plan of Attack</u>, p.87. Condoleeza Rice reputedly thought this was "most clever."
[741] Or refused to consider....

dispute this) due to the American occupation of a Muslim land. There is no room for chicken-and-egg logic before Jesus Christ–George W. and American troops have drawn terrorists in droves to Iraq to fight the infidels for Allah (they weren't all rushing to join Saddam's Imperial Guard before the U.S. invasion). George W. has said that "the violence we are seeing in Iraq today is serious. And it comes from Baathist holdouts and Jihadists from other countries, and terrorists drawn to the prospect of innocent bloodshed."[742] But are these Arab suicide bombers "terrorists drawn to the prospect of innocent bloodshed," or religiously devout though misguided warriors drawn to Iraq by the offense of the shedding of the innocent blood of Muslim women, children and civilians at the hand of America and its WMD/Saddam lust? (Or was it oil? Or liberation? Or world peace? Or to stop terrorism, which is instead more swelled and empowered?)

The September 11 attacks were a direct consequence of eighty-plus years of short-sighted American greed and foreign policy, and the failure of George W. Bush to properly acknowledge the roots of this evolving conflict has agitated the problem and has increased the likelihood of more anti-American sentiment, and of more terrorist attacks against American targets. General John Abizaid, commander of all U.S. troops in Iraq and Afghanistan,

> tends to cast the conflict [against terrorism]…as the "war on extremism" or the "long war." America has

---
[742] Thomas A. Freiling, George W. Bush on God & Country, p. 230.

a chance to confront and stop an Islamic extremist movement akin to fascism or communism in its early stages, the general believes, before it metastasizes and dominates a significant chunk of the world. Before the United States attacked al Qaeda and its Taliban protectors, Afghanistan clearly fit that model; Iraq, on the other hand, did not become a magnet for Islamic jihadists until after the U.S. invasion. CIA Director Porter Goss, in congressional testimony last week, said that Islamic extremists now are "exploiting the Iraqi conflict to recruit new anti-U.S. jihadists. These jihadists who survive will leave Iraq," he predicted, "experienced in and focused on acts of urban terrorism."[743]

George W. has played into al Qaeda's hands, expanding its power base instead of meaningfully undermining it.

The effort to fabricate terrorist connections between Saddam Hussein and al Qaeda also served to avoid the larger question of whether that War has diverted American resources from the war against terrorists, which it very obviously has. This Iraq distraction began pre-9/11, when "Bush had largely ignored the terrorist problem" even though George Tenet "had explicitly warned him about the immediacy and seriousness of the bin Laden threat."[744] Richard Clarke also tried repeatedly to warn the Bush administration of the al Qaeda threat:

---

[743] "A Long, Hard Fight," *U.S. News & World Report*, February 28, 2005, p. 35.
[744] Bob Woodward, <u>Plan of Attack</u>, p. 24.

Richard Clarke presented a detailed memo on January 25, [2001] arguing that bombing al Qaeda's training camps was simple and important....[Rice] promised Clarke that the new administration's terror policy would not continue Clinton's "empty rhetoric that made us look feckless." Rice asked him to develop a new policy paper. Clarke did so, in a long and detailed document, but it languished for months as the new administration lumbered through the transition process.[745]

Congressional efforts to confront the growing terrorism threat were also wasted with the Bush administration in power:

> Hart and Rudman, [who had drafted the U.S. Commission on National Security for the Twenty-first Century,] met separately with Defense Secretary Rumsfeld, Secretary of State Colin Powell, and Condoleeza Rice, urging each to focus more on terrorism....The White House acted as if the Hart-Rudman Commission had never existed.[746]

---

[745] Gerald Posner, Why America Slept: the Failure to Prevent 9/11, pp. 152, 153. Ron Suskind strongly rings the alarm about Bush administration nonfeasance relating to terrorism in favor of salivating attachment to Iraq, summarizing what he calls Richard Clarke's "central point: President George W. Bush and his top officials ignored threats from al-Qaeda in 2001–an assertion that matched neatly with the evidence in this book that the administration was, instead, intensely focused on how to oust Saddam and occupy Iraq." Ron Suskind, The Price of Loyalty, pp. 344-345.
[746] Ibid., pp. 153, 154. Richard Armitage also felt that the focus on Iraq was a bizarre distraction from the war on terror, warning at an April 30, 2001 meeting that "Only al Qaeda...is a direct threat to the United States." Gerald Posner, Why America Slept: the Failure to Prevent 9/11, p. 155.

384   Christian Words, Unchristian Actions

Brent Scowcroft, George H. W. Bush's national security adviser, has been a consistent voice of criticism of this aspect of the Bush administration's foreign policy, declaring prior to the war "that an attack on Iraq could turn the Middle East into a "cauldron and thus destroy the war on terrorism," "[747] and that he "was troubled because he thought the real threat to the United States was not from Saddam but from al Qaeda. He was baffled that Cheney and Rumsfeld were so focused on Iraq."[748] After the invasion, Scowcroft warned that elections in Iraq may only deepen the conflict.[749]

But perhaps the most strident critic of the Iraq War campaign was Colin Powell, whose sobering years of combat experience in Vietnam set him apart from the armchair warriors of the Bush cabinet. This refusal to play ball with the Iraq crowd is what alienated Powell from Bush's inner circle and eventually led to his resignation. But well prior to the military launch of U.S. power into Iraq,

> Powell said the president had to consider what a military operation against Iraq would do in the Arab world. Cauldron was the right word. He dealt with the leaders and foreign ministers in these countries as secretary of state. The entire region could be destabilized–friendly regimes in Saudi Arabia, Egypt and Jordan could be put in jeopardy or overthrown.

---

[747] Bob Woodward, <u>Bush at War</u>, p. 331. "Blunt talk, but Powell basically agreed....It was clear to him now that the context was being lost, the attitudes and views of the rest of the world which he knew and lived with."
[748] Bob Woodward, <u>Plan of Attack</u>, p. 159.
[749] *U. S. News & World Report*, January 24, 2005, p. 20.

> Anger and frustration abounded, war could change everything in the Middle East.
>
> It would suck the oxygen out of just about everything the United States was doing, not only in the war on terrorism, but all other diplomatic, defense and intelligence relationships, Powell said. The economic implications could be staggering, potentially driving the supply and price of oil in directions that were as yet unimagined....The cost of occupying Iraq after a victory would be expensive....[750]

But George W. invaded Iraq anyway, and those doom-and-gloom forecasts look more accurate as the weeks go by, for America cannot afford to simply pull out of Iraq like it did from Vietnam, for Vietnam was not a hole in the dike of Middle East/Arab anti-American sentiment and the world's oil supplies. If America even blinks in Iraq, the dike of both oil dependency and Muslim wrath will burst upon America like the end of the world itself. But George W. insists that Americans are all safer now that the nation has invaded Iraq. Speaking of Hispanic Americans who have served in the U.S. military, Bush has said, "Because of their sacrifices, America is a more secure country. Because of their sacrifices, the world will be a more peaceful place. And because of their sacrifices, people who had lived in bondage under the strong arm of a brutal dictator are now free."[751] Instead, Iraqis are now living "in bondage under the strong arm"

---
[750] Bob Woodward, <u>Bush at War</u>, p.332.
[751] Thomas A. Freiling, <u>George W. Bush on God & Country</u>, pp. 42-42. There is no freedom until there is stability, and Iraq's future forks between two options: continued U.S. occupation, or civil war.

of the United States—at least from their perspective, and that's the one that's supposed to count. And if the United States withdraws and Iraq deteriorates into anarchy, will America be safer?

George W. often preaches this theme of liberation of the Iraqi people, no matter what the situation on the ground, much like the starry-eyed though erroneous visions of Iraqis lining the streets to greet American soldiers as heroes after the U.S. invasion. But rich men's delusions cannot bend reality, though they can cause wars, as we have seen in Iraq. As the situation in Iraq and the Middle East deteriorates, reality will rest on the shoulders of all Americans, and the folly of Bush's naïve tampering will be evident.[752] But the Bible tells us to beware of such false teachers, that in the end times many frauds in Christ will deceive good people into wickedness. However unpleasant a realization for his supporters, George W. Bush is such a deceiver, whether or not consciously—for his delusions about his chosen role as world liberator/dominator and his twisted versions of Christian giving ("trickle down economics" and "compassionate conservatism"), Christian frugality (gala balls, gaudy excesses, Cadillacs), and Christian defense

---

[752] "Bush administration officials who promoted war with Iraq envisioned Americans reshaping the country in their own image after the war. Instead, the reshaping is increasingly being carried out by Iran—the same nation that has provoked a diplomatic furor over its nuclear ambitions….While Tehran has little motive to destabilize Iraq now, its ability to do so could undermine the Bush administration's attempt to stop Iran's nuclear program….If Iran wished to make life difficult for the U.S. and its troops in Iraq, it might draw on the support of Iraqi Shiite leaders." "Iran Plays Growing Role in Iraq, Complicating Bush's Strategy," *The Wall Street Journal*, February 14, 2006, p. 1.

(preemption, bunker busters and systematic torture) are harmful to the world's perception of Christ and to the victims of unchristian policies, however Christian those policies are worded. Paul tells us in 2 Timothy:

> Remember that there will be difficult times in the last days. People will be selfish, greedy, boastful, and conceited;...they will hold to the outward form of our religion, but reject its real power. Keep away from such people....people whose minds do not function and who are failures in the faith. But they will not get very far, because everyone will see how stupid they are.[753]

It is time for Americans to acknowledge how patently stupid was the invasion of Iraq (and tax refunds and NCLB and the decision to authorize torture to extract information), because George W. has already gotten too far and misled too many away from the true face of Christ.

The Imperialist American mission to "liberate" others less fortunate is not novel to George W. Bush and his entourage, but the stakes have never been higher. In the mid-nineteenth century, America went through a similar (and similarly dubious) phase of pompous pseudo-altruism called "manifest destiny." As one historian has summarized:

> "Manifest Destiny"...was a concept cloudy enough to appeal to many needs and hopes, compelling enough to sustain determined leadership. It meant

---
[753] 2 Timothy 3:1-2, 5, 8-9, TEV.

expansion, legitimated by Heaven or the fates, inspired by economic interest, territorial greed, and missionary idealism....That was the alleged purpose of Manifest Destiny–to bring the blessings of liberty and democracy, of Christianity and commercialism, to backward peoples....

Young America mixed nineteenth-century liberal idealism and crassly materialistic expansionism into a heady brew that for a short time helped raise popular consciousness of America's "manifest destiny."....

But liberty, as Americans defined it, seemed to have a variety of meanings and applications–liberty of speech and religion, liberty to take and exploit land, liberty of enterprise, liberty of foreigners to revolt against oppression, liberty of Americans to intercede in such revolts, liberty of Americans to spread liberty. And self-interest often seemed to lurk behind the lofty ideals. Thus William Seward could talk about the nation's "divine purpose" of spreading democracy, and almost in the same breath, of farmers' need of gaining markets for "our surplus meat and bread."....It was this seeming hypocrisy that especially galled foreigners. Punch portrayed a diabolical, cigar-smoking American, pistol in hand, whip tucked under his arm, blowing smoke rings that displayed lynch law, repudiation, dueling, and slavery. The caption: "THE LAND OF LIBERTY."[754]

---

[754] The modern equivalent cartoon would take little doctoring to accurately depict George W. Bush, with eel-skin boots, chewing tobacco, a ten-gallon hat, four-pound belt buckle and arrogant smirk. Oh, and a crucifix and a Bible....His smoke rings would display compassionate conservatism, trickle-down economics, WMD, the USA Patriot Act, and US-mandated elections. The caption: "THE LAND OF LIBERATION."

> The mixed concepts of liberty as liberation, and liberty as exploitation, dominated the goals of American foreign policy in the early [eighteen] fifties.
>
> This was also a time when the President of the United States, instead of predisposed against going to war, was wholly prepared to do so if necessary to protect "American national interests."[755]

So America has been down this moral road before, and she got away with it (at least in this world). But economic gain, the measure used by this world, is not the only standard by which to gauge the success of a venture. Much of America's "manifest destiny" expansion of the past has been financially profitable, but then so was slavery, of which Frederick Douglass observed that American Christian slaveholders were "devils dressed in angels' robes," and complained that the slave master "covers his infernal business with the garb of Christianity."[756] Many Christians did not stand against slavery, or against Hitler, or against America's genocide of the American Indians, but those who did so stood by Christ. Standing with Christ in modern America is exclusive of standing with George W. Bush on a number of issues, most especially the Iraq War and the use of torture.

Richard N. Goodwin discussed the American moral schism when he addressed the employment of "reason" to justify morally dubious ventures such as the Vietnam War:

---

[755] James MacGregor Burns, The Vineyard of Liberty, pp.457, 536, 537.
[756] Frederick Douglass, Narrative of the Life of Frederick Douglass, p. 72.

The alliance of mysticism and science also took more subtle but very effective forms. Given the mystical premise, e.g., the British Empire, defense of freedom, or American self-interest, scientific reason could then be used to prove that certain policies and actions were required. However, the rational pursuit of a mystical idea is not rational and, if carried far enough, loses whatever reason it once contained. The war in Vietnam is an instructive example.

That war began as the rational pursuit of an unexamined, i.e., mystical premise: It was in our national self-interest to help any government threatened by any group which was known or suspected to think of itself as communist. Why?....Because....

[H]ow could we justify the killing of South Vietnamese civilians in the course of protecting them..."Better the death of the body, than the death of the spirit under communism."

The advocates and leaders of the war were undergoing a classical mystical experience. The war for Vietnam was the war for America. South Vietnam was America, their America, them. All the rest—domestic turbulence, economic decline, the decay of shared social purposes—was incidental, an annoyance, or a subversive obstacle to the pursuit of a compelling destiny across the Pacific.[757]

---

[757] Richard N. Goodwin, The American Condition, pp. 50, 51, 51-52. Yet, in an ideological blindness repeated today in Iraq, "As late as 1966, one of the highest officials in the American government remarked that it might be a good idea if some person who understood the Vietnamese people and their culture were asked to attend the meetings where the struggle to win "men's hearts and minds" was being plotted." p. 53.

The current Bush administration brand of mysticism is even more grandiose, envisioning the transformation of the planet into America's image of liberal democratic Shangri-la, as opposed to merely defending the world against the march of communism like the Western Cold War heroes. And of course, scientific reason and self-protection have been interposed as the justifications for this action, not obedience to the will of God as espoused in Scripture and the gift of Christ, the Prince of Peace.

Ronald Reagan, George W.'s idol, developed the "Reagan Doctrine" under similar pretense. But this ideology likewise pretended to a morality higher than Darwinian self-interest:

> The strategic, military and economic advantages flowing to the United States from the support of resistance movements in Soviet client states alone do not validate the Reagan Doctrine. It rests as well on moral principles of the universality of human rights and freedom of human choice–values that are integral to the American ethos.[758]

But the moral ambiguity of these "moral principles" (which do not reference Christ) is revealed by the words of Ronald Reagan (eerie when juxtaposed to the present situation in Iraq), arguing that a primary U.S. objective in supporting "resistance movements" was to support "troubled nations" where the wars are "the consequence of an ideology imposed from without, dividing nations and creating regimes that are, almost from the day they

---

[758] William R. Bode, "The Reagan Doctrine in Outline," <u>Central America and the Reagan Doctrine</u>, p. 254.

take power, at war with their own people." "[759] If the imposition of democratic government structures by the U.S. in Iraq is not "an ideology imposed from without," then neither is Soviet-imposed communism, etc.

Whether in Vietnam or Iraq, the United States government and its zealot bureaucrats-du-jour mask their imperialistic or ideological motivations with paternalistic claims of having the affected populations' interests in mind: "When self-interested considerations have to be dressed up as moral concerns in order to be presentable to the American public, the usual claim is that the United States is concerned with the defense of democracy."[760] George W. Bush resorted to this line of rationalization when the weapons of mass destruction failed to materialize in post-invasion Iraq.

But the creation of democratic institutions in Iraq faces tremendous and most likely insurmountable cultural and religious hurdles which make the idea of an American-imposed "liberation" seem oxymoronic. If Thomas Jefferson was correct that "no nation has ever yet existed or been governed without religion,"[761] then no new government can be sustained in Iraq without religion, and that religion is not inclined to be Christianity. Moreover, many of the western traditions and principles being introduced as part of the American effort to "liberate" Iraq are themselves in direct conflict with the Muslim faith. For instance, how does one impose

---

[759] Ibid., p. 255.
[760] Jeff McMahon, <u>Reagan and the World: Imperial Policy in the New Cold War</u>, p. 22.
[761] David Aikman, <u>A Man of Faith: The Spiritual Journey of George W. Bush</u>, p. 183. "Nor can be," Jefferson is reputed to have said.

freedom of religion and women's rights simultaneously in a Muslim society (as the Bush administration is now confidently attempting), where the vast majority will employ religious freedom to choose a faith which denies equal rights to women? The quandary is illustrated by the early elections in Iraq, which required that "At least 25 percent of the candidates on each list must be women, though there are only a handful of politically prominent women in the country."[762] Perhaps illiterate Iraqi women should be required to fill numerous government posts, in this bizarre creation of surreal ideological fantasy which would be decried by Bush conservatives as perverse reverse discrimination if attempted in the United States. "Democracy and human rights were a distant and tardy third in the President's justifications leading up to the war, and the question of how to advance democracy in post-war Iraq was clearly an afterthought for U.S. war planners. They still have not figured it out."[763]

It would be wonderful, now that the United States has embarked upon the Iraq project, if that country could be transformed into the democratic and peaceful society that Bush W. envisioned. However, such a transformation would not legitimize an unjust war under any logical or Christian moral standard. And

---

[762] Dan Murphy, "Secrecy surrounds Iraq vote," *The Christian Science Monitor*, January 13, 2005, p. 10. Many of the candidates' names were kept secret at the election to protect candidates–were their genders revealed as qualifications for office not based on merit? Has anyone considered how absurd this looks to Muslims?–their view of Americans as *Dallas-*or *Falconcrest-*like was a less alien-looking impression than the current reality of American nation-building and torture.

[763] *Friends Committee on National Legislation Washington Newsletter*, No. 696, April 2005, p. 1.

unfortunately, that scenario is probably a pipe dream—Iraq will only worsen, until the world is increasingly affected by the consequences of a destabilized Middle East. The history of Iraq is one of instability caused by three rival ethnic/religious factions forced into a nation, compelled together in endless conflict. Iraq was "cobbled together" by the British in the 1920s.[764] Saddam Hussein, backed financially and supplied militarily by the United States for many years, created through his brutal reign the most stable situation in Iraq since before World War I. Thus many experts on the Middle East, and countries like Saudi Arabia,[765] felt strongly that Saddam Hussein's removal could lead to chaos in the Gulf region.

The Reagan administration was proactive in its preemption but used American might more to undermine (Soviet-sponsored) regimes than to create new American-sponsored ones, as Bush is doing. Advocating the support of resistance movements, the Reagan Doctrine sought to "bog down and exhaust the enemy's forces."[766] In words that if reversed could easily describe current American vulnerability in Iraq, one conservative commentator noted of the Soviets that because they had so many activities worldwide, the Reagan Doctrine

---

[764] "Reclusive ayatollah speaks softly, carries major clout," *The Christian Science Monitor*, January 20, 2005, p. 10.

[765] The Saudis held "…fears that if Saddam Hussein were deposed, Iraq would disintegrate." George Donelson Moss, <u>Moving On: The American People Since 1945</u>, p. 385.

[766] William R. Bode, "The Reagan Doctrine in Outline," <u>Central America and the Reagan Doctrine</u>, p. 253.

> must concentrate on defeating those salients that either are most vulnerable or most threatening to U.S. interests, while acting in other regions to tie down Soviet resources....Taking the offensive is consonant with economic as well as military criteria.
>
> Moreover, government troops are more costly to train, equip and maintain than are guerilla forces, and the regime-under-attack bears the additional burden of maintaining and guarding the nation's economic infrastructure, part of which is exploited by the guerillas.[767]

Does this perspective, from a pro-Reagan conservative seeking to counter Soviet efforts to expand their ideological and economic influence, suggest that America is now the exporter of ideology, over-reaching as did once the Soviets? The United States will be similarly undermined in stature and in military superiority by its Roman-Empire-like over-reaching.

Iraq must have moral guidance, whatever form its government may take–the structure of a government is the product of a particular society's morality. America's government is founded on religious freedoms and strong ideologies favoring individualism and free markets, etc.: but exporting that government cannot serve to impose America's morality.[768] Most Iraqis will place their religious faith foremost as guide in deciding whether to embrace America's government structures, a faith which is at odds with many of the Western values that

---

[767] Ibid., pp. 253, 253-254.
[768] As Allan Bloom observes, "There must be religion, and reason cannot found religion." The Closing of the American Mind, p. 196.

underpin liberal democratic government. The simple and inevitable consequence of the disparity between the essentially secular American military reconstruction effort and the intensely sectarian Arab culture sought to be transformed, is that any new Western government structures will in time be co-opted by either another dictator or a Taliban-like Islamic movement. (Witness recent Palestinian elections, in which Hamas was democratically elected, but the United States refuses to acknowledge that party's right to rule.)

The U. S. invasion of Iraq cannot be supported on moral grounds, and therefore all death, injury or economic damage that has been caused by that war is immoral, and has itself been caused directly by George W. Bush and those who support and enable him. Consequently, the Iraq War is a stain on Christ's name. Yet George W. Bush carried the name of Jesus Christ on his lips to gain the White House, and then used the oval office to initiate an ungodly war: this president's motto should be "Read my actions." When combined with the neglect of our environment in preference for short-run economic gain, the redistribution of wealth from poor to rich in the name of trickle-down economics, the destruction of America's economy through huge debt and war-bills in the face of welfare cuts dubbed compassionate conservatism, and (worst of all) the systemic governmental torture and illegal detention of thousands of predominantly-Muslim suspects, then the perversion of Christ's message reflected by this system of division and power-lust borders on the Biblical–is George W. Bush the Anti-Christ? Does Revelation 13 refer to George W.?[769]–The fact that the comparison can even tenuously be made demonstrates the hypocrisy which George W. Bush's purportedly-Christian agenda has engendered, with never a word of remorse.

Frederick Douglass addressed in 1845 the hypocrisy inherent in the prevalence of the institution of slavery in a supposedly-Christian nation, saying: "[I am] filled with unutterable loathing when I contemplate the religious pomp and show, together with the horrible inconsistencies, which every where surround me."[770] One is reminded of this degree of hypocrisy in Bush administration actions in Iraq, Abu Ghraib et al., and in the squandering of billions of borrowed dollars that will have to be repaid by today's and tomorrow's American children, laboring in a more globally competitive world, with dwindling natural resources.

---

[769] Biblical interpretation by all Christians is encouraged–all Christians must study the Bible intently to discover its personal truths. But just as food for thought, could the beast's deadly wound which "was healed; and all the world wondered after the beast" (Rev. 13:3, KJV) refer to George's greatest (moral) claim to success, his cessation of drinking? Can it not be said of GWB, more than any man in history, "Who is like unto the beast? who is able to make war with him?" (Rev 13:4, KJV) Perhaps either Dick Cheney or Karl Rove, legendary for their intense loyalty to GWB, is the "other beast" who "exerciseth all the power of the first beast before him, and causeth the earth and them which dwell therein to worship the first beast, whose deadly wound was healed. And he doeth great wonders, so that he maketh fire come down from heaven on the earth in the sight of men." (Rev 13:12-13, KJV) (like modern precision missiles would have appeared to John in his visions?) The fact that analogies between George W. Bush and the Anti-Christ are even possible should be pause for thought by the world's Christians.

[770] Frederick Douglass, <u>Narrative of the Life of Frederick Douglass</u>, p. 71.

Let all Christians beware the possibilities created on this earth by the war between good and evil, and study Scripture for themselves. The Book of Revelation in particular was gifted by God for these times so that Christians would not look away in terror and despair in end times, but would instead be emboldened by clear signs to spread the Good News to others at the very time when those in darkness would be compelled to see. Revelation 13 admonishes "If any man have an ear, let him hear" (Revelation 13:9, KJV). Further, Revelation 1:3 renders a unique blessing to the reader of this Book: "Blessed is he that readeth, and they that hear the words of this prophecy, and keep those things which are written therein: for the time is at hand." (KJV). The Book of Revelation and its particular relevance for modern America's Christians is discussed further in Chapter Ten.

Chapter 9

ABU GHRAIB, THE MODERN SYMBOL OF AMERICA

> When the King of Israel saw them, he shouted to Elisha, "My father, should I kill them? Should I kill them?"
> "Of course not!" Elisha replied. "Do we kill prisoners of war? Give them food and drink and send them home again to their master."
> So the king made a great feast for them and sent them home to their master.
> —2 Kings 6:21-23, NLT, Second Edition

Not only did the abuses at Abu Ghraib prison represent a dramatic departure from America's stated moral values, but it dovetailed perfectly with Arab perceptions of the Great Satan, playing into the hands of the terrorists on both counts. Americans have paid little attention, as usual, to perceptions of the United States outside of America. But these perceptions, always important in promoting trade, Christianity, or goodwill, have never been of more vital concern to America than in the international battle against terrorism. Every foreign heart or mind turned away from sympathy with America is a lost ally or, worse, an increase in the ranks of those who wish her harm.

It is therefore of particular importance in this "day and age" for Americans to understand and engage more with the world, and to be sensitive to other peoples' views of the United States. This requires an honest assessment of our nation's past conduct in foreign lands, through their eyes and not through the rose-colored glasses of American myth-making. This is particularly true for Christian Americans, who must never let the worldly passions of nationalism divide the international brotherhood which is the Body of Christ.

Americans perceive of their country as liberator and freedom fighter, but their government has a track record that is at best spotty. It is hardly surprising that a government which has repeatedly killed or experimented upon its own soldiers and citizens, as the United States government has, may have fallen short in its feigned efforts to aid other peoples. Had America followed through with actions after words of freedom, numerous anti-American, poisonous movements that continue to plague the world would have instead been employed as opportunities to truly spread democracy and freedom. But the American government and the business interests which influence it have cared only for short-term power for economic gain in foreign nations, and have won few hearts and minds in the twentieth century, though many dictators.

To name a few examples:

1) Ferdinand Marcos

The Philippines came under American influence as a direct consequence of military strategic desirability,[771] not liberal democratic altruism. For years, the United States had an opportunity to bring democracy and its much-touted "freedoms" to this nation,[772] but instead millions and millions of U.S.-taxpayer dollars were invested in the Marcos family and in Imelda Marcos' footwear collection[773]–this is the face of democratic influence that the rest of the world has come to expect, and this cynicism has been created by American conduct.

How many polling booths or medical clinics could have been installed using Imelda's shoe-money was never discovered, though the United States paid to escort its puppet dictator safely out of harm's way when the Philippine people ousted Marcos. Neither is America's moral imprint on foreign nations such as the

---

[771] Gerald Segal, The World Affairs Companion: The Essential One-Volume Guide to Global Issues, pp. 194-196: "The Philippines held "close military ties to the United States." "

[772] Reagan did try, though too late, to influence some democratic reform: "The Reagan administration also had to confront a crisis in the Philippines, the former Pacific colony and longtime ally of the United States. For several years, a corrupt military dictator, Ferdinand Marcos, whom the United States had supported, had been losing power....Pressure from U.S. officials forced Marcos to permit elections that had been suspended since he took office." George Donelson Moss, Moving On: The American People Since 1945, p. 349. By this point, it was too late to undo either the inevitable fall of Marcos or the resentment his rule had engendered against the United States.

[773] Doug Bandow summarizes: "The Philippines under Marcos...was a plutocracy...." Beyond Good Intentions: A Biblical View of Politics, p. 199.

Philippines any more popular than its political one: "One long-term consequence of America's military presence in the Philippines is the massive and still growing trade in Southeast Asian girls and young women–a skin trade with which the U.S. military is still involved and which in many cases amounts to modern slavery."[774] The experience of the Philippines with the United States mirrored the experiences of all too many nations which possessed assets or strategic value that the great superpower desired–democratic reforms were not on the agenda, nor was the welfare, health or safety of the people affected by U.S. policies. Thus President Bush's words of liberation for Iraq (though used largely in hindsight to excuse an unjust war) may persuade Americans, but the rest of the world has tired ears. America has not delivered on her grand promises in the past, and George Bush's promises are no less empty.

2) Manuel Noriega

The fact that Mr. Noriega enjoyed American favoritism is well-known, as is his notoriety and subsequent imprisonment. But as much as 50 percent of U.S. imports came through the Panama Canal,[775] making Panama an extremely vital hub of commerce. America's history with Panama is tumultuous, and includes the provision by Manuel Noriega of refuge for the Shah of Iran (fellow puppet) at the behest of the United States, which "fulfilled no Panamanian business or strategic interest, and, for the first time, it opened [Panama] to the

---

[774] Preston Jones, The Best Christian Writing, 2001, p. 159.
[775] Jeff McMahon, Reagan and the World: Imperial Policy in the New Cold War, p. 23.

possibility of terrorist attacks from the Middle East."[776] What could be more clear evidence of the obvious enmity felt toward the United States than Panamanian fear of terrorist reprisals in the 1970s for harboring a U.S. lackey? And thirty years later, President Bush whitewashes American and world history with the simplistic lie that "they hate us because we're free."

In an effort which foreshadowed the failed effort to pressure Saddam Hussein, the United States attempted to exert economic control over Panama via an embargo. And as in Iraq, Iran, and Nicaragua, the effort disproportionately impacted the poor, and compelled Panama to build alliances elsewhere:

> The sanctions were a cynical exercise orchestrated in much the same way that the United States imposed sanctions on Cuba and Haiti….; the effects were felt in reverse proportion to how wealthy someone was. The rich businessmen of Panama City may have suffered economic problems, but it was the poor people of San Miguelito who had less to eat….It was the same cynical approach used by the Americans with Fidel Castro in Cuba: willfully destroy the economy, and then blame the leadership for an inability to maintain proper standards of living….
>
> The Americans used all means at their disposal to discourage their European allies and Japan from doing business with us, so we established ties with the PLO, North Korea and the Soviet Union, looking for diplomatic and economic support.[777]

---
[776] Peter Eisner and Manuel Noriega, America's Prisoner: The Memoirs of Manuel Noriega, p. 97.
[777] Ibid., p. 135.

Noriega, America's "former CIA anti-communist asset,"[778] became an unmanageable maverick who needed to be reigned in, and so Panama was invaded.[779] But once again, no effort, not even a weak effort at pretense, had been made by the United States to spread democratic freedoms or institutions to the people of Panama. And when the puppet was no longer representing the best interests of its American puppeteer, the United States wasted no time taking control of a foreign nation:

> In December, 1989, the U.S. sent military forces into Panama to overthrow dictator Manuel Noriega and to install a pro-U.S. democratic government. Noriega, a former U.S. client, had previously worked with the CIA....Thousands of Panamanians were killed and wounded, many of them civilians, although neither the U.S. government nor the mainstream U.S. news media informed the American public of the massive civilian casualties. Public opinion polls showed the Panamanian intervention, which was of dubious legality, to be overwhelmingly popular with Americans. President Bush's popularity soared.[780]

---

[778] John Kenneth Galbraith, <u>The Culture of Contentment</u>, p. 140. There is no question that Noriega was on the U.S. government's payroll, with funds transferred by the CIA to both Noriega and the Contras through the now-infamous BCCI, a Pakistani bank with terrorist ties. (*see* Posner, p.44)

[779] Manuel Noriega alleges, with logic on his side, that one significant reason that the Bush Sr. administration sought to invade Panama was that "Panama was to assume superintendence of the canal for the first time on January 1, 1990–only twelve days after the U.S. invasion of Panama...." Peter Eisner and Manuel Noriega, <u>America's Prisoner: The Memoirs of Manuel Noriega</u>, p. xv.

[780] George Donelson Moss, <u>Moving On: The American People Since 1945</u>, pp. 380, 381. Twenty-three U.S. soldiers were killed in the attack.

So is America a Christian nation or an Imperialist one? It would seem that the Empire has no clothes, or is dangerously psychotic, for Americans perceive their country to be world liberators and purveyors of Christian faith, whereas their country's actions and the perception of the world bespeak a nation that is far from exemplary in its Christian conduct, that is in fact the greatest Imperialist glutton in world history. America thus wears Christian clothes while it exports actions of violence motivated by greed and by obsession with the interests of self. Christian words, unchristian actions…the wolf in sheep's clothing, feigning Christian faith while acting unfaithfully, leading others to view Christ with disgust because of the evil deeds of His false messengers.

3) Anastasio Somoza

Anastasio Somoza, former President/dictator of Nicaragua, was long a U.S. ally.[781] Indeed, the Somozas were creations of the American imperialist machine, installed in an anti-Communist but certainly undemocratic coup by the United States: "There was a democratic awakening in the 1940s, but it was aborted by the Central Intelligence Agency in the 1950s for fear the Soviets would take advantage."[782] Somoza offered loyalty to America and its economic and military interests in exchange for military, economic and diplomatic support. His family's "power was built on the training

---

[781] Doug Bandow, Beyond Good Intentions: A Biblical View of Politics, p. 192.
[782] Christopher Dickey, With the Contras: A Reporter in the Wilds of Nicaragua, p. 17.

and arms of the United States...."[783] Somoza became a strong U.S. ally, at least to President Reagan and the conservatives:

> He had made himself part of an influential old-boy network of ultra-conservatives in the United States who admired his tough talk and his steadfast hatred of communism so utterly devoid of self-doubt.... In the end, it did not matter how the Nicaraguan people felt about Somoza; what mattered was that his position was one of maintaining the dignity of the United States. That was what Somoza stood for and why he should be supported.[784]

If Somoza stood for the United States, he represented corruption, oppression and malice. Shouldn't the foreign leaders America has so strongly influenced (if not installed) reflect the values of equality, justice and freedom which we say we hold so dear? Have we exported these values to any of these nations? Again, Americans are willing, consumptive pawns in the true Orwellian sense, for they believe the Big Brother lies that reinforce their complacency, at the expense of America's reputation abroad and the victims of American hegemony. Without the modern equivalent of "doublespeak," Americans would be incapable of continuing to ignore the wreckage caused by their nation's short-sighted and distinctly undemocratic foreign policy and the international resentment against America that this has caused. How can any human being with a God-given intellect believe for even an instant that the 9/11 Saudi terrorists blew

---

[783] Ibid., p. 18.
[784] Ibid., p. 45.

themselves up because "they hate Americans because we're free"?–Only with the Satan-given deceptive magic of "doublespeak," so artfully and ubiquitously employed by the United States government in past and present, and of which Karl Rove, Dick Cheney, and George Bush are fluent speakers. Jesus Christ never used doublespeak or deception to lead the lost to truth.

And doublespeak was employed by the United States in its dealings with the Sandinistas. The Reagan administration's obsession with Nicaragua bordered on paranoia, notwithstanding that decades of a U.S. blind eye toward Somoza's conduct had created the environment in which the Sandinista movement thrived. Had America ensured that even a small portion of the U.S. funds sent to Somoza, or a small percentage of Nicaragua's gross domestic product, had been set aside to be used to reduce the country's fifty-percent infant mortality rate, or to build hospitals or schools (as was done by the communists in a successful bid to win the hearts and minds of the Nicaraguan people),[785] then American democracy and freedoms would have been sown in Nicaragua instead of bitter resentment and a receptiveness toward any alternative ideology that might stave off death, poverty, starvation and oppression–for that is what American influence brought to Nicaragua.

---

[785] The success of these efforts by the Sandinistas led to a deliberate campaign by the Contras to undermine such projects. This was accomplished by targeting hospitals and schools, and spreading terror amongst health and education professionals, effected with illegal United States tax dollars: "the anti-Sandinista rebels were covertly funded through a BCCI branch." Gerald Posner, Why America Slept: The Failure to Prevent 9/11, p. 44.

Yet the Reagan administration persisted in the absolutely specious position that Nicaragua was a threat to American national security, a potential Soviet satellite in "America's back yard." Of course, were this true that would be tough luck for America, for there was ample opportunity to "liberate" the Nicaraguan people and make that country a true ally, when our nation instead funneled money blindly to a brutal regime. Once the Sandinistas gained overwhelming popular support, it was quite dictatorial (and grossly undemocratic) of the United States to attempt to undermine them. But for the Reagan administration, "[i]t did not matter that Nicaragua was small and backward....It was cast as a major part of the Soviet threat."[786] Top Reagan officials argued that

> It would be reasonable to assign top priority to those areas in which vital U.S. security interests are at stake. Nicaragua clearly qualifies for this criterion because of the threat to U.S. sea lines of communication posed by Soviet bases in that nation, as well as the specter of subversion and insurgencies directed against other Central American nations and Mexico.[787]

---

[786] Christopher Dickey, <u>With the Contras: a Reporter in the Wilds of Nicaragua</u>, pp. 69-70.

[787] William R. Bode, "The Reagan Doctrine in Outline," <u>Central America and the Reagan Doctrine</u>, p. 256. When will there be accountability for these lies to Americans? Even were these outrageous claims true, the Nicaraguan people are free to choose communism as their form of government, aren't they? Clearly not, if America doesn't like it. The Reagan posse also claimed that "the Nicaraguan resistance [<u>i.e. the U.S.-supported Contras</u>] is being muddied with charges of large-scale drug smuggling and rampant human rights abuses," (Id., p. 259.) when in fact those charges were accurate.

Since the scandalous failure of the Contras to rout the Sandinistas, these "vital U.S. security interests" have never been even remotely threatened by the Sandinistas. The truth is that "...the Nicaraguan revolution represent[ed] a direct challenge to the United States, its values, and its system of global control."[788] As with the Shah of Iran, Ferdinand Marcos, Manuel Noriega, and later Saddam Hussein, America had lost "control" of its own backyard because for the umpteenth time it had ignored the condition of the human beings suffering under its imperialistic domination of a third-world country. In reaction to the uprising of those so oppressed under the Somoza family, the Reagan administration illegally channeled funds[789] to (if not created) the "contras," a rebel force opposed to the Sandinistas. Have America's Oliver North supporters truly examined the truth of what the contras actually represented, and what they actually did?:

> [There was a] clear lack of public support for the contras....That the contras lack popular support is unsurprising given their composition. The main group of contras...in fact consists largely of the remnants of Somoza's hated National Guard whom the Sandinistas allowed to seek asylum in Honduras after the revolution....Somoza's National Guard was legendary for its brutality, and so far the contras have been true to their reputation....their specialties

---

[788] Jeff McMahon, <u>Reagan and the World: Imperial Policy in the New Cold War</u>, p.188.
[789] Saudi Arabia and Israel also contributed funds to the contras. George Donelson Moss, <u>Moving On: The American People Since 1945</u>, p. 352.

include burning villages and crops, and murdering doctors, teachers, and church officials: and they have also performed other feats of military valor such as kidnapping peasant children and attacking and destroying buses, ambulances, and hospitals.[790]

This conduct by America's government forms a pattern which is at odds with America's mythology, that America is "the greatest nation in the world," that America aids the poor and spreads democratic freedoms and the virtues of the free market, etc. But Americans whose allegiance is to Christ will scrutinize their government closely and thoroughly, and hold it to the standard of Jesus Christ. As one writer has dared opine:

> ….General Augusto Pinochet of Chile, who crushed dissent and murdered his opposition; Anastasio Somoza of Nicaragua, who stole millions of dollars in U.S. earthquake relief money in 1973 while his people lived in squalor; Roberto D'Aubuisson in El Salvador, whom a UN commission determined was responsible for the Salvadoran death squads, which

---

[790] George Donelson Moss, Moving On: The American People Since 1945, pp. 183, 184. Hospitals and schools were favorite targets of the Contras, because the Sandinistas, with Soviet aid, invested much energy into building hospitals and schools to win the hearts and minds of those very people whose plight America had ignored: the Nicaraguans. (Iran is now doing the same thing in Iraq, funneling money and other assistance to construct hospitals and schools.) Echoing the highly visible hypocrisy of the current administration, Moss concludes of the Reagan administration that "To summarize, the administration's policy on human rights has been for the most part to ignore human rights violations by friendly regimes, while exploiting the rhetoric of human rights in denouncing its enemies." at p. 104. Sounds familiar….

killed thousands while the United States stood by;[791] collectively, the nameless generals and colonels of Guatemala in the 1980s, responsible for tens of thousands of political murders....All of those men were supported to one extent or another by a succession of American presidents who turned a blind eye to their murderous abuses of power.[792]

These same American presidents then cry foul at the behavior of the successors to America's puppets, as in the Iranian hostage crisis and in Nicaragua; other times criticism is directed at a former American "ally," as in the cases of Manuel Noriega, Saddam Hussein, or bin Laden.[793] But in all cases, America's blind eye benefits short-term gain at the expense of human decency or the "values" we say we represent.

4) the Shah of Iran

The Shah of Iran was America's foothold in the Middle East in the 1960s and 1970s. However, the United States did not capitalize on its influence in Iran

---

[791] *See* Jeff McMahon, Reagan and the World: Imperial Policy in the New Cold War, at page 165, which discusses the United States' support of the government of El Salvador, even though the El Salvadoran government murdered priests using death squads, exterminated whole communities, and suppressed newspapers.

[792] Peter Eisner, in foreword to Peter Eisner and Manuel Noriega, America's Prisoner: The Memoirs of Manuel Noriega, p. xiv.

[793] The Reagan administration had been prominent supporters of the Taliban and bin Laden in their fight against the Soviet effort to occupy Afghanistan, gushing that "the Muhahideen fighters are the only representatives of the Afghan people," that "only the afghan Muhahideen seem invulnerable to criticism," and calling the Muhahideen "afghan freedom fighters." *See* Walter F. Hahn, ed., Central America and the Reagan Doctrine, pp. 294, 259, 268, 248.

during this time to press for democratic reforms, caring only for the (short-term) interest of Gulf oil production. Dana Adams Schmidt wrote in 1974:

> Now that the British no longer stand guard in the Gulf, the United States must replace them as best it may. But the United States cannot reproduce the political and military system the British built up over centuries. American methods must be different but could achieve similar results. Whatever methods are adopted, it seems obvious to me that the first and basic consideration must be to maintain good relations with the Arabs and the Persians in the Gulf. This presents grave problems insofar as the Arabs are concerned, for two reasons. The first is the United States' commitment to Israel. This commitment will raise infinitely greater problems for the United States if and when the traditional regimes of the Gulf are replaced by revolutionary regimes who would be anti-American even if there were no Israel. The second is that the United States appears to be relying on Iran, which had differences with a number of Arab states, to replace the British as keeper of the peace in the Gulf.
>
> To this end the United States in May, 1973, concluded a two-and-one-half billion dollar, five-year arms deal with Iran, including the very latest weapons in every field. The United States has tried to soften the impact of this very real power relationship for its Arab friends, Saudi Arabia and Kuwait, by expressing willingness to sell Phantoms to them too.[794]

---

[794] Dana Adams Schmidt, <u>Armageddon in the Middle East</u>, pp. 95-96.

As one historian has described this development in American foreign policy:

> Washington wanted to involve Iran in American efforts to contain Soviet expansionism into the Middle East. Most important, Nixon and Kissinger intended to use Iran as a stabilizing force[795] within that turbulent region to enable the United States to distance itself from the chronic Arab-Israeli disputes. Washington tapped Iran, led by the Shah, whom the CIA had helped to reclaim his throne[796] in 1953,[797] to become the major U.S. ally in the Persian Gulf region....The United States began importing more oil from Iran and in May 1972, in effect, gave Iran a blank check to buy conventional weaponry from American arms manufacturers.[798] Iran quickly became the preeminent military power in the region and the leading purchaser of American arms. With help from Washington, relations improved between

---

[795] Like the neoconservatives intend to use Iraq as a stabilizing influence–does no one learn from history?: Iraq is an Iran-turned-Vietnam, in which our failed effort at imperialistic domination has transformed into our now-failing effort at military domination, supposedly in defense of the hearts, minds and freedoms of the common folk about whom America's government never gave a rat's whisker.

[796] This "throne" was certainly not a democratic institution, but that didn't cause the United States any reason to pause, any more than in the cases of Marcos, Noriega, Somoza or Saddam Hussein.

[797] "When Iran's Prime Minister, Muhammed Mossadegh, appeared soft on communism...Eisenhower authorized a CIA-financed coup that drove Mossadegh out of office in 1953 and put Shah Muhammed Reza Pahlevi on his path to the throne." James MacGregor Burns, The Crosswinds of Freedom, p. 255. The author notes that in perceiving a Soviet threat, Eisenhower "and his advisers miscalculated, for the real threat was militant Middle Eastern nationalism." Ibid.

[798] *See also* Dana Adams Schmidt, Armageddon in the Middle East, p. 244.

Saudi Arabia and Iran, who historically had been rivals. The rapprochement between the Saudis and Iranians strengthened the Organization of Oil Exporting Countries (OPEC)....[The motivations for U.S. support of Iran] included keeping the Soviets out, stabilizing the region, ensuring Israel's security, maintaining good relations with moderate Arab regimes, and neutralizing the effects of (if not eliminating) the zero-sum game known as the Arab-Israeli conflict.[799]

Unfortunately, America's sale of arms to Iran,[800] though profitable for the United States' military-industrial complex, contributed to an arms race amongst rival Gulf states. Had this "blank check" been issued for hospital, school and infrastructure construction, or for industrial or agricultural investment, perhaps all of the above interests of the United States would be served, and also the Iranian people would have developed a less negative view toward Americans,[801] but surely the Shah would have been more likely to remain in power if unrest had

---

[799] George Donelson Moss, Moving On: The American People Since 1945, pp. 235-236.

[800] Arms shipments to Iran were not limited to weapons. In an eerie parallel to the arming of Iraq and the Taliban, the United States provided nuclear technology to Iran: "Iran's nuclear program began when the Shah purchased a research reactor from the US in 1959....The Shah had big plans for a network of 23 power reactors, but the US did not consider this a danger, because he was an ally...." "Why US doesn't trust Iran on nukes," *The Christian Science Monitor*, January 24, 2006, p.2. Now, having armed Iran, the United States has decided that it has the right to disarm it. Also, how can the US criticize Russia and France for arming its allies (Iran, Iraq?) without obvious hypocrisy?

[801] Like the humanitarian relief provided by the U.S. in the 1940s to the citizens of Germany, France and Italy, amongst others, led to lasting goodwill and respect for America...until recently....

been averted. Instead, the Shah accumulated military toys while his people suffered in abject poverty. Eventually the Iranian people rebelled against both the Shah and his visible handler, the United States of America. The U.S. embassy in Teheran was seized and American hostages taken, by a Muslim people whose motivation was surely not that they "hated us because we're free." Of course, the mother lode of the world's oil supplies was in nearby Saudi Arabia, which was threatened by this instability in Iran:

> Saudi religious leaders were always watching out for Iran, which borders Afghanistan and adheres to the Shiite sect of Islam....If Teheran managed to take over Kabul, their enemy Shiite brothers would hold the key to Central Asia.
>
> Washington shared this analysis. After the 1979 hostage crisis at the American embassy in Teheran, the State Department's most important objective in the region was to support the pro-Western monarchies and weaken the Islamic Republic of Iran.[802]

One historian relates how anti-Western Islam grew in Saudi Arabia and Iran in the 1970s, leading to the ousting of the Shah:

> The heartland of traditional Islam in Saudi Arabia received a major boost in the 1970s with the formation of an effective strategy to raise oil prices and take control of the resource from Western

---

[802] Jean-Charles Brisard and Guillaume Dasquie, <u>Forbidden Truth: U.S.-Taliban Oil diplomacy and the Failed Hunt for Bin Laden</u>, p. 15.

companies. Funds were used to support Islam around the world, undermining both socialist governments in the Arab world, and 'permissive Western practices' in other states....[In Iran, this led to the deposing of] the corrupt, but Western-oriented Shah....But Islam, like any ideology, soon discovered the rude pragmatism of international affairs. While Iran denounced the United States as 'the great satan,' it supported the same anti-Soviet forces in Afghanistan as the Americans.[803]

Yet closer inspection reveals that this perspective is erroneous. There was nothing incongruous about Iranian support of the anti-Soviet Taliban, a Muslim organization fighting another western, secular power: much more awkward was U.S. support of that group. Also, this author avoids addressing that the "major boost [to Saudi Arabia] in the 1970s with the formation of an effective strategy to raise oil prices and take control of the resource from Western companies" was itself a response to increasing Western influence in Muslim lands, and resentment of American support for Israel. And why shouldn't Saudi Arabia "take control" of its own natural resources? They're not the American Indians....

The rise of Islam in the Middle East in the 1970s was a substantial cause of Western expulsion, but, ironically, was fueled in large part by Western intrusion. Thus Mr. Segal's suggestion that the rise in Islam pushed Western influence out of the Middle East is accurate, but discussion of responsibility for that rise is avoided.

---

[803] Gerald Segal, The World Affairs Companion: The Essential One-Volume Guide to Global Issues, pp. 55, 56.

Islam was given strength against the wishes of Saudi and other Arab leaders, who were compelled to ride the popular religious wave of Islam or be devoured by it. But Islam grew because of anti-Western, and particularly anti-American, sentiment which arose in impoverished Arab ghettos as a reaction against Western support for Israel (of which the United States was and remains by far most prominent), Western apathy toward the plight of Palestinians, and a steadily increasing infiltration of Western "culture" and values into Muslim lands. This latter influence was largely unperceived by the West, who believed (as with the American Indians) that they were gifting a wondrous new "progress" to the backward tribal desert residents of the Gulf. But Western television, media, clothes-styles, alcohol, and tobacco were all threatening to an ancient and deeply religious culture: the cultural pressures on the peoples of the Middle East in the twentieth century were both extreme and abrupt, and eventually induced a powerful, defensive, cultural backlash across the Middle East.

This atmosphere caused a deep suspicion of Western culture and values amongst Arab peoples, and this suspicion naturally-enough extended to Christianity also, creating an anti-Christian as well as anti-American backlash:

> The Christian community in Saudi Arabia may well have reached its zenith at Christmas of 1978. In January 1979, the Shah of Iran went into exile and the fortunes of the Christians in Saudi Arabia fell with him. Fear of repercussions from the "Islamic revival" touched off by Khomeini's victory haunted

the House of Saud. As fear of the Shiites escalated so did fear of the Christians....A Saudi's emotional identification with Islam is rooted in the fact that Islam is not just a religion, it is a civilization and a culture; it is fundamental to a Saudi's perception of who he is and what his world is about....[To avoid the fate of the Shah, t]he House of Saud's safety was to be found in promoting religious orthodoxy.[804]

Another consequence of American over-reaching in the Middle East through the disruption of the government of Iran by the installation of the Shah, and his subsequent ouster, was an invitation to Saddam Hussein to seek advantage to further his Gulf ambitions: "Following the Muslim revolution in Iran in 1979 and the resulting instability, Iraq saw an opportunity to reassert its insignificant territorial claim and assert its political aspirations to leadership in the Gulf."[805] Thus the Iran-Iraq War, "the most senseless conflicts since the First World War,"[806] was set in motion.

To this history of failed American meddling in the Middle East we now add George W. Bush, whose attitudes toward Iraqis, Iranians and other Arabs have greatly influenced how the Arab world views U.S. actions in Iraq and treatment of prisoners at Abu Ghraib and elsewhere. And those attitudes have not been helpful. In addition to an overly-ardent and unequivocal public

---

[804] Sandra Mackey, <u>The Saudis: Inside the Desert Kingdom</u>, pp. 95, 98, 99.
[805] Gerald Segal, <u>The World Affairs Companion: The Essential One-Volume Guide to Global Issues</u>, p.254.
[806] Ibid., p. 254.

support of Israel (*see infra*), Mr. Bush has been unnecessarily hostile to Iran. Does America's President not perceive the hypocrisy of the United States, which undermined the Iranian government by covert coup when it installed the Shah, now proclaiming that "The regime in Teheran must heed the democratic demands of the Iranian people or lose its last claim to legitimacy…."?[807] Did America heed the demands of the Iranians when their Prime Minister was replaced by the Shah via CIA influence? What about the demands or needs of the people of Nicaragua as Somoza stifled them while receiving U.S. aid? Of the Panamanians? The people of the Philippines? Of Haiti (Aristide)? Of Venezuala (Chavez)? What of the demands of the Iraqi people while America supplied Saddam Hussein with arms and WMD technology? What of the demands of the Afghani people, as America's CIA financed, armed, and supplied pick-up trucks to the Taliban? What of the demands of his own people, the Americans, whose opposition to the War in Iraq is making Nixon's administration look popular in comparison–can we simply alter Mr. Bush's "words" ever so slightly, to read "The regime in [Crawford, TX] must heed the democratic demands of the [American] people or lose its claim to legitimacy."?

In the Bush administration's readiness to instruct so very many other nations in moral conduct, a haughtiness often present in U.S. foreign policy has been held up for clear view. As Mr. Bush condemns the human rights abuses of other nations, he has yet to answer for

---

[807] George W. Bush, in Thomas A. Freiling, <u>George W. Bush on God & Country</u>, p. 147.

Abu Ghraib. As he admonishes the government of Iran to heed its people, he ignores his own. The Presidency of the United States, under either political party, has grown too powerful, and has been compromised by the overwhelming influence of the military-industrial bureaucracy of which Eisenhower warned. Instead of spreading peace, America has sold land mines and military hardware, and spread war: how can the United States presume to tell other nations about human rights and universal freedoms when it has almost pathologically denied them to others, and when it has unilaterally decided that it can torture detainees without being held to the Geneva Convention or any other international code or standard, not even the Bible?

Allan Bloom writes in <u>The Closing of the American Mind</u>:

> Sometimes the United States is attacked for failing to promote human rights; sometimes for wanting to impose "the American way of life" on all people without respect for their cultures. To the extent that it does the latter, the United States does so in the name of self-evident truths that apply to the good of all men. But its critics argue that there are no such truths, that they are prejudices of American culture. On the other hand, the Ayatollah was initially supported by some here because he represented true Iranian culture. Now he is attacked for violating human rights. What he does is in the name of Islam. His critics insist that there are universal principles that limit the rights of Islam. When the critics of the U.S. in the name of culture, and of the Ayatollah in the name of human rights, are the same persons,

which they often are, they are persons who want to eat their cake and have it, too.

Why, it might be asked, can't there be a respect for both human rights and culture? Simply because a culture itself generates its own way of life and principles, particularly its highest ones, with no authority above it. If there were such an authority, the unique way of life born of its principle would be undermined…..[The] attempt to preserve old cultures in the New World is superficial because it ignores the fact that real differences among men are based on real differences in fundamental beliefs about good and evil, about what is highest, about God.[808]

The Arab world holds profound differences with the West "about what is highest, about God." Americans as Christians must respect the Muslim right to its own culture and its own determination of what human rights are universal. At a minimum, America should be held to its own "highest principles" before it imposes them on other nations without the popular consent of those affected. America possessed tremendous influence over Iran after undermining its legitimate government, failed to use that influence to effect democratic reform or relief from poverty, lost that influence due to a popular rebellion against that very influence, and now attacks the current government of Iran with the stern lecture that it must "heed the democratic demands of the Iranian people." There is no more credibility in this admonition than there have been Christian values in

---

[808] Allan Bloom, The Closing of the American Mind, pp. 191-192.

the way that Iran has been treated by the United States of America. May God forgive the people of our nation who have treated Iran and its citizens so callously for so many decades.

And now, G.W. Bush is preparing to invade or undermine Iran once again, in the name of "freeing" its people. Is the true motive Iran's nuclear ambitions, or Iran's oil? America lacks the moral high ground to dictate to Iran, but that will hardly deter American ideological conviction. Will we soon hear from George W. Bush regarding Iran, that there are no war plans on his desk but that he believes the doctrine of preemption applies?

5) Israel

America has supported the existence of the state of Israel since its creation as a direct response to Hitlerian atrocities.[809] However, this support has often been at the expense of the interests of various Arab peoples, creating resentment against America which was reflected in the September 11 terrorist attacks.

One author has noted that

> [a]s a result of geography, energy needs, religion and history, the Middle East will never be an isolated region. Rather, it will always play an important role in determining the fate of the entire world. It is the home of the biblical site of Armageddon, which carries horrific connotations of the end of the world.[810]

---

[809] John Lukacs, The End of the Twentieth Century and the End of the Modern Age, p.217.
[810] Michael Saba, The Armageddon Network, p. 14. The author characterizes Israel as a U.S. military foothold in the Middle East. (at p. 45)

The author then quotes Ronald Reagan, and subsequently poses an obvious question:

> [Ronald Reagan:] "I think that Israel,…with a combat-ready and even a combat experienced military, is a force in the Middle East that is actually of benefit to us.".… Could the U.S. afford a policy that was so pro-Israel that even our long-time allies in the Arab world would be forced to question our integrity and sincere desire for peace?.…Even Egypt…has recently begun to operate on the premise that American advice and advisors constitute an Israeli Trojan horse in their midst…. While the U.S. budget deficits reach frightening levels, aid to Israel increases year after year, and Israel is permitted to use that aid to develop products which will compete with American products.[811]

America's support of Israel is easy to understand, but Americans, and their federal government, have largely chosen to ignore the resentment that this support has

---

[811] Ibid., pp. 53, 63, 7, 212. "During fiscal years 1978 through 1982, 48 percent of all American military aid worldwide went to Israel. Most of the money Israel received was then used to buy U.S.-made arms." Jeff McMahon, Reagan and the World: Imperial Policy in the New Cold War, p. 94. This author records that "Of the various U.S. regional policemen, the most important is undoubtedly Israel. When the Reagan administration came to power, its Middle Eastern policy, such as it was, focused almost exclusively on the "security" of the Persian Gulf region–that is, it was largely concerned with ensuring continued Western access to the oil resources of the Gulf region in the face of perceived threats from the Soviet Union and from indigenous natural forces. Israel's role in maintaining the security of the Gulf had become particularly critical after the overthrow of the Shah of Iran." p. 93.

fostered amongst Arabs.[812] While a more empathetic, Christian posture toward Arabs would have furthered U.S. economic interests while spreading democracy in the Middle East, the United States chose instead to prop up oppressive puppet dictators:

> As the British presence declined, those of the United States and the Soviet Union rose. And as the United States' commitment to Israel has grown, so have Arab rage and threats of reprisal against American interests.
>
> Why, then, does the United States follow so paradoxical a policy? The answer is to be found, surely, in the nature of Israel and of the United States. In Israel, Americans see what appears to be a little democracy fighting against great odds, a land of refuge for millions of Jews who fled from persecution, a country peopled by idealists. They admire Israeli efficiency, at least by comparison with the Arabs. They see Israel as a David defying Goliath....It is American Jews who annually contribute millions to the support of Israel....Added to this is the fact that millions of Christian Americans believe in the fulfillment of Biblical promise, and will always give the Israelis the benefit of the doubt in any contest with the Arabs....
>
> When the United States was not busy trying to square the circle of Arab-Israeli hostility, it was

---

[812] "...through four wars, multiple domestic economic crises, and persistent territorial expansion, the United States has provided enormous sums of military and economic aid to Israel. In the process, America has become to the Arabs the arch-imperialist of the Middle East." Sandra Mackey, <u>The Saudis: Inside the Desert Kingdom</u>, p. 320.

maneuvering to keep the Russians out of the Middle east....But so far as the Arabs were concerned, only frustration and resentment resulted, and for this simple reason: the Arabs would not–politically and emotionally could not–collaborate with the principle backer of the State of Israel. The more the United States became involved with Israel, the more the Arabs turned to the Soviet Union.[813]

Matters were not helped by the American failure, for decade upon decade, to devote attention to the meaningful improvement of the circumstances of the Palestinian people. This alienated far more than just the Palestinians from sympathy with America:

> Because they are homeless, because they have aspirations and are frustrated, because they suffer and find no solace, the Palestinians are in the Middle East what the Jews have been in similar situations in other parts of the world: catalysts of revolutionary change....Creation of an autonomous Palestinian state would be a breakthrough toward real peace because it would touch the real core of the problem, namely, the fate of the Palestinian people.[814]

---

[813] Dana Adams Schmidt, <u>Armageddon in the Middle East</u>, pp. 195, 196, 197. Mr. Schmidt emphasizes the "paradox ... that the United States, the home of six million Jews, allows its sentimental attachment to the State of Israel to override economic interests in the vast Arab world....From the American point of view–State Department lip service to the aspirations of the Palestinian people notwithstanding–the Palestinians stand in the way of satisfying the aspirations of Israel, the United States' client-state." pp. 226, 237,

[814] Ibid., at pp. 255, 250-251.

Or as one author who spent many years living in Saudi Arabia described of the Arab perspective:

> To the Moslems, God's covenant is with their ancestor, Ishmael. To the Jews, God's covenant is with their ancestor, Isaac....The current hostilities between Jews and Moslems stem from the creation of Israel in 1948 and its territorial expansion in 1967. Saudi Arabia, like the other Arab states, has never recognized the loss of Arab land to the Jewish state. To the Arabs, Israel is a threatening pawn of Western imperialism sitting on Arab sacred land.[815]

The failure of America to respect Arab concerns, for twenty-five years, was a direct cause of the oil crisis of the 1970s: after Egypt was defeated by Israel in the Yom Kippur War in October of 1973, "[t]he aroused Arab world retaliated with an oil embargo against nations friendly to Israel."[816] (And there was no misrepresentation by the United States government that OPEC orchestrated a crippling oil embargo against America "because we're free," like was done after the September 11 attacks.) Yet the volatility of the situation in the Middle East, and the strength of America's ties to Israel, only increased over the next thirty years.[817]

---

[815] Sandra Mackey, The Saudis: Inside the Desert Kingdom, p. 91.
[816] James MacGregor Burns, The Crosswinds of Freedom, p. 574.
[817] The situation was not improved by U.S. bias in Israel's support. "The problem is that...more guns, bombs, and missiles...promise[ ] to exacerbate tensions in an already unstable Middle east. The region seems more and more like a time bomb waiting to explode." Michael Saba, The Armageddon Network, p. 14.

The advent to power of George W. Bush, a man with absolutely no foreign policy experience (except a trip to China with his dad) but eager to win the American Jewish vote, resulted in a marked increase in U.S. favoritism toward Israel. In <u>A Man of Faith: The Spiritual Journey of George W. Bush</u>, David Aikman reports of President Bush's friendship with Ariel Sharon that "[t]heir friendship helps explain why President Bush has been strikingly supportive of the Israeli government in its various dealings with the Palestinian Authority (PA)."[818]

Aikman quotes a Bush W. speech in May 2001 to the American Jewish Committee:

> We will speak up for our principles; we will stand up for our friends in the world. And one of the most important friends is the State of Israel....At the first meeting of my National Security Council, I told them that a top foreign policy priority of my administration is the safety and security of Israel. (Applause.) My administration will be steadfast in

---

[818] David Aikman, <u>A Man of Faith: The Spiritual Journey of George W. Bush</u>, p. 124. The author supports this alliance, arguing that "...Truman's decision to recognize the infant state of Israel in May 1948, in the face of strong opposition from the State Department, reflected an intuitive belief that Israel ought to be there." At pp. 124-125. But supporting Israel's right to exist does not necessitate the denial or denigration of the humanity of the Palestinian people. In fact, had the United States supported equity in the region instead of such blatant favoritism toward Israel, this might have helped Israel and the United States in the long run by planting seeds of goodwill in the Middle East rather than of distrust and resentment. But America was only interested in building democratic freedoms in nations that were perceived to be threatened by communism, like Vietnam, or which presented economic benefit (natural resources, strategic location, etc.) to the US.

supporting Israel against terrorism and violence, and in seeking the peace for which all Israelis pray.[819]

No wonder then that "[d]uring one White House press conference with the president, Israeli Prime Minister Ariel Sharon shouted at the press corps that George W. Bush is the best friend Israel has ever had."[820]

But George W. has not been embraced as such a friend by Muslim nations, who have viewed his close alliance with Ariel Sharon and Israel as proof of the West's lack of true desire to redress Arab grievances,[821] particularly with regard to the Palestinian people. Mr. Bush took a hands-off attitude toward the Israeli-Palestinian conflict when he took office,[822] but has in fact gone further, blaming the Palestinians for their plight,

---

[819] David Aikman, A Man of Faith: The Spiritual Journey of George W. Bush, p. 146. Aikman notes dryly that "George W. had none of the sentimental feelings of affinity for the conservative Arab states that some in his father's administration evinced." p. 157.

[820] Paul Kengor, God and George W. Bush: a spiritual life, p. 111. *See also* Aikman, A Man of Faith: The Spiritual Journey of George W. Bush, who relates that while he was in Israel, "several Iraqis told me, personally, that Bush was "the best American president Israel has ever had."" Aikman, at p. 148.

[821] Even before George W.'s overzealous support of Israel, one author observed: "The result of these "Israel-first" moves has been a dramatic loss of credibility for the United States among Arab countries–especially those considered our friends, such as Jordan and Saudi Arabia....The thrust of previous U.S. foreign policy had been to ensure maximum influence in the region in case of hostilities and a threat to the oil supply. More recent policies, which paid little attention to our friends in the Arab world, however, had severely tarnished our reputation and credibility....This has proved to be a major setback for the United States. Israel, on the other hand, seems to be benefiting from the situation." Michael Saba, The Armageddon Network, p. 213.

[822] *See* Ron Suskind, The Price of Loyalty, at pp. 71-72.

(much like Compassionate Conservatism lays blame for American poverty on the moral shortcomings of the poor):

> For the Palestinian people, the only path to independence and dignity and progress is the path of democracy. And the Palestinian leaders who block and undermine democratic reform, and feed hatred and encourage violence, are not leaders at all. They're the main obstacles to peace, and to the success of the Palestinian people.[823]

Were the Palestinian people to have created a democratic Republic in the American mold when they were displaced by the creation of Israel in 1948, would their plight be improved? The U.S. government failed to effect meaningful resolution of the Arab-Israeli problem since it contributed to the creation of that problem in 1948. More than fifty years later, Bush is lecturing the Palestinians on their leaders' responsibility for their plight. Although Palestinian leaders, particularly Arafat, have been guilty of malfeasance, Mr. Bush's foreign policy answer has been to use those shortcomings as a rationale for American inaction.[824] When this inaction is contrasted with Mr. Bush's demonstrative warmth toward all things Israeli, the salt in Arab wounds is plain to see.

---

[823] George W. Bush, from Thomas A. Freiling, <u>George W. Bush on God & Country</u>, at pp. 147-148.
[824] Indeed, even the so-called "road map for peace" was initiated by the Bush administration only as a concession to Tony Blair for his support of Bush & Co. initiatives in Iraq. *See* Bob Woodward, <u>Plan of Attack</u>, at p. 347.

And what does President Bush have to say to the Palestinian people now that they used the democratic reforms he demanded to elect Hamas, which has sworn to seek to destroy Israel? What can he say? Shall the CIA install an American-friendly regime to "help" the Palestinians? Would that action, consistent with past American conduct, improve the Arab attitude toward America? What will be the American solution if anti-Israeli or anti-American governments are democratically elected in Pakistan, Egypt, Jordan or Syria? The days of American strong-arming are coming to a close, and now the consequences of past shortsightedness will come home to roost. Is it too late for American foreign policy to change its tune?

6) Afghanistan

This rugged, impoverished country has for decades been a pawn in the West's attempts to control energy resources in the Middle East. The Soviet Union was not interested in the welfare or freedoms of the Afghani people when it invaded Afghanistan, nor was Washington when it in turn armed the Taliban and Osama bin Laden against the Soviets (it was imperative to U.S. economic interests that the U.S.S.R. not control Afghanistan). Nor was Washington interested in Afghanis' welfare once the Soviet Union withdrew, nor when the United States helped the Taliban take over the country and its government, nor when the United States invaded to oust the Taliban as reprisal for the September 11 attacks on American soil.

The reason for this convergence on Afghanistan by the world's superpowers is the usual suspect–oil:

> In 1980 the CIA was predicting that the Soviet Union's own energy resources would soon become insufficient to meet domestic needs, so that the Soviet leaders would have a strong temptation to try to gain control of the oilfields of the Middle East. These fears were heightened by the Soviet invasion of Afghanistan.[825]

America did not rush to the aid of Afghanistan's people–it was motivated by a determination to fight the Soviets at every turn, and to protect "the oilfields of the Middle East." Thousands of Muslims, including bin Laden, flocked to Afghanistan to repel what was perceived as an incursion by infidels into Muslim lands. The United States joined Iran and other Muslim nations in supporting Muslim resistance: "…America channeled weapons, training and funding…to the muhadeen, the Taliban, and Osama bin Laden to fight the Russians."[826] And America under the Reagan administration was not very ethical, let alone Christian, in the means employed to support "resistance movements" against the Soviet Union:

> It is a deadly embarrassment to the United States that the war in Afghanistan was in part funded by rebels in the heroine trade. Similarly, pro-US Contra rebels

---

[825] Jeff McMahon, Reagan and the World: Imperial Policy in the New Cold War, p. 119.
[826] Helen Caldicott, The New Nuclear Danger: George W. Bush's Military-Industrial Complex, p. xiii.

in Central America supported their operations by running cocaine and other drugs. The Panamanian strong-man, Manuel Noriega, apparently had been a key part of the South American drug traffic that connected Columbia, the Contras and Panama with markets for cocaine in the United States.[827]

After the Soviet Union was ignominiously ejected from the mountains of Afghanistan, the United States did nothing to help further democratic reform in the shattered nation—no relief efforts, school or hospital construction, or assistance with elections or government organization.[828] The Taliban subsequently overtook the country,[829] and its human rights violations and destruction of ancient relics soon earned the new government international notoriety. But in the United States, the Clinton administration did nothing to "free" the Afghani people, though it actively sought to help large U.S. corporations construct a pipeline[830] through Afghanistan:

---

[827] Gerald Segal, The World Affairs Companion: The Essential One-Volume Guide to Global Issues, p. 87.

[828] "The experts pretty much agreed that after the Soviets had been thrown out in 1989, the mistake was that the United States walked away." Bob Woodward, Bush at War, p. 275.

[829] In the mid-1990s, the United States State Department actually supported the Taliban accession to power. Jean-Charles Brisard & Guillaume Dasquie, Forbidden Truth: U.S.-Taliban Secret Oil Diplomacy and the Failed Hunt for Bin Laden, p. 4. The CIA provided logistical (i.e., weapons, trucks, and cash) support.

[830] Ibid., p. 7: "The pipeline project [from Central Asia, through Afghanistan, to Pakistan] has been planned by American companies since the mid-1990s"

The key to Central Asia's energy reserves, [Afghanistan] had to be run by a strong and uncontested government in order for the United States to peacefully profit from the situation. Which is why, even after the attacks in Nairobi and Dar es Salaam in 1998–when the Taliban was openly protecting Osama bin Laden–the negotiating continued.[831]

These negotiations to construct a pipeline through Afghanistan continued after the transition in America from Clinton to the current administration, with its much closer ties to the oil and oil exploration industries. American business interests sought a windfall in the region, and Osama bin Laden and the Taliban were not morally objectionable in the face of such profit potential. The Taliban very probably used negotiations over pipeline and other resource concessions to distract Washington from the plans of the 9/11 hijackers, which worked very well–the Bush administration, as truthfully alleged by Richard Clarke, did nothing at all to pursue bin Laden or the Taliban prior to the 9/11 attacks. On December 19, 2000, the UN Security Council imposed an arms embargo against the Taliban and imposed sanctions on its leaders for harboring Osama bin Laden and other wanted terrorists.[832] Nevertheless, the Bush administration continued its efforts to advance U.S. commercial interests in the face of this embargo:

What we do know for sure is that from February 5 to August 2, 2001, the United States engaged in private

---
[831] Ibid., p.9.
[832] Ibid., p. xxxiv.

and risky discussions with the Taliban concerning geostrategic oil interests, among other things…. Afghanistan is essential for any country wanting to exercise its supremacy in Central Asia, and has long been coveted by Russia, the United States, and, above all, Saudi Arabia. [For the Al-Saud family,] the Taliban's accession to power was ideal, since it represented an expansion of their zone of influence in Central Asia. Their Wahhabite brand of Sunni Islam goes very well with the kind of Islam espoused by the Taliban. From the beginning, they have regarded these holy warriors as religious brothers who have allowed them to extend their oil-business interests in that part of the world, and above all to contain the hegemony of their neighbor, Iran, whose Shiite values they are trying to combat.[833]

Ronald Reagan had supported the Taliban, calling the Afghani rebels "freedom fighters."[834] Many on the political Right in America favored re-establishing amicable relations with the Taliban government after George W. Bush became U.S. President.[835] In a March 27, 2001 *Wall Street Journal* article, George Melloan wrote:

---

[833] Ibid., xxxiv, xxxv.

[834] In a February 16, 1985 radio address. *See* William R. Bode, "The Reagan Doctrine in Outline," <u>Central America and the Reagan Doctrine</u>, p. 248.

[835] "Within the Bush administration, [the Taliban's] former partners from the anti-Soviet war in Afghanistan were extremely valuable contacts. In the Republican camp, officials who had strongly supported the Islamist guerrillas in destabilizing Russia held key positions yet again." Jean-Charles Brisard & Guillaume Dasquie, <u>Forbidden Truth: U.S.-Taliban Secret Oil Diplomacy and the Failed Hunt for Bin Laden</u>, p. 4.

The U.S. was Afghanistan's ally in the 1980s. But Bill Clinton cut off commercial contact with the Taliban in July 1999 and later that year joined with the Russians to persuade the United Nations to go ground the Afghan national airline, Aryana, cutting off Afghanistan from the outside world. All this because of a Taliban refusal to hand over suspected terrorist Osama bin Laden to the U.S. Mr. Clinton launched a cruise missile attack on Afghanistan in 1998 at the height of the Lewinsky crisis, ostensibly to kill Osama bin Laden but killing nineteen other people instead...the ham-handed policies of the previous administration have done a good job of alienating the leaders of a country that was once a strategic ally.[836]

In 2001, the Bush W. administration continued to press for reconciliation with the Taliban in order to proceed with plans for a trans-Afghanistan oil pipeline:

Both sides understood the interests at stake. In the name of energy policy, Washington would support a progressive effort for international recognition of the Taliban. In exchange, the Taliban would adopt a more peaceful brand of politics, stop harboring Osama bin Laden, and agree to stay in line with the other Sunni fundamentalist states....[837]

After the Taliban-supported Saudi plotters attacked the World Trade Center buildings on September 11,

---

[836] *The Wall Street Journal*, March 27, 2001. Republicans griping about Clinton trying to kill Osama bin Laden....
[837] Jean-Charles Brisard & Guillaume Dasquie, Forbidden Truth: U.S.-Taliban Secret Oil Diplomacy and the Failed Hunt for Bin Laden, p. 8.

2001, the Bush administration could no longer afford to court Taliban leaders for pipelines, as they had only a month prior to the attacks. Having expended very little effort to improve life for the people of Afghanistan in the past, America now invaded that country to prevent al Qaeda from striking again. The United States armed, trained and funded Osama bin Laden, armed, trained and funded the Taliban, and then invaded Afghanistan with America's innocent youth to pursue them both. America had to invade Afghanistan after the September 11 attacks to combat al Qaeda, but America essentially created al Qaeda (unethically) in the first place,[838] and had long ignored the Afghani people, so the United States was directly responsible for creating the conditions which compelled America to now invade Afghanistan.

And the consequences following from America's meddling in Afghanistan are far from Christian: "During the first four weeks of the war, half a million tons of bombs were dropped on Afghanistan. 20 kilos for every man, woman, and child. During eight and a half weeks of U.S. bombing a documented 3,763 civilians were killed."[839] Does just war theory justify America's self-righteous expedition into the Middle East, even into Afghanistan, when the United States has so strongly contributed to the conditions which "necessitate" its

---

[838] In Forbidden Truth: U.S.-Taliban Secret Oil Diplomacy and the Failed Hunt for Bin Laden, the authors attempt "to decipher this badly-controlled nexus...[of] political channels, financial networks, oil stakes, and secret diplomatic deals...without which Osama bin Laden and his companions would have remained just distant, armed cranks praying in the desert." p. xxi.

[839] Helen Caldicott, The New Nuclear Danger: George W. Bush's Military-Industrial Complex, p. xiii.

intervention? Do American Christians pray as readily for Muslim civilian toddlers bombed by U.S. hardware as for American sons and daughters who signed up for military service voluntarily and have been sacrificed by our government in a chess-game for oil? What would Jesus say? Would he say with Paul, "For I have an obligation to all peoples, to the civilized and to the savage, to the educated and the ignorant."[840] Does God not love all His children?

7) Saddam Hussein

America's relationship with Saddam long pre-dates the current War. Because Western industrialized nations have long vied for control of the oil of the Middle East (if only to keep other nations from monopolizing it), and because Iraq possesses substantial oil reserves, America has long sought to influence and manipulate Saddam Hussein. Throughout this time, little if any effort was made by America to become acquainted with the Iraqi people, let alone liberate them from the ruthlessness of Saddam. On the contrary, the United States exhibited cynical heartlessness toward the peoples of both Iran and Iraq:

> The United States feared that a victory by either Saddam Hussein's secular Iraqi regime or Khomeini's Islamic Fundamentalist Iranian government would make the winner the dominant power in the Middle East. To prevent either side from winning the war–a victory that could threaten the political stability of

---

[840] Romans 1:14, TEV.

Saudi Arabia, Kuwait, and other moderate Arab regimes, and disrupt the flow of oil to the United States and its allies—America, behind an official façade of neutrality, secretly aided whichever side appeared to be losing. In the early years of the war, Washington helped the Iranians, but after 1986, the United States backed Saddam Hussein....

During the war, the Iraqis had used poison gas against the Iranians and were feverishly at work developing nuclear weapons. Despite these ominous indicators, the Reagan administration continued to back Iraq, considering that country to be a necessary counterforce to the Iranian threat. American support of Hussein in the late 1980s would be one of the causes of the 1991 Persian Gulf War...., [which] derived in part from some questionable Middle Eastern diplomatic policies. During the long and bitter Iraq-Iranian war, the Unites States had often aided Iraq to prevent an Iranian victory that Washington feared could threaten the oil-rich Saudis. During the late 1980s, America sent the Iraqis nearly $1 billion in agricultural, economic, and technical aid. These aid packages included high-tech equipment, such as computers and lasers, that could be used to create weapons of mass destruction.[841]

Saddam Hussein, empowered with American military equipment and technology, subsequently invaded

---

[841] George Donelson Moss, Moving On: The American People Since 1945, pp. 350, 351, 381. George Bush Senior also supported Saddam Hussein, using Skull &Bones connections to arrange loans to Saddam Hussein in 1990 "in the national interest." Bush Sr. favored helping Saddam build a pipeline to Jordan in order to circumvent Iran's Persian Gulf ports. *See* Alexandra Robbins, Secrets of the Tomb: Skull and Bones, the Ivy League and the Hidden Paths of Power, p.174.

the small country of Kuwait. The United States did not believe that Saddam Hussein would attack Kuwait, and so on the eve of the invasion, "[U.S. Ambassador] April Gilespie…told Saddam Hussein that the United States would not become involved in regional disputes."[842] Saddam took this as tacit American acquiescence in his ambitions to expand his influence in the region, but in fact both sides had miscalculated: after Saddam took Kuwait, it "appeared to threaten Saudi Arabia, long an American ally and possessor of more than a fifth of the world's proven oil reserves."[843] The United States descended on the Gulf to expel Saddam from Kuwait, stationing large numbers of troops in Saudi Arabia and thereby horrifying the Arab world–the infidels had now established a strong military presence in the holy Muslim land.[844] Americans rejoiced that the United States "had

---

[842] George Donelson Moss, Moving On: The American People Since 1945, p. 381.

[843] Ibid., p. 382. This was the true motive for the swift American response in the 1991 Gulf War, not the feigned empathy for the Kuwaitis. America would be in wars weekly if it responded globally to every comparable injustice.

[844] "Saudi Arabia is the cradle of the Islamic religion….As possessors of two of the three holy sites of Islam, Mecca and Medina, the Saudis see themselves as having a certain birthright as defenders of the faith. Therefore, if other Moslems are pious, the Saudis must be even more pious. If other Moslems are faithful to the teachings of the Prophet, the Saudis must be even more faithful….Coupled with their assumed birthright as the elect among Moslems, the Saudis are the Puritans of the Moslem world. They are followers of Wahhabism, a sect that is among the most fundamental, rigid, and intolerant in Islam….For centuries, Saudi Arabia's barren deserts protected its purity from invasion by outside sin. But with the oil boom, the country was suddenly being flooded with thousands of heretics from the Christian West who brought the sins of their decadence with them." Sandra Mackey, The Saudis: Inside the Desert Kingdom, p. 13. Imagine how Saudi Arabians and the Muslim world viewed the stationing of hundreds of thousands of U.S. troops in Saudi Arabia….

asserted its leadership of the world community....They echoed President Bush's talk of forging a "new world order" under American stewardship."[845]

But what was the Christian truth of America's involvement in this engagement? First, our government armed Saddam, including the provision of technology that could be used to produce WMD, at a time when it was known that Saddam was in fact building such weapons. Second, the United States flubbed diplomatically, failing to alert its puppet that he couldn't have Kuwait. Third, whatever Americans thought of the success of this venture, the Arab world was outraged—and since they hold the oil on which all American wallets depend, their hearts and minds do matter. In this sense Saddam won the first Gulf War, and his stature in the Arab world grew exponentially because he had survived a challenge to the U.S. And for the United States of America to have invaded that nation then would have been as unjustified and disastrous as when W. Junior did it in 2003.

America charged into the Gulf, the white knight rescuing the underdog. But the white knight had armed the bully, and in repelling him from Saudi Arabia, only (praise God!) 137 American troops were killed, versus "[a]n estimated 100,000 Iraqi soldiers and civilians."[846] Further, the "underdog" was hardly a democratic nation:

---

[845] George Donelson Moss, <u>Moving On: The American People Since 1945</u>, p. 384. What if the rest of the world abstains from that development? What if other peoples choose to live in societal forms or by cultural values that differ from America's?

[846] Ibid., p. 383.

ABU GHRAIB, THE MODERN SYMBOL OF AMERICA 441

liberating Kuwait also entailed the restoration of a feudal sheikdom to power that exhibited little concern about the welfare of ordinary Kuwaiti citizens and did not appear anxious to extend democratic freedoms to its people. Larger American strategic goals included keeping the vast Middle Eastern oil reserves in friendly hands....[847]

---

[847] Ibid., p. 385. Texe Marrs words it a little more strongly:

....We were told that America fought in the Gulf to bring freedom to Kuwait, but the totally decadent reign of Kuwait's despotic Emir, al Sabah, allows no freedoms. He's the Christian-murdering tyrant whom President Bush reinstated on the throne after some of America's finest young men and women shed their blood in the victorious Persian Gulf battle. It was disgraceful that this indecent Arab Sheik, his tyrannical family bullies, and their Arab cronies were allowed once again to seize power. Predictably, pro-democracy elements inside Kuwait were very quickly cruelly suppressed as the Emir's more hardened loyalist soldiers rounded-up dissenters, raped women and children, and callously carried out assassinations. Worse, with the BCCI bank failure comes the disclosure that all along it has been Kuwait's Emir who has been bankrolling Abu Nidal, the most notorious Arab terrorist in the world. According to the bank fraud investigators, in 1987 alone Kuwait's government deposited $60 million in Abu Nidal's secret BCCI account. Then, in 1989 some $500 million was put into Abu Nidal's account by the Kuwaiti and other Arab sources. Incredibly, *our own CIA knew of these transactions.* Thus, even as President Bush cried crocodile tears over Saddam Hussein's overthrow of Kuwait's Emir and even as he welcomed the Emir back on the throne, *President Bush was keenly aware that this wicked Arab potentate was greatly responsible for such terrorist atrocities as the high-jacking of airliners and ships, and for terrorist bomb attacks around the world.*

Texe Marrs, Dark Majesty: The Secret Brotherhood and the Magic of a Thousand Points of Light, pp. 58-59. [italics in original]

Because of the overwhelming military power brought to bear by the United States in the first Gulf War, the Iraqis were simply obliterated. And contrary to popular American belief, 90% of the bombs employed were in fact conventional ordinance, not the "smart bombs" tightly scripted military films and reports suggested.[848] Not wishing to risk international or domestic censure,

> the U.S. military tightly controlled television reportage, and American TV viewers were allowed to watch only a heavily censored version of the war.... Television journalists, with few exceptions, willingly allowed themselves to be manipulated by the military in exchange for access to war stories.[849]

Of course, America has turned its embarrassments into assets before: witness the public vilification of Manuel Noriega, long-time U.S. ally. But in the case of Iraq, Saddam's defeat had a number of lasting adverse consequences for the United States' all-important "vital" interests. The Arab world was emboldened, and Islamic extremism thrived in the bitter resentment that simmered in the Arab deserts while Americans clapped themselves on the back for their heroic thrust for freedom and human rights. Also: "Ironically, both Syria and Iran, two sponsors of international terrorism, emerged as the dominant powers in the Persian Gulf region in the aftermath of Iraq's shattering defeat."[850]

---

[848] George Donelson Moss, <u>Moving On: The American People Since 1945</u>, p. 384.
[849] Ibid., p. 384.
[850] Ibid., p. 385.

When the current Bush took office, he was already intent to invade Iraq–the U.S. henchman named Saddam could no longer be manipulated as puppet (worse, like Noriega and Osama bin Laden, Saddam had had the gall to turn on his American masters) and became useful instead as scapegoat. The invasion of Iraq by the United States served to 1) permit revenge on Saddam/ complete the first Gulf war; 2) stimulate the United States economy with war spending by feeding the military-industrial-government bureaucracy; 3) secure the "national security interests" of the United States in the Middle East, protecting Saudi Arabia's oil and perhaps gaining access to Iraq's. Because of the known, predominantly Saudi Arabian identities of the hijackers, the September 11 attacks could have been used to justify an invasion of Saudi Arabia with immensely more logic than Iraq, but were used instead to further an existing agenda. And Americans were lied to. Christian words, unchristian actions....

Why al Qaeda and Islamic Extremists Hate America

America's government has been less than forthcoming in accepting responsibility for its past nation-building failures. Often the truth of such matters is not revealed until years after their occurrence. Thus many Americans are not aware of the degree of resentment against their country in many parts of the world, particularly in the Middle East, and when confronted with it, they do not comprehend its source. For individual Americans hold good will toward other peoples, and perceive such hatred against the United States to be quite obviously ill-founded, irrational, even insane.

But the slum-rage of foreign desert cities can easily choke the oil supply that fuels the American way of life,[851] whatever the justifications for American ignorance and lack of compassion. Arab opinions–even ignorant, tribal, Muslim, superstitious, ugly opinions–matter. And the truth is that these opinions, though extreme, have welled up as a direct consequence of "the inadequate, unbalanced nature of United States policy in the entire region of the Middle East...."[852] In 2001 and thereafter, George W. Bush (history major) has proclaimed to Americans that al Qaeda attacks their country over and over again because it hates freedom and because Americans are free. Although Islamic extremists had attacked before, including against the Twin Towers, President Bush told Americans that the 9/11 attacks were unexpected and had no rational motivation. Americans "all of a sudden found ourselves attacked–because we love freedom, because we respect religion, because we honor discourse."[853]

---

[851] Recently, America is re-learning the lessons of the 1970s, "...becoming aware of its growing dependence on the Middle East, and in particular on the countries of the Persian Gulf for its supply of oil, [with]...talk in the United States of "brownouts" and of gasoline rationing." Dana Adams Schmidt, <u>Armageddon in the Middle East</u>, p. 244.

[852] Ibid., p. 241. George W. has also acknowledged "decades of failed policy in the Middle East....No longer should we think tyranny is benign because it is temporarily convenient." Thomas M. Freiling, <u>George W. Bush on God & Country</u>, pp. 228, 229.

[853] Thomas M. Freiling, <u>George W. Bush on God & Country</u>, p. 164. Do we really respect other religions and honor discourse? And was it really "sudden," or does that just support the administration's lie that they could not have anticipated the 9/11 attacks?

But these attacks were not at all unforeseen, nor were their motivations at all in doubt. The problem has been with us for many decades now:

> Eventually–no one can possibly know when–the inexorable march of economic and demographic growth and technological development will have given the Arabs massive material and numerical superiority. And Israel, no matter how great her qualitative superiority, would, in a final test of strength, be submerged unless the United States came to her rescue. This could be Armageddon for the Arabs and the Israelis....
>
> Unless we can reconcile the contradiction between our sentimental interest in the Israelis and our economic interest in Arab lands, we will be inexorably drawn into the successive rounds of the Arab-Israeli struggle....it is a conflict in which neither side can finally prevail. This is a tragedy, on the classic scale, a family struggle between the sons of Isaac and the sons of Ishmael. Israelis and Arabs and their Great Power sponsors are locked in a struggle which will lead to mutual doom."[854]

The United States, supposedly a Christian nation, has had the opportunity to be arbiter in this dispute. The use of Christian morality to address foreign policy in the Middle East for the last 60 years would not have required abandonment of Israel, only warmth, compassion and justice for the Palestinians and for other Arab peoples, as Jesus surely would have demonstrated.

---

[854] Dana Adams Schmidt, <u>Armageddon in the Middle East</u>, pp. 256, 257, copyright 1974.

George W. Bush has said that his foray into the Middle East will not be politics as usual, that his administration is breaking with America's past support of dictators and will press for reform and not just for the maximization of corporate profits:

> Now we're pursuing a different course, a forward strategy in the Middle East. We will consistently challenge the enemies of reform and confront the allies of terror. We will expect a higher standard from our friends in the region....The forward strategy of freedom must also apply to the Arab-Israeli conflict....[By resolving the Arab-Israeli conflict] we will also remove an occasion and excuse for hatred and violence in the broader Middle East.[855]

But there are several problems revealed by Mr. Bush's high-sounding words. First, these words have not been backed up with meaningful action–the Middle East desperately needs a dramatic Camp David-style intercession to save the world, and it hasn't even made it to Camp Crawford. Second, even if well-intentioned, Mr. Bush's plans fail if the Muslim world does not trust and believe him, and the United States' record is abysmal–U.S. Presidents have often expounded their grand plans for liberation, opportunity and freedom as justifications for their imperialist involvement in nations such as Nicaragua, Haiti, Venezuela, or Iraq, but most always those words have been followed by no action in furtherance of those freedoms. And this administration

---

[855] Thomas M. Freiling, <u>George W. Bush an God & Country</u>, pp. 229, 230, 231.

has Abu Ghraib to its credit. Third, Mr. Bush's words sound conciliatory, but in fact to Arab ears they are offensive and immediately reveal this U.S. president's anti-Arab, pro-Israel prejudice–Mr. Bush denigrates and dismisses the Palestinian people and their supporters when he dismisses the Arab-Israeli conflict as "an occasion and excuse for hatred and violence." Is Jewish remembrance of the holocaust an "excuse for hatred and violence"? The Palestinians have legitimate grievances, not just "excuses," and the Arab and Muslim worlds are sympathetic to those grievances. Heavily arming Israel and then dismissing the Arab-Israel conflict as an "excuse" for Arab violence is precisely the type of biased, unchristian foreign policy that has created such intense anti-American sentiment.

Why did the Iraqi people not rise up in the streets with joy at America's arrival in the Iraq War? Why did President Bush and his Cabinet (with the exception of Colin Powell, who served in Vietnam) expect that they would? America has not lent an ear to the voices of the people whose hearts and minds it wishes and needs to win, has not given democratic privilege to those it seeks to "liberate" through democracy. How surprising then to so many Americans who believe the United States is a vehicle for freedom and not imperialist oppression, when the Iraqis (like the Iranians, and the Nicaraguans) and other Arab peoples use their voice of freedom to criticize America and reject its culture:

> ...while the U.S. has contributed to the shift in climate in the Middle East, a real democratic opening, in the short term at least, may not serve

U.S. interests. Most in the region appear angry at America's close relationship with Israel and its invasion of Iraq, and say that statements prodding allies to reform haven't overcome decades of support for Arab dictators.[856]

But this anti-American sentiment is comprehended by everyone except Americans, or else America would invest the minimal energy required to restore its once deserved reputation. But that reputation was built on deeds, not words, and modern America has been grossly lacking in deeds of good will sufficient to overcome decades of false promises coupled with jerky, unbalanced policy. And why don't Americans have more awareness? Perhaps a culture of consumption and recreation has diminished their knowledge level.... Perhaps longer workweeks and increasing individualism are increasing America's isolationist tendencies.... Perhaps politicians don't readily admit their failures, and voters don't really wish to hear them.... Perhaps the American media feed the public the sensationalist news they buy, which rewards coverage of non-fatal accidents or "special-interest" stories at the expense of even basic coverage of world affairs or international disasters....Perhaps the American media similarly provide rationalizations for global anti-American opinion that avoid introspection, for themselves and their complicity in its propagation, as well as for their audiences....Perhaps as long as there is no national accountability and clear moral discourse concerning America's failed foreign policy, America will

---

[856] Dan Murphy, "New Arab rallying cry: 'Enough'," *The Christian Science Monitor*, March 31, 2005, pp. 1, 4.

become even more reviled, lose ever more allies, and elicit less and less sympathy for its decline, like the Roman Empire it ever more closely resembles.

And this self-destructive self-delusion is not confined to one political party–most Americans have been duly indoctrinated into the America-can-do-no-wrong mythology, and to suggest that our "sacred" nation with its "sacred" flag and "sacred" currency acts in error is to be branded unpatriotic. Especially since the Iraq War, there has been pro-American whitewash propaganda throughout the country's news media and across party lines. Consider Mortimer Zuckerman, Editor-in-Chief of *U.S. News & World Report*, in a description of Islamic extremism and radicals who wish "to kill us all–any American, men, women, and children." Mr. Zuckerman, having grabbed the reader's attention with his accustomed fear-mongering, explains that

> [t]he reason this is so difficult for us to understand is that this culture of death is the polar opposite of our culture of life. And it was not created by intervention in Iraq.[857] Iraq may[858] have sharpened the resentments of some radical Islamists and given

---

[857] Obviously not, since al Qaeda attacked America before the Iraq War. Borrowing from his idol, President Bush, Mr. Zuckerman sets up what Ann Coulter aptly describes as a "straw-man" argument. (*See* "Does This Law Degree Make My Resume Look Fat?" Ann Coulter, *The Caledonian-Record*, October 17, 2005, p. A4.) Although it is clear the invasion of Iraq has greatly increased global anti-U.S. feelings, no one has argued that al Qaeda was "created by intervention in Iraq." The only rational reason for Mr. Zuckerman to say this is to create an illusory defense of the Bush administration's invasion of Iraq. But that "intervention" (which has killed tens of thousands of civilians), which no one claims "created" Islamic extremism, *most definitely* exacerbated that extremism exponentially.

[858] What understatement. There is absolutely no "may" about it–of course it did.

them a new excuse,[859] but there was no Iraq war[860] in 1993,[861] when they first tried to blow up the World Trade Center, nor before 9/11, when they did blow it up. The attack on the U.S. Cole took place after U.S. forces contributed to the NATO-led operation in Kosovo that saved the lives of many, many Muslims.[862]

---

[859] As opposed to the "old" excuses of the Arab-Israeli conflict, the one dismissed by President Bush and the West. Again, the comparison to the American Indians is accurate–Americans pushed into their lands in pursuit of resources, corrupted and disrupted their culture and values, and when they fought back (as Americans themselves would, under such circumstances, and probably sooner) to preserve their waning culture, America used that violence as proof that they were savages to be killed, as grounds for the further destruction of their culture and of the sanctity of their native lands. Those Indians were always looking for weak and unfounded "excuses" to rape, pillage and plunder, and the American media was all too willing to feed into fears back east, and to feed the myth. But scalping was a practice initiated by Whites....

[860] How many U.S. soldiers have to perish before this "war" is capitalized? If the body bag count included innocent Iraqi civilians, or if Jesus were consulted, then this is already the Iraq War.

[861] Again wasting space stating the obvious–there was no George W. leading the nation into economic and military disaster in 1993, either, Mort. Now the deeper yet not so adroitly avoided question–what then does Mr. Zuckerman assert is the true motive for Islamic hatred of America? No explanation is given. Those Islamic crazies don't love their kids, they just love death and seek un-named "excuses" to kill innocent white people on the other side of the globe. Just like those vile American Indians....

[862] This information regarding American goodwill in Kosovo is relevant only for propaganda value, making America look like the do-gooder victim and the attackers look particularly heinous (which they are). But it is not at all relevant to the issue Mr. Zuckerman pretends to be discussing–the motivations for these attacks. The American record relating to Serbian Muslims is of little impact to the Arab world's perceptions of how they've been treated. Be cautious, Christians, of writers who spread fear and hate without the benefit of logic.

....The exploding torrent of Muslim energy,[863] something not seen in 500 years, is being fueled by billions of petrodollars coming out of Saudi Arabia in support of an aggressive antiwestern religious teaching called Wahhabism.[864] And it's spreading not just to other Muslim countries but also to the disaffected among the Muslim communities in Europe who can be trained on the Internet in almost every aspect of terrorism.[865]

(There's that fear factor again...) But, one more time: *why* are Wahhabism and other extremist Islamic views spreading so fiercely if America is so spotless? And why is America, first and foremost, the focus of anti-western acrimony? The failure of Americans to answer these questions (and with misleading "help" like

---

[863] That's it, it was an earthquake of Muslim lava-hatred, like a periodic Ice Age that just seeks an "excuse" to pop out of the ground and destroy all civilization. They are all just evil. But Jesus teaches that there are no such things as evil people, just good people who are misled. American business and media interests have misled us all, Muslim, Jew and Christian alike, in the worldly, short-term pursuit of pecuniary gain, masked with an illusory and unchristian ideology.

[864] This is very true, and it rightly should concern Americans that their expenditures for oil will in future directly finance our Muslim enemies–our war machine has been turned inside out, for if we wage war, an incredibly energy-intensive undertaking, we feed our enemy's economy instead of our own, like a Chinese finger trap. But this financing arrangement has been in place since the Gulf War, when America's presence in Saudi Arabia enraged Osama & Co. The Saudi royals have funneled funds to al Qaeda ever since, in return for which al Qaeda has abstained from attacking Saudi Arabia or its oilfields. *See* Gerald Posner, Why America Slept: the Failure to Prevent 9/11, p. 28: "As far as the Saudis were concerned, it was better to encourage young, radical Muslims to fight abroad than to direct their activism toward the Kingdom."

[865] Mortimer Zuckerman, "A Hang-Tough Nation," *U.S. News & World Report*, October 24, 2005.

Mortimer's, their continued failure is likely) will spell their doom, because Arabs don't need oil—no one needs oil—as the Americans do. And propaganda and myth creation don't produce oil, no matter how strident and earnest. Clearly Mr. Zuckerman is much more concerned with the welfare of Israel than that of America.

But Mr. Zuckerman's refusal to answer his own question (which would necessitate criticism of decades of American bias in favor of Israel) is less blatant an effort at deception than the Bush administration's machinations. Paul Kengor writes that "ours is a war against individuals who absolutely hate what America stands for."[866] This is correct but unhelpful, since America "stands for" one thing to Americans, and quite another to many others in the world; a consequence of unchristian U.S. foreign policy. The entire world has been thoroughly exposed to what America thinks of itself, and Americans are surely familiar with the praises of the red, white, and blue. But what has America come to "stand for" to other nations in recent years?

The whole world hears President Bush's periodic proclamations on terrorism and the War in Iraq, and he and America have come to "stand for" hubris, lack of accountability, hypocrisy, dishonesty, extremism, self-interest, excess, and now torture. Mr. Bush has said, "The terrorists are defined by their hatreds: they hate democracy and tolerance and free expression and women and Jews and Christians and all Muslims who disagree with them."[867] This is itself a negative, fearful,

---

[866] Paul Kengor, God and George W. Bush: a spiritual life, p. 140.
[867] Thomas M. Freiling, George W. Bush on God & Country, pp. 242-243.

and hateful construct (like "the Great Satan"), but can be translated to the Muslim perspective by assessing those human beings by their positive rather than negative traits. This translation might read, "The terrorists love their children and mothers, and the agony of watching their Muslim brothers treated miserably by corrupt foreigners led them to passionately devote themselves to Allah, to readily surrender their earthly bodies in the fight against evil, against those who would invade Muslim culture and Muslim lands with an immoral, dominating, godless culture." How do those Arab minds America is supposedly attempting to persuade perceive Mr. Bush's description of their brothers as merely evil hate mongers? Mr. Bush is so busy trying to win over the hearts and minds of Americans that he and his cutesy speechwriters rarely consider the effects of their words on their global audience. Americans have been deceived by his Christian-sounding words, while many in the world have been briskly animated against America and Christianity by both his words and his actions.

George W. Bush has written that "America's foreign policy should respect and nurture our traditional alliances throughout the world and strengthen relations with countries in our own neighborhood."[868] These are sweet-sounding words that don't say much, for presumably this would always be American policy. What is truly telling is how little Mr. Bush's actions in office reflect this statement–his administration has insulted the United Nations, calling it "irrelevant" if it didn't rubber-stamp U.S. war plans in Iraq; offended the world by backing

---
[868] George W. Bush, <u>A Charge to Keep</u>, p. 240.

out of the Kyoto accords, promising a never-materialized and less effective alternative; refused jurisdiction over America for international review of war crimes; renewed the proliferation of nuclear and bioterror weapons; invaded two countries and attempted a coup in Latin America; called several nations "evil," with no apparent goal other than to frighten and stir support amongst Americans; and worst of all, tortured prisoners denied the protection of international or any other human or godly law, and then covered it up with a few scapegrunts. Smooth words, unchristian actions....

Bush has similarly called the terrorists "...enemies of human freedom. They have attacked America, because we are freedom's home and defender. And the commitment of our fathers is now the calling of our time."[869] The commitment of our fathers was to Jesus Christ and our Christian God, and this should always be our calling as Christians. And is this why America was attacked, because it is "freedom's home and defender," (a laughably absurd statement, though quite nationalistic) or was it because the non-American perspective is that America has been the greatest threat to Muslim freedom, imposing its will like a bully, strong-arming underdogs, bolstering tyrants, backing Israel unequivocally, corrupting Muslim faith and Muslim cultures with pornography and materialism? ("As we export American goods and services, we also export American values."[870]) America's Muslim attackers simply did not sit down

---

[869] Thomas M. Freiling, <u>George W. Bush on God & Country</u>, p. 114. (September 14, 2001.)
[870] George W. Bush, <u>A Charge To Keep</u>, p. 237.

one day and determine "let's get America because it's so darned free and our religion commands that we go blow up free people." Again, this was an absurd statement for President Bush to make in the immediate aftermath of 9/11–prideful for Americans, contributive to the American myth–but absurd…and dishonest. And hardly helpful for America's reputation abroad, for resolving the true conflict that led to the attacks, or for the world's view of how Christians behave.

President Bush W. has said, "In our war on terror, we are showing the world the strength of our country…"[871] Or are we proudly showing off our strength? Is this supposed to make Americans feel good, or safer, like after the invasion of Panama or when America ejected Saddam from Kuwait in the Gulf War (only to exponentially compound anti-American bitterness, and mobilize and create support for Osama bin Laden and al Qaeda)? But who in the world doubted America's power?[872] The terrorists employ their means precisely because they and the nations who fund them cannot possibly fight a conventional war against America. It is indeed "our war"–we started it, we decide who is a target in it, and we own it. And by "showing the world the strength of our country," aren't we really playing into the terrorists' plans by expending all our resources in financially-leveraged military over-extension, like the Romans in their final epoch, and like we boast we did to the Soviet Union in our protracted Cold War arms race?

---

[871] Thomas M. Freiling, <u>George W. Bush on God & Country</u>, p. 127.
[872] "Who is like unto the beast? who is able to make war with him?" Revelation 13:4, KJV.

However, not even the United States President can perpetuate America's imperialistic dominance past its current strained breaking point. It is reckoning time for all Americans, long overdue:

> Those of us living in wealthy countries, however, can no longer avoid criticism of the last fifty years of foreign policy, especially oil policy. Our economic development has depended on alliances with oil dictators and has encouraged them in their promotion of the most reactionary beliefs.[873]

It is shocking that it required the September 11 attacks for Americans to perceive the intensity of Arab resentment. (Which was the goal of the terrorists–to draw the attention of the American people to the consequences of their government's actions, of which they are unaware because they are habitually lied to and only care about their own economy.) Islamic anti-American sentiment has been as longstanding as Americans' oblivion to it: "[In the 1980s,] Arab terrorist organizations, dedicated to the destruction of Israel and to attacking its Western supporters, frequently targeted Americans"[874]; "previous [U.S.] administrations believed that authoritarian stability best served the constellation of American interests in the...[Middle East]. In reality, Washington's close connection with Middle Eastern strongmen helped stoke anti-Americanism and contributed to an environment

---

[873] Jean-Charles Brisard and Guillaume Dasquie, <u>Forbidden Truth: U.S.-Taliban Secret Oil Diplomacy and the Failed Hunt for Bin Laden</u>, p. 145.

[874] George Donelson Moss, <u>Moving On: The American People Since 1945</u>, p. 348.

where terrorist organizations can thrive."[875] U.S. efforts to control the Gulf region to protect U.S. interests began, according to one commentator, in 1980 with Jimmy Carter, "…and each successive president would ratchet up military operations in the region (sometimes simply by aiding and abetting dictators like Saddam Hussein), aggravating resentments and tensions as they did."[876]

Alvin Toffler observed in 1990 that

> [d]uring the Cold War, the intelligence agencies of various industrial powers, capitalist and communist alike, sometimes found it in their interest to subsidize Middle Eastern religious extremists.
>
> All these factors kept relighting the fires of religious fundamentalism, ultimately symbolized by the holy frenzy of Khomeiniism, with its all-out attack on the modern world and the secularism it flaunted.
>
> This fanatic attack might have carried less punch if industrial civilization, the home of secularism, were not itself in moral and social crisis, no longer offering a very attractive model for emulation by the rest of the world. Indeed, the industrial states, now torn apart internally, no longer seemed as invincible as they once had. Now hostage-takers, terrorists, and petroleum sheiks were able to jerk them around, seemingly at will.

---

[875] Steven A. Cook, Next Generation Fellow at the Council on Foreign Relations, "To reform broader Middle East, get leaders to trade in epaulets," *The Christian Science Monitor*, January 20, 2005, p. 9.

[876] "The Coming Storms," *U.S. News & World Report*, March 14, 2005, p. 29. (Though such efforts really began in 1953 with the installation of the Shah of Iran, and even earlier via the powerful cultural and economic influence of huge American oil corporations.)

> As the smokestack era ended, therefore, its reigning secular philosophy was attacked from within and from without, from many sides at once, and fundamentalism and religion in general took wing....
>
> What is happening is a sky-darkening attack on the ideas of the Enlightenment which helped usher in the industrial age.
>
> While all these religious movements are...different,...all of them–Christian or New Age, Judaic or Islamic–are united in one thing–their hostility to secularism, the philosophical base of mass democracy.
>
> Today, therefore, in country after country, secularism is in retreat. What do advocates of democracy have to put in its place? So far the new, high-tech democracies have renovated neither their outdated mass democratic political structures nor the philosophical assumptions that underlie them.[877]

Religious extremism in the Middle East narrowed its sights fully onto America, fueled by a perfect storm of poverty (which America created or ignored in many, many cases, securing only its own short-term needs), a strong U.S.-Israel alliance (which focused resentments at the plight and suffering of the Palestinians against America for decades), and a perception that America was

---

[877] Alvin Toffler, <u>Powershift: Knowledge, Wealth and Violence at the Edge of the Twenty-First Century</u>, pp. 366-367, 368. This is because secular, democratic governance holds no moral compass–the inevitable consequence of moral relativism and liberal decay is social breakdown and anarchy, as witnessed by the fall of the Roman Empire before the collapse of the American one. Toffler may not prefer Christianity as the answer to Western amorality, but it's the only sane game in town.

invading the Persian Gulf: physically and militarily, but also culturally and spiritually: "originally welcomed as liberators, the Westerners in time came to be regarded as an army of occupation bent on destroying the Saudis' traditional values."[878]

The U.S. presence in Saudi Arabia in the Gulf War was considered by the Muslim world to be an invasion of the Middle East by American infidels. Most Arabs, already suspicious of U.S. motives, were much more alarmed by such large numbers of Western troops in holy lands than they were by Saddam's behavior. (The intensity of this sentiment contributed to the first George Bush's decision not to pursue Saddam Hussein in that conflict.) Osama bin Laden and al Qaeda, along with other extremist Islamic groups, were greatly strengthened, in personnel and in finances, by this wave of alarm. According to an August 14, 1996 State Department Factsheet on Bin Laden, in August, 1995,

> Osama bin Laden call[ed] for a guerilla campaign targeting American forces stationed in Saudi Arabia in an open letter to King Fahd….[On August 23, 1996,] Osama bin Laden launche[d] a declaration of war against the United States, demanding that American troops leave the Arabian peninsula, that the holy sites be liberated, and that the Saudi regime be overthrown, and call[ed] on fundamentalist groups to join his battle.[879]

---

[878] Sandra Mackey, The Saudis: Inside the Desert Kingdom, p. 24.
[879] Jean-Charles Brisard & Guillaume Dasquie, Forbidden Truth: U.S.-Taliban Secret Oil Diplomacy and the Failed Hunt for Bin Laden, pp. 151-152.

And so U.S. foreign policy "exploited and created an extremist Islamic mercenary army that eventually turned on its creators. [After 9/11, p]eople will no longer joke about the power struggles and petty rivalries that plague our planet. Everyone must be mindful of the consequences of a hatred left to rot on the other side of the world...."[880] But Americans, and their government, can hardly "be mindful" or institute corrective action when the only explanations given for this seething resentment is that the terrorists "hate us because we're free," "because we are freedom's home and defender," or "because we love freedom, because we respect religion, because we honor discourse," all phrases employed by President Bush in a patent and deliberate deception of the American people. Should supporters of this lying President maintain their willful ignorance of this reality, there is a whole world of human beings who have not been deceived by a lifetime of bias and insularity from recognizing both the roots of terrorism in America's past foreign policy and the blatant dishonesty of the current administration. Moreover, America (i.e. President Bush) persisting in denial about its conduct particularly galls the very Middle Eastern peoples whom America has long-wronged, without repentance even now. A recent poll revealed

> that 18 of 21 countries surveyed considered the world to be less secure because of Mr. Bush's reelection....the global distrust-America trend...largely resulted from America's 2003 decision to launch a preemptive war in Iraq without UN approval....

---

[880] Ibid., pp. x, xxiii-xxiv.

Among those nations with the most negative views were some of America's closest allies....Just under half of all respondents (47 percent) said they now view U.S. influence in the world as mostly negative, while an average 42 percent said that Bush's reelection had made them feel worse toward the American people.[881]

Americans' utter ignorance of their government's complicity in creating the terrorist furies that now threaten the entire world will continue to seed more and more violence until the camel's back is crushed and the entire (one-billion-plus) Muslim world rises up to smite America, just as wealthy Americans' greedy accumulation of wealth will continue until the United States collapses under the strain of class strife—it is Americans' conviction that their country is invincible and beyond reproach that blinds them to the disaster stirring under its foundations. While the United States deludes itself that it is furthering "freedom's march" throughout the world, others may decline that brand of freedom, have been alienated against America and her capitalistic values for decades, and will likely use those very freedoms to revolt against American hegemony:

---

[881] Scott Baldauf, "Most Indians say 'thumbs up' to second Bush term," *The Christian Science Monitor*, January 21, 2005, p. 7. In Mexico, Mr. Bush gained a favorable rating from only 4 % of respondents; in Turkey, 6 % of opinions were positive, versus an 82% negative rating. India responded positively, according to a reported source, because "George Bush has done a lot to rehabilitate the language of pure national self-interest [here]...." Is this a Christian message to the world? Note also how the title of this article puts a positive gloss on a negative picture–almost all nations surveyed said "thumbs down" to Bush's reelection, but India made the headline.

"America's conviction that its rhetoric will help secure its interests in the region often clash [sic] with the anti-US leanings of many of the Arab world's democracy activists, who generally belong either to Islamist parties or to the left-leaning, anti-US groups."[882]

America ignores this reality, like the realities of global warming, unsupportable debt, wealth disparity and economic decline, at its peril. Frankly, it's simply too late to overcome these liabilities now that George W. has made the nation's course one of no return–America is in irreversible, secular, worldly decline, and the world has no new secular model of government to take its human, worldly, "evolution" further. Only the coming "government" of Jesus Christ, with integrity, love, and perfection, will release the world from its failures and save the good from the evil consuming the planet. America is just a nation–one that has squandered its numerous opportunities at that–and Jesus Christ has absolutely zero loyalty to soul-less nations: Christians who do not readily perceive this must review their Scripture, then repent of false idol worship (and throw in the American flag, the U.S. constitution, the American dollar and modern technology while they're at it).

ABU GHRAIB

If America's credibility and international (and self-) image had not been sufficiently tarnished by the Kyoto withdrawal or the Iraq War (and the missing WMD fiasco surrounding it), this President led the country to its

---

[882] Dan Murphy, "New Arab rallying cry: 'Enough'," *The Christian Science Monitor*, March 31, 2005, pp. 1, 4.

most heinous immoral conduct in modern history–the deliberate, premeditated, and unchristian torture of so-called "enemy combatants." One history text has noted: "The most important potential impact of terror is that liberal democratic governments will descend to the level of terrorists, impose draconian laws and restrict civil liberties. So far…there is little evidence that the terrorists have achieved this much."[883] Or as Gregory Peck's character, Captain Millory, explains to Major Franklin (played by Anthony Quinn) in *The Guns of Navarone*:

Captain Millory:

"The only way to win a war is to be just as nasty as the enemy. The one thing that worries me is that we're liable to wake up one morning and find out we're even nastier than they are."

Major Franklin:

"Can't say that worries me."

Captain Millory:

"Well, you're lucky."[884]

George W. Bush cannot be a Major Franklin, and also remain true to Christ. The entire concept of morality, of a moral code, is premised on boundaries of conduct. Christianity regards the practice of torture to be intolerable without exception–there is no "just torture" doctrine in Christianity. There is no question that the United States government has detained non-American human beings as prisoners, and that they have in very large numbers been denied the protections of the

---

[883] Gerald Segal, The World Affairs Companion: The Essential One-Volume Guide to Global Issues, p.122.
[884] *The Guns of Navarone*, Columbia Pictures Corp., 1961.

Geneva Convention or any other international standard, denied the right to trial, and denied the rights of the U.S. constitution, indefinitely. There is also no question that they have been denied the standards of Christ. There is no question whatsoever that Alberto Gonzales, close and longtime Bush W. associate, drafted, or caused to be drafted, documents as White House counsel, at White House request, the sole purpose of which was to justify detention and interrogation techniques not sanctioned by international or domestic law. There is no question that the cases of abuse of U.S.-held prisoners numbered many hundreds, extended simultaneously to numerous facilities on different continents, and utilized many of the same barbaric techniques. When combined with America's history in the Persian Gulf and Bush's impetuous launch into Iraq, it is hardly surprising that the Arab Muslim peoples of the world do not believe that America has entered their hemisphere with good intentions. (A substantial number of Americans don't either.) And George W. has managed to dismiss this horrible malfeasance to the American people as the acts of a few bad apples. But these bad apples were created by the legal recipe of the Gonzales memos, drafted and implemented at the direction of George W. Bush: hundreds of U.S. service people didn't suddenly and simultaneously create S & M warehouses around the world on their own initiative: "In these times of terror alerts and shadowy threats, let us be most vigilant about what might be lurking in the shadows within ourselves."[885]

---

[885] Reader's letter from *The Christian Science Monitor*, April 27, 2005, p. 8.

How does this American conduct, since President George W. Bush gained office on Jesus' platform, compare to the words of Paul?: "Do not let what you regard as good get a bad name....So then, we must always aim at those things that bring peace and that help strengthen one another."[886] When the President trumpeted to the world that "Either you are with us or you are with the terrorists"[887] (again concerning himself with domestic approval ratings more than foreign perceptions), did he purposely intend to bastardize the words of Mark 9:40 that "Whoever is not against us is for us."?[888] This is the Bible being tampered with, this is the Word of God being mutated to fit the uses of the world–for the two statements have very different meanings, the one a war-like connotation, the other peaceable. Who speaks for God but His Word? Who dares? "We must always aim at those things that bring peace…"

America's image in the world was certainly in decline before George W. arrived on the scene. But Mr. Bush's

---

[886] Romans 14:16, 19, TEV. The King James Version cautions "Let not then your good be evil spoken of…," reminding Christians of the duty they carry with the honor of serving Jesus–if Christians act in ways which conflict with Christ's teachings, their hypocrisy discourages others from seeking Jesus. Christians fully understand that the Truth of Jesus should not be judged by the example of His sinning modern followers, but by the standard of Christ Himself. But Muslims today, and others, will be converted to the power of Christ only when His followers lead–where they demonstrate the intensity of their faith in the way they live their own lives, according to the clear precepts of Christian fellowship. Non-Christians judge Jesus by His followers, and a planet full of non-Christians are judging Jesus now, in these end times, in light of the actions of modern America and its current leader.

[887] Even the Nazis weren't this harsh, or Switzerland would have been destroyed by Hitler. And Spain was neutral in World War I.

[888] TEV.

466 Christian Words, Unchristian Actions

Christian promise is what rallied (barely) enough Americans, in hope, to position him to employ a moral code that would perhaps stem the nation's social decline. Most Americans still hold an image of their nation formed by the country's benevolence in World War II, and justly so, but times (and behaviors) have changed:

> In 1945 the power and prestige of the United States…were enormous. Forty or fifty years later that image has become weaker, if not altogether gone. On the lowest levels of popular "culture" America is still emulated, and will continue being so for a long time, but for reasons that have nothing to do with the virtues of American political traditions. On other, more important levels more and more people are uneasily aware of America's own troubles, inherent in institutions and practices that they no longer wish to emulate.[889]

Americans cannot rationally expect other nations to embrace their political system and values in the face of their own nation's obvious failures. George W. Bush could perhaps have resuscitated America's bygone moral reputation with an infusion into the United States Government of Christian piety, integrity, and acts of good will, especially in the wake of the 9/11 attacks when the world held great compassion for America.

Instead, the world was shown the so-called virtues of liberal democracy (with "Christian" leadership) by the example of Kyoto, exception from jurisdiction of

---

[889] John Lukacs, <u>The End of the twentieth Century and the End of the Modern Age</u>, p. 219.

international law over U.S. actions, the bullying of smaller nations, incessant criticism of the United Nations, protectionist trade practices, war-mongering and subsequent invasion of two other nations, and the detention, presumed guilt, imprisonment or torture of thousands of Arabs. Mr. Bush, though, has often been the sharp critic of others. He called Jacques Chirac a "bully," and "maintained [that] the French seemed so dogmatic."[890] Prior to the invasion of Iraq, Colin Powell and Richard Armitage were "attempting at every possible turn to soften the appearance–and reality–of unilateralism and arrogance in Bush administration foreign policy."[891] Bob Woodward relates that President Bush "…understood that his early actions on global climate change and national missile defense had rattled U.S. allies in Europe. America's friends feared the administration was infected with a new strain of unilateralism, a go-it-alone attitude, looking inward rather than engaging the world as the lone superpower might be expected to do."[892] The world view toward the Iraq War is that such unilateralism by America (and particularly by its hawkish President) was hasty and uninformed, if not outright hostile. President Bush was repeatedly and clearly warned by Colin Powell that this would be the case if there were no credible evidence linking Saddam Hussein to the 9/11 attacks. When Iraq was raised as a possible target immediately following the 9/11 attacks (how much evidence of Iraqi involvement did the administration have at this early

---

[890] Bob Woodward, <u>Plan of Attack</u>, p. 346.
[891] Ibid., p. 433.
[892] Bob Woodward, <u>Bush at War</u>, p. 44.

date, except none?): "Powell objected. You're going to hear from your coalition partners, he told the president. They're all with you, every one, but they will go away if you hit Iraq. If you get something pinning September 11 on Iraq, great...."[893] But George W. went to war despite this counsel, and world opinion turned sharply against America as a consequence.

It is not partisan politics but an honest recognition that America needs to improve its ethical stature in the world that leads many to speak out against this administration's Reagan-on-steroids unilateralism. This is not unpatriotic, but the opposite–failure to hold America's government accountable to standards of fair play and decency is a disservice to the nation's youth (as with the budget deficit and pollution) and military personnel: "Despite the noble efforts of our soldiers, sailors, and pilots, and a brightening outlook for democracy overseas, the way we have conducted ourselves has so offended others that America's reputation abroad has plummeted."[894]

An area of particular concern to the rest of the world is America's pursuit of nuclear weapons. America, having deployed nuclear weapons in Japan, assumes with smug arrogance that it could never be the vehicle for the world's doom, that the United States only ever acts to further the cause of goodness. But those ignorant foreigners, especially the Muslims, just don't seem to trust what is such a confident certainty to Americans. The war on terror has been presented by the Bush administration

---

[893] Ibid., p. 84.
[894] David Gergen, *U.S. News & World Report*, p. 60.

as the greatest threat in the history of the world. Is that threat greater than the threat posed by Japan in World War II, necessitating nuclear assault? America didn't torture the Japanese....

The Bush administration, whether through a desire to bolster businesses that manufacture weapons, or simply from an ignorance of the consequences of its actions, pushed to develop nuclear "bunker busters," despite potent international opposition. Any tactical military enhancement offered by these types of weapons is dwarfed by the costs in loss of American goodwill and the guarantee of a renewed global nuclear arms race if this course continues. In April, 2005, the Arms Control Association in Washington and the Carnegie Endowment for International Peace

> issued [a] statement, signed by prominent former officials and nuclear-weapons experts, warning that the world is on the "threshold" of a new round of proliferation that next month's NPT review must address....
>
> "One of the key issues of the conference will be how the nuclear states are doing at fulfilling their own nuclear disarmament commitments," says the Arms Control Association's Mr. Kimball.
>
> The administration wants to go ahead with feasibility studies that could result in a new generation of replacement warheads within a decade. But that runs contrary to disarmament commitments the US made at NPT reviews in 1995 and 2000, Kimball says. "For the U.S. to ask others to take on additional commitments while disregarding its own commitments to

the NPT is a recipe for division," he says. "You're basically assuring a lack of progress toward the very goals the U.S. says it supports."[895]

But President Bush's ideological intensity is not deterred by grassroots opposition, at home or abroad. If only the intensity with which he stirs up fear and war-passion were applied to the glory of Jesus Christ. George Orwell spoke directly to the problems of over-zealous ideologues in <u>1984</u>, and if one were not too quick to dismiss Orwell's book as science fiction hype, a warning about our present circumstances is loud and clear:

> It is precisely in the Inner Party that war hysteria and hatred of the enemy are strongest. In his capacity as an administrator, it is often necessary for a member of the Inner Party to know that this or that item of war news is untruthful, and he may often be aware that the entire war is spurious and is either not happening or is being waged for purposes quite other than the declared ones; but such knowledge is easily neutralized by the technique of doublethink. Meanwhile no Inner Party member wavers for an instant in his mystical belief that the war is real, and that it is bound to end victoriously, with Oceania the undisputed master of the entire world.
>
> All members of the Inner Party believe in this coming conquest as an article of faith. It is to be achieved either by gradually acquiring more and more territory and so building up an overwhelming

---

[895] Howard LaFranch, "New gaps in controlling the spread of nuclear arms," *The Christian Science Monitor*, April 27, 2005, pp. 1, 4.

preponderance of power, or by the discovery of some new and unanswerable weapon. The search for new weapons continues unceasingly….[896]

The Bush administration and its supporters believe "as an article of faith" that the Iraq War "is bound to end victoriously, with [the United States] the undisputed master of the entire world," achieved by the spread of democracy and continued U.S. economic hegemony, and hopefully aided "by the discovery of some new and unanswerable weapon" (like bunker busters). America's technological supremacy has been used tirelessly to develop new weapons since World War II, always in the name of "defense" but always ultimately commercializing new discoveries–new technologies are inevitably obtained by other world powers and then employed in new, ever-more-sinister ways in the name of their defense. Carpet bombs and landmines are sold by the United States worldwide in opposition to efforts at their abolition: these are hardly defensive in nature; hardly Christian for such a "Christian" nation.

What is America's Christian example to the world? Is America furthering the world toward an emulation of Jesus Christ and His Goodness? Allan Bloom wrote:

> This is the American moment in world history, the one for which we shall forever be judged…. [I]n politics the responsibility for the fate of freedom in the world has devolved upon our regime….The gravity

---

[896] George Orwell, 1984, p. 159.

of our given task is great, and it is very much in doubt how the future shall judge our stewardship.[897]

But of course "the future" is no one's judge. There either will or won't be a divine judgment, though, and Americans currently face a choice between the despair of there being no God (in which case America and its inhabitants will perish soul-less, and this book is without meaning), or the despair of there being one (in which case the over-indulgent, over-consumptive, overly selfish waste of American Christian opportunity will be judged by clearly enunciated standards, with eternal consequences). As Americans and their President thrust their chests out to the world, proclaiming how God-fearing, freedom-protecting, and "good" America is while alienating most of the world's inhabitants from both America and Christianity with weapons of mass destruction, war and threats of war, and widespread torture and imprisonment, the New Testament stands silently ignored: "…anyone who does not help me gather is really scattering."[898]

The United States would not consider itself to be on a "Crusade" in the Middle East, though the Muslims are

---

[897] Allan Bloom, <u>The Closing of the American Mind</u>, p. 382.
[898] Luke 11:23, TEV. The King James Version states: "He that is not with me is against me: and he that gathereth not with me scattereth." This language appears incongruous with Jesus' admonition in Mark 9:40, "For he that is not against us is on our part," but is repeated in Matthew 12:30. Read in context, there is no incongruity–Christians who do not work for Jesus are "against" Him because they can actually turn others away from Jesus by their hypocrisy, but non-Christians who do not work for Jesus are potential converts and therefore not "against" Him. Otherwise, the greater incongruity would be in Christ's admonition to love our enemies.

very clear about the nature of their current jihad against the United States—have Americans considered that the appearance of their actions in the Middle East are precisely consistent with the term "Crusade," especially to Islamic eyes? The way prepared by massive bombings with many civilian casualties,[899] America's soldiers, many of them Christian, with Christian crucifixes and Bibles in their possession, have been launched into a passionate campaign to spread democracy and the Western way of life and government, into the heartland of Christianity's historic arch-rival, Islam, with massive technological armaments, against the hearts and minds of the Muslim towel-head infidels. Spreading havoc everywhere with their massive military superiority, these conquering Christian invaders burn the Koran, flush it down the toilet, desecrate the Islamic Holy Word of God. They imprison without rights like any other barbaric infidel society, they torture their prisoners, they even desecrate women by using their whorish she-soldiers to humiliate righteous Muslim husbands. How sick can these American Satan-servers be, and still proclaim their Christian faith?....This is how much of Islam is coming to view the United States.

---

[899] Tens of thousands of civilians, including women and children, have been "liberated" in Iraq by American ordnance since the invasion of Iraq. The U.S. media has not been very quick to cover this aspect of the war. A demonstrative case is that "...of Ali Abbas, a 12-year-old Iraqi who lost his entire family and both his arms when a US rocket hit their house. The boy, who went to London for treatment, got extensive press coverage in Europe and became the poster child of sorts for the British Boy Scouts. In the US, his name is barely known." Susan Llewelyn Leach, "How to tell story of the dead without offending the living," *The Christian Science Monitor*, January 19, 2005, pp. 11, 12. (The American press was instead covering the "heroic" tale of Jessica Lynch.)

Under the definition of crusade in <u>The Westminster Dictionary of Christian Ethics</u> is found, *inter alia*, the following:

> The idea of the crusade, or "holy war," is described by Roland Bainton as one of three Christian attitudes toward war, alongside pacifism and the just war idea. Bainton identifies the crusade by four characteristics: holy cause, belief in divine guidance and aid, godly crusaders and ungodly enemies, and unsparing prosecution. Other writers (e.g., Thomas Fuller) have stressed the close connection between the just war and crusade ideas....Some apologists in the Puritan revolution argued that their soldiers' godliness implied scrupulously merciful treatment of the enemy; yet extreme cruelty and devastation sometimes appeared in this war and were generally characteristic of the Continental religious wars. The evidence is not that all crusades are necessarily unsparing, but that a transcendent cause tends to justify extreme measures in its service. Modern ideological wars share the characteristics of the crusade and present the same dangers.[900]

Is there any question that America's incursion into the Middle East meets this definition? To "spread democracy and freedom throughout the world" is an ideological cause, period. Bush thinks God wanted him to run for president, and believes God wants him to carry his ideology to the world ("holy cause" and "divine guidance and aid"). He and his "prayer warriors" believe

---
[900] James F. Childress and John Macquarrie, <u>The Westminster Dictionary of Christian Ethics</u>, p. 139.

God is on America's side and that the "insurgents" or "terrorists" (or other propagandistic noms-du-jour) are "evil," "the forces of evil," etc.; that is, they believe in "godly crusaders and ungodly enemies." Finally, Bush has sworn "unsparing prosecution" in the "war on terror," a concept too wide even for the Crusaders of the Middle Ages–he has vowed that America will never yield, that America will "protect civilization itself,"[901] and he has backed up these words with the most powerful and technologically advanced military force in the history of the world. So America's youth are dying in a war that fits precisely the theological definition of a Crusade, a dirty word–the Iraq Crusade.

In World War II, Americans were famous for their beneficence: for humanitarian relief supplied to both enemy and ally, for mercy in battle, for granting honorable terms of surrender; but most striking to the Allies' enemies was the civil, humane treatment received by prisoners in Allied captivity. This stood in dramatic contrast to the treatment of prisoners by Germany, Japan and the Soviet Union. Yet despite the overwhelming horrors and magnitude of the Holocaust, and the sub-human treatment and torture of prisoners of war by the Japanese, in general the United States and Great Britain, and those countries' soldiers and prison guards, treated Japanese prisoners of war as they would treat any

---

[901] "And you need to know that we're going to defend ourselves, and defend that which we hold dear, and at the same time, protect civilization itself." George W. Bush, in Thomas M. Freiling, <u>George W. Bush on God & Country</u>, p. 164.

other prisoners, with humane decency.[902] Their prisoners returned home after the war with true stories of Allied treatment, that the British and Americans acted like what they said they were—"the good guys."

Now sixty years later, young (Christian) American soldiers allegedly decided to take the immoral initiative to torture and humiliate hundreds of U.S. "enemy combatants" in Iraq and elsewhere in the name of the war on terror, even though no links whatsoever, even circumstantial, had been established between that country and the 9/11 attacks. Denied the presumably protective classification "prisoner of war," the Bush administration's bureaucratic, Clinton-like (as in, define what "is" means) redefinition of the status of these human beings meant that they no longer were required to be treated as human beings, seized by an Orwellian State which created an indefinite limbo for its uncharged enemies. Further, this arrangement unilaterally and imperiously denied any international, congressional or constitutional accountability. Gulag. A surreal America.

The logical, algebraic construct of the American government's torture of predominantly Arab "detainees" is as follows:

---

[902] C.S. Lewis, in <u>The Screwtape Letters</u>, records the (fictitious) complaint of a demon, frustrated that the English talked big and expressed vindictive feelings toward the Germans, but were soft when they met their enemies face-to-face: "The results of such fanciful hatred are often most disappointing, and of all humans the English are in this respect the most deplorable milksops. They are creatures of that miserable sort who loudly proclaim that torture is much too good for their enemies and then give tea and cigarettes to the first wounded German pilot who turns up at the back door." p. 17.

1) George W. Bush instructed Alberto Gonzales to massage the law to avoid the U.S. Constitution, avoid international law, and permit the Bush-directed U.S. military et al. to employ methods of interrogation that grammar-school children would readily identify as torture.
2) Human beings created by God and beloved by Jesus Christ were systematically tortured, both physically and psychologically, and in some cases killed. The Koran was desecrated by American interrogators,[903] but such stories, though true, were covered with lies because the truth was far too damaging.
3) The Bush administration denied that it tortured anyone, and (vaguely) changed its (warped) interpretation of the law. A "few bad apples" were blamed for the prisoner abuse. The administration continues to seek to hold thousands of detainees, uncharged, without trial, for life. A "few bad apples" are publicly convicted as scapegoats; no senior officers or government officials are held accountable. Alberto Gonzales is posted to the position of United States Attorney General to reward loyal support and for helping make torture possible. (Like with George Tenet, promotion is an effort to impart an imprimatur of legitimacy on actions which were grossly not so, and to reward loyalty).
4) The rest of the world is unamused, the enthusiasm of many of America's allies wanes, and al Qaeda sees the Great Satan aroused to a Christian Crusade.

---

[903] "…a *Newsweek* report, later retracted but generally corroborated by Red Cross sources, that the Koran had been defiled by US interrogators at Guantanamo Bay…." Ibrahim N. Abusharif, "Snares and symbols," *The Christian Science Monitor*, May 25, 2005, p.9.

5) Jesus Christ is weeping for the sorrow and hatred sown by those who carry His name on their bloodthirsty lips, while they find moral excuse, then legal means, then physical method to systematically torture imprisoned human bodies.[904]

Americans can protest the above recounting of facts 'til they're blue in the face, but the burden of proof on America in the international community on these issues is identical to the burden placed on "detainees"–America is guilty of the above, until proven otherwise (guilty until proven innocent). In fact, America would lose any effort at defense quite quickly under almost any standard, because all of the above is incontrovertibly true in the absence of the deployment of cognitive dissonance/denial. If ignorance is bliss, American refusal to acknowledge what is much more than a simple "scandal" is no doubt blissful, but American Christians know that ignorance, particularly "willful" ignorance, is sinful and eternally punishable. Christians, then, ought not to be so easily bought off by waves of the hand and vague dismissals–Christians who are true to Jesus Christ do not torture animals, let alone human beings, ever.

Amazingly, the American public has not raised much outcry against this unconscionable, unchristian conduct

---

[904] "In the Abu Ghraib setting, people saw a confirmation of the linkages between power and corruption embodied in the torture and molestation of scores of weak, incarcerated Iraqis at the hands of a few but powerful military personnel." Ibrahim N. Abusharif, "Snares and symbols," *The Christian Science Monitor*, May 25, 2005, p. 9.

by its government.⁹⁰⁵ Perhaps this is what occurs when the largest moral bloc in the country sacrifices their loyalty to Jesus Christ on the altar of American politics. But Americans will be held accountable for this conduct even though their political leaders may not, for world opinion and Christ's judgment will both take accurate inventory of modern American behavior.

---

⁹⁰⁵ This is starting to change, thanks in part to the determination of Senator John McCain, may God bless him and his family. But Mr. McCain's efforts have not gone far enough, because of the failings of political compromise. Bush's persistence in keeping detainees in secret locations, and reports of numerous suspicious deaths of detainees, have exposed Bush for the liar he is, blaming a few American soldiers for his own conduct. Fortunately he is not as clever as his ego would have him believe. *See*, e.g., Farredd Zakaria's frank discussion of the White House's torture policy in "Pssst...Nobody Loves a Torturer," *Newsweek*, November 14, 2005, p. 36:

> We now have plenty of documents and testimonials that make plain that the administration created an atmosphere in which the interrogation of prisoners could lapse into torture....What angers [America's friends abroad] is that no one beyond a few "little people" have been punished, the system has not been overhauled, and even now, after all that has happened, the White House is spending time, effort, and precious political capital in a strange, stubborn and surely futile quest to preserve the option to torture."

This unchristian action is unsurprising in an unchristian liar, a man who has never been told "no." It's time that America's Christians stood up for their Christ and told George W. Bush "no" to torture–he must no longer be permitted the unilateral power to effect heinous, unchristian practices.

Having decided that the "war on terror"[906] justified the use of extreme methods of interrogation (clearly without any troublesome consultation with the New Testament or the writings of Oswald Chambers, who Bush says he reads, but obviously either does not read or does not understand), George W. Bush, ignorant Christian, instructed Mr. Gonzales to "get around" those pesky American and international human rights laws. The result was barbaric. Americans waiting for the DNA evidence on this blue dress will wait too long–the conduct of this administration is blatant and overwhelmingly criminal, and no test tube science is required to "judge" these actions–and Jesus Christ calls every Christian to do so, at peril of losing one's soul for failure.

Prior to Alberto Gonzales' testimony before the Senate Judiciary Committee relating to his appointment as United States Attorney General, Vermont Senator Patrick Leahy

---

[906] Do Iraqi children experience terror when American rockets destroy their homes, families, and bodies? Does Jesus permit a "Christian nation" to terrorize such innocent victims based on the morally spurious logic that the Old Testament recites that there would always be wars (there will always be sin, bestiality, and rape, but God does not thereby imply that Christians should undertake such actions, ever). It is sinful to dismiss Jesus' teachings with such shallow illogic–Jesus came to change the Law, so reliance on the Old Testament to overcome His words of peace, that we must love our enemies, is a rejection of Christ and what he represents. The Iraq War is not a just war, it is an immoral, criminal, unjust, unchristian engagement in which therefore every soul lost is the responsibility of the individual citizens of the United States–every single life sinfully extinguished is a mortal sin, and God will not be judging America's idols: its government, its flag, or its hallowed soul-less halls. To God, America is not defined by her worldly accomplishments, but by her heavenly ones; and she is not defined by idols and worldly trappings or edifices, but by the condition of the human souls who inhabit her.

said Gonzales would have to explain "the role he has played in formulating the administration's policies." Leahy added that "somewhere in the upper reaches of the executive branch a process was set in motion that rolled forward until it produced this [prisoner abuse] scandal." White House spokesman Trent Duffy said last week that the president wholeheartedly supports Gonzales. When Bush nominated him in November, the president said Gonzales's "sharp intellect and sound judgment have helped shape our policies in the war on terror." That sounded good then....[907]

Bush publicly praised Gonzales for the legal positions he codified which originated the Bush torture loophole, and then continued to stand behind this embarrassing appointment even after the Abu Ghraib scandal broke. And despite Leahy's inquiries, Gonzales did not give straight answers in his subsequent testimony, only more legal squirming, and so the word "torture" is never linked to the lips of George W. Bush.

Again, when the stakes are so incredibly high, a much greater burden should have been, but was not, placed on the Bush administration to explain its conduct.[908] This is especially so for an administration which held the standards of Jesus Christ aloft to win two elections–the Bible teaches repeatedly that flying the banner of Jesus Christ commits one to a higher standard than others.

---

[907] "A Lingering Prison Scandal," *U.S. News & World Report*, January 10, 2005, p.31.
[908] Ann Coulter wrote of the President that "It is his constitutional duty to take care that the laws be faithfully executed." High Crimes and Misdemeanors: the Case Against Bill Clinton, p. 301. (The *laws*, not the *prisoners*....)

Christian Words, Unchristian Actions

But many Christians in America have sinfully abdicated their Christian voices to the powers of a worldly, fear-spreading, bureaucratic government to which they continued to give a green light even after public exposure of torture and other human rights abuses. Do they think God is blind?

When the story of Abu Ghraib broke (the torture practices having been employed for some time with impunity until that point), there was great alarm in America and abroad:

> …various government memoranda since 9/11 related to torture and the rules of war send a signal that the norms are different than in the past, and that new standards for interrogation are not yet clear. At the same time, some in legal and political circles are suggesting that torture could be justified under certain circumstances–a position others view with alarm….
>
> Both President Bush and his attorney general nominee, Alberto Gonzales, say they abhor torture and that the U.S. does not engage in it. Yet other leaders–from Republican Sen. Lindsay Graham to retired Army Gen. John Shalikashvili, former chairman of the Joint Chiefs of Staff–suggest that the country has lost the moral high ground.
>
> Legal experts acknowledge that defining torture is a difficult task, but say that the Bush administration's reframing of the legal context for US policy sparked

the debate.⁹⁰⁹ Before 9/11, the US followed the Convention Against Torture and the Geneva Conventions on rules of war. Memos by Mr. Gonzales, counsel to the president, and Justice Department staff have since argued that the US faces an unprecedented situation–fighting an enemy that violates the rules of war, an enemy that does not merit the protection of the rules.⁹¹⁰

In a January 2002 memo, Gonzales called parts of the Geneva Convention "quaint" and "obsolete." Although Secretary of State Colin Powell vigorously protested, Mr. Bush directed that detainees at Guantanamo, Afghanistan, and other secret sites be held as unlawful combatants unprotected by the conventions, though "treated humanely."⁹¹¹

The most strenuous objections have come from those with military experience....

In August 2002, a Justice Department memo defined torture so narrowly that it eliminated anything

---

[909] Interesting that George W. Bush should employ man's laws without recourse to God in determining his and our nation's course in this regard. It's a shame that the words of Pope John Paul II, spoken directly from the Pope's mouth to this president's ear, were not heeded: "A free and virtuous society, which America aspires to be, must reject practices that devalue and violate human life at any stage from conception until natural death." Reprinted in Thomas M. Freiling's George W. Bush on God & Country, at p. 254.

[910] Japan, North Vietnam, and Germany were also such enemies, but this argument was never employed in those conflicts to justify torture: what has become of America's moral compass?

[911] Presumably, they were "treated humanely" in between torture sessions. But to detain men in prison indefinitely (i.e., for life) without the requirement of evidence or trial, is considered inhumane under international law, *for obvious reasons.*

short of inflicting pain equal to that "accompanying serious physical injury such as organ failure, impairment of bodily function, or even death."….
And last month the White House pressed Congress to drop legislation that would have imposed restrictions on the use of extreme interrogation measures by intelligence officers.

[Says Hurst Hannum, professor of international law at Fletcher School of Law and Diplomacy in Medford, Mass.] "….There has to be some decision as to what kind of a society we are."

Many in the legal community see America's values and its reputation at stake. "The standards of interrogation have been muddied…since the invasion of Afghanistan," says Washington lawyer Eugene Fidell, president of the National Institute of Military Justice. "The administration has done incalculable damage with all the bobbing and weaving…treating as debatable things that should not be debatable. I don't think our country is willing to give up its value system."

….Perhaps the murkiest areas involve CIA interrogations at secret overseas sites, as well as the practice of sending some captives to countries such as Syria and Egypt, where they are likely to be tortured—a practice that is illegal in international law.

….[Cases of abuse] sully America's reputation as a promoter of universal human rights and even endanger US citizens around the world. The US, [military and legal experts] argue, needs to treat others as it would expect others to treat Americans. Until recent years, the army taught its interrogators that they should use only those methods that would be considered lawful if an enemy used them on Americans.[912]

To "sully America's reputation as a promoter of universal human rights" is to simultaneously sully Christ's message of universal truth. And for George Bush and Alberto Gonzales to state that they "abhor" torture, while they unilaterally and surreptitiously change American law to permit it, is to lie. Christian words, unchristian actions....

The widely-publicized Abu Ghraib photos of American abuse of prisoners shocked Americans, but such treatment was by no means confined to that facility. The enormous number of demonstrated cases of prisoner abuse, which simultaneously occurred at disparate locations, using similar techniques of "interrogation," compel the conclusion that this behavior was the consequence of policy set at the top. Only the most woefully and willfully ignorant can even attempt to assert that these prisoner abuses were the result of the actions of a "few bad apples:" this requires both a disregard for the huge numbers of cases of abuse ("hundreds of bad

---

[912] Jane Lampman, "US stand against torture: firm enough?," *The Christian Science Monitor*, January 19, 2005, pp. 11, 13. At his subsequent confirmation hearing, Gonzales was pressed "on his role in an August 2002 memorandum on the rules of torture, which was officially repudiated on the eve of his nomination hearing....Critics say the memo [,written at Gonzales's request,] opened the door to the abuses at Abu Ghraib prison and that, despite the later retraction, the Gonzales nomination sends the wrong signal to human rights groups worldwide." Gail Russell Chaddock, "Democrats flash steel at Gonzales," *The Christian Science Monitor*, February 1, 2005, p. 2.

apples"), and also a belief that hundreds of American personnel suddenly abandoned their oaths of loyalty to their nation, simultaneously, in numerous different locations, and began to deliberately and systematically disobey orders and inflict horrible treatments upon other human beings. In other words, believing that a "few bad apples" inflicted these injuries to human beings and to America's image is to disrespect American troops, and accuse them of mass immorality and mutiny. How far the Bush administration will go to avoid responsibility for the consequences of its actions/policies has yet to be determined, but clearly it includes using young, honest, loyal U.S. troops as shields, staining the honor of the entire American military and its history, and putting soldiers' lives and welfare at risk by blaming them for the direct consequences of Bush administration policies.[913]

Employing the methodology that he once criticized, President W. Bush is quick to take advantage of bureaucratic structure to avoid accountability. There is no smoking gun or DNA evidence to link his hand to the war crimes in American detention facilities, but common sense is sufficient for those who care for truth:

---

[913] These policies create a risk to American lives in addition to the obvious increase in the likelihood that U.S. personnel will be subject to torture in future conflict. Enemy soldiers are less likely to surrender, and likely to fight much more fiercely, when motivated by stories (or photos) of American treatment of prisoners–better to die than surrender. Of course, past U.S. policies of humanitarian, lenient treatment of those who surrender often saved American lives by undermining enemy morale and resolve in battle (as when Iraq was invaded, and many of Saddam's soldiers surrendered without resistance)–for some enemy soldiers, defeat looked better than victory, because American captivity was better than their "normal" existence. But no longer....

…several former military officers and legal experts say the numbers of complaints will probably multiply as long as the United States maintains a presence in Iraq, and as long as the definition of what constitutes torture remains somewhat ambiguous–in a global war on terror that is amorphous itself.

….FBI documents…indicated its agents complained of military abuses of detainees at Guantanamo Bay, Cuba, as early as late 2002. This was about a year before the scandal broke at Abu Ghraib.

….So far, the Pentagon says, 137 members of the military have either been disciplined or face courts-martial for abusing detainees….the two studies commissioned by the Pentagon–the Taguba report and the Schlesinger report–both found responsibility lay with higher-level officers.

"Washington continues to establish policies that are very important as guidelines," says a former Army general who still works for the Pentagon. "But it is almost always impossible to draw a straight line from a Washington policy to a specific act or series of acts in a prison in Iraq…."

"….There's been so much of this in so many places that you have to look at what was being said and done at the top to have affected this behavior," says Patrick Lang, former head of Middle East intelligence at the Defense Intelligence Agency.

At the time, the government's policy on what constituted torture was outlined in an August 2002 memo. Interrogators were allowed to use pain up to the "equivalent in intensity to the pain accompanying

> serious physical injury, such as organ failure, impairment of bodily function or even death."
>
> ...."There are two issues that are bothersome to people here," says Hurst Hannum...."One is the administration's early suggestion that torture might have been OK. The second is that the administration seems to be trying to leave itself total discretion to take what action it needs when confronted with terrorists." ....Yet most disturbing to critics are the moral issues and questions of accountability.[914]

Ironically, the military was used to investigate abuses which were in fact clearly committed in the execution of military duty, i.e. pursuant to orders. Like a dog chasing its own tail, the military "investigated" itself in an effort to re-establish the credibility it lost via the behaviors it was investigating....Further, the military knew full well that those hundreds of soldiers were following orders and policy correctly, and so its investigations are a farcical (if successful) effort by the big brass to join the Bush administration in making scapegoats of the little guys once again:

> Thanks to probing by the Pentagon and others,[915] the public knows that Abu Ghraib did not represent

---

[914] Faye Bowers, "In US stand on torture, more trials to come," *The Christian Science Monitor*, January 18, 2005, p. 3. The article also reports that FBI agents said that aggressive interrogation tactics "generally aren't effective in eliciting information."

[915] Where was the probing two-plus years earlier, when FBI agents filed complaints of excessive tactics such as putting lit cigarettes into the ears of detainees? *See*, e.g., *The Christian Science Monitor*, January 18, 2005, p. 3.

a few isolated cases. The abuse has stretched in an arch from the US military prison in Guantanamo Bay, Cuba to Afghanistan. The cases of abuse number in the hundreds and include at least two dozen suspicious deaths.[916]

How dare President Bush blame the U.S. military for policies he ordered them to carry out,[917] and then make the military clean up the mess to boot?

The Bush public relations team has wasted no time seeking to deflect criticism of its torture policies by dismissing the cases of abuse as perpetrated by a few errant criminals, never explaining what were the new interrogation techniques that the Gonzalez memo was designed to permit, if not the behaviors and techniques exhibited by hundreds of soldiers and depicted in hundreds of photos. Did the Gonzales memo, defining as permissible interrogation techniques those which caused pain equal to that "accompanying serious physical injury such as organ failure, impairment of bodily function, or even death," refer to some other interrogation techniques not yet revealed to the American public? How can George W. Bush give the order to create this new definition of

---

[916] "Abu Ghraib: Questions Linger," *The Christian Science Monitor*, May 4, 2005, p. 8: "The images [of a pyramid of nude prisoners] shocked the nation and the world. The images portrayed not only the harm inflicted on the prisoners, but the damage done to America's credibility as a torchbearer for human rights."

[917] This diversion of responsibility, an unchristian action, contrasts with Mr. Bush's accountability words, that "There is a concept that you are responsible for your behavior. You can't shirk off your problems on somebody else. You must handle them yourself." George W. Bush, quoted in Stephen Mansfield's The Faith of George W. Bush, at p. 11.

prisoner treatment, give the order that this new standard be carried out, lie and say he "abhors" torture, promote the torture-memo draftsman to one of the highest and most important legal positions in the country,[918] and call himself a follower of Lord Jesus Christ?

Instead of answering legitimate questions about its role in setting the tone for the new American preemptive torture doctrine, the Bush spin machine shifted blame to the grunts who gave effect to that doctrine. John Yoo, a former Justice Department lawyer who helped draft the memos, "…insist[ed] the Bush administration is being clear that torture is not permitted. "There are always people who will go beyond their authorization."…."[919] And

---

[918] This even though "a dozen retired military officers criticized Gonzales for a series of memos" that created a " "new kind of war" against terror." George Hunsinger, a professor at Princeton Theological Seminary in New Jersey, remarked that "If a person such as this is placed in the position of being the attorney general of the United States, what kind of message does that send to the rest of the world, especially the Arab world?" Gail Russell Chaddock, "Gonzales likely to be confirmed as AG, but faces sharp questions," *The Christian Science Monitor*, January 5, 2005, p. 2. But George W. and the Americans who support him and his actions, at their and the whole world's peril, are not interested in the opinions of non-Americans—the country is nation-centric, and wanted a "politically correct" Hispanic more than integrity, Christianity, or a favorable world opinion of America. Like it owns Iraq, America now owns its newfound reputation; and like in Iraq, it will take decades to reform that new American image. Or is Gonzales America's AG for the sole qualification of nepotism: general counsel to Governor Bush, later promoted (by then Governor Bush) to Texas Secretary of State, then appointed to the Texas Supreme court, which he left to join the Bush administration as counsel to the president. Ibid. Like a true bureaucrat and Bonesman, Bush constantly rewards loyalty over merit.

[919] Jane Lampman, "US stand against torture: firm enough?," *The Christian Science Monitor*, January 19, 2005, pp. 11, 13. Like President Bush in Iraq?

Paul Kengor, in his re-write of history <u>God and George W. Bush: a spiritual life</u>, wrote indignantly that

> A few sick, unprofessional soldiers–whose crimes had been exposed by fellow troops–had thereby caused immense harm to the U.S. effort....The situation was indeed the classic case of a few bad apples rotting the whole barrel. Critics exploited the photographs for political purpose, and tried to extend the tentacles all the way to the Oval Office.[920]

A "few" soldiers are blamed for a widespread practice that involved hundreds of cases, and "critics" are immediately dismissed as "exploiting" the situation "for political purposes," ignoring Republican critics and not allowing for the possibility of truth that the "tentacles [<u>extended</u>] all the way to the Oval Office"–of course they did, for a child can trace the connection. And is objection based on the definitive theological Christian prohibition of the use of torture a "political purpose"? Kengor allows for no legitimate moral right to object, relying on the patently specious and fully discredited "bad apple" argument and dismissing moral conscience as politically motivated.[921]

Mr. Kengor continues with undisguised partisan loyalty to dismiss those who would challenge Bush war policies, including Nick Berg's father:

---

[920] pp. 308, 309.

[921] In contrast, Robert H. Schuller calls upon Christians to walk the walk of Jesus Christ: "What is our Lord's greatest passion for his church today? I believe that he wants his followers to respect themselves as equal children of God and to treat all other human beings with that same respect." <u>Self-Esteem: The New Reformation</u>, p. 47.

The beheading brought perspective to the Abu Ghraib scandal:[922] the humiliation of the POWs was intolerable mistreatment, the action against Nick Berg an unspeakable atrocity. The Berg beheading made it abundantly clear that the war on terror was being fought in Iraq.[923]

---

[922] Beware such false logic: comparing heinous crimes for relative heinousness is something serial murderers do, not Christians–Mr. Kengor is engaging here in the most offensive and Satanic form of moral relativism, suggesting that American torture of prisoners was acceptable or of "lesser" evil when contrasted with a beheading. He is also connecting the two, which is morally absurd–the Abu Ghraib detainees did not behead Nick Berg, and Americans do not sacrifice their whole history of moral behavior because of the moral wrongdoings of others. This same immoral logic has been employed repeatedly by different members of, and spokesmen for, this administration: in the case of allegations that American prisoner abuse was akin to the Soviet Gulags, Dick Cheney and others were furious, pointing out that nothing like that number of prisoners were affected by Abu Ghraib-like practices, drawing attention away from the fact that although quantitatively different, the two were qualitatively identical. In the case of Iraqi children and other civilians destroyed by war, their bodies and souls are spared remorse or even words of acknowledgement by Mr. Kengor's "perspective"–clearly their deaths are viewed by Mr. Kengor as the consequence of Saddam Hussein's intransigence and not American bungling.

[923] No, what is abundantly clear is that Paul Kengor and George W. Bush both sought to make political hay of Nick Berg's death–his death as equally made clear that the war in Iraq was creating a seething grassroots backlash that would threaten many more Nick Bergs. It appears that it was abundantly clear to the young man's father that his son died because the Bush administration has inflamed those anti-American sentiments, feeding the fires that fuel al Qaeda, swelling the extremist ranks of Muslim jihadists and playing into the hands of Osama bin Laden once again. America's invasion of Iraq drew the terrorists there, not the other way around.

ABU GHRAIB, THE MODERN SYMBOL OF AMERICA 493

Not everyone[924] interpreted[925] it that way. Rather than interpreting his son's beheading as vindicating the Bush war on Islamic terror,[926] Nick berg's father blamed the murder squarely on the president. "My son died for the sins of George Bush and Donald Rumsfeld...."[927]

Perhaps Mr. Bush's Bible is missing a few pages, and in their stead has fallen an extract from the moral philosophy of Machiavelli:

> Therefore, a prince ought not to care about the infamy of cruelty with respect to keeping his subjects united and faithful;...And of all princes, it is especially impossible for a new prince to avoid

---

[924] No, only neo-cons and other willful deniers.

[925] "Interpreting" is used to supplant truth–Mr, Kengor's "interpretation" here is that Nick Berg's beheading "vindicated the Bush war on Islamic terror." Yet the terrorists had no links to Saddam Hussein, and to call Nick Berg's beheading a "vindication" of the policies of the man who got him killed (Bush) is a strained "interpretation" at best. But of course, "not everyone sees it" the way I do, just the majority of Americans who have seen that the Iraq War has become a vile stain on their country...and Nick Berg's father.

[926] Clearly that interpretation never occurred to the gentleman, but it is nice of Mr. Kengor to offer that offensive-if-fictitious consolation to Mr. Berg, Sr. This is another moral contortion–that Mr. Berg is essentially admonished that he should see his son's horrifying execution as a "vindication of the Bush war on Islamic terror." The nerve to tell a parent how to grieve for their child, what their "political" view of that death should be. The Bush administration has consistently welcomed parents of deceased service personnel who agree with its decision to invade Iraq to prominent seats at events, and to speak in support of the war; but has even refused to meet with parents of a differing political view, like Cindy Sheehan. Is this Christian? Is this the free exchange of ideas in a democracy?

[927] Paul Kengor, p.310. After acknowledging this detraction by Nick Berg's father, Kengor offers no position as to how this poor man is mistaken.

> the name of cruelty, because new states are full of dangers. And Virgil, through the mouth of Dido says: "Difficult things and a new reign force me to take such measures, and to defend the boundaries all around."[928]

Or perhaps George is just following his early training with his unrenounced Skull & Bones comrades, using the powers of light or darkness at will to achieve his rise to worldly power….

For one thing is certain: George W. Bush has not acted in a Christian manner in permitting, let alone promoting, torture and indefinite detention without trial. The only moral argument permitting torture, that it is acceptable when necessary to protect a larger good, is simply unavailable to Christianity, period. Perhaps George W. will direct Gonzales to draft a new memo on the definition of suicide, or of abortion—would Christ be consulted, or ignored again?

George W., as usual, talks a good Christian talk:

> We believe that protecting human dignity and promoting human rights should be at the center of America's foreign policy….and how we respect human rights is another way we'll be judged by history. We'll be judged by history on how we defend our freedoms. We'll be judged in history by how we help our people prosper and grow. And we'll be judged by history as to whether or not we defend the universal values that are right and just and true.[929]

---

[928] Niccolo Machiavelli, The Prince, p. 100.
[929] Thomas M. Freiling, George W. Bush on God & Country, pp. 83, 166.

Where does the Bible speak of this judge named "history"? Jesus Christ will be our judge, and He will not be judging "how we defend our freedoms," nor "how we help our people prosper and grow," nor "whether or not we defend the universal values that are right and just and true." He will be judging whether we defended Him, whether we helped Him to prosper and grow, and whether we defended the universal truths that are Him. And as to this George W. is correct, for he, and all Americans who turn a blind or approving eye to excessively harsh interrogation techniques, will be judged by Jesus Christ for Abu Ghraib et al., for "how we respect human rights."[930]

Mr. Bush can hardly be held "accountable" for his behavior by the standards of this world, of politics and bureaucracy–this is the world of Machiavelli, where the ends justify the means, where personal "vision" replaces God's desires. But surely George W. Bush has offered repeatedly, in fact has implicitly promised to the American people, the world, and God, that he will abide by the rules and regulations enunciated by God and His servants in the Bible–George W. Bush has said that he is a follower of Jesus, and the Bible repeatedly instructs Christians (see Chapter One) to hold their Christian

---

[930] Mr. Bush's actions always speak more clearly than his deceitful words. Did he respect human rights when he authorized the use of white phosphorous, or was this done behind his back by a few bad apples who manufactured and transported this vile substance behind his back? (Like the Plame leak?) Has this student of history forgotten history so thoroughly that we must relive World War I and its horrors in this century? "The U.S. acknowledged using white phosphorous as a weapon against insurgents in last fall's Fallujah battle." *The Wall Street Journal*, November 16, 2005, p. 1.

CHRISTIAN WORDS, UNCHRISTIAN ACTIONS

leaders to His standards. So let us examine the standards of Christianity when applied to the use of torture at Abu Ghraib and elsewhere.

This administration has created controversy over the existence and appropriate response to global warming, over WMD in Iraq, over the renewal of the nuclear arms race via a driven determination to develop nuclear bunker busters, and over what should be the definition of torture. But all of these issues had been largely resolved by general international consensus before Mr. Bush began fiddling around with his ignorant monkey wrench. When it came to torture, Mr. Bush developed a novel, sickening definition of acceptable conduct by American personnel, gave effect to its use, then changed the definition to a still-nebulous standard and stated that he "abhorred" torture. Liar. The U.S. "peacekeepers" have been documented to have committed the following actions, amongst others, while representing the United States of America on Mr. Accountability's watch: sexual humiliation and waterboarding,[931] "poked cigarettes in detainees' ears, deprived them of food and sleep, and used dogs, among other cruel and sexually humiliating tactics,"[932] and "executions or physical assaults of prisoners in Iraq, theft of their cash or private property, and shackling without

---

[931] Water-boarding "makes a prisoner think he is drowning." "US stand against torture: firm enough?," Jane Lampman, "US stand on torture: firm enough?," *The Christian Science Monitor*, January 19, 2005, p. 11.
[932] Faye Bowers, "In US stand on torture, more trials to come," *The Christian Science Monitor*, January 18, 2005, p. 3.

food or water."[933] This in addition to the well-publicized photos of stacked naked prisoners, hooded victims with electrodes attached to their flesh, or prisoners held with a leash. (The worst photos have been withheld from the public and the world to avoid the additional outcry that revealing the truth would occasion: it says a lot when America conceals its actions to avoid the consequences of truth-telling.)

At a time when America is proclaiming that it will better the world with democratic liberties, it is directly in the global spotlight for its hypocritical human rights abuses, and is becoming ever more unpopular in the Middle East:

> "Saddam…deserves what he gets, but the pictures [of a humiliated Saddam Hussein, in his underwear] show that if a person is behind US-controlled bars, then anything can happen to him. It's clear now that America isn't very different from the Arab states in this," [said Samir Nagrub, manager of a Cairo mobile phone company.]…A report earlier this month from the Council on Foreign Relations summarizing a series of focus groups in Morocco, Egypt, and Indonesia found that America's efforts to win hearts and minds aren't working.…"The growth of hostility to America in Muslim countries increases recruitment and support for extremism and terror," the authors write.[934]

---

[933] This information was garnered from "hundreds of pages of Army records obtained under the Freedom of Information Act.…The documents implicate both regular and Special forces soldiers.…" *The Christian Science Monitor*, December 23, 2004, p. 20.

[934] Dan Murphy, "For Arab press, Hussein photos reinforce view of US," *The Christian Science Monitor*, May 23, 2005, p. 7.

CHRISTIAN WORDS, UNCHRISTIAN ACTIONS

Is the Chinese government doing to Christians what this administration caused to be inflicted on defenseless prisoners? Armageddon is imminent and Christ will judge us all, and our country's morality is being governed by the Machiavellian laws of secular evolution. If the latter is the case then "We are apparently near the end of a degenerative phase of an evolutionary process—a long way from any large-scale regeneration."[935]

Yet this "degenerative phase" of evolution will lead non-Christians to despair, hopelessness, and the recognition of the failure of mankind and its technologies, the failure of "Progress." But to Christians, who have already accepted man's failures as certain without God and have studied the Scriptures which foretell in astonishing detail of our current condition, the "devolution" of the world and its man-made conventions does not instill fear but confirmation that God keeps His promises. George W.'s efforts to instill terrorist-phobias in the American people are worldly exhortations that one would expect from a man who says he believes in Jesus Christ but expands military might at every turn, enlarges the federal government and its powers at every opportunity, covets secrecy, and is an unrecanted alumnus of the Satanic Skull & Bones cult.

Where is the accountability for the torture of helpless victims? (their being Muslim is not relevant to this characterization, only to those who, like the Nazis, would employ rationalizations that they are sub-human

---

[935] Wendell Berry, <u>The Unsettling of America: Culture and Agriculture</u>, addressing the deterioration in the American institution of marriage and accompanying virtue of fidelity, at p. 120.

or animalistic enemies who do not deserve human or Christian treatment–Christ does not distinguish, and America never used to, either). Some (bad apple) pawns have been sacrificed, but the Bush chess game is far from ended. Americans find comparisons of their country's conduct with evil-doers of the past to be distasteful and objectionable, but some of the comparisons are far too stark to be ignored, and surely those reminders are not lost on the citizens of the world who endured or have clear memories of great evil in the past.

Americans do not appreciate their country being compared to the Soviet Union, but America's current interrogation methods and regard for human rights could have been extracted from a Gulag instruction manual. The Bush administration Defense Department plans to put some 500 Guantanamo Bay prisoners in foreign detention facilities:

> The Defense Department's proposal could very well be a lost chapter out of George Orwell's timeless novel <u>1984</u>: potential lifetime sentences for the hundreds of people now in military and CIA custody at a prison yet to be built outside the US, and thus beyond the reach of its constitutional protections on due process.
>
> ....Who are these prisoners? They are men who have outlived their usefulness as intelligence sources and against whom the government lacks sufficient evidence to charge them in courts.
>
> ....However, under the rules set forth, these prisoners are guilty first, and will never have an opportunity to prove otherwise....The prisons are likely to be in

> countries where torture can be administered without legal consequence....
>
> This is the kind of conduct that was practiced in the Soviet Union's Lubiyanka prison, where people were held interminably without ever facing their accusers. Indeed, it's the kind of treatment often doled out in Saddam Hussein's palace of punishment–Abu Ghraib prison....
>
> This proposed policy is unpardonable not only because it robs potentially innocent people of the chance to stand before justice; it potentially robs America of its right to call itself a just nation. The Bush administration has essentially thrown its precious rule of law out the window and let it land on the Constitution with a thud.[936]

The best the Bush administration can do to distance its practices from those of the dreaded USSR is argue that the American abuses are much smaller in number. This artful dodge is moral relativism again, and certainly not Christian. Is one's sin measured by the greater sins of others in the eyes of Jesus Christ? Does the world measure America's conduct against that of the Russians and Nazis and forgive it because "not that many" people have been tortured, humiliated, and treated as sub-human in precisely the same manner as those nations? Those quick to dismiss analogies to the Soviet gulags when discussing American treatment of detainees would benefit from a cursory review of the

---

[936] Cathryn J. Prince, "Terror detainees and America's gulag," *The Christian Science Monitor*, January 18, 2005, p. 9.

writings of Aleksandr I. Solzhenitsyn, who described his experiences in Soviet gulags, including witnessing or experiencing instances of: torture;[937] humiliation;[938] deprivation of legal counsel;[939] indefinite imprisonment;[940] secret courts;[941] deprivation of food, water or sleep;[942] the extinguishment of lit cigarettes on skin;[943] military courts;[944] the use of propaganda;[945] and the administration of deliberate trauma to male sex organs,[946] amongst other techniques. His highly intelligent mind having survived years of the very worst face of human malice and suffering, Mr. Solzhenitsyn wrote extensively in an earnest effort to expose Soviet horrors so as to warn the world and prevent a repeat of such horrible behavior (much like survivors of Nazi terror often devote themselves to the prevention of tyranny).

---

[937] Aleksandr I. Solzhenitsyn, The Gulag Archipelago, 1918-1956, Volume One, p.103 et seq.: "...the so-called *light* methods ...[proved that] the actual boundaries of human equilibrium are very narrow, and it is not really necessary to use a rack or hot coals to drive the average human being out of his mind."
[938] Ibid., p.104. The author relates cases of inmates being forced to lay on the floor for extended periods, and of female inmates being stripped naked and then subjected to the jeering appraisals of male jailers.
[939] Ibid., p. 121: "The principal of our interrogation consists further in depriving the accused of even a knowledge of the law."
[940] Ibid., p. 301.
[941] Ibid., p. 286-287.
[942] Ibid., pp. 111-113. Also cold and heat. Starvation, see p. 114.
[943] Ibid., p. 108.
[944] Ibid., pp. 293-298.
[945] Ibid. At page 299, Solzhenitsyn writes that "...things repeated on the radio day after day drill holes in the brain." Sounds like the Bush link between terrorism and Iraq.
[946] Ibid., e.g., p. 128.

Solzhenitsyn offers Americans and Christians remarkable insights into the origins of torture and the dangers of bureaucracy. In considering the Alberto Gonzales memos, the Soviet jurisprudential methodology employed by Stalin to justify torture is instructive:

> It turns out that in that terrible year [of 1937] Andrei Yanuaryevich (one longs to blurt out, "Jaguaryevich") Vyshinsky, availing himself of the most flexible dialectics (of a sort nowadays not permitted either Soviet citizens or electronic calculators, since to them, yes is yes and no is no), pointed out in a report which became famous in certain circles that it is never possible for mortal men to establish absolute truth, but relative truth only. He then proceeded to a further step, which jurists of the last two thousand years had not been willing to take: that the truth established by interrogation and trial could not be absolute, but only, so to speak, relative.[947] Therefore, when we sign a sentence ordering someone to be shot we can never be absolutely certain, but only approximately, in view of certain hypotheses, and in a certain sense, that we are punishing a guilty person. Thence arose the most practical conclusion: that it was useless to seek absolute evidence—for evidence

---

[947] This is not as great a jurisprudential leap as to define torture to include anything other than the deliberate infliction of pain to the level of organ failure, death, etc. as was done by the Bush administration, hiding behind Gonzales et al.–lawyers are trained to create legal support for *any* position to which they are assigned (or hired). The Bush administration torture memo is easily recognizable as a hired argument, a contrived straw-grasping; one not subject to the review of a judge or Congress, but barely sufficient (and the only thing they could come up with without plagiarizing Jaguaryevich) as an ass-coverer and torture-enabling philosophy.

is always relative–or unchallengeable witnesses–for they can say different things at different times.[948] The proofs of guilt were relative, approximate, and the interrogator could find them, even when there was no evidence and no witness, without leaving his office, "basing his conclusions not only on his own intellect but also on his Party sensitivity, his moral forces" (in other words, the superiority of someone who has slept well, has been well fed, and has not been beaten up) "and on his character" (i.e., his willingness to apply cruelty!)....

Thus it was that the conclusions of advanced Soviet jurisprudence, proceeding in a spiral, returned to barbaric or medieval standards.[949]

---

[948] Though bizarre, this argument, which pretends to be scientific at arriving at a determination of guilt without trial but also pretends to be extending justice to human beings, is actually less unchristian than the policies of detainment without trial of the Bush administration, which does not even pretend that it treats detainees as human beings–they are "evil." Of course, this is the necessary component which distinguished Stalin's conduct from a Crusade–Stalin did not perceive his genocidal actions as serving the godly against the ungodly, nor that he was in a holy cause or told by God to take the country's helm.

[949] Aleksandr I. Solzhenitsyn, The Gulag Archipelago: 1918-1956, Volume One, pp.100-101. Stalin also employed the state bureaucracy and the terrified loyalty of subordinates to accomplish his purposes without leaving a trail to implicate him, like George W. employed the loyal Gonzales: "...Stalin did not pronounce that final word, and his subordinates had to guess what he wanted....Stalin had to remain innocent, his sacred vestments angelically pure." Ibid., p. 102. This is also presumably the method Bush W. employed to expose Valerie Plame–or would he have Americans believe that on his incredibly tight and loyal ship that 1) two staff, including Karl Rove, violated federal law behind his back, 2) as loyal as they are, they continued in a lie to the President and refused to admit their actions, and 3) he (the president) did not know who leaked this CIA agent's identity to the press, and has not known all this long time? Which is President Bush–incompetent or dishonest?

But more important than Solzhenitsyn's recounting of the legal fictions concocted to justify the denial of human rights in Stalinist Russia, is his warning about the moral or spiritual condition of human kind which permits such barbarity to occur:

> Ideology–that is what gives evildoing its long-sought justification and gives the evildoer the necessary steadfastness and determination. That is the social theory which helps to make his acts seem good instead of bad in his own and others' eyes, so that he won't hear reproaches and curses but will receive praise and honors. That was how the agents of the Inquisition fortified their wills: by invoking Christianity; the conquerors of foreign lands, by extolling the grandeur of their Motherland; the colonizers, by civilization; the Nazis, by race; and the Jacobins (early and late), by equality, brotherhood, and the happiness of future generations.
>
> Thanks to ideology, the twentieth century was fated to experience evildoing on a scale calculated in the millions. This cannot be denied, nor passed over, nor suppressed. How, then, do we dare insist evildoers do not exist? And who was it that destroyed these millions? Without evildoers there would have been no Archipelago....
>
> But the evildoer with ideology does cross [the line the Shakespearean evildoer could not cross]..., and his eyes remain dry and clear....
>
> Evidently evildoing also has a threshold magnitude. Yes, a human being hesitates and bobs back and forth between good and evil all his life. He slips, falls back,

clambers up, repents, things begin to darken again. But just so long as the threshold of evildoing is not crossed, the possibility of returning remains, and he himself is still within reach of our hope. But when, through the density of evil actions, the result either of their own extreme degree or of the absoluteness of his power, he suddenly crosses that threshold, he has left humanity behind, and without, perhaps, the possibility of return.[950]

Is it possible that George W. Bush can draw back over this threshold of evildoing, and simply repent of allowing or causing torture or human rights violations? I pray in Jesus' name that it should be so, and also for those who in error support George W.'s unchristian actions.

The Bush administration's interrogation techniques, as well as its detention of suspects without counsel, trial or any rights of due process, are reminiscent also of the Khmer Rouge of Cambodia:

> Arrest presupposed guilt....The Khmer Rouge utilized a wide range of torture techniques–electric shocks, asphyxiation, immersion in water, forcing the consumption of feces and urine, stringing prisoners up in the air, and prolonged bodily stress–that have echoes today. These brutal methods got results: Most prisoners were eventually willing to confess to almost anything.
>
> Now, as we learn more about Bagram, Abu Ghraib, Guantanamo, and sites of rendition, the violent

---

[950] Ibid., pp. 174, 175.

> practices of the Khmer Rouge warn us that the information extracted through torture is highly unreliable and that those who turn down this dark path start to resemble the evil they are pursuing.[951]

The overwhelming evidence is indeed that torture does not produce reliable information, and so the Bush administration's policies are destroying American goodwill around the world for a failed method which yields dubious results, if any–and for no gain or a loss to the desired policy objective (like NCLB, the Kyoto withdrawal, the Iraq War, trickle down economics, and nuclear proliferation).

National uproar has been caused by the comparison of American conduct under the Bush presidency with the behavior of German World War II Nazis, but what distinguishes German torture from American torture, Bush's (non-Christian) ideological rationalizations from Hitler's? As one writer has observed:

> Here is a German soldier in a World War II film who says that he believes in Hitler: we automatically condemn him, he is a bad sort. There is an American soldier who says that he believes in democracy and that he hates Nazis: we think that he is a good sort. That is too simple. That German soldier might treat an enemy civilian or a prisoner kindly. The American soldier may not. What matters is what they do, how they behave. The ideas of the German and the ideas of the American are not inconsequential; but

---

[951] Alex Hinton, "Lessons from killing fields of Cambodia—30 years on," *The Christian Science Monitor*, April 14, 2005, p. 9.

let me insist, again and again, that what people do
with their ideas is more important than what their
ideas do to them.[952]

America built its reputation, and a favorable world
opinion toward its democratic traditions, on decades of
ethicality–on charitable help to other nations (not just
military aid), on food relief for its enemies after World
War II, on decent treatment of its prisoners, on leading
the world in fighting human rights abuses. The nation
managed to maintain this opinion despite its failed foreign policy in the Middle East, until it invaded Iraq in
response to the completely unrelated 9/11 attacks. The
detention of men and women without trial, and the
approval of the use of interrogation techniques never
before used by the United States, have accomplished the
reverse–a decline in U.S. popularity and in the world's
trust of our democratic model.

But to Christians, there is in fact a glaring difference between the torture committed by Nazis and the
torture and human rights abuses (lack of Geneva Convention protections, indefinite detentions without trial
or counsel, assumption of guilt, relocations to countries
that employ torture) committed by America's government under the direction of Mr. Bush–Adolph Hitler
did not purport to be Christian, did not rise to power
on a Christian platform or supported by Christians,
and therefore did not raise a Christian banner to war.
Consequently, Adolph Hitler, whose rise to power drove

---

[952] John Lukacs, The End of the Twentieth Century and the End of the Modern Age, p.218.

many to God or Jesus in hope for deliverance from the threat of fascism, did not turn human souls away from the truth of Jesus Christ in the manner in which George W. Bush and recent American actions have. Christians are warned in 2 Peter 2:2: "And many shall follow their pernicious ways; by reason of whom the way of truth shall be evil spoken of."[953]

Many Americans have simply scoffed at prison abuse allegations, dismissing such conduct as an acceptable consequence of war. They argue that what America has done to these prisoners is insignificant when compared to the atrocities of other nations in the past. And the 9/11 attacks are often used as a justification, both for torture and for the deaths of civilians. But these arguments are directly against the teachings of Jesus, and America has never found occasion to lower its standards this dramatically before: in World War II, the Germans were working to develop an atomic or nuclear weapon ahead of the allies, and in the Cold War, the Soviet Union threatened the United States with nuclear weapons and a godless, totalitarian ideology, but neither urgency formed a basis for Americans and the allies to debase their own humanity by stooping to the level of torture. As stated in a letter from retired Army General John Shalikashvili and 11 retired military officers to Congress, protesting U.S. abuses in Abu Ghraib and elsewhere:

> "Repeatedly in our past, the United States has confronted foes that, at the time they emerged, posed threats of a scope or nature unlike any we had

---

[953] KJV.

previously faced. But we have been far more steadfast in the past in keeping faith with our national commitment to the rule of law." The letter contends that recent detention and interrogation policies have undermined intelligence-gathering and increased risks facing US troops overseas.[954]

What of "keeping our faith" to Jesus Christ?
George Orwell did not distinguish between ideologies in their capacity to create the conditions for genocide, torture, or oppression. His fiction was too close to modern reality to be taken lightly. In 1984, in a world of constant government surveillance, changing enemies but constant war, a toxic environment, extreme wealth disparity and overpopulation, and a large, bureaucratic government, George Orwell explored the morality of modern man that permitted the employment of technological and industrial methods to torture and kill human beings. Famously, Big Brother and the Party could determine a person's worst fears and then design a torture specifically custom-tailored to that fear, and for that person. The book's dark message, of the failure of modern man to evolve morally and the dangers of the use of mass media and mass production to control populations, has increasingly become reality, especially since George W. Bush took the American helm, with national registration and testing of students, the USA Patriot Act, "moral" justification for neglecting the underclass, the use of the military in domestic police actions, Homeland Security and terror alerts, and a "war on evil."

---

[954] Jane Lampman, "US stand against torture: firm enough?," *The Christian Science Monitor*, January 19, 2005, pp.11, 13.

The message of George Orwell is that the face of man's most hideous evil can be Russian, German, Japanese, Iraqi, Cambodian, Iranian or American; that evil does not discriminate, in that it will infect any people. Christians know this, but do American Christians have a blind eye to their country's current appearance? Are America's Christians blind to unchristian, evil action in their midst because the perpetrators are "Christian Americans"? Is "Christian" a label easily adorned in "the world," or an honor achieved by difficult and earnest action and sacrifice?

For the world envisioned by George Orwell and gradually unfolding in modern American conduct is hardly a Christian haven:

> …war hysteria is continuous and universal in all countries, and such acts as raping, looting, the slaughter of children, the reduction of whole populations to slavery, and reprisals against prisoners which extend even to boiling and burying alive, are looked upon as normal, and, when they are committed by one's own side and not by the enemy, meritorious. But in a physical sense war involves very small numbers of people, mostly highly trained specialists, and causes comparatively few casualties. The fighting, when there is any, takes place on the vague frontiers whose whereabouts the average man can only guess at….

> ….And in the general hardening of outlook that set in round about 1930, practices which had been long abandoned, in some cases for hundreds of years–imprisonment without trial, the use of war

> prisoners as slaves, public executions, the use of hostages and the deportation of whole populations–not only became common again, but were tolerated and even defended by people who considered themselves enlightened and progressive....[955]

Today, America's battles are fought in far-off lands against vague enemies that are not allied with nations, and the news of war crimes by Americans (if reported) does not raise many eyebrows–surely not as many as it should, for America's Christians should be raising more than eyebrows at this conduct–Christian voices must be raised to separate world opinion of Christ from world opinion of Bush, to separate American loyalty to Christ from American loyalty to Bush. But perhaps most of all, Christians must demand that this unrepentant man, who won Christian trust and support for his bid for the Presidency, stop engaging honest, loyal young American men and women to perform horrible, unchristian tasks and then condemn and blame them for that very conduct when it is revealed by people of conscience. Christians empowered George W. Bush in America and in the world, and Christians must reign in their Frankensteinian crusader before he kills any more foreign babies, or tortures any more of God's children, guilty or innocent. America and its Christians must do more than appoint commissions to do studies while two or three scapegoats do brief jail time and the officers and policymakers who directed them fade behind the administration curtain,

---

[955] George Orwell, <u>1984</u>, pp. 153, 168-169.

erasing the trail of responsibility.[956] Americans must demand and exact accountability from all its leaders, but especially its Christian ones.

George W. Bush believes that he has "a charge to keep," that he has been selected by God (an even higher accolade than being a Bush or a Bonesman!) to lead America on a righteous path. He says he believes that he is doing good for the world at personal self-sacrifice, but the more his conduct deviates from unequivocal Christian standards, the more the integrity of his attention to Jesus Christ and His glory is in doubt. George Orwell pondered the motives that drive men to wish to control the destinies of other men: when being tortured, the protagonist of 1984, Winston Smith, is asked to tell his captor (O'Brien) why the Party wants power:

> ...Winston did not speak for another moment or two. A feeling of weariness had overwhelmed him. The faint, mad gleam of enthusiasm had come back into O'Brien's face. He knew in advance what O'Brien would say: that the Party did not seek power for its own ends, but only for the good of the majority. That it sought power because men in the mass were frail, cowardly creatures who could not endure

---

[956] John Kenneth Galbraith has observed that in large bureaucracies, accountability diminishes with increases in scale: "The culture of organization runs strongly to the shifting of problems to others–to an escape from personal mental effort and responsibility....The delegation process...adds ineluctably to the layers of command and to the prestige associated with command....[e]specially in the higher levels of an organization..., diminishing the role of thought itself." The Culture of Contentment, pp. 69, 68. This actually explains the current federal bureaucracy quite accurately–one of the largest bureaucracies in the history of man, with perhaps the least accountability.

liberty or face the truth, and must be ruled over and systematically deceived by others who are stronger than themselves. That the choice for mankind lay between freedom and happiness, and that, for the great bulk of mankind, happiness was better. That the Party[957] was the eternal guardian of the weak, a dedicated sect doing evil that good might come, sacrificing its own happiness to that of others....

"You are ruling over us for our own good," he said feebly. "You believe that human beings are not fit to govern themselves, and therefore—"

He started and almost cried out. A pang of pain had shot through his body. O'Brien had pushed the lever of the dial up to thirty-five.

"That was stupid, Winston, stupid!" he said. "You should know better than to say a thing like that."

He pulled the lever back and continued:

"Now I will tell you the answer to my question. It is this. The Party seeks power entirely for its own sake. We are not interested in the good of others; we are interested solely in power. Not wealth or luxury or long life or happiness; only power, pure power. What pure power means you will understand presently. We are different from all the oligarchies of the past in that we know what we are doing.[958] All the others, even those who resemble ourselves, were cowards and hypocrites. The German Nazis and the Russian Communists came very close to us in their methods,

---

[957] Jesus Christ is the eternal guardian of the weak. No nation and no ideology but Christianity can substitute for Him.
[958] Ah, neo-conservatives!

but they never had the courage to recognize their own motives. They pretended, perhaps they even believed, that they had seized power unwillingly and for a limited time, and that just round the corner there lay a paradise where human beings would be free and equal. We are not like that. We know that no one ever seizes power with the intention of relinquishing it. Power is not a means; it is an end. One does not establish a dictatorship in order to safeguard a revolution; one makes the revolution in order to establish the dictatorship. The object of persecution is persecution. The object of torture is torture. The object of power is power. Now do you begin to understand me?"[959]

Surely Christians see in this passage the despair of man left to self, the void of power without love. But Orwell's search into the motivations for the desire for power raises interesting worldly contrasts to the Christian perspective. Why would a good Christian seek worldly power?[960] God uses imperfect vessels, but those vessels have souls—God does not require the instruments of worldly government or human laws to spread the news of His Son. God's servants work in the trenches

---

[959] George Orwell, <u>1984</u>, pp.216-217. "We are the priests of power," he said. "God is power...." Skull and Bones teaches initiates that they are the world's elite, gods of reason, whose destiny is to wield worldly power. *See* Chapter Ten.

[960] Stephen L. Carter opines in <u>The Culture of Disbelief: How American Law and Politics Trivialize Religious Devotion</u>, that "...religions are at their best when they are forms of resistance. One way of losing the power of resistance is to have the state take it away; another is to surrender it willingly in the rush to become part of the very state against which the religions should ideally serve as a bulwark." p. 82.

with Jesus and the lepers, with Mother Theresa and the poor and ill–not in the corrupt corridors of power, in corporate boardrooms or Wall Street brokerages, the workplaces of the Pharisees.[961] Surely, Christ will answer any knock at his door, but He does not ask His servants to compromise their faith by working in a brothel or by seeking the highest office in worldly government–he who is least is greatest, and he who is greatest is least. Were God to select a mouthpiece to head a Christian nation, then a millionaire, arrogant, Ivy League, Skull & Bones, Texas oilman would indeed be an eye-catcher of a choice, but why have him run for president? The most corrupt institution in the world, the pinnacle of politics, will bend its worldly ways to accommodate a true Christian? The corporate elite and military-industrial powers-that-be would not permit a player who brought his own rules. Christians can only serve one master, and can not walk in both the dark and the light. The place to serve Jesus Christ is in the Body of Christ, not in the Body of American Politics. George W. has not exhibited Christian integrity in his political battles (Plame, O'Neill, Clarke). Only an iron fist in a Christian glove of velvet, always removed from his deeds by the likes of Rove, Rumsfeld, Gonzales, or Cheney. And where is there any effort, ever, even in the trumped up Bush biographies, of an effort by this man, supposedly chosen by God, to save souls?

---

[961] This is not to say that there are not good Christians in these environments, but that these environments are not Christian. Particularly in modern America, corporate boardrooms are bound to an ethic of maximizing profits, perhaps within the bounds of the "law," but rarely driven by any moral code but that of capitalism.

My words may seem harsh to those who support George W. Bush and believe in his integrity. But instead of constantly making excuses for this administration's conduct (or worse, denying that conduct), perhaps more of America's Christians should turn their eyes to their professed Lord Jesus Christ both for prayer to seek truth in this matter, and for moral guidance in what is acceptable conduct for a Christian nation. Consider for instance the following words from the Book of Matthew:

> Watch out, and do not let anyone fool you. Many men, claiming to speak for me,....will fool many people....countries will fight each other....There will be famines and earthquakes everywhere. All these things are like the first pains of childbirth..... Then many false prophets will appear and fool many people. Such will be the spread of evil that many people's love will grow cold....false prophets will appear; they will perform great miracles and wonders in order to deceive even God's chosen people, if possible.... All who take the sword will die by the sword.[962]

Who is trying to fool Christians, he who detains and punishes in violation of both God's and man's laws, or he who admonishes Christians to heed the Gospels? If God says those will come to deceive Christians and they had better be on guard, then those will come who will deceive Americans, and Christians had better be on guard. Who

---

[962] Matthew 24:4, 7, 11, 12, 24; 26:52. TEV

is misleading Christians, he who leads young men and women hastily into war based on contrived evidence, or he who condemns all war as unchristian? He who reorganizes government to provide more worldly wealth to the worldly wealthy, or he who presses government to respond to the needs of the poor, mentally compromised, or dysfunctional?[963] He who advocates consumption and unlimited oil-driven expansion without concern for the crisis created thereby, or he that presses for frugality and conservation? A. W. Tozer observed that "Where faith is defective the result will be inward insensitivity and numbness toward spiritual things. This is the condition of the vast number of Christians today."[964] Unfortunately, though "believing" himself godly, this "inward insensitivity and numbness toward spiritual things" is the condition of George W. Bush today. This is why there is absolutely no glimmer of remorse or repentance in this President, let alone a Christian demonstration of confession that would both model Christian humility and be an actual action of accountability.

Jesus Christ taught his followers to refrain even from the evil of harsh words–He certainly never condoned torture, nor indefinite imprisonment without charges or

---

[963] Matthew 25:43: "I was sick and in prison but you would not take care of me...." TEV. Does anyone contend that Jesus intended to exclude certain categories of prisoner? Is the door to Christ not open to Muslims?
[964] A.W. Tozer, The Pursuit of God: the Human Thirst for the Divine, p. 50.

trial.⁹⁶⁵ <u>The Westminster Dictionary of Christian Ethics</u> contains the following information regarding torture:

> Torture is one of the very few things that are absolutely prohibited in international law....Why should torture be absolutely prohibited? What about the textbook problem of the terrorist who can be forced to reveal the whereabouts of a nuclear bomb only by torture? In theory, one could apply something like just war criteria to argue that torture would be licit in such a case, but in practice legalizing any exceptions would be exploited to legitimize practices going far beyond the hypothetical extreme case.⁹⁶⁶

This is precisely what happened under Bush leadership—"legalizing an exception" in practice was used to extend to many, many people. But though George W. Bush acted quickly to instruct Alberto Gonzales to avoid the strictures of the Geneva Convention and the U.S.

---

⁹⁶⁵ "See that no one pays back wrong for wrong, but at all times make aim to do good to all people." 1 Thess 5:15, TEV. Perhaps George W. will direct Alberto Gonzales to draft a new passage to better clarify what Paul meant by "all people," to exclude "enemy combatants" or those who worship Islam or join al Qaeda as non-human, as "evil." Or perhaps he will dismiss Paul's words as just more political disgruntlement, like Richard Clarke, Joseph Wilson and Paul O'Neill were dismissed and maligned when they all spoke the truth. And many Americans also scorned them and their truth without inquiry, as many will no doubt scorn this book. Who am I to speak for Jesus Christ? Who was Tozer? Who was Chambers? Who was Paul? What did they all do, and what did they all instruct His servants to do? Flip tables, and tell the truth in Christ, not to judge but to liberate. And they all had strong words for weak or false Christians. We are all called to be ministers, and to hold our ministers and each other accountable to our faith, in truth and love always.

⁹⁶⁶ James F. Childress and John Macquarrie, <u>The Westminster Dictionary of Christian Ethics</u>, pp. 627-628.

Constitution, he has not publicly addressed the applicability of the laws of Jesus Christ to the subject policy change. Where are the Christian actions in this behavior by America's president? Where are even the Christian words, as in the Word of the Bible? Because this shift in U.S. policy was clandestine, there was no pretense of Christian reflection; and because the U.S. government and the American legal system are increasingly godless entities, there was certainly no avenue for Christian logic to influence the process. But George W. was not seeking spiritual truth, only a means to an end–the torture memo was not created as a spiritual search, but as a legal tool. Did George W. bring a candle of Christian light into the darkness of the world of politics? Where is the Christianity in this decision-making process? What decision could more vitally require it? Christian words, unchristian actions....

But though Christ's opinion on the use of torture was not sought by the Bush administration when it determined to use the ignorant methodology of the savage, Satan's argument was readily publicized; that the use of evil in the detention and interrogation of adversaries was necessary to accomplish good. Non-Christians may not hold a moral code which would question this–even some unwary Christians may be beguiled in fearful times to acquiesce in such spurious logic. And at least some legal scholars have bought into this slippery slope argument:

> The US is using torture, says Alan Dershowitz of Harvard University Law School, who deplores what he calls the hypocrisy of official statements

on the topic. A better method, he suggests, would be to legitimize torture in limited instances, such as "ticking bomb" scenarios when a prisoner may have information that could prevent an impending disaster.[967]

The Bush administration decided to employ torture to "defend" Americans in a "preemptive" war against a bedraggled army which had no capabilities to travel to America, no weapons that could be fired upon America, and absolutely no ties to the 9/11 terrorist attacks other than those created by Republican propaganda. It decided to employ torture even though the FBI and others have determined that it is not effective. Perhaps it did so thinking it would not be caught. Perhaps it did so with disregard to the safety of American troops or the reputation of America if such conduct became public.

---

[967] Jane Lampman, "US stand against torture: firm enough?," *The Christian Science Monitor*, January 19, 2005, pp. 11, 13. It would be amusing that liberal law professors supported the (immoral) limited use of torture, if it weren't so terrifying. But even in this article's language are already seen the seeds of the moral decay that inevitably attends the use of torture–torture would be "legitimate" (making the immoral moral?) "when a prisoner *may* have information…." [italics added]. How broad is the potential list of people who "may" have "information" (an intangible the existence of which cannot be known without torture)? What is "may"? (Subjective–Big Brother and the thought police, or "Jaguaryevich" and the equality of trial and interrogation for reliability because they are both "relative," i.e. subjective.) Who decides who is on the list? Who decides what is an acceptable technique of torture? Who decides when the torture shall be discontinued because the recipient has experienced a level of pain bordering on that akin to organ failure or death? Does America really need its untrustworthy federal government detaining human beings indefinitely who "may" have "information," picking into human brains and psyches like Big Brother or Stalin?

And when the cases of abuse did become public, the Bush administration response was two-pronged: blame the cases of abuse on the deviant behavior of a few pawn grunts; and redraft the revised torture language (that didn't encourage the bad apples to rot) so that there is still no international, Constitutional, or Christian standard applicable. The "moral" response of torture-proponents to complaints of ambiguity is the only one available without the wisdom and guidance of Jesus Christ, the one specifically repudiated in <u>The Westminster Dictionary of Christian Ethics</u>:

> Yet, overall, the [new] policy still remains ambiguous. Supporters say that is appropriate, even necessary.[968] If the US had someone in custody who knew about an imminent terrorist attack–say, one involving a

---

[968] It is "necessary" that the policy remain ambiguous? What enormous faith in government and man. The Nazis had faith in the necessity of secrecy and ambiguity, as did Stalin. Where is this in the Bible? As Ann Coulter observed of the Clinton administration, "The White House's secretive actions could not help but create the impression that there was something worthy of being kept secret." (<u>High Crimes and Misdemeanors: The Case Against Bill Clinton</u>, p. 185) What then of Cheney and energy policy, of the Gonzales memos, or of Bush Jr.'s silent lips on Skull & Bones? What of the wiretapping of American citizens, which so outraged George W. when it became public? GW Bush is the most secretive president in US history, and resists public accountability. He wasn't nearly as upset over the Plame incident, in which laws were broken by him or members of his Cabinet: he reserved his fury for when his own law-breaking was "leaked."

nuclear device–it would want to use aggressive tactics to get that information out of him.[969]

There is always a seemingly rational argument to support sin—even to support torture by the government of the United States of America, and even while that government is being tightly controlled by a person who purports to be devoted to the rules of God's law, to Jesus Christ. The wolf in sheep's clothing who comes in the end times will be like all false prophets, masking unchristian actions with Christian words, leading good Christians astray and non-Christians to judge Christ by such evil hypocrisy.

---

[969] Faye Bowers, "In US stand on torture, more trials to come," *The Christian Science Monitor*, January 18, 2005, p.3. This statement once again reveals the deceptive chicken-and-egg nature of what sounds like a reasonable argument: it assumes the rational foundation for torture, when the existence of that foundation is unknown until after torture is administered (if then). The problem is, and the door immediately opens to abuse and evil, where the government sets up a massive bureaucracy to "take [people into] custody who knew about an imminent terrorist attack": how does the government create rules to determine what a person knows? We're back to Big Brother mind-reading again.

Chapter 10

BONESMAN OR CHRISTIAN?

> ....fierce wolves will come among you, and they will not spare the flock. The time will come when some men from your own group will tell lies to lead the believers away after them.
>
> ....You are to open their eyes and turn them from the darkness to the light and from the power of Satan to God....
>
> —Acts 20:29, 30; 26:18. TEV

George W. Bush's history of association with an unchristian, dark cult is most likely of no consequence to those who, because they do not believe in God, are not fearful of "superstitious" dark forces–such worldly associations are viewed as akin to Halloween dress-up or spooky fraternity pranks. But even to these people Mr. Bush's unchristian conduct is instructive as to his persistent, sly dishonesty.

Christians, however, have sworn allegiance to the Son of God–to be true to Him, to be honest in His representation, and (in His love) to hold other Christians accountable to His standards (for their own salvation as well as the defense of His Church). And because the Bible–the Word of God and the Law of Christianity–is clear and direct as to what are the standards of God and Christ, Christians learn that the occult is not for idle dabbling, and part of the early transformation of any sincere follower of Jesus is a renunciation of any such ties, along with other past worldly sinful associations. But George W. has, rather clumsily, failed ever to take Christian responsibility for this aspect of his past. Though Christian repentance is a personal experience between each person and Christ, Christian leaders who have widely-publicized ties to Satanic cults have a duty to publicly repent of those contacts and to ask Jesus for forgiveness. George W. Bush, champion of the religious right, has failed to do this.

Perhaps the rest of God's souls on the planet Earth, ignored as they are by a majority of Americans, might also take exception to such associations in the leader of the free world and of the world's lone remaining superpower, especially if that leader talks of a "crusade" or invades impoverished but oil-rich countries that America previously armed, or directs thousands of soldiers to engage in the systematic torture of secretly hidden captives, all the while lying to the world and Americans that such actions are for good, for freedom and liberation, for safety and preserving the American way of life. Christians should be concerned about the perception of Christ that these cumulative actions portray.

Christianity and Satan-worship do not mix. Of course, even non-Christians readily perceive this glaring truth, but Christians are cautioned over and over to avoid dark forces, and to avoid those who commune with such evil–in the Bible, "[a]ll forms of witchcraft and demonolatry are explicitly denounced."[970]

An examination of the available evidence about the Skull & Bones cult reveals that this organization is no place for a Christian. Skull & Bones has its roots in German demonic worship, in the Illuminati: "Many witches, wizards and Satanists are involved in a hierarchy of four stages and perhaps a fifth, known as the Illuminati."[971] Not only was George W.'s father, George Herbert Walker

---

[970] Kenneth Boa, <u>Cults, World Religions and the Occult</u>, p. 148.
[971] Ibid., p. 149.

526 CHRISTIAN WORDS, UNCHRISTIAN ACTIONS

Bush, a Bonesman,[972] but so were both his maternal and fraternal grandfathers.[973] And many of George's business and political contacts on the way to personal fortune and the presidency were Bonesmen. John Kerry is a Bonesman, ensuring in the 2004 election that a Bonesman would sit in the White House (the first time ever that both presidential candidates have been Bonesmen).[974] The American people, and Christian Americans in particular, have a right to accountability from their highest elected or appointed leaders, but to date there has

---

[972] Texe Marrs, in <u>Dark Majesty: The Secret Brotherhood and the Thousand Points of Light</u>, p. 192, goes so far as to (convincingly) assert that the senior Bush was assisted by his Bones contacts to attain political office, even at the expense of those Bonesmen's supposed ties to established religion, including Christianity. He also records this information regarding the elder Bush:

> ....In 1981, Bush [<u>Sr.</u>] asked Potter Stewart to swear him in as Vice President of the United States at his inauguration ceremony. Stewart was delighted to accommodate his fellow Bonesman. Through these two men, the Brotherhood was to send the entire conspiratorial network a powerful symbolic message of harmony and favored status accorded brother elitists. To reinforce this symbolic connection, the Bible from the altar of the Masonic lodge of New York City, first used in the inauguration of George Washington, was transported all the way to the White House steps so that Bush could lay his hand on it and be sworn in. Unlike other King James versions of the Bible, the Masonic version has an introductory section which meticulously explains that Masonry is *not* a Christian society but, instead, supports *all* religions and creeds." (at pp. 193-194.)

[973] David Aikman, <u>A Man of Faith: the Spiritual Journey of George W. Bush</u>, p. 21.

[974] How was a Christian supposed to exercise his or her vote in a Christian manner in an election between two Bonesmen?–This is a gift, a clear sign for Christians not to seek justice, truth, or Christianity in modern America's political process. It also echoes the secular crisis facing America, in which both parties have betrayed their constituencies.

been little open discussion of Mr. Bush's lifelong, and apparently continuing, association with Skull & Bones, nor of what being a member of that organization entails. Mr. Bush has always ducked this simple inquiry, noting in his autobiography (in keeping with the laws of Skull & Bones, that their sinister dealings not be revealed) that "My senior year I joined Skull and Bones, a secret society so secret I can't say anything more."[975]

What is known of Skull & Bones should greatly concern Christians who seek truth, because what is reflected is an organization with extremely unchristian origins, no positive teaching, and an apostate theology. Had he been born again as a Christian and then converted to Satan worship, George W. might not have been embraced so warmly by America's Christian Right. Having created his personal theology in the reverse order, what guarantee is there that he does not still serve his old master, a wolf in sheep's clothing–for Satan worship, under the guise of faith in "self" or "reason," permits its adherents to proclaim any other of the world's religions, including Christianity. But the Bonesman is sworn not to do two things–to embrace any one religion in exclusion to others, or to renounce his life-bonds to the Skull & Bones cult: like the mafia, once you're in, you cannot resign. And George W. has kept that oath–he has evaded renouncing the group, and he has hidden behind the excuse of politics as to why he never mentions Jesus in

---

[975] George W. Bush, <u>A Charge To Keep</u>, p. 47. Mr. Bush cleverly attempts to have his cake and eat it too–to impress potential supporters with the exclusivity and elitism of his membership, without renouncing his ties thereto, and without revealing what that mysterious honor is supposed to mean on his resume.

his speeches, but instead extols all religions as great and wondrous.[976] Thomas M. Freiling gushes of Bush's faith that Bush "…has mentioned the Almighty in literally hundreds of speeches and proclamations,"[977] but in the thirty-four Bush speeches reprinted in Mr. Freiling's book, covering some 250 pages, Jesus is mentioned by name only two times.[978]

All writers agree that many of Skull & Bones' secrets are still unknown, but what *is* known is disturbing and commands Christian vigilance. Alexandra Robbins, in <u>Secrets of the Tomb: Skull and Bones, The Ivy League, and the Hidden Paths of Power</u>, which Bush W. biographer David Aikman dubs "an informative

---

[976] "For sound diplomatic reasons, President Bush cannot state publicly a view of Israel that might be considered theological." David Aikman, <u>A Man of Faith: The Spiritual Journey of George W. Bush</u>, p. 126. I.e., he must walk in the dark and the light, place Christ behind him on the political podium: the faith he proclaims does not animate his actions. Christ must be first and last for Christians, the Alpha and Omega–but not for politicians, for they are somehow granted "a Christian accountability exemption." And not for Bonesmen, because they have sworn that self and "reason" shall always be their priority, and walking in the dark (of politics) and at the same time in the light (of feigned Christianity) is not only acceptable, *it is from whence they draw their power.*

[977] Thomas M. Freiling, <u>George W. Bush on God & Country</u>, p. 13.

[978] At p. 83 ("For many people, Jesus' admonition to care "for the least of these" is an admirable moral teaching. For many Baptists, it is a way of life.") and at p. 97 ("For many people, Jesus' admonition to care for "the least of these" is an admirable moral teaching. For many Hispanic Americans, it's a way of life.") Besides demonstrating how shallowly Bush employs Jesus to win votes (from Baptists and Hispanics, in these cases), these quotes, especially in view of Bush tax and budget policies that have dramatically favored the wealthy over the poor, raise the contrast of Bush's own actions with the teachings of Christ. When will George demonstrate the Christian way of life he extols, rather than the simplistic "admirable moral teaching" lukewarm Christianity he has employed in American public policy? Christian words, unchristian actions….

history of Skull and Bones,"[979] writes about how Skull and Bones members at debates would commonly employ "…the Yorick, the skull divided into compartments from which the initiates drink blood,"[980] and how "Skull and Bones is deferential to Eulogia; at functions, a speaker addresses the membership by beginning, "Most Sacred Goddess Eulogia, Uncle Toby, and Knights of Eulogia,""[981] and they sing "sacred anthems" which include lyrics such as :

> The Soul is too Ethereal
> Too viewless, light and airy.
> Its home is not on the Earth at all
> Of day it soon grows weary.
> The flesh with the Devil is aye in league
> His sway it too often owns, boys–
> Then let it go–who cares a fig
> For aught but the Skull & Bones boys.[982]

Of no concern to Christians? George W. Bush dismisses his Skull & Bones commitments as "a chance to meet fourteen new friends,"[983] but neglects to mention that they drank blood, lay naked in a sexually perverse coffin ritual, worshipped unholy idols, and sang songs worshipping evil and darkness while banging (human?)

---

[979] David Aikman, <u>A Man of Faith: The Spiritual Journey of George W. Bush</u>, p. 45.
[980] Alexandra Robbins, <u>Secrets of the Tomb: Skull and Bones, the Ivy League and the Hidden Paths of Power</u>, p. 134.
[981] Ibid., p. 132.
[982] Ibid., p.149. Written in 1843.
[983] George W. Bush, <u>A Charge To Keep</u>, p. 47.

bones on the table.[984] Unconfirmed rumor has it that George W.'s grandfather Bonesman and Nazi financier,[985] Prescott Bush, obtained the Bonesmen's most prized and "sacred" relic, Geronimo's skull, as an Army Captain in late May 1918.[986]

Ms. Robbins also records of Skull & Bones the following:

> One major difference between Skull and Bones and the other secret societies is that Bones does not use its wealth and connections to help the community.... Skull and Bones does not just condone stealing, it actually encourages it....For Bonesmen, "crooking" doesn't exactly feel like stealing. With a kleptomaniacal thrill, the knights rationalize that anything they take they are taking as a conquest for the society. Crooking is a light-hearted activity that is viewed within the society as just another Skull and Bones tradition, in tribute to the goddess who inspires them....[In a Skull and Bones marriage ceremony

---

[984] Alexandra Robbins, <u>Secrets of the Tomb: Skull and Bones, the Ivy League and the Hidden Paths of Power</u>, p. 138. *See also*, Texe Marrs, <u>Dark Majesty: The Secret Brotherhood and the Magic of a Thousand Points of Light</u>, Chapter 11.

[985] "...Hitler's financier stowed $3 million in the Union Banking Corporation, a bank that counted amongst its seven directors Prescott Bush."; "Through these companies, Skull and Bones provided financial backing to Adolf Hitler because the society then followed a Nazi–and now follows a neo-Nazi–doctrine." Alexandra Robbins, <u>Secrets of the Tomb: Skull and Bones, The Ivy League and the Hidden Paths of Power</u>, pp. 188, 6. *See* Texe Marrs, <u>Dark Majesty: The Secret Brotherhood and the Magic of a Thousand Points of Light</u>, pp. 202-203, for a more detailed discussion of this subject.

[986] Ibid., p. 144-145. There is a quite detailed historical account of this excursion in Robbins' book, un-provable but allegedly provided by a Bonesman.

partly witnessed in the 1960s,] the Bonesmen wore black, hooded robes and intoned chants in strange languages....You can't resign from Skull and Bones. You are a member for life....The patriarchs [of Skull and Bones] are the publicists, leaking gossip to the columnists; they are the politicians, spinning stories as distractions; they are the magicians, directing patter to enhance the sleight of hand....They adopted the numerical symbol 322 because their group was the second chapter of the German organization and founded in 1832. They worshipped the goddess Eulogia, celebrated pirates, and plotted an underground conspiracy to rule the world....The secret society is now, as one historian admonishes, 'an international mafia'...unregulated and all but unknown. In its quest to create a New World Order that restricts individual freedoms and places ultimate power solely in the hands of a small cult of wealthy, prominent families, Skull and Bones has already succeeded in infiltrating nearly every major research, policy, financial, media, and government institution in the country. Skull and Bones, in fact, has been running the United States for years....A rebel will not make Skull and Bones; nor will anyone whose background in any way indicates that he will not sacrifice for the greater good of the larger organization....No one has publicly breathed a word about his Skull and Bones membership, ever....Skull and Bones' corporate shell, the Russell Trust Association, owns nearly all of the university's real estate, as well as most of the land in Connecticut. Skull and Bones has controlled Yale's faculty and campus publications so that students cannot speak openly about it. "Year by year," the campus's only anti-society publication stated during its brief tenure in 1873, "the deadly evil is growing."....The knights (as the student members are called) learn quickly that their allegiance to the society must supersede all else: family, friendships, country, God. They are taught that once they get out into the world, they are expected to reach positions of prominence so that they can further elevate the society's status and help promote the standing of their fellow Bonesmen....Skull and Bones members control the wealth of the Rockefeller, Carnegie, and Ford families.[987]

Additionally, this author notes of Skull and Bones that George H. W. Bush used its connections[988] to obtain loans for Saddam Hussein in "the national interest": Bush Sr. favored helping Saddam "build a pipeline to Jordan in order to circumvent Iran's blockade of Persian

---

[987] Alexandra Robbins, <u>Secrets of the Tomb: Skull and Bones, the Ivy League and the Hidden Paths of Power</u>, pp. 141, 147, 147-148, 156, 199, 200, 3-4, 4, 5, 6.

[988] These connections were established through BCCI, of which Texe Marrs records that John Kerry acted while U.S. Senator to quell investigations into this corrupt international bank (pp. 188-189); and that BCCI was "[t]he preferred bank of Philippine despot Ferdinand Marcos, Iraq's Saddam Hussein, Panama's Manual Noriega and Columbia's murderous Medellin drug cartel, BCCI also serviced the Central Intelligence Agency.... Closer to home, there are charges the bank was used by the CIA as a link to Nicaraguan Contras, Afghan rebels and a host of cloak-and-dagger operatives overseas." <u>Dark Majesty: The Secret Brotherhood and the Magic of a Thousand Points of Light</u>, pp. 53-54. Of course, George H. W. Bush must be quite aware of the dealings of BCCI with the CIA, having headed the CIA himself, another well-placed Bonesman.

Gulf ports."[989]; that the Taft family is "the one family with more Bones members than the Bushes."[990]; that the society's formal name is "the Brotherhood of Death"[991]; that the group "fought for slavery"[992]; that "this society also encourages grave robbing."[993]; and that "Eulogia" is "the Greek goddess of eloquence."[994]

Kevin Phillips asserts that "Skull and Bones was an especially powerful initiation into the etiquette of keeping secrets and declining to discuss one's activities with outsiders,"[995] and records that "at Yale, "the most legendary of all college clubs was Skull and Bones. To be tapped by Bones in that era was akin to canonization....The clocks [at Bones] were set five minutes fast to symbolize that Bonesmen started life a leg up." "[996]

---

[989] Robbins, Secrets of the Tomb: Skull and Bones, the Ivy League and the Hidden Paths of Power, pp. 174, 174 (footnote). It is amazing that God created the bulk of the world's oil in the region of the world described in the Bible as Armageddon, which region over time has come to be inhabited by followers of one of the world's great religions, Islam; and that precious, vast, oil "wealth," worldly energy, is most greatly needed by the followers of one of the world's other great religions, Christianity, who have wed themselves to the world in depending on oil and money before God.
[990] Ibid., p. 180.
[991] Ibid., p. 3.
[992] Ibid., p. 7.
[993] Ibid., p. 7.
[994] Ibid., p, 84. Texe Marrs notes (in Dark Majesty: The Secret Brotherhood and the Magic of a Thousand Points of Light, at p. 205) that "Religious heresy seems to be a staple of the alumni of Skull & Bones."
[995] Kevin Phillips, American Dynasty: Aristocracy, Fortune, and the Politics of Deceit in the House of Bush, p. 198.
[996] Ibid., p.26, quoting Isaacson and Thomas, *The Wise Men*, p. 29.

Ominously, Skull and Bones was originally formed as a branch of a German society.[997] Its founder, William H. Russell,

> ...came from an inordinately wealthy family that ran one of America's most despicable business institutions of the nineteenth century: Russell and Company, an opium empire....While in Germany, Russell befriended the leader of an insidious German secret society that hailed the death's head as its logo; he soon became caught up in this group, itself a sinister outgrowth of the notorious eighteenth-century society the Illuminati. When Russell returned to the United States, he found an atmosphere so Anti-Masonic that even his beloved Phi Beta Kappa, the honor society, had been unceremoniously stripped of its secrecy. Incensed, Russell rounded up a group of the most promising students in his class—including Alphonso Taft, the future secretary of war, attorney general, minister to Austria, ambassador to Russia, and father of future president William Howard Taft—and out of vengeance constructed the most powerful secret society the United States has ever known.[998]

Texe Marrs also warns against the machinations of the Skull & Bones men. In <u>Dark Majesty: The Secret Brotherhood and the Magic of a Thousand Points of Light</u>, Marrs outlines from a spiritual or Christian perspective the ungodly philosophy of the Illuminati, which

---

[997] Texe Marrs, <u>Dark Majesty: The Secret Brotherhood and the Magic of a Thousand Points of Light</u>, p. 82.
[998] Alexandra Robbins, <u>Secrets of the Tomb: Skull and Bones, the Ivy League and the Hidden Paths of Power</u>, p. 3.

ties in strikingly with the practices and teachings of its branch, Skull and Bones:

> These men, Illuminati doctrine holds, are those who are endowed with something called "reason." The man whose sole god is Reason has himself become a superman, a type of deity....They practice a pagan religion which acknowledges and venerates the ancient sun god; yet they claim that all gods are the same and that their ritualistic worship of ancient deities is only symbolic....While Lucifer, the "light bearer," is in reality their ultimate deity, most do not directly profess him as Lord....The illumined person is considered one who is able to wield the spiritual energies of both sides of reality—the good and the evil, the light and the darkness. Such a man becomes superman. He becomes his own deity, a master magician, a prince among princes, and a king over many....Since the Illuminati have no special regard for or devotion to any specific deity, it stands to reason that Christianity—or any other organized religion—holds no special merit either. Therefore, the Secret Brotherhood favors no organized religion, but instead recognizes all as coequal....This universalist, all-encompassing view of deity means that the initiate of the Secret Brotherhood is welcome to join and participate in any religion he chooses. But what he cannot do is claim exclusivity or uniqueness of that religion. This would be the ultimate heresy for tolerant, universalist illumined man.
>
> Thus, a brother of the Order can freely profess Christianity and Christ; he can talk a good game of "Christianity" and show all outward respect and

fervent adherence to the God of the Bible. But in fact, he is not worshipping the same Christ and God as the true Christian, nor does he hold the Bible in the same high, exalted regard.[999]

This chilling description is precisely warned against in the Bible. Paul cautions Christians: "Remember that there will be difficult times in the last days. People will.... hold to the outward form of our religion, but reject its real power. Keep away from such people."[1000] To this narcissistic, apostate creed can be contrasted the Christian ethic of meekness and true humility before God: "Who made you superior to others?....We are the scum of the earth to this very moment."[1001]

And where better to locate such an organization than in the spiritually dead, ultra-liberal former Christian institution of Yale University? William F. Buckley, Jr. summarized the moral decay of Yale, and the resultant compromise and thus diminution of Christian faith at that institution, in <u>God and Man at Yale</u>:

> Such a utilitarian conception of Christianity, coupled with this brand of self-effacement and steadfast refusal to proclaim Christianity as the true religion (which is what all genuine Christian leaders proclaim it to be, thus committing themselves logically to the proposition that other religions are untrue) is a sample of the adulteration of religion to the point that it becomes nothing more than the basis for

---

[999] Texe Marrs, <u>Dark Majesty: The Secret Brotherhood and the Magic of a Thousand Points of Light</u>, pp. 211, 213, 215.
[1000] 2 Timothy 3:1,2,5, TEV.
[1001] 1 Corinthians 4:7, TEV.

"my most favorite way of living." The instincts are fine, and a good life is inevitable for such persons, but so long as what they profess can be subscribed to wholeheartedly by an atheist, we have not, really, got religion at all.[1002]

This is the condition of much of what is accepted by modern Americans as "Christian Living," in which people pay lip service to Christ, but true belief has not entered their lives. It is also the condition of spiritual vulnerability most prized by Satan, and which is inculcated at Yale through Skull and Bones membership.

One of numerous well-timed (for the re-election campaign) "Christian" biographies of George W. Bush notes that "[t]hough George W. certainly kept in touch with some of his fellow Bonesmen, he has affected an almost insouciant unawareness of the institution's recent or current activities….George W. responded to a question about Bones by ABC News by saying: "Does it still exist? The thing is so secret that I'm not even sure it still exists." "[1003] This reflects both the deceptiveness and dishonesty of this self-proclaimed Christian president—and what a thing to lie about. Mr. Bush avoided this question by feigned ignorance, answering a question with a question, while he knows full well that this almost two hundred year old institution did not disband or dissolve—he employed his own and his family's Skull and

---

[1002] At pp. 25-26.
[1003] David Aikman, A Man of faith: The Spiritual Journey of George W. Bush, p. 45.

Bones connections[1004] over and over again in his failed oil ventures and other business enterprises, and to climb politically.[1005] His father still visits the "Tomb," as Skull and Bones' New Haven meeting place is called.[1006]

But rather than renounce or condemn his Satan-worshipping past, Mr. Bush has deflected questions about Skull and Bones by playing dumb. Also, in 2004 he employed his bevy of revisionist writers to create a spiritual smokescreen between his unchristian conduct and the

---

[1004] Texe Marrs reports of such connections that "older Skull & Bones families have formed blood alliances with wealthy families such as the Rockefellers," quoting Fritz Sprinmeister's "thoroughly documented book," Be Wise as Serpents.

[1005] See, e.g., Bill Minutaglio, First Son: George W. Bush and the Bush Family Dynasty, in which the author recounts the litany of Bush and Walker names in Skull & Bones' membership rolls (p. 103); that Skull & Bones "...had evolved, above all else in the sometimes uncertain times, into a business network–a ready resource for big investment capital and a source of stock-buying advice and management jobs." (p. 24); that rumor had it that George H. W. Bush had personally "tapped" his son for Skull & Bones, reflecting the solemn commitment of the Bush family to this supposedly non-existent network: "...the symbolism of the story is what is really important, the very possibility that George W.'s father might have personally urged the hesitant first son to stay the Bush-Walker course, not to veer from his legacy, his destiny." (p.105); and that "Bush was at his tomb every Thursday and Sunday night." (p. 105). And yet, Mr. Bush continues to pretend that the most exclusive club in the country–in which his family has been more involved than almost any other, which was part of his "legacy" and "destiny"–has had no impact on his views or provided numerous business and political contacts: "Does it still exist? The thing is so secret that I'm not even sure that it still exists." Skull & Bones met, sacrilegiously, on Sundays, and included regular Satanic rituals–of course he'd like to avoid recognition of such contacts, but he wants also to eat his cake, and continue to benefit from those very connections. Christian words, unchristian actions.

[1006] "...his father ...was at a Bones Tomb celebration as recently as 1998." David Aikman, A Man of Faith: The Spiritual Journey of George W. Bush, p. 45.

American people whose votes he sought to curry. David Aikman was one of those authors. In a high-sounding tome called <u>A Man of Faith: The Spiritual Journey of George W. Bush</u>, with the ubiquitous propagandistic cover photo of a pensive George W. with an American flag in the background, Mr. Aikman dismissed Bush's flirtation with Skull and Bones:

> In his junior year, George W. was "tapped" (invited by existing membership) for Skull and Bones, the well-known Yale senior-year secret society that was founded in 1832 and has been the focus of wild, indeed sometimes paranoid, conspiracy theories ever since. Skull and Bones is the most famous of the Yale societies, which admit a dozen or so juniors as lifetime members....The prestige of Skull and Bones membership and the fear of its alleged power among many of the society's critics are products of the secrecy in which the society has operated from the outset and the unmistakable achievement of generation upon generation of Bonesmen[1007]....The Skull and Bones initiation ritual—which appears never to have been fully and credibly penetrated by outsiders—does seem to involve some hocus-pocus

---

[1007] Or perhaps this "fear of alleged powers" is grounded in solid Christian doctrine–the Bible is ignored in Mr. Aikman's excuse-making for Skull and Bones, and those who would raise concern about dark worship are dismissed as "paranoid" conspiracy theorists. Perhaps integrity would dictate that Mr. Aikman address the specific and undisputed facts from what he calls an "informative history of Bonesmen" (Alexandra Robbins' Book) or other writings, which summarize a host of evil, gothic rituals and practices.

ceremonials,[1008] but almost certainly[1009] not of any genuinely "spiritual"[1010] significance. It focuses on stripping initiates of any pretence or barriers of reserve about who they really are[1011]—a process that, in its turn, is likely to reinforce a sense of

---

[1008] What deceptive understatement! The descriptions of these dark rituals are uncontested, so the initiation ritual in fact includes Satanic ritual–it doesn't just "seem" to. And the worship of self and demons, which in fact goes on in the world and is specifically described repeatedly in the Bible, is dismissed by this non-Christian writer as "hocus-pocus ceremonials." Could George W. find no Christian writers to write his "Christian" biography? How is the title served, "the spiritual journey of George W. Bush," if Mr. Bush's life is re-painted as a Christian one, and his "spiritual journey" through an ancient Satan-worshipping sect is dismissed simply as "hocus-pocus"? In the trademark Bush deception, Mr. Bush gets to have his cake and eat it too–he is a supposedly Christian man who worships God, but his intimate associations with evil are dismissed as unreal: is God real or not? Is evil real or not? Is baptism *real*, but sacrifices inside of pentagrams are "*hocus-pocus*"?

[1009] This is more than surmise–it is fabrication. Hollywood horror-movie rituals have hellish scenes akin to those described as occurring in the Tomb: thus these rituals "almost certainly" *do* possess genuine "spiritual" significance.

[1010] Why is this in quotation marks? All things of this world have genuinely spiritual significance.

[1011] Actually, more than barriers are stripped, and Aikman has once again glossed over, even re-defined, the "genuinely "spiritual" significance" of these activities. In actual fact, as part of the initiation ceremony the initiates "...lie naked in coffins, masturbate, and reveal their innermost sexual secrets. After this cleansing the Bonesmen give the initiates robes to represent their new identities as individuals with a higher purpose." Alexandra Robbins, <u>Secrets of the Tomb: Skull and Bones, the Ivy League and the Hidden Paths of Power</u>, p. 5. *See also* Bill Minutaglio, <u>First Son: George W. Bush and the Bush Family Dynasty</u>, p.23. This unchristian, sinful indulgence is transformed by Aikman to be "stripping initiates of any pretence or barriers of reserve about who they really are," a worldly interpretation he concocted, and which makes no theological sense (though it makes excuse for Bush W.).

bonding[1012] among the fifteen "knights," as the newly tapped members are called, for the rest of their time at Yale and, for many Bonesmen,[1013] for the rest of their lives....Bush's ambivalence[1014] about Skull and Bones probably[1015] is in part explained by the general suspicion of alleged East Coast supra-governmental conspiracies against American freedoms concocted by Ivy League elitists like Bonesmen, by members of the New York-based Council on Foreign Relations,

---

[1012] Christians call this "sense of bonding" soul-ties, and such ties are in this context unchristian and Satanic. True acceptance of Jesus Christ requires a sincere severing of all such ties. Contrast this with Aikman's description of Bush's subsequent Christian ties as "deep and lasting spiritual relationships."

[1013] For all Bonesmen, according to Robbins and their own oaths.

[1014] Deliberate deception, not ambivalence.

[1015] This is surmise—in writing the biography, did Aikman ever *ask* his subject what were his motivations, rather than fill in his own interpretation of the man's entire life with "probablys" and "almost certainlys"?v

or by the Trilateral Commission[1016].…There are two other possible explanations for Bush's seeming lack of interest in the secret society of his senior year at Yale.[1017] One is that his own Christian experience later in life, an experience replete with deep and lasting spiritual relationships over many years with close Christian friends, has eclipsed whatever friendship bonding occurred at Skull and Bones.[1018] The second

---

[1016] So Bush doesn't think Skull and Bones no longer exists, he just wishes to distance himself from the "conspiracy theories" that attend to it? Then why doesn't he simply renounce his connections to any such activity or entity? What has he got to lose? And why did he refuse to testify under oath before his own 9/11 Commission? "After all, a conspiracy occurs in secret and the thugs who perpetrate it always do their best to keep their hideous acts under concealment. Naturally, they would attempt to downplay and discredit any talk of conspiracy." Texe Marrs, <u>Dark Majesty: The Secret Brotherhood and the Magic of a Thousand Points of Light</u>, p. 59. David Aikman assists in such an effort, calling people who question the Bush family ties to the Council on Foreign Relations or Skull and Bones "conspiracy theorists." Marrs (and the Bible) foretold of such people, that "[t]hey would encourage the media to snicker at the conspiracy "theorists" among us. They would teach the media to proclaim that all of this is simply "wild talk." Crazy stories invented by strange people who need such mind games for entertainment during long, lonely, cold winter nights or steamy, hot summers." (Marrs, p. 59) And Mr. Aikman alleges that these conspiracy theories were "concocted" by the Council on Foreign Relations, the Trilateral Commission, or Bonesmen: were they? Is there evidence of such concoctions? Why would they do such a thing?

[1017] Or maybe yet another–i.e., he is a member of a secret society, and feigns a lack of interest because that society's nefarious activities are unchristian, elitist, and secret. But despite Alexandra Robbins' detailed descriptions of Skull and Bones practices, Aikman apparently fails to see even the "possibility" that Bush is still an active Bonesman who wishes to maintain the secrecy and low Bonesman profile to which he swore an oath long ago.

[1018] Then why can't America's devout Christian President say so himself? Of course, this sounds like baloney, given that George has maintained his Skull and Bones contacts through the same period.

is George W.'s apparently lifelong[1019] distaste for the pretensions of much of the predominantly liberal world-view of many of the students and faculty on Ivy League campuses.[1020]

Mr. Bush's book-writing servants conducted an effective public relations campaign in 2004 to polish Mr. Bush's spiritual credentials with history re-writes and specious logic like Mr. Aikman's.[1021] Paul Kengor, who wrote God and George W. Bush: a spiritual life, never even mentions Bush's stint at Skull and Bones in his supposed account of Bush's "spiritual life." How nice to control a book so that it appears objective but only presents the asset side of the subject's spiritual balance sheet. Are America's Christians really so easily fooled by such patent propaganda? Does anyone read these books at all, let alone critically, or is the objective

---

[1019] Apparently not through those parts of his life spent at Andover, Yale, Harvard, at Delta Kappa Epsilon, and in Skull and Bones. And Mr. Bush's alleged "distaste" for pretensions apparently does not extend to his penchant for Cadillacs and wasteful, gala balls.

[1020] David Aikman, A Man of Faith: the Spiritual Journey of George W. Bush, pp.44, 45, 46. This does not jibe though with the tremendous Ivy League influence with which this president has surrounded himself: Scooter Libby attended both Andover and Yale, and Paul Wolfowitz was a Yale professor. *See* "A Rough Road for Scooter?" *U.S. News & World Report*, October 31, 2005, p. 16.

[1021] Aikman's embarrassing stretches to impute faith to Bush while he was a partying playboy include observations like this one: while at Yale, "…George W. even then seemed to have an interest in Christian things. He kept a copy of The Living Bible open by his bedside in his parents' home in Houston." (p. 42) Mr. Aikman "seems" to accept this as spiritual, but leaving your Bible home while you go away for a year is hardly religious devotion (no matter what page is left open), especially when one has gone away to worship in unchristian, heretical rituals. Mr. Aikman repeatedly grasps at such "spiritual" straws.

accomplished simply by coupling the words "faith," "God," or "spiritual" with a picture of a pious-looking George W. Bush on the cover, using images without substance. Paul Kengor filled some 350 pages of paper with biographical information supporting President (and then-candidate) Bush as a devout Christian, without ever even addressing years of unrepentant, intimate contacts and a deep family involvement in an elitist Satanic cult like Skull & Bones.

Stephen Mansfield, another Bush spiritual propagandist with absolutely no theological qualifications, also whitewashes this president's Skull and Bones involvement (similarly employing surmise and imputed/fabricated motives for Bush's actions) in his 2004 book <u>The Faith of George W. Bush</u>:

> This lack of inner fire plagued Bush for some time. It may have been one of the reasons he was so eager to enter Skull and Bones, a secret society at Yale. Designed for "converting the idle progeny of the ruling class into morally serious leaders of the establishment,"[1022] Skull and Bones accepted fifteen seniors each year with the goal of making them "Good Men," known as "Bonies," a play on the

---

[1022] What a quaint gloss to be put on Satan worship. Though Mr. Bush has not been baptized since his adult conversion to Christ (why not?–this is only more curious in view of his unrenounced membership in a secret society of the occult), were he to be baptized or take communion, would Mr. Mansfield regard those ceremonies as legitimate in view of his facile dismissal of drinking blood and worshipping evil as "converting the idle progeny of the ruling class into morally serious leaders of the establishment"? Worshipping Satan is "morally serious" indeed.

French word for "good."[1023] The club reportedly began in a break with the Phi Beta Kappa honor society over the issue of secrecy. The dissidents[1024] met in a chapel adorned with skull and cross-bones, which gave them both their name and their emblem. That they met in a building called "the tomb" only added to their mystique.[1025]

Myths have long surrounded the society, including that they brand their members, that they pledge themselves to one world government, and that they secretly study the black arts.[1026] Conspiracy theorists

---

[1023] Skimmed over is that that "play" is deceptive, presenting the collection and ceremonial employment of human bones as "good" ("Bonies"), and the participants in such activities (along with grave-robbing, stealing and bizarre sexual and other unchristian ceremonies) as "Good Men." Doesn't Mansfield mean "privileged, elitist, immoral men?"

[1024] "*dissident*: somebody who disagrees: somebody who publicly disagrees with an established political or religious system or organization." Of course, Bonesmen are religious dissidents (from Christianity), but they are not political dissidents but the opposite–political idolaters.

[1025] "*mystique*: a special quality or air that makes somebody or something appear mysterious, powerful, or desirable." The significance of this word choice may be lost on the spiritually dead, but what Mr. Mansfield affirms is the very evil power that both he and George W. continue to employ. Mansfield himself employs the word to capitalize on suggestions of mysterious power and secrecy, the tools of the Bonesmen and of George W. Bush (who avails himself of its mystique and secret benefits, not renouncing Skull & Bones while disingenuously suggesting it no longer exists, adding to the mystique and pushing the "club" back into secrecy at the same time. Skull & Bones does not like scrutiny, but it likes "mystique.")

[1026] Well, don't they? Mr. Mansfield's only logical grounds for disagreement with these allegations is the simple conclusive assertion that they are "myths." Mr. Mansfield offers no factual support for this characterization, much like the logic employed by George W. in linking the 9/11 terrorists to Saddam Hussein: make the conclusion over and over, without content, truth, or factual support.

abound,[1027] and there are websites that claim to have "exposed" Bush's involvement. However, as Helen Thorpe has written for Texas Monthly, "The truth is rather mundane: It's a club of fifteen students who meet regularly to learn more about each other." What Skull and Bones probably[1028] did for Bush, other than providing him with a moneyed old boy network, was to expose[1029] him to Bonies of vastly different backgrounds. Among members in his day were men like Donald Etra, an orthodox Jew, and Muhammad Saleh, a Jordanian Arab.[1030]

[1027] Really? Why? Who are they? What do they allege? And the most Mansfield does to respond to what might be genuine Christian concerns about dark worship, is to offer up Helen Thorpe and her dismissive excuse for Bush, who should have answered for himself long ago. Informed Christians do not treat such things lightly, and the Bible is neither myth nor conspiracy theory, so this shallow sleight of hand by Mansfield is insulting to Christians and their God. For Christians, devil worship is not so easily dismissed as "a moneyed old boy network" or a social club for members to simply "learn more about each other"–evil is real, Satan is real, and dabbling in a relationship with Satan and his worldly network of minions is serious spiritual business.

[1028] There's that "probably" guesswork again. Doesn't Mr. Mansfield "know"? Didn't he ask his subject? If not, on what Christian or journalistic ethic is he surmising? On what factual or investigative foundation is he relying to write his book? Where's the beef in this book purportedly exploring "the faith of George W. Bush"? Are America's future hopes hanging on so slender a reed of Christian introspection?

[1029] I'll say!

[1030] To Christians, Bush's education in cultural diversity in Skull & Bones should be of less interest than the moral tenets embraced there and their subsequent repudiation, or lack thereof. Obviously people of any religious background can swear fealty to evil in their worldly desire to reach great heights through institutions such as Yale and Skull & Bones–Marrs warns that this is one of the hallmarks of the Illuminati, that they can profess loyalty to any religion, so long as they do not elevate any as highest. Mansfield's attempt to make excuses for George does nothing to address the core Christian questions surrounding Bush's membership in this organization.

Bush's mention of the society in his book, <u>A Charge To Keep</u>, has not served him well.[1031] He writes, "My senior year I joined Skull and Bones, a secret society, so secret I can't say anything more." It is hard to imagine a sentence better designed to awaken suspicion.[1032] He should have known better.[1033] During his vice presidential campaign, the senior Bush was compelled to resign his membership in the Trilateral Commission when errant suspicions[1034] arose that he served the political agenda of the Council on Foreign Relations in pursuit of a "New World Order." George W. had already fielded dozens of

---

[1031] So perhaps Mr. Mansfield can reform Bush's defense for him, since the President has admittedly failed to answer for himself.

[1032] No, it's very easy to imagine such a sentence: try "My senior year I joined Skull and Bones, a secret society, so secret I am sworn by my soul to silence, and so secret that I can't say anything more out of fealty to that oath, and of course I can't renounce such a magical, powerful secret group, but vote for me, I'm a Christian–just look at all the pseudo-books written about how devoted to Christ I am. (But these are just words–by all means do not look at my actions.)" That would do it, and it would "probably" be honest, too.

[1033] Why didn't he? Is this not a reflection of his spiritual character? Who are all these guys making excuses for him? But Mansfield's criticism of Bush is not a Christian one–that he should have known better as a servant of Christ than to attempt to continue to benefit from connections with darkness–but a political one: that those conspiracy theorists he and Bush blame for questioning his unchristian past would use his poor choice of words to fabricate wild fantasies about dark forces and the establishment. So Mansfield makes a political excuse for Bush, that he has been persecuted politically by nut-cakes, in a book pretending to address "the Faith of George W. Bush." If the moral yardstick of that faith is Mr. Mansfield's political one, then it's small wonder that there is almost no Scripture or Christian teaching reflected in his deceptive book.

[1034] How are they "errant"? Why did they arise?

questions[1035] about such matters both as a candidate himself and in his father's campaigns. He could have handled the matter more wisely.[1036] Still, though the Skull and Bones legacy would haunt[1037] both Bushes throughout their careers,[1038] the network it gave them[1039] opened important doors.[1040]

Of course it did, and these doors were not open to common folk, or to Christians.[1041]

[1035] Has he ever actually answered those questions, or just dodged them? Why are they being asked? From whence come these "errant suspicions"? Skull & Bones is connected to these institutions, and plans for world domination may be confined to a few elitist fruit loops, but such plans have been attempted and American movement toward world domination has surely quickened under the hands of both Bushes.

[1036] Or as a Christian.

[1037] Poor boys.... But this political "haunt" is different from the true, haunting pangs of Christian repentance that should instead be haunting these men.

[1038] Because neither realized they would need to woo the religious right while they were worshipping Satan?

[1039] Which George W. coyly suggests he no longer knows exists.

[1040] Stephen Mansfield, The Faith of George W. Bush, pp. 48-49. But George W. says he doesn't even know whether it still exists....

[1041] "In 1970, while Bush Senior was seeking President Nixon's strong backing for a run for a Senate seat in Texas, George W. was picked up at his base in Valdosta, Georgia, by a United States government aircraft and flown to Andrews Air Force Base in Maryland. The purpose? A dinner date with the older of Nixon's two daughters, Tricia." (Aikman, pp. 50-51.) How impressive to the worldly, but how empty as to George W. being "A Man of Faith," the book's title. Corruptly wasting American tax dollars is just not spiritually impressive, nor is Mr. Bush's Christian stature improved by such examples of success based not on the American Way of rags to riches but on power, access, birthright: his "legacy" and "destiny." Jesus' world is a meritocracy–this example shows the reader a world of advance by connections and bureaucracy: a use of Satan's powers, of government's powers; of the types of power used by Big Brother, Saddam Hussein, and Bonesmen.

Mr. Bush's ability to be such a prominent Bonesman and yet proclaim his Christian integrity without renouncing ties to evil has been accomplished by a lack of Christian accountability, and the use instead of others to make excuses for him. His own words again come to mind: "You can design a system so that nobody is held accountable."[1042] But this only applies to worldly systems, for there is no such deception and avoidance of accountability in God's world.

Mr. Bush's actions consistently mirror the ethical conscience of a Machiavelli, which is not as evil as Skull & Bones (though Machiavelli favored self-interest, he didn't toast the powers of darkness with blood from a skull), the other moral code that fits this president's behavior. For this man invested much time learning, and swore allegiance to, a moral code which abandons good in favor of self; which conditions men not to feel remorse in employing any means to further their worldly ambition. Bonesmen are taught to use powers of darkness or light, theft or Christian piety, in the pursuit of their own glory and that of fellow soul-mates in "The Brotherhood of Death." Bush quit drinking, but he has not renounced Skull & Bones, a patently unchristian group. Myron Magnet argues that if a person commits a crime while intoxicated, the wrong is doubled, for "…he has willfully deprived himself of the human reason that distinguishes right from wrong and makes him more than a beast."[1043] Skull and Bones conditions men to be "beasts" morally

---

[1042] Bob Woodward, Bush at War, p. 244.
[1043] Myron Magnet, The Dream and the Nightmare: The Sixties Legacy to the Underclass, p. 51.

even when sober—for the Christian, surely quitting this immoral heresy is more important than quitting drinking. A.W. Tozer writes that "The spiritual faculties of the unregenerate man lie asleep in his nature, unused, and for every purpose dead."[1044] When awakened to Christ, these "spiritual faculties" transform the unregenerate man—but by definition the unregenerate Bonesmen are specifically encouraged to feign Christian faith to use its influence for personal aggrandizement, so how does one know if a former Bonesman is a true Christian and not a Satanic deceiver? By observing their actions, and by learning the Word of God.

Mr. Bush's actions reflect spiritual ignorance if not spiritual death. The Republicans resent anyone raising Bush's "Mission Accomplished" fiasco at the commencement of the War in Iraq, when the president cowboyed his way onto an aircraft carrier with the conveniently placed (if blatantly and shamelessly propagandistic) banner which reflected his gross ignorance of the hearts and minds of the Muslim world, and also his startling overconfidence. As a worldly president, what moral code of politics prohibits a man admitting he made a mistake? And as a Christian, why has he never expressed regret for such grandstanding? Perhaps because as a Bonesman his ego is conditioned away from remorse for any action other than an action which reduced his worldly power. Bush is overly proud of his connections to Texas, "one of the most self-congratulatory states in the nation" where

---

[1044] A. W. Tozer, The Pursuit of God: the Human Thirst for the Divine, p. 49.

"people were tired of being ashamed...."[1045] It has been observed of him that "Once on a course, he directed his energy at forging on, rarely looking back, scoffing at–even ridiculing–doubt and anything less than 100 percent commitment."[1046] Christians must be cautious of those who claim to serve their Lord, for the Bible teaches that some proclaim Jesus Christ "from a spirit of selfish ambition."[1047]

In Ephesians 5:15, Paul admonishes Christians: "Don't live like ignorant people, but like wise people."[1048] But Paul refers to wisdom of a spiritual nature, not a worldly wisdom. And Christians must pray for guidance for that spiritual wisdom, and remember that false prophets and deceivers shall be known by their actions. Thomas A. Kempis notes that Grace "shuns public appearances" and "shuns private interest"[1049]: clearly George W. shuns neither. In fact, were one to ignore for a moment Mr. Bush's claim to faith and analyze the consequences of a continuing loyalty to self and the Skull & Bones creed, a picture does indeed emerge of

---

[1045] Bill Minutaglio, First Son: George W. Bush and the Bush Family Dynasty, p.240. And as stated earlier, he has said he was never one to feel "guilty" about his wealth or privilege. What a perfect candidate for America's newest "culture of contentment," in which God chooses America to wage war and Americanize the world, approves consumption and capitalism, and agrees those poor people just need to be kicked off welfare to rejuvenate their moral failings.

[1046] Bob Woodward, Bush at War, p. 256. For those who work under him, Bush is well-known for his temper and intolerance of criticism: "Any hint of less than full trust would be devastating. They served at his pleasure." Bush at War, p. 262.

[1047] Philippians 1:17, TEV.

[1048] TEV.

[1049] Thomas A. Kempis, The Imitation of Christ, pp. 170, 169.

an elitist effort to control as many of the world's levers of power as possible, guided by an immoral compass. George Orwell's description of Big Brother morality in <u>1984</u> describes such a world, in which the masses struggle in poverty in a toxic soup, and an unaccountable bureaucracy fueled by ideological zealots controls their every move, and even controls thought (like torture seeks to discover the subjective):

> For the secret of rulership is to combine a belief in one's own infallibility with the power to learn from past mistakes[1050]....Big Brother is the guise in which the Party[1051] chooses to exhibit itself to the world. His function is to act as a focusing point for love, fear, and reverence, emotions which are more easily felt toward an individual than toward an organization.[1052]

George W. Bush is the fabricated human face of compassion, cloaked in a fraudulent Christian piety, used by the military-industrial, political, and class "establishment" to deceive Americans that their myth is alive and well. Orwell describes an anti-Utopia that is anti-Christian, and that vision is becoming reality, accelerated by Bush the Second.

[1050] The most important "past mistake" that George W. Bush learned from was that he could not attain political office as a Conservative without the support of the Christian community: "Long before the Christian Coalition was a force to be reckoned with, Bush received a baptism by fire into the world of fundamentalist politics and learned firsthand the perils of running afoul of religious zeal." Patricia Kilday Hart, "The Bush Report," *Texas Monthly*, September, 1999, quoted in David Aikman, <u>A Man of Faith: The Spiritual Journey of George W. Bush,</u> p. 60.
[1051] The Bonesmen? The forces of evil?
[1052] George Orwell, <u>1984</u>, pp.177, 171.

This also explains Bush's intense insistence on "loyalty" (to him, not to truth or Christ) and intolerance of dissent: Paul O'Neill was fired (he refused to cooperate with the Bush lie that he "resign," for he is a man of integrity) because he spoke out against large, uncontrolled budget deficits. O'Neill performed his job as Treasury Secretary using decades of financial knowledge, but Bush demands lackeys, not independent thinkers, and puts people in his Cabinet to do as he instructs, not as they in their professional judgment deem appropriate. The entire administrative branch of government has been severely compromised in this manner by this president–Christie Todd Whitman was ignored and circumvented for holding honest views about global warming, and others do what they're told and are rewarded for toeing the party line, not for integrity, honesty or independent thought. Thus George Tenet and Alberto Gonzales are rewarded and praised for their "loyal" incompetence.[1053]

If George Bush's presidency in fact resembles in some aspects the totalitarian leanings of Big Brother and Skull & Bones, then the simple solution would be for him to repent of and denounce his own past associations with Skull & Bones and its undisputed veneration of Satan. Perhaps this explains Bush's mantra that he will not answer for "youthful indiscretions," a means to avoid discussion not just of his alcoholism, drug use

---

[1053] George Orwell described such a Skull & Bones government when he wrote 1984, in 1948: "What opinions the masses hold, or do not hold, is looked on as a matter of indifference. They can be granted intellectual liberty because they have no intellect. In a Party member, on the other hand, not even the smallest deviation of opinion on the most unimportant subject can be tolerated." p.173.

and promiscuity, but also his heretical devil-worship. Such dabblings (and Bush appears to have done much more than dabble) are not a trifling matter to children of God; they are quite serious. For Christianity does not regard the dark arts as "hocus-pocus" or fantasy, but as the true corollary to the powers of light–there is no Jesus without a very real, powerful and malicious Evil which God named Satan.

C.S. Lewis addresses the moral state of a wayward, deceived Christian in <u>The Screwtape Letters</u>, described from the perspective of the forces of evil, in terms that mirror the moral state of the unrepentant member of Skull & Bones:

> As long as he retains externally the habits of a Christian he can still be made to think of himself as one…whose spiritual state is much the same as it was….And while he thinks that, we do not have to contend with the explicit repentance of a definite,

fully recognized sin....It increases the patient's reluctance to think about the enemy.[1054]

But Christ and God call us to "contend with explicit repentance," an experience of deep remorse and tears, self-realization and shame. But it is through this process of seeing truthfully the darkness in ourselves that Christians "transform" to be more like Jesus–this is the mark of true faith, "For the sadness that is used by God brings a change of heart that leads to salvation."[1055]

George W. Bush represents that he is a student of Oswald Chambers, one of the most inspiring and widely

---

[1054] C.S Lewis, The Screwtape Letters, p. 34. This book reflects on George W. in many ways. Mike Moore's (liberal and therefore to be dismissed by many "conservative" Christians without reflection) movie *Fahrenheit 911* contains footage of George W. at a white-tie dinner making jokes about the failure of the administration to find the much-touted Weapons of Mass Destruction in Iraq: "No weapons here," George jokes, feigning to look under tables.... Is such gross error (as the missing WMD) humorous? Just to the wealthy beneficiaries of tax refunds and enhanced worldly power. Our country went to *war* over these fictitious WMDs, and now the nation's "Christian" leader makes light of that deception/failure unrepentantly. Jesus is not amused. As C.S. Lewis notes, "Only a clever human can make a real Joke about virtue....every serious subject is discussed in a manner which implies that they have already found a ridiculous side to it....it deadens, instead of sharpens, the intellect." The Screwtape Letters, p. 33. Mike Moore did not fabricate this footage, or this Bush trait, and Christians repeatedly give Bush a pass on such grossly insensitive reminders of the immorality that Bush supposedly shed with his youth. Christians are instead supposed to hold Christian leaders to *higher* standards, not let them walk the bases unchallenged simply because they have "Jesus" on their uniform.

[1055] 2 Corinthians 7:10, TEV. Oswald Chambers prods about remorse that "...produced in [the rich young ruler of Luke 18:23] a sorrow that had not any words. Have you been there?" My Utmost For His Highest, August 18.

read devotees of Jesus. Oswald Chambers addressed the experience of repentance in detail, and often:

> Have you ever heard the Master say a hard word? If you have not, I question whether you have heard Him say anything. Jesus Christ says a great deal that we listen to, but do not hear; when we do hear, His words are amazingly hard….Our Lord knows perfectly that when once His word is heard, it will bear fruit sooner or later. The terrible thing is that some of us prevent it bearing fruit in actual life…. All spiritual history must have a personal knowledge for its bedrock. To be born again means that I see Jesus….The true character of the loveliness that tells for God is always unconscious. Conscious influence is priggish and unchristian….It is possible to know all about doctrine and yet not know Jesus….Have I been asking God for liberty while I am withholding it from someone…?…as a child of God I am only good as I walk in the light. Prayer with most of us is turned into pious platitude, it is a matter of emotion, mystical communion with God….It is no use praying unless we are living as children of God.[1056]

What Oswald is describing includes the spiritual state of the Bonesman, attaching Jesus to their creed in "conscious influence" which is "priggish and unchristian"; knowing "all about doctrine" but not knowing Jesus.

George W. Bush pretends to read Chambers' book: where is his repentance?:

[1056] Oswald Chambers, <u>My Utmost For His Highest</u>, August 18, August 15, August 21, August 24.

Maintain a continual watchfulness so that nothing of which you would be ashamed arises in your life....

....Repentance always brings a man to this point: I have sinned. The surest sign that God is at work is when a man says that and means it. Anything less than this is a remorse for having made blunders, the reflex action of disgust at himself.

The entrance into the Kingdom is through the panging pains of repentance crashing into a man's respectable goodness; then the Holy Ghost, Who produces these agonies, begins the formation of the Son of God in the life. The new life will manifest itself in conscious repentance and unconscious holiness, never the other way about. The bedrock of Christianity is repentance....If ever you cease to know the virtue of repentance, you are in darkness. Examine yourself and see if you have forgotten how to be sorry.[1057]

And what of George W. Bush's Christian supporters? Their support, based largely on his façade of Christian sincerity, has enabled him to gain the White House twice; destroy the Kyoto protocols or any other response to global pollution; expand the federal government, its powers, and the national debt; exempt the United States from international law, including the Geneva Convention; dramatically compound both the wealth of the very rich and the despair of the very poor; indefinitely detain thousands without evidence; cause hundreds of loyal American troops to commit torture; and commit the nation to an endless war that cannot be won, in

---

[1057] Oswald Chambers, My Utmost For His Highest, September 15, December 7.

contravention of Christian just-war doctrine. Christian Bush supporters have an "indirect participation in war through their prayers for their emperor."[1058] According to one conservative commentator, Iraqi civilian deaths from the Iraq War have exceeded 25,000.[1059] Though the number is surely much larger, and grows daily, even one life destroyed—even one Iraqi soldier's life destroyed—in an unjust war in the name of Jesus Christ, is a reprehensible desecration of His name and of all that is good.

Have Bush W.'s Christian supporters tested this man's faith before putting their faith in him? If not, they have placed faith in a human being and his ideology before their faith in Christ. For those who belong not to this world but truly to Jesus Christ, Jesus calls us to do more than simply believe, for His love makes us yearn to share His promise with as many others as we can reach, and he admonishes us repeatedly that this is a vital Christian duty. As to George Bush and his Christian supporters, then, and as to the view of Christ and America that they have presented to the world,

> Has it ever dawned on you that you are responsible for other souls spiritually before God?….My life as a worker is the way I say "thank you" to God for His unspeakable salvation. Remember it is quite possible for any one of us to be flung out as reprobate silver—"…lest that by any means when I have preached to others, I myself should be a castaway."[1060]

[1058] James F. Childress and John Macquarrie, eds., <u>The Westminster Dictionary of Christian Ethics</u>, p. 446.
[1059] John Leo, *U.S. News & World Report*, August 1, 2005, p. 62. (+/-24,865 Iraqi civilian deaths).
[1060] Oswald Chambers, <u>My Utmost For His Highest</u>, February 15.

It is with this view toward our individual responsibility to Jesus that George W.'s sincerity and actions must be critically but fairly assessed by every Christian. His soul is not ours to judge, but our failure to judge his actions, if unchristian, places us in greater peril than the German citizens who dared not raise voices of protest to the Nazi rise to power. George Bush spent much youthful energy in worldly pursuits, consistent with his (and Skull and Bones') apparent moral code at that time–that man is his own measure. The timing of Bush's conversion to Christ is dubious because of the obvious political motivations which prompted it–he was at the time assisting his father with his bid for the presidency:

> The elder Bushes' motives [in arranging a meeting between their son and Billy Graham] may have had little to do with modifying their son's behavior. In his efforts to build a winning coalition, the Vice President had failed to secure the unequivocal backing of the increasingly important Christian Right. Doug Wead, an Amway executive and Assembly of God Evangelist with close ties to Jim and Tammy Baker–among other questionable characters–would be given the task of forging a bridge between Bush and the evangelical movement. His handler: George W.
>
> But before he could be handed this formidable job, it only seemed appropriate that W. should undergo a conversion of his own....[So George W. met with Billy Graham on the beach at his parents' home in Maine]...Conveniently, W. became a vocal

born-again Christian just as he was masterminding the effort to lure evangelicals into the Bush fold.... George W. gave no outward sign of having become a changed man.[1061]

Bill Minutaglio reports similarly:

[George W.'s] tasks were narrowed down, and a decision was reached to have him serve as a loyalty monitor for his father and also to become instrumental in bridging the gaps to the unpredictable but gathering political power bloc that his father feared the most and understood the least: the far Right of the Republican Party, especially the Christian Right....[Bush, Sr.] made a video about his versions of a Christian conversion experience....[Doug Wead in June 1985 prepared a 58 page analysis of Bush Sr. and the evangelical movement. In December 1985, he presented a 35-page] operations manual entitled "The Vice President and the Evangelicals: A Strategy"....One of Wead's first, most serious orders of business was meeting with the first son and other advisers and deciding how to get the elder George Bush on the cover of a magazine that would solidify the elder Bush's Christian credentials....Barbara Bush...was as interested as anyone else in drawing closer to the Christian Right....[Bush and Wead met to determine how to seal Team Bush ties to the Christian Right wing]...–how to do it the way that Reagan had done it–and they were also talking about

---

[1061] Christopher Anderson, George and Laura, pp.277, 278. According to Mr. Anderson, the younger Bush continued without pause in his *very* well-known routine of drinking and chain smoking, and "to fly into purple-veined rages." (p. 278)

BONESMAN OR CHRISTIAN? 561

the book he was helping oversee with Doug Wead that would serve as one of the "authorized" Bush campaign publications. Aimed at evangelicals and right-leaning conservatives, it would be entitled Man of Integrity, and the eager-to-please Wead was working closely with the first son....The first son's and the family's strategy to prove the elder Bush's mettle to the evangelicals...[included] publicly disclosing meetings with Billy Graham....Wead told people that he believed that only the father and George W. adequately understood the importance of currying favor with the evangelicals. <u>George Bush: Man of Integrity</u>,...[was] the paean to the evangelicals that the family and Wead were working on....George W. returned to Houston, knowing his father would win and satisfied that he had done his job crisscrossing the country, playing hardball and salesman with hundreds of evangelicals, paving the way for the Christian Right and the ultraconservatives.[1062]

People come to Christ for different reasons, often in despair or suffering, but George W. was led to Christ by political motives, and has consistently used Christ for political ends. If politics did not bring him to Christ, was it the famous meeting on the beach with Billy Graham, the one that Billy Graham has said he doesn't recall? The one in which "George W. today swears he cannot remember specifically what Graham said...."?[1063]

And then there are the books. The Reagan-Wead book-writing method was an effective means to put

---

[1062] Bill Minutaglio, <u>First Son: George W. Bush and the Bush Family Dynasty</u>, pp. 210-211, 211, 213, 213-14, 215, 219, 227, 227, 232.
[1063] Ibid., p. 22.

Jesus into Republican propaganda, and helped lift both Reagan and Bush, Sr. into the Oval Office. Bush's autobiography, titled, with Biblical reference, <u>A Charge To Keep</u>, appeared in time for his 2000 election bid. <u>A Man of Faith</u>, by David Aikman; <u>The Faith of George W. Bush</u>, by Stephen Mansfield; <u>God and George W. Bush: a spiritual life</u>, by Paul Kengor; and <u>George W. Bush on God and Country</u>, edited by Thomas Freiling (who, the reader is told by the cover, was "Author of <u>Reagan's God and Country</u>")–all of these books were released in 2004, for maximum effect on the election. They were not motivated by service to Christ but service to politics, and this is reflected in the empty spirituality, false excuses, and selective memory they contain. All purport to be "spiritual," but all are motivated by a political apparatus controlled by Bush, and none are written by theologians or from a truly critical Christian perspective.

Thomas M. Freiling's book, titled <u>George W. Bush on God and Country</u>, is adorned with an American flag, the commingling of Christ and nationalism popular with Mr. Bush's campaign. The author fills in the moral gaps for the president, glowingly praising the president for his spiritual insight in the Iraq War (that Bush says God did not guide), saying that Bush "even talks about [<u>his faith</u>] in terms of foreign policy, as he defends freedom and leads the fight against terrorism."[1064] How much did George W. Bush talk about his faith in determining to enter Iraq against the specific plea of Pope John Paul II? No matter, he has Mr. Freiling to explain it away to

---

[1064] At p. 9.

the American people in one of four conveniently-timed books, all spiritual white-washers.

So what are the actions of this devout leader who duped the Christian Right?:

—He has lied to the American people about the use of torture by U.S. forces, saying he is opposed to torture while he personally instructed Alberto Gonzales and the forces of the U.S. government to craft a strained and contrived legal position that permitted policies of indefinite detention without trial (itself a violation of international law), and of extreme, virtually unlimited infliction of physical and psychological interrogation methods (i.e., torture).

—He lied to Americans and the world about Iraq:

> The president and his team sold the Iraq War to Congress and to the American people as a conventional war to prevent nuclear war. Their pitch was that Iraq President Saddam Hussein had chemical and biological weapons of mass destruction (WMD), a program to develop nuclear weapons, and contacts with members of al Qaeda who might use these terrible devices to threaten the United States. Subsequent events have proven that none of this was true.[1065]

But George W. did not lie about the absence of any Christian doctrine to support his Iraq venture, saying of the War in Iraq: "I'm surely not going to justify war based on God. Understand that."[1066] If a war is not "of God," it is evil. If a Christian leader, who says he daily

---
[1065] *Friends Committee on National Legislation Washington Newsletter*, May 2005, No. 697, p.1.
[1066] Bob Woodward, <u>Plan of Attack</u>, p. 379.

reads the Bible and Oswald Chambers, refuses to reflect upon the Christian implications of thrusting a so-called Christian nation into a bloody, dirty war, then what exactly are the Christian virtues that his faith promised in worldly office? As a self-proclaimed representative of Christ, his actions (especially when not "justified by God") are wounds to Jesus Christ: "The insults which are hurled at you have fallen on me."[1067]

—He lied to Americans when, on April 24, 2004, he stated that "Any time you hear the United States government talking about wiretap, it requires–a wiretap requires a court order. Nothing has changed, by the way. When we're talking about chasing down terrorists, we're talking about getting a court order before we do so."[1068] At this time, Mr. Bush was very purposefully circumventing federal law and legal process, and this lie demonstrates that he knew this conduct was unlawful. And there is no excuse that lying was necessary to preserve national security (as implied by the administration's institution of an investigation into who leaked the truth), for terrorists are not depending on court delay to protect their communications, and the law could be changed by the democratic/constitutional process if it was insufficient. Americans who trust government carte blanche have given over their constitutional and legal protections, and the Rule of Law, to politicians.

—By abandoning God's counsel in his decision to go to war in Iraq (and presumably in his decisions to

---

[1067] Romans 15:3, TEV.
[1068] Quoted by Jonathan Alter, "The Political Power of Truth," *Newsweek*, February 6, 2006, p. 41.

employ torture, reward the wealthy, abandon the poor, etc.), George W. clearly ignores Oswald Chambers, who wrote:

> Never look for justice in this world, but never cease to give it....If we look for justice, we will begin to grouse and to indulge in the discontent of self-pity–Why should I be treated like this? If we are devoted to Jesus Christ we have nothing to do with what we meet, whether it is just or unjust. Jesus says–Go steadily on with what I have told you to do and I will guard your life. If you try to guard it yourself, you remove yourself from My deliverance. The most devout among us become atheistic in this connection; we do not believe God, we enthrone common sense and tack the name of God on to it. We do lean to our own understanding, instead of trusting God with all our hearts....
>
> Naturally, if a man does not hit back, it is because he is a coward; but spiritually if a man does not hit back, it is a manifestation of the Son of God in him.... Every time I insist upon my rights, I hurt the Son of God; whereas I can prevent Jesus from being hurt if I take the blow myself. That is the meaning of filling up that which is behind of the affliction of Christ. The disciple realizes that it is his Lord's honour that is at stake in his life, not his own honour.
>
> Never look for right in the other man, but never cease to be right yourself. We are always looking for justice; the teaching of the Sermon on the Mount is–Never look for justice, but never cease to live it.[1069]

[1069] Oswald Chambers, <u>My Utmost For His Highest</u>, June 27, July 14.

—Nor did President Bush heed the words of the New Testament in his hasty rush to a perverse war: "...do not fight from worldly motives. The weapons we use are not the world's weapons but God's powerful weapons, which we use to destroy strongholds. We destroy false arguments."[1070] And the Bible teaches Christians that we are not to "...handle God's message as if it were cheap merchandise."[1071] But George W. tells the world simply, "I'm surely not going to justify war based on God. Understand that." Thus Bush admits the War in Iraq is not justified by God: God's message is cheap merchandise in Bush's hands.

—George W. used taxpayer funds to promote partisan propaganda, political corruption in violation of the law:

> Federal auditors said...that the Bush administration violated the law by buying favorable news coverage of President Bush's education policies, by making payments to the conservative commentator Armstrong Williams and by hiring a public relations company to analyze media perceptions of the Republican Party.
>
> In a blistering report, the investigators, from the Government Accountability Office, said the administration had disseminated "covert propaganda" in the United States, in violation of a statutory ban....
>
> The Education Department flouted the law by telling [a public relations company] to use Mr. Williams to "convey a message to the public on behalf of the government, without disclosing to the public that the

---

[1070] 2 Corinthians 10:3, TEV.
[1071] 2 Corinthians 2:17, TEV.

messengers were acting on the government's behalf and in return for the payment of public funds," the G.A.O. said.[1072]

—George W. Bush's words: " "Look," said the president, "I oppose using the military for nation building. Once the job is done, our forces are not peacekeepers...." "[1073] This was clearly Bush's expectation in Iraq, as reflected by his "Mission Accomplished" confidence. But his expectation was based on a narrow world view untempered by either experience or education. And now the War Against Terror, Americans are told, will extend 'beyond their lifetimes;' and American soldiers in Iraq, many already tapped beyond their original commitments by unilateral service extensions, and many diverted there from the National Guard (and from America's domestic defense), will be there for at least ten more years. Christian words, unchristian actions...Though many make excuses for such failed promises, do any of Mr. Bush's promises mean anything if they all end up in the excuse pile? Do American Christians really believe that God chose George W. Bush to lead America to do good, so that he could drag the nation into the series of scandals that he has? For the Iraq War and the weapons of mass destruction contrived to initiate it is a scandal; the torture of helpless humans by America's once-reputable soldiers in uniform is a scandal; giving money to the wealthy at the expense of the poor is a scandal; dismissing Richard Clarke's, Joseph Wilson's,

---

[1072] "Buying of News by Bush's Aides is Ruled Illegal," *The New York Times*, October 1, 2005, pp. A1, A9.
[1073] Bob Woodward, <u>Bush at War</u>, p. 237.

and Paul O'Neill's words, let alone attacking their patriotic motives, is scandalous; telling Americans not to conserve energy was scandalous, as was treating the dollar as phony money and running up the national debt. These and others, are they God's scandals? Does God like scandals and unchristian war and torture, and so "chose" George W. Bush to be a politician? None of these scandals is Christian, and God never calls his servants to worldly but to spiritual service.

—This president has never renounced his continuing ties to Skull and Bones, instead repeatedly dodging inquiry, and feigning ignorance of its continued existence. The Bible warns us (and warns George W., the so-called "First Son"[1074]) "…do not…use your freedom to cover up any evil…."[1075] The Bonesmen "freely" seek to use Jesus Christ Himself to achieve their ends, and George W. Bush rallies the cry for freedom in his war-mongering, and even in defense of torture and the indefinite detention without legal rights of those abroad he chooses. He used the freedom of Christ to capture two worldly elections, to cut benefits to the poor, to increase the wealth of the rich, and to further bloat the military-industrial federal government behemoth.

[1074] Only Jesus Christ is the First Son, except perhaps for His bastard nemesis, the "First Son" of Satan, Antichrist. A majority of today's Christians believe the Antichrist is now walking the earth–the Bible teaches that this Antichrist will delude thousands of Christians with false words while he takes over the world, pretending to be Christian….Who could it be? By definition, he will be someone Christians come (wrongly) to trust, someone in great political power and dramatic global visibility and prominence, someone who will lead Christians into sinful actions….

[1075] 1 Peter 2:16, TEV.

George W. Bush uses his Christian front to cover up evil that he creates.

—He has made the poor poorer and the rich richer, through the two-pronged, unchristian onslaught of tax refunds that favor the wealthiest Americans, and program cuts justified by the failed and deceptive propaganda of "compassionate conservatism." Trickle-down economics is a proven dud for long-term growth, so the country has really only expanded its long-term debt with Bush's giveaways. America is declining economically, and can't just build weapons forever–George W. Bush & Co. have ensured that America's decline will not be reversed without economic shock. (People are not angered by doctors who tell them the truth regarding the inevitability and severity of bird flu, so why do Americans chafe so when the fundamental weaknesses of their economy are pointed out?) .

—Mr. Bush has done nothing to treat the environment with respect, despite his false claims that the environment is cleaner now than in the past. Christians who wish to plunder the earth's resources for the short-term, willfully ignoring the environmental costs of their gluttonous consumption, take God's blessings for granted in their support of economic growth at any cost.

—Another patently unchristian behavior indicative of a Bonesman rather than Christian morality was this administration's treasonous disclosure of Valeria Plame in a deliberate vendetta against her husband for attempting to reveal the truth about Bush Iraq WMD lies–for that's what they were. This action was not only vicious, illegal, and a threat to committed CIA operatives, it also reveals that this administration will stoop to any means to accomplish its ends, like Machiavelli and the Bonesmen. George Bush has not been linked to this embarrassing, treasonous action, but there is absolutely no question that he authorized this action if not directed it–this man retains extremely tight control of his Cabinet via intense secrecy and a demand for the strictest loyalty, so are Americans to believe that his devoted staff broke ranks and acted behind his back? That he didn't know about this action?[1076] Yeah, and Clinton didn't have sex with "that woman" either. Willful ignorance is a sin–wake up, American Christians, and worship Jesus Christ instead of this pathologically dishonest, corrupt, worldly Fraud.

—Also particularly ugly is the widespread decline in U.S. popularity as a direct consequence of many of Bush's policies. This is saddening not so much because America's reputation has been permanently stained, but because Jesus Christ has been dragged into the mud with her. A nation is not blessed by God: a people though may choose God as their guardian and guide. This relationship can be unilaterally terminated at any time–but not by God, only by the actions of people who have turned away from Him. George W. Bush has unilaterally withdrawn the American nation from the Kyoto accords, unilaterally withdrawn the American nation from the Geneva Convention and the International Convention on Human Rights, and unilaterally

---

[1076] If Bush didn't know (ludicrous!), then apparently he also didn't have the leadership or discipline to determine who had committed such a leak before that information was discovered by the special prosecutor.

withdrawn America from its perceived covenant with God. America has been turned from a "house of prayer" into a "hideout for thieves."[1077]

George W. Bush and Modern America

Nationalism contains the seeds of potential over-zealotry in any nation, America included. One can love one's country–patriotism is not malignant. But nationalism in its extreme form can infect any people: "nationalism:...3. <u>Excessive devotion to nation</u>: excessive or fanatical devotion to a nation and its interests, often associated with a belief that one country is superior to all others." Do Americans deny familiarity with the phrase "The Greatest Country in the World"? How often has America sacrificed its moral code to "protect national interests"? For moral relativists, evolutionary theorists, atheists or luke-warm Christians to ascribe to such an ideology is perhaps of no consequence to their "moral code" (or amoral code). But for true Christians, allegiance to nations at the expense of other human souls is not acceptable: "Primary loyalty for the Christian is not to any nation, but to the kingdom of God."[1078] Oswald Chambers instructs the earnest Christian that "As soon as God becomes real, other people become shadows."[1079] Are soul-less nations then to retain their substance for Christians, when God is to be elevated above ties to men? Mr. Chambers inquires:

[1077] Mark 11:17, TEV.
[1078] "The Politics of the People of God," *Christianity Today*, September, 2005, p. 85.
[1079] Oswald Chambers, <u>My Utmost For His Highest</u>, January 19.

> His purpose…is to simplify our belief until our relationship to Him is exactly that of a child–God and my own soul, other people are shadows. Until other people become shadows, clouds and darkness will be mine every now and again.
>
> ….Is there anyone "save Jesus only" in your cloud? If so, it will get darker; you must get to the place where there is "no one any more save Jesus only."[1080]

There are ample champions for America and her greatness under any circumstances, their nationalistic fervor and enslavement to a worldly ideology blinding them to, infuriating them by, any criticism. Do I better myself in life without self-analysis and remorse, or do these introspective assets help me be a better human being to others, and to myself? The dismissal of calls to correct America's course as unpatriotic is itself extremely dangerous, unpatriotic, and threatening to all the freedoms that America once stood for–the survival of a democratic republic depends on an informed populace, which requires critical and open debate. America was once the land of the spirit of Voltaire, "I disapprove of what you say, but I will defend to the death your right to say it."[1081] Partisan division in recent years, aggravated by Bush W. and his controversial, unchristian policies, has stifled meaningful spiritual/ethical debate across the nation. Christians are even divided into worldly labels of "liberal" or "conservative"–how absurd and

---

[1080] Oswald Chambers, <u>My Utmost For His Highest</u>, July 29.
[1081] Voltaire, per <u>Random House Webster's Quotationary</u>, Leonard Roy Frank, Editor, Random House, New York, NY, 1999, p. 296.

shallow. Rather than resolve doctrinal disputes, perhaps the next classification to divide the Body of Christ will be "Independent" Christians. Or how about "moral relativist Christians" or "neo-Nazi Christians?" Christ is desecrated and once again tormented on the Cross when His words are selectively employed, compromised for the comfort of a worldly ideology–any ideology or Orwellian Party. We see zealous nationalism in the neo-conservative ideology embraced by this White House, at the expense of God.

All worldly ideologies are as sinful as the humans who create them. All governments will be fallible and corrupt, as the base humans who run them, until Jesus arrives to bring perfection to world order. But for those with no true moral code, nationalism is a simple mysticism to embrace, though a snare of Satan. Michael Barone, regular secular contributor to *U.S. News & World Report*, criticizes those who embrace one universal moral standard for man, intending to tarnish liberal multiculturalists but unwittingly insulting Christianity. Mr. Barone says in effect that all cultures are not equal, that America's is better: "But all cultures are not equal in respecting representative government, guaranteed liberties, and the rule of law."[1082] But Mr. Barone's selection of values is immediately seen as relative and selective: what of the values of materialism, capitalism, and corporate/industrial dominance that accompany modern American culture? Are other nations permitted by our great superiority to choose to decline to embrace all or any part of American culture, especially when those

---

[1082] *U.S. News & World Report*, August 15, 2005, p. 26.

values enumerated by Mr. Barone have not prevented the moral deterioration and impending disaster which is America? Perhaps others in the world view America as the canary in the coal mine, the lead guinea pig in the relatively recent development of mass industrialism; another failed Empire to be ravaged after her fall, but not followed into darkness.

Whatever the views of others, our American creed supposedly grants other nations the freedom to choose, but beliefs like Mr. Barone's, which have long been employed by American nationalism in places like Nicaragua, Iran, Iraq, and Vietnam to ignore and treat as "backward" or "third-world" those nations' cultures, are only slightly different from those of, e.g., Hitler's Nazis. The Nazis "believed" that they were a "super Aryan race"; no more absurd than America's silly claim to hold the world's supreme government structure, culture, or model society. If America's Amish are free not to watch television, can foreign societies not elect likewise?

Mr. Barone's nationalist superiority complex, no doubt born of an ideologically-compromised indoctrination through life, is now shared by a dangerous number of Americans, because moral debate and human relationships are being destroyed by modern technologies and mass media.[1083] One need not be Christian to see the logical failing of such a proud claim–what is the difference between "cultural" and "biological" superiority? Is it that Americans wish to expand throughout the world and share their great Way of Life with everyone? The Bible again gives clear instruction: "…you neglect to

---

[1083] *See* Richard Goodwin, <u>The American Condition</u>.

obey the really important teachings of the Law, such as justice and mercy and honesty."[1084] As America praises itself for its "respecting representative government, guaranteed liberties, and the rule of law," have its actions conveyed to the world the "important teachings of the Law, such as justice and mercy and honesty"? One is a standard of worldly laws, the other the standard of Christ; one is fallible, human and imperfect, the other the opposite. Christianity and nationalism are mutually-exclusive belief systems, and no flag or currency or human document will lead one to moral truth and admit one to heaven: quite the opposite, they lead astray.

The Islamists demonstrate this passion. Confusing to Americans looking for national borders to define their enemy, the "…new Islamism mocks the borders of nations and the very idea of nationality."[1085] This is the same religious devotion that leads Muslims to seek to dominate the world with Islam. But is this not the goal and promise of Christian doctrine too? Are America's nationalistic Christians paying the same level of priority and devotion to their Christ? Christianity, too, is not confined by borders or nations.

But George Bush's actions speak "crusade." His good versus evil rhetoric, combined with his constant assurances that he'll prosecute the war on terror forever, etc., place his unchristian belief system squarely in the definition of "crusade," a spiritual offense to God and a threat to men's souls. Bob Woodward records Bush's response to the 9/11 attacks:

[1084] Matthew 7:21, TEV. Where are justice, mercy and honesty in the Iraq War, or in Abu Ghraib? In compassionate conservatism?

[1085] Fouad Ajami, *U. S. News & World Report*, July 25, 2005, p. 26.

"But our responsibility to history is already clear: To answer these attacks and rid the world of evil." The president was casting his mission and that of the country in the grand vision of God's master plan. [The president went on to say that this new conflict] "...will end in a way, and at an hour, of our choosing."....Powell asserted that everyone in the international coalition was ready to go after al Qaeda, but that extending the war to other terrorist groups or countries could cause some of them to drop out.

The president said he didn't want other countries dictating terms or conditions for the war on terrorism. "At some point," he said, "we may be the only one's left. That's OK with me. We are America."

[Powell said:] "Don't go with the Iraq option right away, or we'll lose the coalition we've been signing up. They'll view it as bait-and-switch–it's not what they signed up to do...." Nobody could look at Iraq and say it was responsible for September 11. It was important not to lose focus. "Keep the Iraq options open if you get the linkages...but [I] doubt you'll get the linkages."[1086]

[The next day, Donald Rumsfeld said that any] "...argument that the coalition wouldn't tolerate Iraq argues for a different coalition."

[On September 16, 2001, Bush spoke to the press and called the war on terror a "crusade,"] a blunder because of its serious negative connotations in the Islamic world, where it is still associated with invading medieval European Christian armies.

[1086] This was on September 15, 2001.

[Later, of Afghanistan Bush said] "We are going to rain holy hell on them. You've got to put lives at risk...." "I will not relent in waging this struggle for freedom and security for the American people."[1087]

Is it any wonder that the hornet's nest of Islam is stirred up, and the ranks of extremists are swelling in response to the threat of Christianity in Islam? Will the whole world be turned against America, and Jesus Christ, because of the doctrine of "preemption" or Bush's "Christian war machinery"? Who dares put Christ's name on their battle shield in offensive, unjust war? Bonesmen, apparently.

Are American Christians, many blinded to the superiority of Christ by their "faith" in their nation, blinded also thereby to the desecration of His holiness by their current government? If they cannot face their nation's evil, can they face the possibility that their revered nation is addressed harshly in the Book of Revelation?:

> ...MYSTERY, BABYLON THE GREAT, THE MOTHER OF HARLOTS AND ABOMINATIONS OF THE EARTH....[the nations of the beast with ten horns] shall hate the whore, and shall make her desolate and naked, and shall eat her flesh, and burn her with fire....And the woman which thou sawest is that great city, which reigneth over the kings of the earth....For all nations have drunk of the wine of her fornication, and the kings of the earth have committed fornication with her, and the merchants of the earth are waxed rich through the abundance

---

[1087] Bob Woodward, Bush at War, pp. 67, 81, 87, 88, 94, 98, 99, 108.

of her delicacies….For her sins have reached unto heaven, and God hath remembered her iniquities.

Reward her even as she rewarded you, and double unto her double according to her works: in the cup which she hath filled fill to her double.

How much she hath glorified herself, and lived deliciously, so much torment and sorrow give her: for she saith in her heart, "I sit a queen, and am no widow, and shall see no sorrow."

….And the merchants of the earth shall weep and mourn over her; for no man buyeth their merchandise any more.

….And the fruits that thy soul lusted after are departed from thee, and all things which were dainty and goodly are departed from thee, and thou shalt find them no more at all.

"…Thus with violence shall that great city Babylon be thrown down, and shall be found no more at all.

….for thy merchants were the great men of the earth; for by thy sorceries[1088] were all nations deceived."

[1088] The Good News Bible, Today's English Version, employs this language: "…"Your merchants were the most powerful in the world, and with your false magic you deceived all the peoples of the world!" " Perhaps these "sorceries" and "false magic" are references to television, computers, and other modern technologies, innovated largely by American industry and employed by America to extend its culture, infecting other peoples with the negative and sinful effects of materialism, consumption, and techno-dependency, ultimately terminal. American Christians might not be comfortable with the idea of life without television, but a) that discomfort should not dull insight; b) there will be no television in heaven.

FOR TRUE AND RIGHTEOUS ARE HIS JUDG-
MENTS: for he hath judged the great whore, which
did corrupt the earth with her fornications, and
HATH AVENGED THE BLOOD OF HIS SER-
VANTS AT HER HAND.[1089]

Are America's Christians not willing to apply the same Christian sanctification and repentance to their nation as that which the Bible, and Jesus Christ, demand of individuals? Are American Christians spiritually comfortable with what their nation has become? For America has become the world's capital of drug-use, alcoholism, abortion, pornography, pedophilia, family-breakdown, homosexuality, tobacco, prostitution, capitalism and materialism. And now out on a Crusade to tell others how to live, to "liberate" them.... Many Americans had best hope the evolutionists are correct, for at least then when their nation falls they can look forward to a mortal death, and escape eternal judgment.

Texe Marrs warns that:

> Democracy may indeed be the best that man has to offer. But in the end the democratic governments of this globe will be converted into a hellish dictatorship ruled with an iron hand by an Antichrist, the Son of Perdition (II Thessalonians).
>
> Peace and democracy will ultimately fail, because it is built on the vain greed and ambition of men such as the Bilderbergers.[1090]

[1089] Revelation 7:5, 16, 18; 18:3, 5, 6, 7, 11, 14, 21, 23; 19:2, KJV.
[1090] Texe Marrs, <u>Dark Majesty: The Secret Brotherhood and the Magic of A Thousand Points of Light</u>, p. 113. Or such as the Bonesmen....Or the Bushes....

Christian Americans, God calls you now in this vital time to your Bibles, to test the truth of my words. For those critical of my renunciation of some of the more salient "actions" of George W. Bush and his fellow ideologues, I call upon Jesus to judge the truths of this book: hold both George W. and me to the standards of Christ, and stop giving him a "pass" based solely on flowery, deceptive words. God will hold all of us to account, and so I pray that I am not in error. God is real, and George W. Bush and many of America's Christians have shamelessly abandoned and desecrated His Son and His teachings: for the actions of George W. Bush in creating war, torture, and poverty for America recounted in this book do not accord with the teachings of Jesus Christ by any interpretation.

Paul warns us in Romans 16:17: "Watch out for those who cause division…." Has anyone caused more division through their individual action than this career politician? Will Christians listen to Paul, or be governed by their stifling worldly political loyalties?

Paul also warns Christians, in Ephesians 4:14 (TEV),[1091] to avoid the "teaching of deceitful people, who lead others into error by the tricks they invent." Tricks such as new definitions of rights and interrogation techniques, leading honest Christian soldiers and a trusting Christian nation to perpetrate unchristian torture? Deceit such as fabricating or exaggerating the existence of weapons of mass destruction, and also of non-existent

---

[1091] The King James Version warns "That we henceforth be no more children, tossed to and fro, and carried about with every wind of doctrine, by the sleight of men, and cunning craftiness, whereby they lie in wait to deceive;"

Iraq connections to al Qaeda, in order to trick Americans and their allies into an endless and unwinnable unjust war that has inflamed our enemies and alienated our allies? Deceit like failed trickle-down economic theory employed to reward wealthy supporters; federal testing in education encouraged by illegal propaganda paid for by U.S. taxpayers, for a costly system that does little other than expand federal dominance over Americans; tricks like including, in the NCLB legislation, requirements that schools must permit access to military recruitment; tricks like telling Americans they have to comply with new, invasive, computer chip passports because they are required by international standards, omitting that the Bush administration insisted on those standards over international objection; deceit like "compassionate conservatism," where Christian-sounding words are employed to reduce economic assistance to America's poorest citizens; deceit like magnifying federal spending with promises of a plan for future cuts that never arrive (unless to programs that benefit the poor); deceit of the world and future generations of American children, by withdrawing from Kyoto, raping resources, and cutting environmental regulation; deceptions like Bush pretending he doesn't know a Satanic cult called Skull & Bones still exists, when he has routinely availed himself of connections to that entity in his worldly climb, and is its most prominent alumnus ever?

John 7:18, 8:47 instruct us:

> Those who speak on their own authority are trying to gain glory for themselves. But he who wants

> glory for the one who sent him is honest, and there is nothing false in him….He who comes from God listens to God's words.

Is it listening to God's words to initiate (and fabricate grounds for) a war which is "surely not justified by God"? Is preemption doctrine on Bush's own authority, or God's? Is a man who prints baseball cards with his picture on them "trying to gain glory for himself"? George did this, *after* supposedly finding Jesus.

I listen to God's words. He calls me to repent of my sin, and he calls me to worship Him instead of money, politicians, ideologies or nations. He calls me to keep Jesus close to my heart throughout every day. He also compelled me to write this book (is that different from George W.'s claim that God wanted him to run for presidential office?), because His sorrow is great at the perversions that have been committed in His Son's name, and because he wishes for true Christians to lead those in darkness back into His light.

The matter is really quite simple–I call George W. Bush to repent, publicly, for the patently unchristian actions that he has committed in Christ's name. In the name of Jesus Christ, I demand it, or in the alternative a Christian defense of war, torture, and the increase in wealth disparity that has occurred under his stewardship. I also call Christians who have supported this false prophet of darkness to accountability before their God for the consequences of their blind, willful ignorance–they have allowed fear and worldly matters to tarnish their Lord, and they must return to Him now in repentance. I ask God to help me correct any errors that might be in this work, for it is my fervent desire to serve Christ who is Truth, not falsehood. If my motives are not Christian but worldly in writing this book, or if I am mistaken in my criticisms of the "First Son of the Brotherhood of Death," then I beg God to correct me in mercy, and guide me to His Light.

"If we say that we know [God], but do not obey His commands, we are liars and there is no truth in us." (1 John 2:4)

1 John 3:10 tells us "those who do not do what is right or do not love others are not God's children."

And again, because its command is so clear and simple:

> My dear friends, do not believe all who claim to have the Spirit, but test them to find out if the Spirit they have comes from God.... Those false prophets speak about matters of the world, and the world listens to them because they belong to the world.
> —1 John 4:1, 5, TEV

I claim to "have the Spirit" of God in writing these words–I request that all Christians test my words, and look to their Jesus. I have felt His infinite love which evaporates fear, and I have spent countless hours feeling His sorrow at the loss of souls which George W. Bush's actions have produced. Do not belong to this world any longer, Christian brothers and sisters, but look only to the words and Promise of God and His Holy Son. Should my nation desecrate our Lord Jesus Christ, I will abandon my nation–America's moral decline can only be reversed by the Words of Jesus Christ, and I fear for so many frightened souls who do not heed Him, or who mock and desecrate His Truth. God Bless America...if she earns it. Otherwise, God's Will be done, whatever hardship that may bring.

Chapter 11

DO THE END TIMES JUSTIFY THE MEANS?

The End Times signify the return of Christ the Redeemer and the triumph of His Truth. These times are an affirmation of the supremacy of good over evil, of love over hate, of compassion over selfishness, of spirit over technology, of peace and comfort over war and pestilence. But by definition, the End Times are also about judgment, and judgment by Christ is a judgment of human "means"–how we made our passage through this world, how we treated others, etc.[1092] Christ already knows the "End," and our free will determines our course thereto (or not). But in Christianity, the ends do not justify the means–just the opposite.

This moral premise, not coincidentally, applies also to America's democratic institutions. As one political scientist has summarized:

[1092] In Christian morality, the Christian conduct aspired toward is both means and ends.

> The <u>emphasis on means</u> in democratic life is based on the realization that ends lead no existence apart from means but are continually shaped by them. The totalitarian makes a clear-cut distinction between means and ends. He is absolutely certain what the ends are, and possessing this certainty, he pays little attention to the nature of the means. [<u>Jury trials, habeas corpus and due process are all "means"-related doctrines of American jurisprudence</u>.]
>
> At present, the danger in democratic societies lies in the possible waning of this awareness that differences over means are the heart of the difference between democracy and totalitarianism. In opposing a totalitarian system like fascism or communism there is a natural tendency to imitate their means, and because the tendency is natural, special efforts must be made to guard against it. In defending democracy, some persons are willing to use means that are bound to destroy the very thing they seek to defend.[1093]

George W. Bush and his over-confident, fear-mongering, neo-conservative entourage are the embodiment of this "danger in democratic societies." Worse, their actions are decidedly unchristian–America has been duped.

Yet George W.'s words are consistent with democracy: he says that "we must not forget that even the

---

[1093] William Ebenstein, <u>Today's Isms: Communism Fascism Capitalism Socialism</u>, pp.170, 171. *Emphasis in original.*

most noble ends do not justify any means."[1094] What then are the noble ends that justified the "means" of Abu Ghraib? The invasion of Iraq? Even by his own words George W.'s actions are condemnable. What are the limits of the means he is willing to employ? Clearly he does not feel constrained by "the most fundamental principle of medical ethics, that no human life should be exploited or extinguished for the benefit of another."[1095] Perhaps George W. is described by the ends-oriented ethical lapses of which Ann Coulter accused the Clinton administration:

> It is essentially impossible to have democracy if elected leaders do not tell the truth, everyone knows they do not tell the truth, and no one cares. Presidents who by their deceit spread such cynicism actually do commit "offenses that subvert the system of government."
>
> Clinton will have established a new standard for the entire country....We adore a lovable rogue. And we are very, very tolerant. The only thing we won't tolerate is a loser. Nothing matters except winning, and it is fine to lie and cheat and manipulate because

---

[1094] Thomas M. Freiling, George W. Bush on God & Country, p. 104. Nor does George W. comply with the ethical standards one might expect of scientific researchers: "The good scientist, moreover, rejects the use of people as instruments, as means to an end....Resolving moral dilemmas in science, however, involves not merely isolated choices but a committed pattern of behaviour, long-term resistance to compromise leading to feelings of self-respect: integrity." John Cornwell, Hiltler's Scientists: Science, War and the Devil's Pact, p. 462.

[1095] George W. Bush, quoted in Thomas M. Freiling, George W. Bush on God & Country, at p. 105. Nice "words," but the human lives of American troops and foreign civilians have been "exploited or extinguished" by the Iraq War and U.S. torture practices.

honor is just a word, just hot air, and the country doesn't really believe in it.[1096]

But Christianity is an end, a faith which then determines all means for the Christian loyal to Christ. Violent means never justify Christian ends,[1097] and Christian means never lead to violent ends. C.S. Lewis described the trap of using Christianity as a means to worldly ends from the perspective of the darker forces. He wrote in The Screwtape Letters that Satan's servants want

> [t]o make men treat Christianity as a means; preferably, of course, as a means to their own advancement, but, failing that, as a means to anything–even to social justice. The thing to do is to get a man at first to value social justice as a thing which the enemy demands,[1098] and then work him on to the stage at which he values Christianity because it may produce social justice. For the Enemy will not be used as a convenience. Men or nations who think they can revive the Faith in order to make a good society might just as well think they can use the stairs of Heaven as a shortcut to the nearest chemist's shop.[1099]

George W. Bush used the name of Jesus Christ as a convenience to gain the political throne, and his actions

---

[1096] Ann Coulter, High Crimes and Misdemeanors: The Case Against Bill Clinton, pp. 21, 21-22, 22.

[1097] In contrast, Aleksandr I. Solzhenitsyn wrote of the instructions/guidelines provided to Soviet interrogators: "*And it was simply stated*, orally but often, that any measures and any means employed were good, since they were being used for a lofty purpose…." The Gulag Archipelago, 1918-1956, Volume One, p. 102 (italics in original).

[1098] Like the insistence that God would have America transform the planet into a free, liberal democracy with food and justice for all.

[1099] C.S. Lewis, The Screwtape Letters, p. 69.

have shone with the shadows of darkness accordingly. Christians follow false prophets at their own peril–Christ is Truth, the Almighty One, and it is He who is to be followed, and He alone.

Texe Marrs lists the following events as some of those which the Bible teaches will occur in the last days before Jesus returns:

> Mass Hypnosis: The people of the world will be given a "strong delusion" so that they will believe "the Lie." (II Thessalonians 2; Isaiah 28, 29; Revelation 13:14)....The conspirators will gain their wealth and riches by defrauding working people....
>
> Occultism: "Craft" (witchcraft) and magic will be employed by the conspiracy to seduce the masses. (Isaiah 44; Daniel 8:23-25; 11:37-38; Timothy 4:1-3).[1100]

Many in the neo-conservative camp are, if Christian, of the "conservative" variety, meaning that they support a strong military and economic America. Unfortunately, the same ideology often views Christian cheek-turning as weakness instead of Christ-like: "Democracy meant weakness. Democracy limited your means and questioned them."[1101] This mutated "brand" of

---

[1100] Texe Marrs, <u>Dark Majesty: The Secret Brotherhood and the Magic of a Thousand Points of Light</u>, p. 48.

[1101] Christopher Dickey, <u>With the Contras: A Reporter in the Wilds of Nicaragua</u>, p. 10. Yes, constitutional protections and prohibitions of torture "limit your means," but that's the whole idea of democracy, and a democracy can't have its cake and eat it too, can't walk in darkness and in light–if democracy did not "limit your means and question them," it would not be a democracy.

Christianity spreads distrust of America and consequently of Christianity, and for good reason–it subverts the very trust and benevolence America has always associated with itself. So is George W. Bush errant (a bad apple), or is he simply the properly-elected, business-as-usual hypocrite that Americans wanted while they went about their complacent, consumptive delusion of worldly comfort?

Perhaps Machiavelli, handbook-writer for tyrants, described best the non-Christian moral alternative which faith in science and self above God presents:

> And if with respect to all human actions, and especially those of princes where there is no judge to whom to appeal, one looks to the end. Let a prince then win and maintain the state–the means will always be judged honorable and will be praised by everyone; for the vulgar are always taken in by the appearance and the outcome of a thing, and in this world there is none but the vulgar.[1102]

And thus Americans wait to judge George W. Bush's performance in Iraq based on "the appearance and the outcome," waiting to see whether the ends justify the means, which they never do, in Christ. Interestingly, this moral pattern also accords perfectly with the Skull & Bones creed of using the powers of light or darkness to accomplish one's worldly ends: "Serving the lesser gods permits ethical lapses under the broad heading, "the end justifies the means." "[1103]

[1102] Niccolo Machiavelli, The Prince, p. 109. Sounds like Bonesmen again....
[1103] Pat Robertson, The New World Order, p. 234.

Who are Americans to determine that they are "good" or "right" without God? Who made them superior? American torture, like the Iraq War, is not compatible with Christ's teachings. But both the Iraq War and torture, and all other of Bush's actions which fail to conform to the moral standards expected of a Christian leader, are "morally pure" under Skull & Bones morality, which is "similar...[to] Hitler's Aryan race theory."[1104] Like the German nationalism before theirs, Americans haughtily view the world as their oyster, and feel compelled to further their "manifest destiny" to induce others into economic slavery to capitalism and materialism and the chronic depression and moral decay that accompany them–the fate of the American Indians. America's Christians will be judged by Christ, who knows who is true and just. Repent, America, and command your Commander-in-Chief to match his Christian rhetoric with Christian action, including his own public repentance–repentance of an unjust, fraudulent war, of torture hidden behind legal shenanigans, of an uninterrupted association with an unchristian cult named Skull & Bones....Repent, and all is forgiven: "...renounce the whole thing until there is no hidden thing of dishonesty or craftiness about you."[1105] Repent, and a Christian example will be shown to the world, by Christians and by George W. Can America return to its path of goodness in its world leadership? Time is very short....

[1104] Texe Marrs, <u>Dark Majesty: The Secret Brotherhood and the Magic of a Thousand Points of Light</u>, p.210.
[1105] Oswald Chambers, <u>My Utmost For His Highest</u>, September 15.

William F. Buckley, Jr., criticizing the sacrifice in American universities of truth in the face of moral relativism, made the following, now-very-relevant observations about truth and America:

> ...the most casual student of history knows that, as a matter of fact, truth does not necessarily vanquish. What is more, truth can never win unless it is promulgated. Truth does not carry within itself an antitoxin to falsehood. The cause of truth must be championed, and it must be championed dynamically. Moreover, as President Howard Lowry of Wooster College points out, truth can win only where people are temperamentally and intellectually disposed to side with it, for the mere act of recognizing it as such does not entail the willful act of attaching allegiance to it.
>
> ....But the people of Italy, in 1922, did have the opportunity to learn better than to allow Mussolini and his blackshirts to march upon Rome and preempt the power of the people's government. The people of Germany had had what seems like ample opportunity to embrace truth and scorn error when they nevertheless gave the Nazis the largest party vote in an election.
>
> Both of these "revolutions," to be sure, were wrought by complex forces acting in complex ways; but it is nevertheless a tragic fact that truth did not triumph, and that this was not because the truth had not been made known. It was rather because (a) not enough people recognized the truth, (b) those who did recognize it did not exert themselves sufficiently in its behalf, and (c) many people saw the truth, but were indifferent to it.

The denial of truth in Italy and Germany, coupled with the refusal of Japan to ally herself with truth, resulted in a devastating world war. The continued refusal of Russia to scorn error bids fair to bring an end to truth everywhere in the world.

These examples are perhaps gaudy; but, still and all, they are certainly historical instances of the way in which contempt for truth can lose the battle, if not the war, to the idolatry of falsehood. It would seem that the will of man has never been confronted more dramatically between a choice of black and white, and yet how explain the loyalty that Stalinism commands among millions of people all over the world?

….It is unquestionably the case that the people of America, with a dynamic tradition of freedom, are less easily deceived. But it does not follow that there should be a total abdication of responsibility, a lapse into complacency, in giving impetus to values that we consider to be good, that we consider most closely to approximate truth, or perhaps, even, to be truth itself. The communication of values is, after all, the raw stuff of democracy.[1106]

Is Christianity, then, an idea to be "propagandized…to attract consumers to their platform"? And is George W. Bush's ideological conviction based on Christianity, or on America's nationalism, materialism, and capitalism? Is George W.'s cause righteous? Paul, and Jesus, teach us that the purity of God's word is not to be compromised by worldly or political motives.

[1106] William F. Buckley, Jr., God & Man at Yale, pp.140-143.

But this is exactly what George W. Bush and the Republican Party have corruptly done. Jesus Christ is not the badge of a worldly political party. America's Christians should have known better, and now they have a duty to their God and Christ to fix a spiritual disaster of their own manufacture. George W.'s extraordinary expansion of federal and presidential powers, his devolution to moral standards more to be expected from a Bonesman than a Christian, has been, like Mussolini, to "preempt the power of the people's government." But the infinitely greater nightmare is that George W. Bush has, repeatedly and blatantly, preempted the truth of Christ.

Am I to be attacked by Bush's worldly idolators for my words? Are my words true to my Christ and God? I invite George W. Bush and my detractors to withhold their barbed lies about my motives in these criticisms, and to instead of attacking me as their defense, present a Christian rationale to the world's Christian community, and by direct relation to Jesus Christ Himself, for this administration's actions criticized in this book. Simply put, reflective Christians most assuredly must wish to hear, from the president they have trusted with the word and errand of God, Christian theological justifications for:

1) lying repeatedly in high political fashion. (Do I really need to list them all?)
2) continued association with the nation's most powerful and well-known Satanic cult, together with a deliberate attempt to shield that entity from scrutiny. Choose a Lord, George W. Bush, and commit.

(An adult baptism might in fact have the holy power to sever Mr. Bush's extensive and intimate ties to Satan, but it depends on what he really did in that coffin, etc., etc.)

3) the War in Iraq. If not based on God, as George has said his decision to invade was not, then admit the only rationalizations for the war have been worldly (and generally fraudulent), repent (publicly, and to the world) of abandoning Jesus Christ as guide in such a world-changing decision, and surrender future decision-making to God.

4) Abu Ghraib and other torture and human rights violations. Just try to justify torture and indefinite detention in Christian theology, George W. Bush, and feel your sin. Repent, and quit lying to the world and to Jesus Christ about the heinous things you've caused to be done to human beings, while feigning Christian fealty. Torture by America is unchristian, and I pray that God will forgive America's deceived souls who let fear and falsehood sway their hearts from the truth of Jesus Christ, the Almighty Son, to follow such unchristian perversion, and ignore the sorrow of God. Hitler was allowed to advance in power with vile falsehood on his lips: now has been America's time to allow nationalism to be their "idolatry of falsehood."

5) Let America's Christians, and the world's, hear in detail of "the spiritual journey" by Mr. Bush that avoided scripture and Jesus in favor of Marvin Olasky, Myron Magnet, and the falsehood and deception of "Compassionate Conservatism" to justify huge financial benefits to America's most wealthy at the direct expense of America's poorest. And our nation is now nearly as financially as it is morally bankrupt.

All of a Christian leader's actions must be measured before the standards of Jesus Christ, and none other. Romans 13 was written by Paul to avoid persecution of Christians by worldly government powers, and to recognize and acknowledge that God is always in control. Paul encouraged Christians to pray for and not challenge their worldly leaders. But that is an entirely different matter from allowing those who purport to speak for Christ to go unchallenged if they err, of which Paul is perhaps the Bible's most vocal proponent. Repeatedly Paul condemns and warns against false teachers and false prophets like George W. Bush, and like those who would bring homosexual "marriage" into Christ's holy body, dividing His Church in the End Times. Unite, Christians, and surrender to Jesus Christ our Lord, for through prayer He will unveil falsehood and reveal truth. Test my humble book against the actions of George W. Bush: an error is all the greater if swept under the carpet. This book has made some sharp observations in the name of Jesus Christ, but it does so in complete faith in the promises and word of our Holy God, and His Word can indeed be incisive: "For the word of God is quick, and powerful, and sharper than any two-edged sword, piercing even to the dividing asunder of soul and spirit, and of the joints and marrow, and is a discerner of the thought and intents of the heart."[1107]

Let us all turn to the Word of God in these End Times, Christians, for as Mr. Buckley observed in 1951 (in words that fall naively to the ground in contrast to

---

[1107] Hebrews 4:12, KJV.

today's America), "It would seem that the will of man has never been confronted more dramatically between a choice of black and white...." This is immensely more true in 2006, and it's time to choose. The only choice for "white" is Jesus Christ, in His pureness and not adulterated by worldly comfort and worldly deception.

"But will the Son of Man find faith on earth when he comes?" Luke 18:8[1108]

"I Jesus have sent mine angel to testify unto you these things in the churches. I am the root and the offspring of David, and the bright and morning star....Surely I come quickly." Revelation 22:16, 20.[1109]

"...if thou warn the wicked, and he turn not from his wickedness, nor from his wicked way, he shall die in his iniquity, but thou hast delivered thy soul"[1110]

Jesus Christ offers love and peace to all who seek Him. Praise God for the glory and righteousness of His Son. It is to Jesus and Jesus alone that man must turn in these End Times, and in so doing find relief from all worldly sorrow and worldly fear. His yoke is light.... The End Times do not justify unchristian, worldly means. We are called to match Christian words with *Christian* actions.

Please give this book to another
to read, to thereby combat false arguments with truth.

[1108] TEV.
[1109] KJV.
[1110] Ezekial 3:19, KJV.

Bibliography

1) <u>Holy Bible</u>, King James Version, Thomas Nelson Publishers, Nashville, TN, 1977.
2) <u>Good News Bible</u>, Today's English Version, Second Edition, Thomas Nelson Publishers, Nashville, TN, 1993.
3) Charles Adams, <u>Those Dirty Rotten Taxes: The Tax Revolts That Built America</u>, The Free Press, New York, NY, 1998.
4) David Aikman, <u>A Man of Faith: The Spiritual Journey of George W. Bush</u>, W Publishing Group, Nashville, TN, 2004.
5) Frederick Lewis Allen, <u>Since Yesterday: The 1930's In America, September 3, 1929-September 3, 1939</u>, Perennial Library, New York, NY, 1939, 1968.
6) Christopher Anderson, <u>George and Laura</u>, HarperCollins Publishers, Inc., New York, NY, 2002.
7) Doug Bandow, <u>Beyond Good Intentions: A Biblical View of Politics</u>, Crossway Books, Westchester, IL, 1988.

8) Donald Bartlett and James B. Steele, <u>America: What Went Wrong?</u>, Andrews and McMeel, Kansas City, KS, 1992.
9) Joseph D. Beasley, M.D., <u>The Betrayal of Health: The Impact of Nutrition, Environment, and Lifestyle on Illness in America</u>, Times Books, New York, NY, 1991.
10) Wendell Berry, <u>The Unsettling of America: Culture & Agriculture</u>, Avon Books, New York, NY, 1977.
11) Kenneth Boa, <u>Cults, World Religions and the Occult: What They Teach, How to Respond to Them</u>, Chariot Victor Publishing, Colorado Springs, 1977, 1990.
12) Catherine Drinker Bowen, <u>John Adams and the American Revolution</u>, Little, Brown and Company, Boston, MA, 1950.
13) Allan Bloom, <u>The Closing of the American Mind</u>, Simon & Schuster, Inc., New York, NY, 2002.
14) William R. Bode, "The Reagan Doctrine in Outline," <u>Central America and the Reagan Doctrine</u>, Walter F. Hahn, ed., United States Strategic Institute, Lanham, MD, 1987.
15) Jean-Charles Brisard & Guillaume Dasquie, <u>Forbidden Truth: U.S.-Taliban Secret Oil Diplomacy and the Failed Hunt for Bin Laden</u>, (translated by Lucy Rounds), Thunder's Mouth Press/Nation Books, New York, NY, 2002.
16) William F. Buckley, Jr., <u>God & Man at Yale</u>, Regnery Publishing, Inc., Washington, D.C., 1986.
17) James MacGregor Burns, <u>The Crosswinds of Freedom</u>, Vintage Books, New York, NY, 1989.
18) James MacGregor Burns, <u>The Vineyard of Liberty</u>, Vintage Books, New York, NY, 1983.
19) George W. Bush, <u>A Charge To Keep</u>, William Morrow and Company, Inc., New York, NY, 1999.

20) Helen Caldicott, <u>The New Nuclear Danger: George W. Bush's Military-Industrial Complex</u>, The New Press, New York, NY, 2002.
21) Stephen L. Carter, <u>The Culture of Disbelief: How American Law and Politics Trivialize Religious Devotion</u>, Anchor Books, New York, NY, 1993.
22) Oswald Chambers, <u>My Utmost For His Highest</u>, Barbour Books, Uhrichsville, OH, 1935.
23) James F. Childress and John Macquarrie, eds., <u>The Westminster Dictionary of Christian Ethics</u>, Philadelphia, PA, 1986.
24) John E. Chubb and Terry M. Moe, <u>Politics, Markets, & America's Schools</u>, The Brookings Institution, Washington, D.C., 1990.
25) Richard A. Clarke, <u>Against All Enemies: Inside America's War on Terror</u>, Free Press, New York, NY, 2004.
26) Lynne Cook and Peter Wollen, eds., <u>VISUAL DISPLAY: Culture Beyond Appearances</u>, Bay Press, Seattle, WA, 1995.
27) John Cornwell, <u>Hitler's Scientists: Science, War and the Devil's Pact,</u> Viking, New York, NY, 2003.
28) Ann Coulter, <u>High Crimes and Misdemeanors: The Case Against Bill Clinton</u>, Regnery Publishing, Inc., Washington, D.C., 1998.
29) James Dale Davidson and Sir William Rees-Mogg, <u>Blood in the Streets: Investment Profits in a World Gone Mad</u>, Summit Book, New York, NY, 1987.
30) Christopher Dickey, <u>With the Contras: A Reporter in the Wilds of Nicaragua</u>, Simon & Schuster, Inc., New York, NY, 1985.
31) Frederick Douglass, <u>Narrative of the Life of Frederick Douglass</u>, Dover Publications., Inc., New York, NY, 1995.

32) William Ebenstein, Today's Isms: Communism Fascism Capitalism Socialism, Prentice-Hall Inc., Englewood Cliffs, NJ, 1970.
33) Peter Eisner and Manuel Noriega, America's Prisoner: The Memoirs of Manuel Noriega, Random House, New York, NY, 1997.
34) Al Franken, Lies and the Lying Liars Who Tell Them: A Fair and Balanced Look at the Right, Dutton, New York, NY, 2003.
35) Thomas M. Freiling, George W. Bush on God & Country, Allegiance Press, Fairfax, VA, 2004.
36) John Kenneth Galbraith, The Culture of Contentment, Houghton Mifflin Company, Boston, MA, 1992.
37) Robert A. Goldberg, Grassroots Resistance: Social Movements in Twentieth Century America, Wadsworth Publishing Company, Belmont, CA, 1991.
38) Richard N. Goodwin, The American Condition, Bantam Books, New York, NY, 1974, 1975.
39) G. Edward Griffin, The Creature From Jekyll Island: A Second Look at the Federal Reserve, American Media, Westlake Village, CA, 1994.
40) Molly Ivins and Lou Dubose, Shrub: The Short But Happy Political Life of George W. Bush, Vintage Books, New York, NY, 2000.
41) C. G. Jung, Synchronicity: An Acausal Connecting Principle, (R. F. C. Hull, translator), Princeton University Press, New York, NY, 1960.
42) Thomas A. Kempis, The Imitation of Christ, Penguin Books, Middlesex, England, 1952, 1980.
43) Paul Kengor, God and George W. Bush: a spiritual life, ReganBooks, New York, NY, 2004.
44) Russell Kirk, The Roots of American Order, Third Edition, Regnery Gateway, Washington, D.C., 1991.

45) Tim Lahaye and Jerry B. Jenkins, Are We Living in the End Times?, Tyndale House Publishers, Inc., Wheaton, IL, 1999.
46) Christopher Lasch, The True and Only Heaven: Progress and its Critics, W.W. Norton & Co., New York, NY, 1991.
47) William E. Leuchtenburg, The Perils of Prosperity, The University of Chicago Press, Chicago, 1958, 1966.
48) C.S. Lewis, Mere Christianity, Collier Books, MacMillan Publishing Company, New York, NY, 1943.
49) C.S. Lewis, Reflections on the Psalms, Harcourt, Brace & World, Inc., New York, NY, 1958.
50) C.S. Lewis, The Screwtape Letters, Bantam Books, New York, NY, 1982.
51) John Lukacs, The End of the Twentieth Century and the End of the Modern Age, Ticknor & Fields, New York, NY, 1993.
52) Niccolo Machiavelli, The Prince, (Leo Paul S. de Alvarez, ed.), Waveland Press, Inc., Prospect Heights, IL, 1980, 1989.
53) Sandra Mackey, The Saudis: Inside the Desert Kingdom, Houghton Mifflin Company, Boston, MA, 1987.
54) Myron Magnet, The Dream and the Nightmare: the Sixties' Legacy to the Underclass, Encounter Books, San Francisco, CA, 1993.
55) Stephen Mansfield, The Faith of George W. Bush, Charisma House, Lake Mary, FL, 2003.
56) Nicholas A. Masters and Mary A. Baluss, The Growing Powers of the Presidency, Parents' Magazine Press, New York, NY, 1968.
57) Texe Marrs, Dark Majesty: The Secret Brotherhood and the Magic of a Thousand Points of Light, Living Truth Publishers, Austin, TX, 1992.

58) Jeff McMahon, <u>Reagan and the World: Imperial Policy in the New Cold War</u>, Monthly Review Press, New York, NY, 1985.
59) Thomas Merton, <u>Bread in the Wilderness</u>, The Liturgical Press, Collegeville, MN, 1953.
60) Bill Minutaglio, <u>First Son: George W. Bush and the Bush Family Dynasty</u>, Three Rivers Press, New York, NY, 1999.
61) Thomas Moore, <u>Care of the Soul: A Guide for Cultivating Depth and Sacredness in Everyday Life</u>, Harper Perennial, New York, NY, 1992.
62) Samuel Eliot Morison, ed., <u>Sources & Documents illustrating the American Revolution 1764-1788 and the formation of the Federal Constitution</u>, Second edition, Oxford University Press, London, 1923.
63) George Donelson Moss, <u>Moving On: The American People Since 1945</u>, Prentice Hall, Englewood Cliffs, NJ, 1994.
64) Joseph Nocera, <u>A Piece of the Action: How the Middle Class Joined the Money Class</u>, Simon & Schuster, New York, NY, 1994.
65) Marvin Olasky, <u>The Tragedy of American Compassion</u>, Regnery Publishing, Inc., Washington, DC, 1992.
66) George Orwell, <u>1984</u>, Signet Classic, New York, NY, 1948.
67) Thomas Paine, <u>Rights of Man</u>, Wordsworth Editions Limited, Hertfordshire, England, 1996.
68) Louise Perrotta, <u>All You Really Need to Know About Prayer You Can Learn From the Poor</u>, Charis Books, Servant Publications, Anne Arbor, MI, 1996.
69) Kevin Phillips, <u>American Dynasty: Aristocracy, Fortune, and the Politics of Deceit in the House of Bush</u>, Viking, New York, 2004.

70) Kevin Phillips, <u>Arrogant Capital: Washington, Wall Street, and the Frustration of American Politics</u>, Little, Brown and Company, Boston, MA, 1994.
71) Kevin Phillips, <u>The Politics of Rich and Poor: Wealth and the American Electorate in the Reagan Aftermath</u>, Random House, New York, NY, 1990.
72) Gerald Posner, <u>Why America Slept: the Failure to Prevent 9/11</u>, Random House, New York, NY, 2003.
73) Pat Robertson, <u>The New World Order</u>, Word Publishing, Dallas, TX, 1991.
74) Alexandra Robbins, <u>Secrets of the Tomb: Skull and Bones, the Ivy League and the Hidden Paths of Power</u>, Back Bay Books, Boston, MA, 2002.
75) Paula S. Rothenburg, <u>Race, Class & Gender in the United States: An Integrated Study</u>, Second Edition, St. Martin's Press, New York, NY, 1992.
76) Michael Saba, <u>The Armageddon Network</u>, Amana Books, Brattleboro, VT, 1984.
77) Dana Adams Schmidt, <u>Armageddon in the Middle East</u>, The John Day Company, New York, NY, 1974.
78) Robert H. Schuller, <u>Self Esteem: The New Reformation</u>, Word Books, Waco, TX, 1982.
79) Gerald Segal, <u>The World Affairs Companion: The Essential One-Volume Guide to Global Issues</u>, Touchstone, New York, NY, 1987, 1993.
80) William Shakespeare, <u>The Tragedy of Hamlet</u>, Washington Square Press, Inc., New York, NY, 1966.
81) Renald E. Showers, <u>What On Earth Is God Doing?: Satan's Conflict With God</u>, Loizeaux Brothers, Neptune, NJ, 1973.
82) William E. Simon, <u>A Time For Truth</u>, Reader's Digest Books, New York, NY, 1978.

83) Peter Singer, <u>The President of Good and Evil: Questioning the Ethics of George W. Bush</u>, Penguin Group (USA) Inc., New York, NY, 2004.
84) Aleksandr I. Solzhenitsyn, <u>The Gulag Archipelago, 1918-1956</u>, (Thomas P. Whitney, translator), Harper Perennial, New York, NY, 1973, 1991.
85) Alvin Toffler, <u>Powershift: Knowledge, Wealth, and Violence at the Edge of the 21st Century</u>, Bantam Books, New York, NY, 1990.
86) A.W. Tozer, <u>The Pursuit of God: The Human Thirst for the Divine</u>, Christian Publications, Inc., Camp Hill, PA, 1982, 1993.
87) Bob Woodward, <u>Bush at War</u>, Simon & Schuster, New York, NY, 2002.
88) Bob Woodward, <u>Maestro: Greenspan's Fed and the American Boom</u>, Simon & Schuster, New York, NY, 2000.
89) Bob Woodward, <u>Plan of Attack</u>, Simon & Schuster, New York, NY, 2004.
90) Donald Worster, <u>Dust Bowl: The Southern Plains In the 1930s</u>, Oxford University Press, New York, NY, 1979.

To order additional copies of

CHRISTIAN WORDS, UN-CHRISTIAN ACTIONS

Have your credit card ready and call:

1-877-421-READ (7323)

or please visit our web site at
www.pleasantword.com

Also available at:
www.amazon.com
and
www.barnesandnoble.com

Printed in the United States
55684LVS00001B/1